Lecture Notes in Computer Science　　　3555

Commenced Publication in 1973
Founding and Former Series Editors:
Gerhard Goos, Juris Hartmanis, and Jan van Leeuwen

Tullio Vardanega   Andy Wellings (Eds.)

Reliable Software Technology – Ada-Europe 2005

10th Ada-Europe International Conference
on Reliable Software Technologies
York, UK, June 20-24, 2005
Proceedings

 Springer

Volume Editors

Tullio Vardanega
University of Padua
Department of Pure and Applied Mathematics
via G. Belzoni 7, 35131 Padua, Italy
E-mail: tullio.vardanega@math.unipd.it

Andy Wellings
University of York
Department of Computer Science
Heslington, York, YO10 5DD, UK
E-mail: andy@cs.york.ac.uk

Library of Congress Control Number: 2005927232

CR Subject Classification (1998): D.2, D.1.2-5, D.3, C.2-4, C.3, K.6

ISSN   0302-9743
ISBN-10   3-540-26286-5 Springer Berlin Heidelberg New York
ISBN-13   978-3-540-26286-2 Springer Berlin Heidelberg New York

Springer is a part of Springer Science+Business Media

springeronline.com

© Springer-Verlag Berlin Heidelberg 2005
Printed in Germany

Typesetting: Camera-ready by author, data conversion by Scientific Publishing Services, Chennai, India
Printed on acid-free paper   SPIN: 11499909   06/3142   5 4 3 2 1 0

Preface

Started on the inspired initiative of Prof. Alfred Strohmeier back in 1996, and spawned from the annual Ada-Europe conference that had previously run for 16 consecutive years, the International Conference on Reliable Software Technologies celebrated this year its tenth anniversary by going to York, UK, where the first series of technical meetings on Ada were held in the 1970s.

Besides being a beautiful and historical place in itself, York also hosts the Department of Computer Science of the local university, whose Real-Time Group has been tremendously influential in shaping the Ada language and in the progress on real-time computing worldwide. This year's conference was therefore put together under excellent auspices, in a very important year for the Ada community in view of the forthcoming completion of the revision process that is upgrading the language standard to face the challenges of the new millennium.

The conference took place on June 20–24, 2005. It was as usual sponsored by Ada-Europe, the European federation of national Ada societies, in cooperation with ACM SIGAda. The conference was organized by selected staff of the University of York teamed up with collaborators from various places in Europe, in what turned out to be a very effective instance of distributed collaborative processing. The conference also enjoyed the generous support of 11 industrial sponsors.

This year's conference was very successful indeed. It attracted the largest number of submissions in years, from as many as 15 countries worldwide, which made the selection process tougher than ever. Overall, the conference program included 21 carefully selected and refereed papers assigned to 8 thematic sessions spanning a variety of high-profile subjects. The technical program included an industrial track, a first in the conference's history, which encompassed 10 contributions illustrating challenges faced by a cross-section of high-integrity software industry in Europe and the US. As usual, the conference program was itself bracketed by two full days of tutorials, with a special half-day presentation on the new Ada 2005 language, offered by four of its lead designers: John Barnes, Alan Burns, Pascal Leroy and Tucker Taft. Furthermore, three keynote presentations, delivered by John McDermid, Martin Thomas and Bev Littlewood, respectively, marked the opening of each of the main conference days. Finally, much in keeping with the well-established tradition of the conference series, the program made provisions for an excellently populated vendor exhibition and for a half-day vendor session, in which participants were able to catch up with the latest advances in reliable software technology products.

Let us now go into the details of some of the conference highlights.

The invited talks were as follows:

- Prof. John McDermid, University of York, UK
  Model-Based Development of Safety-Critical Software
  where the opportunities and challenges of model-based development were discussed.
- Prof. Martyn Thomas, Thomas Associates, UK
  Extreme Hubris
  where the principles of Extreme Programming were critically examined and an alternative
  manifesto for dependable software development was proposed.
- Prof. Bev Littlewood, City University, London, UK
  Assessing the Dependability of Software-Based Systems: a Question of Confidence
  where the controversial contention was made that dependability claims ought to be associated with a probability-based assessment of the inherent uncertainty about the truth of the
  claim.

The technical sessions of the program ranged from the illustration of successful
applications and distributed systems, to the discussion of design, analysis and implementation methodologies, to formal methods, certification and verification, through to
the latest advances with Ravenscar technology, to finish with Ada-related concerns regarding education and language implementation issues.

The tutorial program gathered the following assortment of topics and international
expert speakers

- **Developing Web-Aware Applications in Ada with AWS**, Jean-Pierre Rosen, *Adalog,
  France*
- **Correctness by Construction — A Manifesto for High Integrity Systems**, Peter Amey
  and Neil White, *Praxis High Integrity Systems, UK*
- **Real-Time Java for Ada Programmers**, Benjamin M. Brosgol, *AdaCore, US*
- **SAE Architecture Analysis and Design Language**, Joyce Tokar, *Pyrrhus Software, US*
  and Bruce Lewis, *US Army*
- **High-Integrity Ravenscar Using SPARK**, Brian Dobbing, *Praxis High Integrity Systems,
  UK*
- **Software Safety Cases**, John McDermid and Rob Weaver, *University of York, UK*
- **Requirement Engineering for Dependable Systems**, William Bail, *The MITRE
  Corporation, US*
- **Software Fault Tolerance**, Patrick Rogers, *AdaCore, US*
- **Programming with the Ada 2005 Standard Container Library**, Matthew Heaney, *On2
  Technologies, US*

in addition of course to a special half-day session where four of the lead designers
of Ada 2005, John Barnes, Alan Burns, Pascal Leroy and S. Tucker Taft, provided an
extensive overview of the new features introduced by the language revision.

A number of people crucially contributed to the success of the conference. First and
foremost the authors of all the papers, talks and presentations, for it was from their
contribution that the conference was put together. The Program Committee members
helped promote the conference in their own circles and also successfully solicited submissions from a variety of authors. The same members along with a number of others
also devoted considerable effort to refereeing the submissions in a thorough and timely
fashion. The program itself was put together by a smaller group including the Conference Chair, Alan Burns, the Program Co-chairs, Tullio Vardanega and Andy Wellings,

the Tutorials Chair, Iain Bate, the Exhibition and Industrial Track Chair, Rod Chapman, and Dirk Craeynest, representing Ada-Europe. Selected PC members also undertook to shepherd some papers to their final versions. All of these people deserve our gratitude, along with the local organizers, in particular Ian Broster, also in charge of the conference publicity along with Dirk Craeynest, and Sue Helliwell, who oversaw the administrative details of the registration process.

We trust the attendees enjoyed both the technical and social program of the conference, and we close this volume with the confidence of a job well done and the satisfaction of a thoroughly enjoyed experience.

June 2005   Tullio Vardanega

Organization

Conference Chair

Alan Burns, University of York, UK

Program Co-chairs

Tullio Vardanega, University of Padua, Italy
Andy Wellings, University of York, UK

Tutorial Chair

Iain Bate, University of York, UK

Exhibition and Industrial Track Chair

Rod Chapman, Praxis High Integrity Systems, UK

Publicity Co-chairs

Ian Broster, University of York, UK
Dirk Craeynest, Aubay Belgium, Katholieke Universiteit Leuven, Belgium

Local Organization Administrator

Sue Helliwell, University of York, UK

Ada-Europe Conference Liaison

Laurent Pautet, ENST Paris, France

Other Program Commitee Members

Lars Asplund, Mälardalens Högskola, Sweden
Alejandro Alonso, Universidad Politecnica de Madrid, Spain
Janet Barnes, Praxis High Integrity Systems, UK
Guillem Bernat, University of York, UK
Johann Blieberger, Technische Universität Wien, Austria
Bernd Burgstaller, Technische Universität Wien, Austria
Ulf Cederling, Vaxjo University, Sweden
Alfons Crespo, Universidad Politecnica de Valencia, Spain
Raymond Devillers, Université Libre de Bruxelles, Belgium
Michael González Harbour, Universidad de Cantabria, Spain
Andrew Hately, CEATS Research Development Simulation Centre, Hungary
Günter Hommel, Technischen Universität Berlin, Germany
Stefan Kauer, EADS Dornier, Germany
Hubert Keller, Institut für Angewandte Informatik, Germany
Yvon Kermarrec, ENST Bretagne, France
Jörg Kienzle, McGill University, Canada
Fabrice Kordon, Université Pierre & Marie Curie, France
Albert LLamosi, Universitat de les Illes Balears, Spain
Franco Mazzanti, Istituto di Scienza e Tecnologie dell'Informazione, Italy
John McCormick, University of Northern Iowa, USA
Javier Miranda, Universidad Las Palmas de Gran Canaria, Spain
Juan A. de la Puente, Universidad Politecnica de Madrid, Spain
Erhard Plödereder, Universität Stuttgart, Germany
Alexander Romanovsky, University of Newcastle upon Tyne, UK
Jean-Pierre Rosen, Adalog, France
Edmond Schonberg, New York University and AdaCore, USA
Jörgen Winkler, Friedrich-Schiller-Universität, Germany

Referees

Alejandro Alonso
Las Asplund
Khaled Barbaria
Janet Barnes
Guillem Bernat
Johann Blieberger
Maarten Boasson
Ben Brosgol
Ian Broster
Bernd Burgstaller
Alan Burns
Ulf Cederling

John Clark
Dirk Craeynest
Alfons Crespo
Raymond Devillers
Claude Dutheillet
Javier Esparza
Michael González-Harbour
Andrew Hately
Günter Hommel
Erik Hu
Jerome Hugues
Alexei Iliasov

Stefan Kauer
Hubert Keller
Yvon Kermarrec
Jörg Kienzle
Fabrice Kordon
Albert Llamosi
Moreno Marzolla
Franco Mazzanti
Javier Miranda
John McCormick
Laurent Pautet

Juan A. de la Puente
Erhard Plödereder
Alexander Romanovsky
Jean-Pierre Rosen
Bo Sandèn
Edmond Schonberg
Tullio Vardanega
Thomas Vergnaud
Andy Wellings
Jörgen Winkler

Table of Contents

Ada and Education

Certification and Verification

Distributed Systems

Language Issues

Ravenscar Technology

ILTIS - The Legacy of a Successful Product

Neville Rowden

Siemens Switzerland Ltd., Transportation Systems,
Industriestrasse 42, CH-8304 Wallisellen, Switzerland
neville.rowden@siemens.com

Abstract. ILTIS is probably the most versatile modern railway control and supervisory system available today. From its initial conception in 1990 to the present day, Siemens has been upgrading ILTIS with further functionality while maintaining the quality of original product. The aim of this paper is to analyse what have been the contributing factors in ensuring this success and how this success can be maintained for the future.

Abbreviations

CMMI	Capability Maturity Model Integrated
CTC	Centralised Traffic Control
DEC	Digital Equipment Corporation
GUI	Graphic User Interface
HP	Hewlett Packard
ISO	International Organization for Standardization
LAN	Local Area Network
MMI	Man/Machine Interface
OSF	Open System Foundation
SBB	Swiss National Railways (Schweizerische Bundesbahnen)
SIL	Safety Integrity Level

1 Introduction

ILTIS (an acronym in German for "Integrated Traffic Control and Information System"; it also German for polecat) is a centralised traffic control (CTC) system developed initially for the Swiss National Railways (SBB). All of the software has been written in Ada83 and was originally targeted to DEC's OpenVMS operating system using Alpha computers. On average, 20 developers are employed with ILTIS at any given time adding further functionality to the system.

From humble beginnings, ILTIS has expanded beyond all expectations. Not only is the system currently targeted to OpenVMS (now HP OpenVMS) but also to Microsoft's Windows. The customer base has also expanded dramatically including not only all SBB operating centres, but also those in Austria, Malaysia (national and a private railway), Hungary, Slovenia, Poland, Vietnam and many of the myriad private

T. Vardanega and A. Wellings (Eds.): Ada-Europe 2005, LNCS 3555, pp. 1–12, 2005.

railway companies in Switzerland. Several other countries around the world are also expressing interest.

Software projects do not have a good reputation. As a general rule, the larger the project, the greater the chance of failure. ILTIS projects manifest themselves as releases producing additional functionality with respect to the previous release, with projects continuing for an average of 12 months (depending on the complexity of the new features) from the formulation of the system requirements to the final validation.

A recent survey in the United States (see Reference 1., Chapter 1) has found that the cost of an average project ranges from $430,000 to $2,300,000. ILTIS releases can, therefore, be considered as larger than average projects. The following statistics were also presented from the same survey:

- only 16% of projects are completed on schedule
- 31% are cancelled, primarily because of quality problems
- 53% cost more than planned, exceeding their budgets by an average of 189%
- projects that reach completion delivered an average of only 42% of the originally planned features.

Experience with ILTIS has shown that it continually bucks the trend (as yet, there have been no major failures) and it would perhaps be interesting to look back and analyse why ILTIS projects have enjoyed so much success.

2 ILTIS Basics

The control and supervision of a railway network requires the acquisition and provision of all data relating to the state of the tracks within the area of responsibility. To accomplish this, CTC (Centralised Traffic Control) computers store and process information, which is received from the local interlocking and the remotely controlled stations. They enable a simple and exact overview of all train movements in the controlled area to be presented to the stationmaster.

A CTC can cover a radius of about 100 km and manages several stations - 30 is a typical number, although there are installations, which control 75 stations.

A CTC system has three basic functions, viz.:

1. the central control of the interlockings, e.g.:
   - routing trains,
   - controlling individual elements (points, signals, etc.),
   - blocking/clearing the routes for train traffic,
   - blocking/clearing the operation of points,
   - emergency commands to override the interlocking in the event of a breakdown.
2. the automation of train traffic:
   - tracking trains,
   - automatic routing,
   - transferring train position information to a higher level management centre
3. the display of train information for passengers.

Before ILTIS's conception, existing CTC systems and their previous generations were generally developed piecemeal, based on *ad hoc* requirements of a customer's needs. They were loosely coupled together over a LAN (Local Area Network). Every computer in the network was usually dedicated to fulfilling a particular task within the CTC system, e.g. a computer dedicated to tracking trains, another dedicated to the display of train information, etc. The stationmaster was then confronted with a working environment, in which commands to the control system had to be issued via one of the several terminals available to him, each terminal given access to a particular CTC computer. In addition to the ergonomic disadvantages of these CTC systems, there are also inherent disadvantages in the design caused by:

- heterogeneous infrastructure,
- duplication of configuration data (although this in itself is not a problem, there was a danger of inconsistencies appearing in the data unless tight controls were incorporated to prevent it), and
- duplication of resources such as printers, one of which needed to be connected to each computer to register errors.

ILTIS is composed from a network of (upto 40) computers. It was designed from scratch as a totally integrated CTC system, based on the experiences of developing previous CTC systems. Instead of dedicating computers to a particular function, the CTC functions were freely distributable within the available computers. No computer was dedicated to one particular task.

Another radical departure (at least in 1990) was that the stationmaster's work place was to be based on a workstation with a single PC-keyboard and a pointing device (e.g. a mouse). Each workstation can control upto 6 full-graphic colour screens.

All dataflow in the system is over the LAN, making it accessible to every computer connected to the LAN. Information to and from the interlockings is also transmitted directly over the LAN. Similarly, peripheral devices that utilise serial interfaces (such as printers and the system clock) communicate with the LAN through a terminal server. This characteristic enables each computer in the system to take over the functionality of another computer in the event of hardware problems.

3 ILTIS Man/Machine Interface

Probably the most important component of a CTC system is its MMI (Man/Machine Interface). It is of the utmost importance that the MMI can provide clear, concise information concerning the state of the interlockings, and enable the stationmaster to issue error-free commands quickly and efficiently.

3.1 Display Information

The stationmaster has, depending on the system configuration, a number of graphic displays available to him. Using standard window techniques, various windows are accessible to provide clear presentations of the state of the total system and allow any necessary modifications to the system to be made. These windows can be displayed when required and removed from the screen when they are no longer needed, facilitating rapid access to target windows. Earlier CTC systems used screens onto which information defining the state of the interlockings was displayed as a collection of semigraphic symbols. This severely restricted the amount of information that could be displayed onto a single screen. Even average-sized stations would be forced to be placed onto two screens.

ILTIS is in a position to manipulate full-graphic, colour symbols. Much more information can therefore be concentrated onto a single screen, reducing the need to split stations over several screens. Indeed, using standard window technology, several stations can be displayed simultaneously onto one screen. When necessary, windows can be readily overlaid by the user on top of each other.

The display of the interlocking state information is uniform for each type of interlocking, whether it is a relay-based interlocking or an electronic interlocking. All important messages in the system are displayed by a central message manager in a window containing four sections dedicated to:

- operating requests,
- operating messages,
- faults, and
- system messages.

It is also possible to configure individual messages so that they are emphasised with different audio tones. Once the message has been noted, it can be acknowledged or cancelled by the stationmaster.

3.2 Commands

Commands are issued via the mouse without any keyboard being involved (commands in earlier CTCs were entered as coded text). Entering commands with a mouse not only increases the speed at which commands can be sent, but also reduces the chances of executing any incorrect commands through typing errors. Interlocking commands are issued by pointing the cursor at the target element with the mouse. With a single mouse click, a popup menu displays the commands, which are currently valid for that element. The available commands are not only determined by the element type (i.e. if it is a barrier, or a main signal, etc.) but also by its current dynamic state. It would, for example, be meaningless offering a command to open a particular barrier, if that barrier were already open.

Once a command has been selected, it is displayed in a text format within the window. The stationmaster has then to acknowledge this command with a single mouse-click before the system allows the command to be executed by the interlocking.

3.3 Language

Another important characteristic of a MMI is the ability to present textual information in the language of the user. This problem is particularly acute in countries like Switzerland, which boasts four national languages. It is, therefore, important that each work place in the CTC system is able to switch online to the language of the current user. Of course, the choice of language should not be restricted to the Latin character set, but should be able to handle the full gamut of character sets (e.g. Cyrillic, Arabic, etc.).

Multilanguage MMI was a basic design consideration in ILTIS and it was a surprisingly much underestimated problem in software development before the concept Unicode existed. In ILTIS, a user can not only define in which language the workstation should present text, but can also decide in which language the various log files (e.g. system log files, fault log files, critical command log files, etc.) should be printed out.

3.4 On-line Maintenance

ILTIS has its own maintenance software integrated into the design. When a maintenance engineer has the necessary privileges, he is able to supervise or modify certain aspects of the running system. This is particularly useful in localising any unexpected problems and for collecting information, which can be analysed at later time by the system developers.

4 ILTIS Architecture Requirements

The ILTIS architecture was required to satisfy the following basic requirements:

- Safety
- Availability
- Scalability
- Portability
- Maintainability
- Generic software

4.1 Safety

In certain installations (e.g. in Switzerland and Austria), it is necessary to be able to by-pass the inherent safety of an interlocking to provide an uninterrupted service even in the event of hardware faults and breakdowns.

In these installations, it is essential that a CTC system is able to fulfil certain safety-related functions, i.e.

- it has to ensure that the station-master does not make life-endangering decisions based upon faulty information presented to him by the CTC system,
- it has to ensure that so-called critical commands (i.e. the commands which by-pass the safety of an interlocking) cannot be inadvertently executed, and
- critical commands have to be correctly executed.

4.2 Availability

The availability of a CTC system is becoming an increasingly important factor as railway networks become more and more dependent upon them. Current systems usually tackle this problem by having redundant computers, which can be manually switched into service whenever they are needed. From experience, it has been seen that this design suffers from a number of drawbacks, viz.:

- The redundant computers are not in active service. When a situation arises where they need to be brought into service, they themselves could have developed technical problems, which, as the redundant computers are dormant, have gone unnoticed.
- As each computer in the distributed system needs to have a similarly configured redundant computer, this effectively doubles the number of required computers if a full stand-by capability is needed.

In ILTIS the necessary redundancy has been built into the software architecture. No ILTIS task is dedicated to a particular computer but can execute on any available computer in the system. In this way, ILTIS uses a technique of redundant software instead of redundant hardware.

4.3 Portability

ILTIS was designed to be in service for at least 25 years. As it has now passed the halfway point in its life cycle and is not showing any signs of age, ILTIS will be probably reach this goal. In 1990 (as now), it was impossible to predict how the target platforms would change. It was, therefore, important to choose a development language that would facilitate porting to different hardware platforms and operating systems.

4.4 Maintainability

Again, in order to satisfy the expectation of a 25-year product life, ILTIS needed an architecture, which would allow ease of extending functionality without degrading existing functionality.

4.5 Generic Software

ILTIS has not been developed for a single target installation. It is a generic system, which has to be instantiated onto a target installation using configuration data. The software that runs in every Swiss installation is exactly the same as that running, for example, in the Malaysian installations.

Configuring ILTIS installations is not trivial and requires considerable engineering effort. Because of the complexity of configuring target installations, a configuration tool was also developed in parallel to ILTIS.

5 Success Stories

5.1 Ada as Development Language

- Ada was predestined for this development. ILTIS is a SIL 2 system and Ada is highly recommended for developing such systems (see Reference 2., Table A.15). In 1990, it was clear that Ada should be chosen as the development language but even today, no other language is available that can compete with Ada when safety is a factor.

- The cleanly defined constructs in Ada (strong typing, package structure, etc.) not only helps in the area of safety, but also when the target system needs to be robust and of a high quality. ILTIS must be in service 24 hours a day, 7 days a week. The railway traffic in Switzerland never stops and it is essential that a CTC is always in service. Even short breaks in service would have devastating consequences in a country that has the densest railway-traffic in the world. Software quality and reliability are, in effect, prerequisites for any system that has safety requirements.
- In a project of ILTIS's magnitude (3 million lines of code and still counting) and longevity, ease of maintenance is an important factor in the success of the product. Again, Ada's constructs support the developer when he is required to make changes in existing code.

    Changes are brought about not only by customers changing requirements but also by the fact that ILTIS is in a continuous state of further development (the latest release contained 46 new features). Development for new markets in other countries often requires changes in sensitive parts of the system as each individual country usually has its own methods for handling railway-traffic. Again, such changes can only be made with confidence if the development language offers the necessary support.
- The target operating system for the first ILTIS installations (OpenVMS on Alpha platforms) is approaching the end of its life. In addition, many customers want to use the cheaper Windows platforms for their installations. Because of these market forces, it was necessary to port ILTIS from OpenVMS to Windows. Portability was built into the original system architecture and, as Ada is operating system independent, it was possible to port the vast majority of the code without any significant problems. Of course, the GUI caused problems and calls to the operating system (which were minimised and isolated in the original architecture) had to be specially handled, but all problems were resolved. ILTIS is now currently supported under OpenVMS and Windows.

    The goals of the port actually went further than the ILTIS target platform. A complete development environment for ILTIS is now available under Windows. This has also helped to keep the product alive by reducing the cost of workstations and increasing productivity by using the more advanced development-tools under Windows such as graphical editors.

    The port in itself was not totally without problems. Operating system specific code needed to be handled with conditional compilation through a pre-processor, which needed to be custom-developed by Siemens. DECnet connections needed to be replaced with TCP/IP and, although an Ada95 compiler was used for Windows, new code still needed to be restricted to the Ada83 constructs to allow compilation for the target OpenVMS systems.

    Interestingly, the Windows Ada95 compiler has a switch, which should have enforced Ada83 compatibility. This, unfortunately, did not cover all cases. A sub-contractor for Siemens (the company White Elephant) resolved this problem by customising the editor to perform a syntax check for Ada83 compatibility before submitting it to the compiler. This check could have only been otherwise possible by compiling directly on an OpenVMS system.
- With the risk of appearing to be a Luddite, the fact that Ada is not at the forefront of modern technology is, in fact, a Godsend for developers. Perpetual change is a

nightmare for the maintenance of large systems. Changes in a compiler or operating system result in the need to repeat the full suite of system tests (especially relevant for SIL 2 systems). With Ada's stability, problems or language restrictions are well known and can usually be worked around.

With respect to stability, ILTIS has been doubly blessed. Not only does Ada offer a stable compiler but the main target operating system (OpenVMS) has also offered a stable and robust platform on which ILTIS can be developed and run. It has been a winning combination for the last 15 years, which has only recently been disrupted by the planned phasing out of OpenVMS.

5.2 On-site Customer

- Another factor in the success of ILTIS was having the customer (initially the SBB) involved in all stages of the original development. The concept of the on-site customer is one of the basic tenets of Extreme Programming and it has much to recommend it. Of course, not all projects can afford the luxury of an on-site customer but his advice and perpetual availability for clarification of requirements expedited the development significantly. Unfortunately, this is no longer possible. ILTIS is now being targeted to many customers (not just the SBB) and there is powerful trend within Siemens to satisfy the more formal methods of CMMI.

5.3 Clearly Defined Architecture

- The aim for all system architectures should be to keep it as simple as possible while allowing for the flexibility for further development. The key to the ILTIS architecture was to integrate the concepts of reliability (in the form of redundant components) and of safety (in the form of dual-channelled processing when required) within the basic system architecture. As these concepts were embedded in the system architecture, it necessitated the component developers to take these factors into account within each component design.

5.4 Enforced Component Structure

- All basic component functions in ILTIS (inter-component communication, processing of configuration-data, component start-up, etc.) can only be undertaken by instantiating generic system software. This not only facilitated central points of reference for error localisation and monitoring but also enforced a similar basic design structure for all components. As ILTIS currently contains over 60 components, maintenance and ease of understandability for new developers in the project has been enhanced by the similar design structure of the components.

5.5 Use of Standards

- As portability was always an issue in the ILTIS development, standards were used wherever possible. This was most evident not only with Ada but also with the GUI where OSF Motif was chosen for all interactions with the user. Again this facilitated the porting of ILTIS to Windows where the Ada bindings in the ILTIS code were correspondingly modified.

6 Lessons Learnt from Bitter Experience

6.1 Development Resources Should Be Available in the Future

- To contrast with all the advantages of developing within a stable environment, the world has unfortunately not stood still. As Ada is no longer flavour of the month, it has become increasingly more difficult to find experienced developers. In addition, although there are many tools to help in the development of Java, etc., there is almost nothing available for Ada.

  Even porting to Windows presented its own set of problems. The number of available Ada compilers for Windows was definitely limited and, at end of the day, there was not much to choose from. The consequences of changing compilers in a project are that all system tests need to be repeated. This was necessary for the port from OpenVMS to Windows. For cost reasons, this is an exercise that can be undertaken only when it is absolutely necessary. Under OpenVMS, ILTIS is still being developed using Ada83. Although the code in Windows compiles with an Ada95 compiler, all new code still needs to be Ada83 compatible so that it can also compile under OpenVMS.

6.2 Manage Changes of Development Processes

- As with most large companies, Siemens has a penchant for changing its development processes. ILTIS is now experiencing:

  - its 3rd development process, and
  - its 3rd document management system.

  The original ILTIS documents were written in DECwrite. The current documents are written in Word. In ILTIS, the problems of progressing to the next development process, or for using another text-processing tool were never properly addressed. These changes cost time and money, and need to be thought through properly. Such effort is always given a lower priority than new development but eventually everything becomes so cumbersome that further progress is extremely inefficient. ILTIS is addressing this problem at the moment but no satisfactory solutions have been found.

6.3 Invest in a Practical Test Environment

- As ILTIS has been continually extended with further functionality over the previous 15 years, each release has resulted in additional costs for regression testing. These costs have increased exponentially with time and it has been increasingly difficult to maintain the original ILTIS quality whilst keeping the costs to an acceptable level.

  The main problem is that the vast majority of the tests are carried out manually. It is, in fact, extremely difficult to automate tests for distributed systems when the real-time aspects and the correctness of the graphical display need to be taken into account. In addition, the generic nature of ILTIS means that endless variations need also to be tested (it can safely be assumed that no two installations are the same).

Nevertheless, these problems should have been foreseen and addressed during the design phase of the project. Again, no satisfactory solutions have been found. Various attempts with off-the-shelf test automats have not been particularly successful and thought is now being given in developing a custom-built test automat.

6.4   Extract Text Management from Code Development

- It is unbelievable how something as trivial as handling text in different languages could be so difficult. Of course, the aim of the project was always to extricate the text from the code so that installation engineers would be free to define text without impacting the released software. Unfortunately, this was not always possible (most evidently in OSF Motif's UIL files). These file are an integral part of the release and any text corrections in the UIL files, no matter how trivial, result in a new release with the consequent validation process and approval from the governing body.

   Also, it is not sufficient to translate text into the target languages. Thought has to be given to window layout which may change due to an increase or decrease in text length. ILTIS currently supports 10 languages and any further text from new functionality needs to be tested for each supported language.

   The hope that, by using OSF Motif, all language problems would be consequently solved also proved to be illusionary. ILTIS, Ada83 and OSF Motif all preceded ISO 10646 where most of these issues were finally addressed. Languages covered by ISO Latin 1 were never a problem but it is only in the last release that support has also been provided for ISO Latin 2. Languages such as Cyrillic and Arabic remain a pipe dream.

6.5   Design Tools for Remote Maintenance

- Remote maintenance has become of increasing importance as the number of installations in service increases. This function began as a throwaway feature in the first release and its limitations today are now patently obvious. Although important aspects such as access protection were taken seriously and resolved, not enough time was spent considering how the feature could be designed to be most effective. Remote maintenance was also developed on an *ad hoc* basis without much thought being given to strategy. It is still a useful tool but it would have had an even greater potential if more time had been spent developing a unified design within the system architecture.

6.6   Limit the Scope of Generic Code

- ILTIS code is generic. The same code runs in every installation in Switzerland and the rest of the world. The code needs to be instantiated for each installation using system data (which is also installation-independent) and installation-specific configuration data. The generation of the configuration data is a science unto itself and can only be undertaken by trained engineers. A data generation and management tool has been developed in conjunction with ILTIS, without which it would be impossible to map an installation's characteristics onto ILTIS-friendly data.

Unfortunately, there was a tendency among developers to relegate unclear specifications to the configuration data, i.e. if it was uncertain what the customer wanted, the choice would have been made configurable. Although this results in much flexibility and versatility, it also causes headaches during the regression test phase where all variations need to be tested. If the variations are not actually used in any installation, this is clearly a waste of resources and also increases the potential for creating errors.

6.7 Standards Can also Be a Millstone

- The reverse side of the standards' coin is that they lose their effectiveness when they are poorly supported. OSF Motif is a case in point. Although OSF Motif may have seemed to be the way forward in 1990, it is anything but today. OSF Motif was an uncomfortable fit with Ada on OpenVMS and it is has been almost perverse using it with Windows today. With OSF Motif on Windows, ILTIS has now become heavily dependent on the whims of another third-party product that, in turn, adds to the complexity of release management.

7 Conclusion: From Cutting Edge to Legacy

After many successful years of ILTIS development and deployment, the SBB want to go one step further. Currently, an ILTIS CTC is used to control, on average, 30 stations. The SBB want to connect all ILTIS systems in Switzerland together, creating 12 new control centres (reduced from today's 23 control centres) encompassing 38 cells from which the whole country can be controlled. In the long term, this could even be reduced to just one railway control centre. In order to achieve this, a new project, ILTIS-Netz (or ILTIS-Network in English), was started in 2003 and this is planned to go into service in 2007.

ILTIS-Netz uses ILTIS as its basic component, a cell. The current ILTIS-architecture has been decomposed into its respective layers (3-tier). A new GUI is being developed, which presents the information on the stationmaster's work place by connecting many cells together. The development is being undertaken in Java and it will be interesting to observe how the Ada development interacts with the Java development. The aim of ILTIS-Netz is to replace the View Layer (currently integrated with the Presentation Layer) by a new 5-tier architecture.

As a consequence, ILTIS appears to be heading into the last phase of its life cycle. With respect to ILTIS-Netz, it will be a legacy product. However, there will still be further life in ILTIS as the SBB have many features that they want to be developed in ILTIS in the future. Because of the additional requirements from ILTIS-Netz, future development will be even more demanding than it is today.

References

1. Software Factories – Jack Greenfield and Keith Short – Wiley Publishing, Inc. 2004
2. Deutsche Norm EN 50128 – Bahnanwendungen: Telekommunikationstechnik, Signaltechnik und Datenverarbeitungssysteme Software für Eisenbahnsteuerungs- und Überwachungssysteme - November 2001

A Reference Control Architecture for Service Robots Implemented on a Climbing Vehicle*

Francisco Ortiz, Diego Alonso, Bárbara Álvarez, and Juan A. Pastor

Universidad Politécnica de Cartagena, Spain
{francisco.ortiz, diego.alonso}@upct.es

Abstract. Teleoperated robots are used to perform hazardous tasks that human operators cannot carry out. The purpose of this paper is to present a new architecture (ACROSET) for the development of these systems that takes into account the current advances in robotic architectures while adopting the component-oriented approach. The architecture is currently being used, tested and improved in the development of an heterogeneous family of robots in the context of the EFTCoR project. It is also presented the Ada'95 implementation of ACROSET for a climbing robot.

1 Introduction

Teleoperated robots are used for extending human capabilities in hazardous and inaccessible environments. Recent progress in mechatronics, perception and computing is opening up a number of new application domains for tele-robotics, but at the same time, the complexity of the applications grows due to the domain characteristics: high variability of functionality and physical characteristics, large variety of execution infrastructures, sensors, actuators, control algorithms, degrees of autonomy, etc.

Despite these differences, teleoperated systems are normally similar from a logical point of view, having many common requirements in their definition and many common components, both logical or physical, in their implementation. As stated in [1], one way of dealing with this complexity is *to use architectural frameworks and tools that embody well defined concepts to enable effective realization of systems to meet high level goals.* Such an architectural framework allows rapid development of systems and reuse of a large variety of components, with concomitant savings in time and money. There are numerous efforts to provide developers with architectural frameworks of this nature, such as [2, 3, 4].

The objects of this paper are twofold: to present an architectural approach to the development of control units for these kind of systems and to present an example of its use in the development of a real system. The architectural

---

* This work has been partially supported by European Union (GROWTH G3RD-CT-00794) and the Spanish Government programs CICYT (TIC2003-07804-C05-02) and Seneca (PB/5/FS/02).

T. Vardanega and A. Wellings (Eds.): Ada-Europe 2005, LNCS 3555, pp. 13–24, 2005.

approach, ACROSET, is based on the latest advances in robotic architectures and adopts a component-oriented approach. ACROSET offers a way to re-use the same components in very different systems by separating the functionality from the interaction patterns. It also provides a common framework for developing robot systems and for integrating intelligent behaviours. ACROSET has been implemented and tested in different systems, such as a PLC of Siemens (series 300) and a small FPGA (*Field Programmable Gate Array*), which is a kind of re-programmable hardware. Actually, it is being implemented in Ada'95.

2   A Climbing Vehicle in the EFTCoR Project

The *Environmental Friendly and Cost-Effective Technology for Coating Removal* (EFTCoR) project [5, 6] is part of the European Industry current effort to introduce environmental friendly ship maintenance. It addresses the development of a solution to the problem of retrieval and confinement of the subproducts obtained from the ship maintenance operation (oxide, paint and adherences mainly). A glance at Fig. 1 shows the difficulty of designing a general purpose system, or even defining a common body of general requirements that could be applied to all systems because: hull dimensions and shapes differ widely, the different areas of any given hull impose very different working conditions for robotic devices, working areas differ in different shipyards or even within the same shipyard and the particular businesses and cultures of shipyards impose different requirements and priorities.

This tremendous variety generates very different problems, which require different robotic systems, each adapted to the specific problem. To solve these problems, a common design pattern has been followed for every robot of the EFTCoR family: they generally consist of a primary positioning system capable of covering large hull areas and a secondary positioning system mounted on

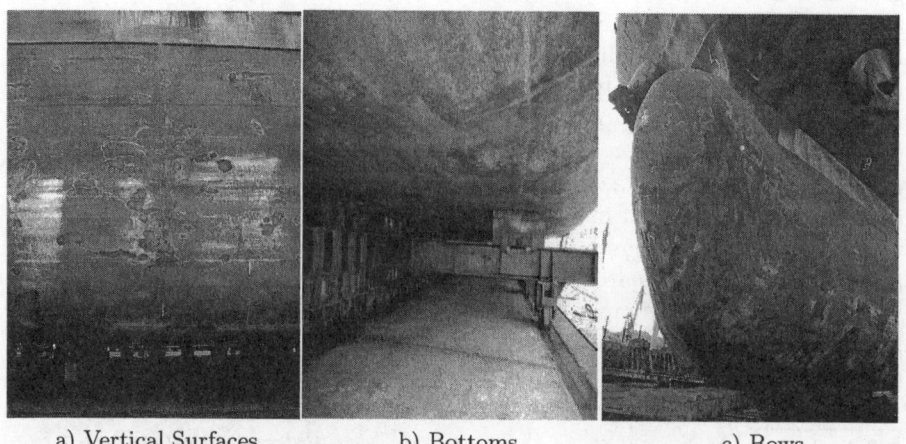

a) Vertical Surfaces   b) Bottoms   c) Bows

Fig. 1. Different hull shapes in the operational domain

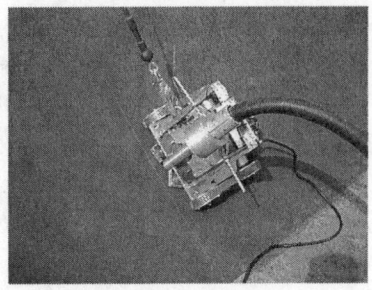

a) CAD model   b) Real model

Fig. 2. Different views of the Lázaro vehicle

the primary system that can position a tool over a relatively small area (4 to 16 m^2). Different combinations of primary/secondary/tool have been considered and tested. Finally, it is important to stress that the EFTCoR is an industrial project and as such should use components that are common in industrial facilities (PLCs rather than work-stations, field buses rather LANs).

One of the members of the EFTCoR family is the Lázaro vehicle. Lázaro is a caterpillar vehicle capable of scaling a hull thanks to permanent magnets (see Fig. 2), carrying a manipulator that holds a cleaning tool. Like all members of the EFTCoR family, the vehicle can be driven by a human operator and also performs some autonomous tasks, such as obstacle avoidance and simple pre-programmed sequences.

The execution platform is an on-board embedded PC with a PC/104 expansion bus. Its based on an Intel, ultra low voltage Celeron microprocessor. The PC/104 bus is a widely used industrial standard with many advantages, such as vibration-resistance, modularity, mechanical robustness, low power consumption, etc., so its an excellent bus for embedded systems. The expansion system is formed by an analog and digital I/O board featuring 8 analog inputs, 4 analog outputs, 3 timer/counter and 24 general pourpose digital lines, and a PCMCIA expansion interface.

The Lázaro robot has two servomotors to move along the ship hull. The control of each servomotor is performed with the help of both incremental encoders. Besides this, the robot also has a ring of bumpers and infrared sensors to stop in case it gets near an obstacle or collides with it.

The chosen operating system is Real-Time Linux [7], which makes it possible to have a real-time application running while retaining all the power of a Linux distribution (though with some restrictions) underneath. The Industrial IT Group at the Universidad Politécnica de Valencia has made a GNAT Ada compiler port for the RTLinux operating system [8].

3   The ACROSET Reference Architecture

Considering the differences among systems as noted in sections 1 and 2, a central objective of the proposed architecture must clearly be to deal with such variability. A more precise analysis of the differences among systems [9] reveals that most of them relate not only to the components of the system but to the interactions among these components. Therefore, when designing the architecture the following points (architectural drivers, AD) should be borne in mind:

AD1: Very different instances of the architecture should be able to share the same virtual components.

AD2: The designer should adopt policies that allow a clear separation between the components as such and their patterns of interaction.

AD3: The implementation of such virtual components may be software or hardware; it is highly advisable that such components can be *Commercial off the Shelf* (COTS) components.

AD4: It should be possible to derive concrete architectures for both deliberative (operator-driven) and reactive (autonomous intelligent) systems.

ACROSET (*Arquitectura de Control para Robots de Servicio Teleoperados[1]*) was designed as a solution to the variability problem found on the EFTCoR project that takes account of the already mentioned architectural drives. It aims to be a reference architecture for teleoperated service robot control units. The architecture emerged from previous works at the DSIE (*División de Sistemas e Ingeniería Electrónica, Universidad de Cartagena, Spain*) [10, 11] and is currently being used, tested and improved in the EFTCoR project.

ACROSET (see Fig. 3) is supposed to make it possible for very different systems to use the same components. Therefore, the first step was to define the rules and common infrastructure that would allow components to be assembled or connected. To that end, the concepts of component, port and connector were adopted as defined in [12] and they are the keypoints of ACROSET. A brief description of these concepts is given in section 5.1. The notation followed to describe components, ports and connectors is inspired by the 4 views of Hofmeister [12] and ROOM [13], which extends the UML notation with stereotyped classes and special symbols.

The first subsystem of the architecture is the *Coordination, Control and Abstraction Subsystem* (CCAS). The CCAS abstracts and encapsulates the functionality of the physical devices of the robot. The CCAS is composed of *virtual* components, which can be implemented in either software or hardware. The CCAS breaks down into several components, distributed in hierarchical layers (see 3.1). Many of the components used in a robot control unit can be found on the market either as hardware devices and control cards or software packages for a given platform. Where COTS components are used, ACROSET offers the designer two possible solutions: he can define its *virtual* counterpart or he can use

---

[1] Control Architecture for Teleoperated Service Robots.

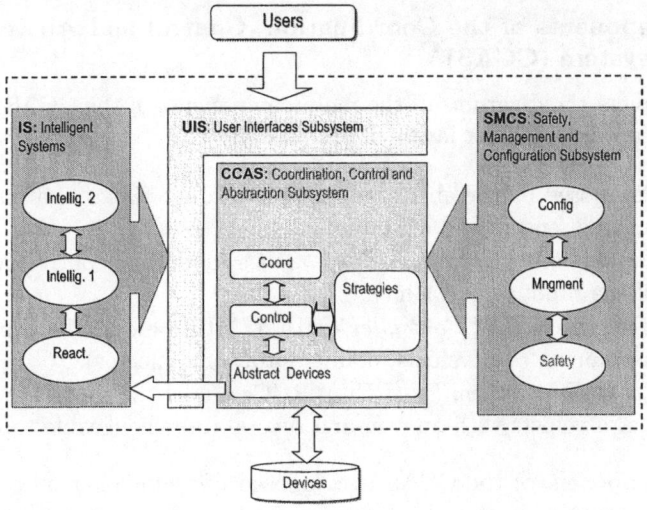

Fig. 3. An overview of ACROSET subsystems

the *Bridge* pattern to map an existing virtual component to the actual COTS interface.

To deal with operator-driven and semi-autonomous systems an *Intelligence Subsystem* (IS) is proposed. This way, autonomous intelligence can be added if necessary, to act as another user of the CCAS functionality. This separation of intelligence and functionality enhances the modifiability and adaptability of the system to new missions and behaviours. The intelligence can be combined with the operator commands depending on the application or mode of operation.

A *User Interaction Subsystem* (UIS) is proposed to interpret, combine and arbitrate between orders that may come simultaneously from different users of the system functionality (CCAS), since the system does not concern itself with the source of the order.

Other important aspects besides the functionality or the intelligence of the system include the safety and the possibilities of configuration and management of the application. To differentiate between functionality *per se* and the monitoring of such functionality, a *Safety, Management and Configuration Subsystem* (SMCS) is proposed. Another function of this subsystem is to manage and configure the initialisation of the application.

A complete description of ACROSET and one of its instantiations is too extensive to be included in this paper, so only details from one of the subsystems will be presented in the remaining sections. The CCAS has been the selected subsystem because its the most representative and complex subsystem of ACROSET, since it abstracts the robot functionality.

3.1   Components of the Coordination, Control and Abstraction Subsystem (CCAS)

Figure 4 depicts the diagrams of the main components of the CCAS, which are defined and grouped in four layers of granularity:

Layer 1: Composed by the abstraction of the characteristics of atomic components, such as sensors and actuators.

Layer 2: *Simple Unit Controller* (SUC). SUCs model the control over one actuator of the robot (e.g. a joint).

Layer 3: *Mechanism Unit Controller* (MUC). MUCs model the control over a whole mechanism (e.g. vehicle, manipulator, end effector).

Layer 4: *Robot Unit Controller* (RUC). RUCs model the control over a whole robot (e.g. a vehicle with an arm and several interchangeable tools).

Every component of the CCAS is composed of two similar objects. On the one hand, it contains a *statechart manager*. This statechart manager decides, depending on the component current state, whether a recently issued command should be executed or not or if the state of the component should change in response to an external signal. It also controls every task created by the component. On the other hand, the object that carries out the component main purpose is interchangeable. This object follows a *Strategy* pattern, so the component behaviour can be modified even at runtime to adapt to a new state and new behaviours can be added later.

Figure 4-a depicts the *SUC* component. SUCs are meant to control actuators, so the `ControlStrategy` is the interchangeable object in this case; for example, the `ControlStrategy` of a given joint may be a traditional control algorithm (PID) or may be changed for a fuzzy logic one. SUCs usually need to accomplish hard real-time requirements and are therefore generally implemented in hardware. When they are implemented in software, they impose severe real-time constraints on operating systems and platforms. In such case, SUCs also need

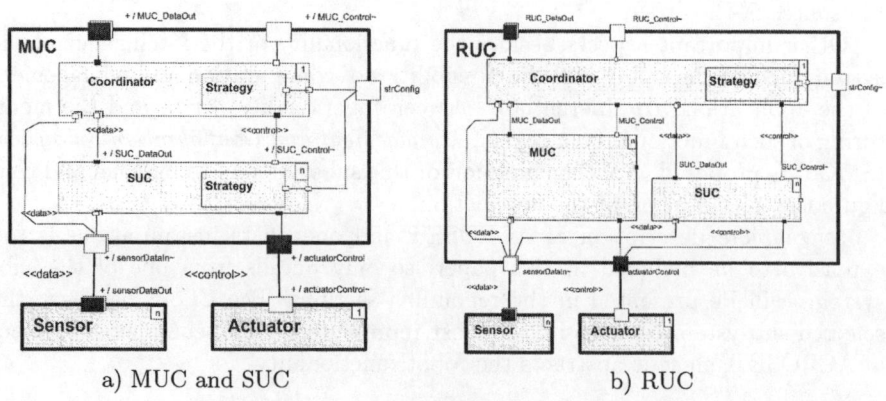

a) MUC and SUC   b) RUC

Fig. 4. CCAS components diagrams

a task to periodically generate the control signal according to the algorithm present in the `ControlStrategy` object.

Figure 4-a also depicts the *MUC* component. MUC components are logical entities composed of an aggregation of SUCs and a coordinator, which coordinates SUC actions according to the commands and information it receives. The interchangeable object of the MUC is the `CoordinationStrategy`; for example, the `CoordinationStrategy` of a given manipulator may be a particular solution for its inverse kinematics. Although the architecture defines MUCs as relational aggregates, they can actually become components (hard or soft) when the architecture is instantiated to develop a concrete system. ACROSET allows the designer decide whether the MUC interface provides access to its inner components or not. In fact, although MUCs may be implemented in either hardware or software, they are very commonly commercial motion control cards that constrain the range of possible commands to its internal components.

Finally, Fig. 4-b shows the *RUC* component. RUCs are an aggregation of MUCs and a global coordinator that generates the commands for its MUCs and coordinates their actions. As in the case of MUCs, the `CoordinationStrategy` is the interchangeable object. For example, the `CoordinationStrategy` of a robot composed of a vehicle with a manipulator could be a generalised kinematics solution that contemplates the possibility of moving the vehicle to reach a given target. Like MUCs, RUCs are logical components that can become physical components depending on the concrete instantiation. In general, RUCs are quite complex, comprise both hardware and software elements and can expose a wide variety of interfaces.

4   Instantiation for the Lázaro Vehicle

Figure 5 shows the CCAS instantiated for this system. As can be seen in the figure, two different MUCs have been implemented: one to control the vehicle and another to control the manipulator. The first contains one SUC to control each of the electrical motors that move the vehicle. The manipulator MUC coordinates two SUCs, one for each manipulator axis. The vehicle uses a tool that consists of an enclosed nozzle for making the blasting and recovering of residues.

The motion controllers have been implemented by means of Ada packages that implement the interfaces defined by ACROSET. In this case, the implementation allows direct access to the hardware without the mediation of any SUC. Two different intelligent behaviours have been added to the IS: obstacle avoidance and simple pre-programmed sequences. The components of the IS that implement these behaviours obtain the information they need from the vehicle sensors and generate commands to the CCAS. Integration between these commands and the operator commands is resolved by an arbitrator in the UIS.

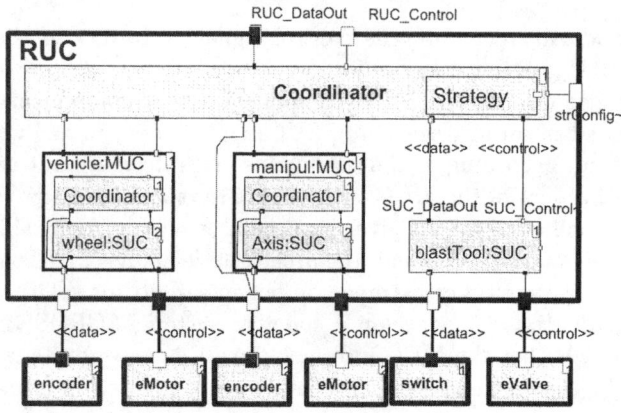

Fig. 5. Components of CCAS in climbing vehicle Control Unit

5   Implementation of the Architecture

In the implementation phase, the conceptual view must be mapped to a module view [12]. We have chosen the object-oriented paradigm and Ada95 to implement the architecture, so components, ports and connector will be mapped to classes, objects, associations and dependencies. In this section, some important aspects of the implementation will be presented.

5.1   Ports and Connectors

As mentioned in section 3, ACROSET follows a component-oriented approach. Two important concepts when talking about components are the concepts of *port* and *connector*. Connectors communicate two compatible ports of two components. Only the functionality offered by the ports of the component can be invoked, using for that the communication protocol encapsulated by the connector. This way, the content of the message is separated from how it is sent.

The concept of *port* is similar to that of interface, but with two differences: ports involved both the operations offered and required by the component and they implement the necessary services to fulfil the communication protocol appropriate to its connector. *Connectors* allow the flow of information between components, and can be as simple as pipes and events or as complex as the client-server protocol.

Changing a connector basically implies the change of the communication protocol between the ports it connects. This variation should be reflected in the modification of the port services referred to the communication, but not of those referred to the component functionality, which is accessed through the port. To separate these concepts (separation of concerns strategy [12]), ACROSET defines as many port types as possible communication ways exist. Port types are defined according to the functionality that they must fulfil (Control Input Port for a SUC, Out Data Port and Input Data for a sensor, etc). Defining the

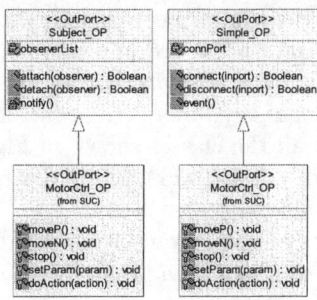

Fig. 6. Ports and connectors implementation

communication protocol for these last ports is as simple as inheriting from the desired protocol port, as showed in Fig. 6.

5.2   SUC Implementation

For the same reason that a complete description of ACROSET cannot be described in this paper, only an example of a component implementation is presented in this section. The chosen component is a SUC to control one motor as a representative part of the system (see Fig. 7).

The Motor_SUC class contains the ports showed in Fig. 6 with stereotypes ≪*InPort*≫ and ≪*OutPort*≫, to get data (`Data`) or produce control (`Ctrl`) and to configure the SUC (`Config`). Ports belong to the component and they are created and destroyed with it, so they have a composite relation, as Fig. 7 shows.

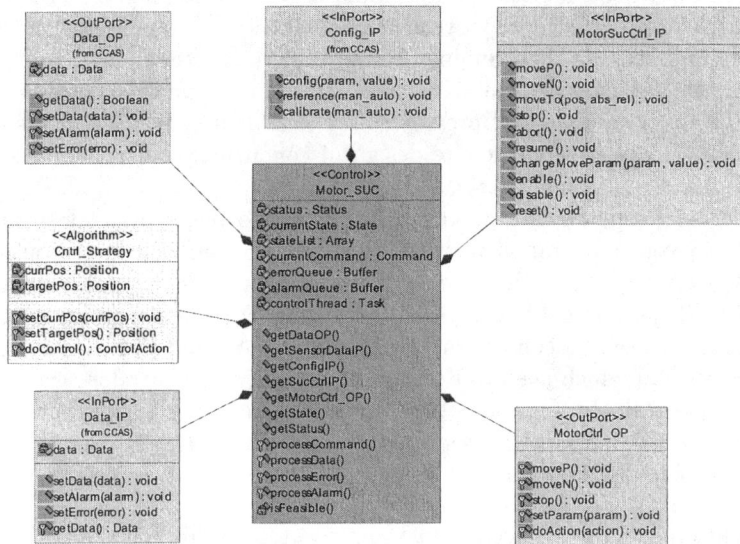

Fig. 7. Class diagram of the Motor_SUC

The operations offered by the control ports match with the events sent by other components to the SUC. Data ports are implemented as generics, showing the same interface to any component. Besides ports, class Motor_SUC contains the interchangeable `ControlStrategy` object (the control algorithm).

In case of a Tool_SUC, all the classes shown in Fig. 7 remain with the same interface, excepting control ports (`Ctrl`). These ports must be adapted to the control events related to this particular tool.

The rest of components of the instantiation of ACROSET for Lázaro have been built in a similar manner, extending their interfaces to the needs of the system. Notice that the SUC interface remains similar in every component thanks to the method `processCommand()`, which process any incoming event in its particular control inport, of course, the implementation of that method is different for SUC, MUC and RUC.

5.3   Execution View

Following the 4 views of Hofmeister [12] notation, the execution view describes the structure of a system in terms of its runtime platform elements (tasks, processes, address spaces, etc). In this view, the objects identified in the module view of the system are mapped to a concurrent tasking architecture, where concurrent tasks, task interfaces and interconnections are defined. The driving forces behind the decisions for designing the execution architecture view are performance, distribution requirements and the runtime platform, which includes the underlying hardware and software platforms.

Too many tasks in a system can unnecessarily increase its complexity because of greater inter-task communication and synchronisation, and can lead to increased overhead because of additional context switching. The system designer has to make tradeoffs between introducing tasks to simplify and clarify the design and keeping their number low so that the system is not overloaded.

To help the designer determine the concurrent tasks and to make these tradeoffs, the COMET method [14] provides a set of heuristics which capture expert designer knowledge in the software design of concurrent and real-time system, so called *task structuring criteria*.

Hofmeister proposes as a good starting point to begin by associating each high-level conceptual component with a set of execution elements. Considering that the main objects of the system have been proposed as an instantiation of ACROSET (see Fig. 5), the task structuring criteria might be applied to determine which of the components in the IS, CCAS and SMCS may execute concurrently, and which need to execute sequentially and therefore are grouped into the same task. In a second stage, the task clustering criteria are applied, with the objective of reducing the number of tasks. Figure 8 depicts the task diagram obtained by applying the following task clustering criteria:

Temporal clustering. Since the tasks involved in controlling the I/O show no sequential dependency and their activation periods are multiples, they have been grouped in one task.

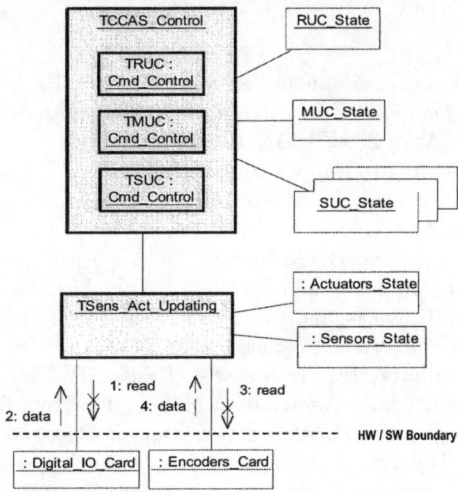

Fig. 8. Task diagram after clustering

Task inversion. Instead of using a task for each SUC, all identical tasks of the same type have been replaced by one task that performs the same service. Each object state information is captured in a separate protected object. Although SUCs have been grouped, the tasks that perform their concurrent control activities (e.g. a periodic control algorithm) remain as separate tasks, with the task type Cmd_Control. The same happens with MUC and SUC command control.

Sequential clustering. To avoid overloading the system, all the *UC* state control tasks have been grouped in the CCAS task because the information flows up and down always in a sequential order.

6   Conclusions

The use of a common architecture for a domain or family of systems allows rapid developments and the reuse of components. This paper has presented a common architectural framework for the development of teleoperated service robots control units (ACROSET) and also an application example in the context of the EFTCoR project (the Lázaro vehicle), that shows the ability of ACROSET to cope with the needs and requirements of very different systems.The separation of the conventional functionality of the systems (CCAS) from the intelligent behaviours (IS) greatly facilitates the addition of new functionalities and the maintenance of applications.

Perhaps, the main contribution of ACROSET to the current state of the art is the conceptual component oriented approach, which makes the components independent to the implementation language or hardware/software partition. This has allowed implementing those components as PLC blocks, not only as objects and classes, e.g. as CLARAty [2] does.

References

1. E. Coste-Manière and R. Simmons. Architecture: the Backbone of Robotics Systems. In *Proc. of the 2000 IEEE International Conference on Robotics & Automation*, pages 67–72, April 2000. ISBN: 0780358864.
2. I. Nesnas, A. Wright, M. Bajracharya, R. Simmons, T. Estlin, and W.S. Kim. CLARAty: An Architecture for Reusable Robotic System. March 2003. Jet Propulsion Laboratory, NASA.
3. K.U. Scholl, J. Albiez, and B. Gassmann. MCA – An Expandable Modular Controller Architecture. In *4th Real-Time Linux Workshop*, 2001.
4. H. Bruyninckx, B. Konincks, and P. Soetens. A Software Framework for Advanced Motion Control. Draft version, January 2002.
5. C. Fernández, A. Iborra, B. Álvarez, J.A. Pastor, P. Sánchez, J.M. Fernández-Meroño, and N. Ortega. Co-operative Robots for Hull Blasting in European Shiprepair Industry. *IEEE Robotics & Automation Magazine (Special Issue on Industrial Robotics Applications & Industry-Academia Cooperation in Europe - New Tendencies and Perspectives)*, November 2004. ISSN: 1070-9932.
6. EFTCoR Official Site. http://www.eftcor.com/.
7. M. Barbanov. *A Linux-based Real-Time Operating System*. PhD thesis, New Mexico Institute of Mining and Technology, June 1997.
8. M. Masmano, J. Real, I. Ripoll, and A. Crespo. Running Ada on Real-Time Linux. In *Reliable Software Technologies - Ada-Europe 2003*, volume LNCS 2655, pages 322–333. Springer-Verlag, June 2003.
9. J.A. Pastor Franco. *Evaluación y desarrollo incremental de una arquitectura software de referencia para sistemas de teleoperación utilizando métodos formales*. PhD thesis, Technical University of Cartagena (Spain), 2002.
10. F. Ortiz, A. Iborra, F. Marín, B. Álvarez, and J.M. Fernández-Meroño. GOYA: A teleoperated system for blasting applied to ships maintenance. In *3rd International Conference on Climbing and Walking Robots*, October 2000. ISBN: 1-86058-268-0.
11. A. Iborra, J.A. Pastor, B. Álvarez, C. Fernández, and J.M. Fernández-Meroño. Robots in Radioactive Environments. *IEEE Robotics and Automation Magazine*, 10(4):12–22, December 2003. ISSN: 1070-9932.
12. C. Hofmeister, R. Nord, and D. Soni. *Applied Software Architecture*. Addison-Wesley, January 2000. ISBN: 0-201-32571-3.
13. B. Selic, G. Gullekson, and P.T. Ward. *Real-Time Object-Oriented Modelling (ROOM)*. John Wiley and Sons, 1994. ISBN: 0471599174.
14. H. Gomaa. *Designing Concurrent, Distributed, and Real-Time Applications with UML*. Object Technology. Addison-Wesley, 2000. ISBN: 0-201-65793-7.

An Ada Framework for QoS-Aware Applications

Luís Miguel Pinho, Luis Nogueira, and Ricardo Barbosa

Department of Computer Engineering, ISEP, Polytechnic Institute of Porto,
Rua Dr. António Bernardino Almeida, 431, 4200-072 Porto, Portugal
{lpinho,luis,rbarbosa}@dei.isep.ipp.pt

Abstract. In this paper we present a framework for managing QoS-aware applications in a dynamic, ad-hoc, distributed environment. This framework considers an available set of wireless/mobile and fixed nodes, which may temporally form groups in order to process a set of related services, and where there is the need to support different levels of service and different combinations of quality requirements. This framework is being developed both for testing and validating an approach, based on multidimensional QoS properties, which provides service negotiation and proposal evaluation algorithms, and for assessing the suitability of the Ada language to be used in the context of dynamic, QoS-aware systems.

1 Introduction

Quality of Service (QoS) is considered an important user demand, receiving wide attention in real-time multimedia research [1][2]. However, in most systems, users do not have any real influence over the QoS they can obtain, since service characteristics are fixed when the systems are initiated. Furthermore, multimedia applications (and their users) can differ enormously in their service requirements as well as in the resources which need to be available to them [3]. These applications present increasingly complex demands on quality of service, reflected in multiple attributes over multiple quality dimensions.

At the same time, the use of laptop computers coupled with wireless network interfaces is growing rapidly. Recent technological development lead to the fusion of wireless ad-hoc networks, peer-to-peer computing and multimedia content. As devices move within the range of each others a local ad-hoc network forms spontaneously, creating a new, highly dynamic and decentralized environment for multimedia applications.

Such an environment is expected to be heterogeneous, consisting of nodes with several resource capabilities. For some of those there may be a constraint on the type and size of applications they can execute with user's acceptable quality of service. For example, video conferencing systems often use compression schemes that are effective, but computationally intensive, trading CPU time for limited network bandwidth. A mobile client with limited CPU and memory capacity, but sufficient link speed, with nearby more powerful (or less congested) devices, can divide the computational intensive processing into tasks and spread it among different neighbours.

T. Vardanega and A. Wellings (Eds.): Ada-Europe 2005, LNCS 3555, pp. 25–38, 2005.

It is obvious that these requirements for more flexible QoS-aware applications impact on the available support from the underlying environment (language, middleware, operating system). In what languages are concerned, Ada has been for a long time considered suitable for the development of traditional, static, real-time applications, but is often considered to be limited concerning the support to more dynamic real-time applications. It is our belief that this latter idea is not true, and, moreover, that Ada is an enabling technology for supporting QoS-aware type of real-time applications

Therefore, in this paper we present a framework which is currently being built for testing and validating a QoS applications support approach which is currently being specified [4]. This framework is being implemented in Ada, using the currently available mechanisms, which will allow providing sufficient insight on the suitability of the language. The rest of this paper is structured as follows. The next section provides a brief description of the considered model for the system, and the used approach for QoS requirements representation and service requests. Section 3 presents an overview of the Ada framework, considering its structure and main functionalities, while sections 4 and 5 present, respectively, how negotiation and acceptance of services is performed, and how resource managers are implemented. Finally, section 6 presents some conclusions.

2   System Model

In this work, we consider a system where wireless/mobile nodes may dynamically enter the range of each other, and of wired infrastructures (even clusters of nodes [5]), opportunistically taking advantage of the local ad-hoc network that is spontaneously created, forming a temporary coalition for service execution (Figure 1). Coalition formation is necessary when a single node cannot execute a specific service, but it may also be beneficial when groups perform more efficiently when compared to a single node performance.

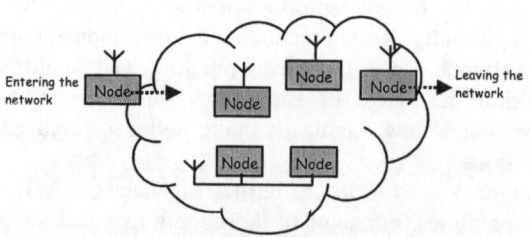

Fig. 1. System Overview

Ad-hoc networks, i.e., networks without any fixed network infrastructure (such as base stations, etc.) are gaining much interest in research as well as in industry. With ad-hoc network mechanisms, clients that are in sufficiently close proximity are able to communicate directly without the need of further, externally provided, infrastructure. At first glance, an individual mobile device may not have sufficient capacity and computation power for an effective integration in a distributed multimedia processing environment. However, if we exploit the aggregated mobile power instead of single, individual power and consider the exponential rise of mobile devices and the continuous developments in wireless technology, then one may conclude that this collaborative processing can be a valid solution.

This provides a generic model that enables a distributed service allocation, i.e., without a central authority distributing the services among nodes. Given a set of services, a distributed environment must seek the maximization of the associated QoS constraints. The nodes shall reach efficient service allocation by themselves, seeking a maximal outcome. This will be achieved via the formation of a temporary group of individual nodes (coalitions), which, due to its higher flexibility and agility, is capable of effectively respond to new, challenging, requirements.

It is clear that such a group presents very significant challenges, especially at the architectural level. Major developments are required in the fields of communications protocols, data processing and application support. Our goal is to develop the architecture which enables the creation of a new generation of mobile nodes that can effectively network together, providing a flexible platform for the support of distinct network applications. In this model, QoS-aware applications must explicitly request the service execution form the underlying QoS framework, thus providing explicit admission for controlling the system, abstracting from existent underlying distributed middleware and from the operating system. The model itself abstracts from the communication and execution environments.

2.1 QoS Requirements Representation

In [4], QoS requirements are described through a scheme that defines dimensions, attributes and values, as well as relations that maps dimensions to attributes and attributes to values:

$$QoS \rightarrow \{Dim, \ Attr, \ Val, \ DA_r, \ AV_r, \ Deps\}$$

where Dim is the set of QoS dimensions (e.g. Video, Audio), $Attr$ is the set of attributes identifiers and Val is the set of attribute's values identifiers. DA_r is the relationship that assigns to each dimension in Dim a set of attributes in $Attr$, AV_r is the relationship that assigns to each attribute in $Attr$ a specific value in Val and $Deps$ is a set of relationships defining the dependencies between attributes' values. Values are represented by a type (integer, float, enumeration) and domain (discrete, continuous).

As an example of this requirement description, a video streaming application may define a set of dimensions (and their attributes) that might be associated with a particular application (the following list is not intended to be exhaustive):

```
Dim  = {Video Quality, Audio Quality}
Attr = {color depth, frame rate, sampling rate, sample bits}
Val  = {{1,integer,discrete},{3,integer,discrete},...,
        {[1,...,30],integer,continuous},...}
```

It is clearly infeasible to make the user specify the utility of every quality choice, for all the QoS dimensions of a particular application. There are simply too many choices. Instead, a preference order is imposed over the dimensions, its attributes and their values on user's service request [4]. While a semantically rich request is provided, so that the system tries to achieve a service the more closely related to user's preferences, a user is actually able to express his preferences in his request.

Suppose that, in a remote surveillance system, video is much more important to the user than audio. Assuming that for a particular user a grey scale, low frame rate is fine for video, his request could be as follows:

```
1. Video Quality
     (a) frame rate    : [10,...,5], [4,...1]
     (b) color depth   : 3, 1
2. Audio Quality
     (a) sampling rate : 8
     (b) sample bits   : 8
```

The relative decreasing order of importance imposed in dimensions, attributes and values expresses user's preferences, that is, elements identified by lower indexes are more important than elements identified by higher indexes. In the example above, video is more important than audio, and frame rate is more important than color depth in the Video Quality dimension. In a similar way, the audio sampling rate is more important than the sampling size. For each of these attributes, a preference order for the QoS values is as well expressed.

3 The Ada QoS-Aware Framework

Figure 2 presents the structure of the proposed framework. Central to the behaviour of the framework, is the *QoS Provider*, which is the responsible for all the process of both distributed and local resource requests.

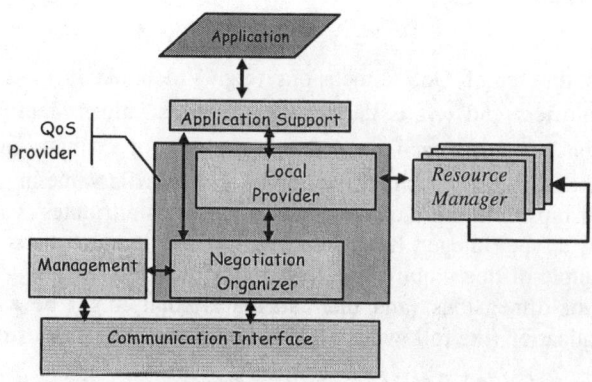

Fig. 2. Framework Structure

The *QoS Provider*, rather than reserving resources directly, contacts the *Resource Managers* to grant specific resource amounts to the requesting task. It is the *QoS Provider* which receives the user's preferences for all the QoS dimensions of a particular application, which are then distributed among the *Resource Managers*.

Within the *QoS Provider*, the *Negotiation Organizer* is the responsible for the collaboration of all of the current nodes in the system, by implementing the negotiation and proposal evaluation algorithms of [4], atomically distributing service requests, receiving the individual nodes' proposals for each service and deciding which node(s) will provide the service. Note that for now we consider the existence of an atomic broadcast mechanism [6] in the system, thus by guaranteeing that all nodes will receive the same service requests and proposals in the same order, we guarantee that the decision will be the same in all nodes of the system.

The *Local Provider* is responsible for replying to negotiation requests, by making a proposal using a heuristic algorithm [4] inspired in the local QoS optimization heuristic of [7]. This module is also responsible for maintaining the state of the resource allocations and services provided in each node.

The *System Manager* module will be responsible for maintaining the overall system configuration, due to the dynamics of nodes entering and leaving the system, and for detecting coalition operation and dissolution. The *Resource Managers* are the modules that manage a particular resource. These modules interface with the actual implementation in a particular system of the resource controllers, such as the device driver for the network, the scheduler for the CPU, or by software that manages other resources (such as memory). It is obvious that, although we consider a collaborative environment, proper resource usage must be monitored in run time [8], in order for system resource managers be able to decide based on the actual resource usage of the system, not only on the resource assumptions of executing services.

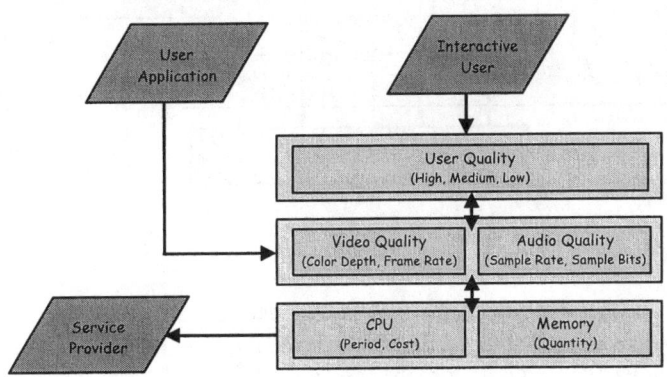

Fig. 3. Resource Managers Layering

One important issue is the ability of resource managers to use each other, in order to allow systems to be built supporting QoS requirements either from the point of view of the user (*e.g.* high quality), of applications (*e.g.* frame rate) or of the system (e.g. period and cost). Nevertheless, special care must be taken that a service request is not performed with accumulative resource requests on these different levels.

As an example, a particular system may provide the resource manager layering of Figure 3. With this layering, an interactive user application could be more friendly and easier to use by providing only high-level user perceptive quality, whilst other user applications could be programmed to use application-related QoS constraints. Finally, service providers would collect the service requirements at the system level.

4 The QoS Provider

Figure 4 presents the structure of the *QoS Provider* module. New service requests are made by the communication interface (applications call this interface in order to guarantee the order of service requests). Applications may request information concerning the actual QoS values of currently executing (in this node) services. The module also receives/sends proposals from/to other nodes concerning a service being negotiated.

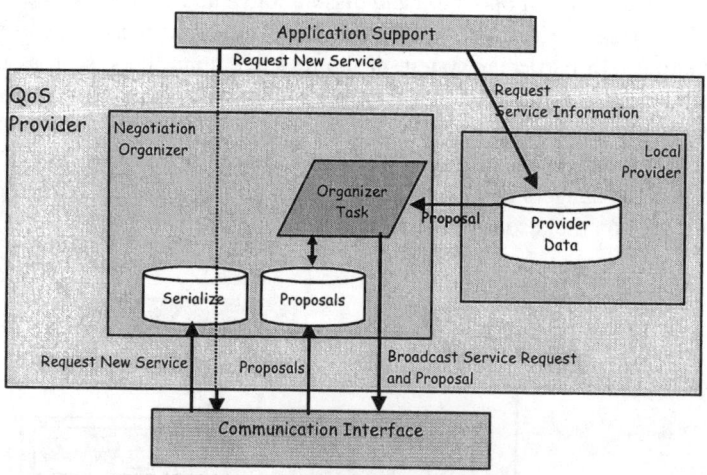

Fig. 4. *QoS Provider* structure

In order to guarantee that new service requests are serialized in the provider, a protected object is used (Figure 5). New service requests queue on the *New_Service* entry, in order to request for the service. Then, requests are re-queued on *Wait_New_Service*, waiting for the end of the negotiation process. Note that while this process takes place, the barrier in *New_Service* is closed.

Concerning the proposals (Figure 6), there is no need to serialize access to deliver a proposal, therefore only mutual exclusion is provided, but an entry is provided for the *Organizer Task* to wait for the arrival of the proposals of the other nodes.

```
protected Serialization is
    entry New_Service(Preferences      : in  QoS_Values_Type;
                      Accepted_Values  : out QoS_Values_Type;
                      Accepted         : out Boolean;
                      Id               : out Service_Id);

    entry Get_Service(Preferences : out QoS_Values_Type);

    procedure Service_Answer(Accepted : in Boolean;
                             Proposal : in QoS_Values_Type;
                             Id       : in Service_Id);
private
    entry Wait_New_Service(Preferences : in  QoS_Values_Type;
                           Accptd_Val  : out QoS_Values_Type;
                           Accepted    : out Boolean;
                           Id          : out Service_Id);

    Pref, Acc          : QoS_Values_Type;
    Accepted_Service   : Boolean;
    Serv_Id            : Service_Id;

    New_Service_Request   : Boolean := false;
    New_Service_Response  : Boolean := false;
    Organizer_Available   : Boolean := true;
end Serialization;
```

Fig. 5. *Serialization* protected object

```
protected Proposals is
    procedure Set_Proposal(Node     : in SM.Nodes_Type;
                           Proposal: in QoS_Values_Type);

    procedure Clean;
    entry Wait_Decide(Accepted_Values : out QoS_Values_Type;
                      Accepted        : out Boolean;
                      Node            : out Nodes_Type);
private
    Proposals : Nodes_Proposals;
    Proposed  : Nodes_Proposed := (others => false);
    Complete  : Boolean        := false;
end Proposals;
```

Fig. 6. *Proposals* protected object

The *Organizer Task* (Figure 7) is normally blocked in the *Get_Service* entry of the *Serialization* object. Upon a service request is made, the task atomically broadcasts it to the system, and requests a proposal to the *Local Provider*. Note that the broadcast of the proposal thus not need to be atomic, since there is no necessity of order between the proposals. The task then blocks waiting for a decision of the *Proposal* object. It then informs the *Local Provider* of the state of the request. Note that since the decision is the same in all nodes then it is not necessary to broadcast it. The *Local*

```
task body QoS_Organizer_Task is
  -- declarations
begin
  loop
      Serialization.Get_Service(Preferences);
      Comm.Atomic_Broadcast(Preferences);
      Local.Service_Request( Preferences,
                                My_Node_Proposal,
                                Id);
      Comm.Broadcast(My_Node_Proposal);
      Proposals.Set_Proposal(This_Node,
                                My_Node_Proposal);
      Proposals.Wait_Decide( Decided_Values,
                                Accepted,
                                Node);
      if Node = This_Node then
         Local.Accepted_Service(Id);
      else
         Local.Rejected_Service(Id);
      end if;
      Serialization.Service_Answer( Accepted,
                                       Decided_Values,
                                       Id);
  end loop;
end Qos_Organizer_Task;
```

Fig. 7. *Organizer* task

```
protected Provider_Data is
   procedure Register(Resource  : in Manager_Access;
                      Dimension : in QoS_Dimensions_Type;
                      Old       : out Manager_Access);
   procedure Service_Request(Pref : in QoS_Values_Type;
                             Prop : out QoS_Values_Type;
                             Id   : out Service_Id);
   procedure Rejected_Service(Id : in Service_Id);
   procedure Accepted_Service(Id : in Service_Id);
   procedure Terminated_Service(Id : in Service_Id);

   function Get_Service_Parameters(Id : SM.Service_Id)
       return QoS_Values_Type;
   function Get_Resource_Manager(D : in QoS_Dimensions_Type)
       return Manager_Access;

private
   Resources : Resources_Set := (others => null);
   Used_Service_Id : Service_State_Array := (others => Free);
   Services :  Service_Array;
end Provider_Data;
```

Fig. 8. *Local Provider* protected object

Provider (Figure 8) is a simple mutual exclusion object, protecting the manipulation of resource managers and services information. Note that Resource Managers must register with the provider upon initiation, in order to be asked for proposals concerning their particular dimension.

5 Resource Managers and Attributes

Resource attributes are supported by providing a tagged abstract type (Figure 9), which can be extended by resource managers, to define particular resource attributes.

```ada
type Attribute_Value is abstract tagged null record;

type Attribute_Value_Access is access all
    Attribute_Value'Class;

function Difference(Preference, Proposal : Attribute_Value)
    return Float is abstract;

package Attr_List is new
    List(Attribute_Value, Attribute_Value_Access);
```

Fig. 9. *Attribute_Value* tagged type

```ada
type Manager_Type(Dim : QoS_Dimensions_Type) is abstract tagged
record
        Dimension: QoS_Dimensions_Type := Dim;
end record;

type Manager_Access is access all Manager_Type'Class;

-- Resource Managers must call register
procedure Register_Manager(Resource : Manager_Access;
                           Old       : out Manager_Access);

-- Services to implement
-- Depend of the particular Resource Manager
procedure Evaluate_Service(Resource    : in Manager_Type;
                           Preferences : in Attr_List.List;
                           Proposal    : out Attr_List.List;
                           Id          : in Service_Id)
    is abstract;
procedure Accepted_Service(Resource : in Manager_Type;
                           Id        : in Service_Id)
    is abstract;
procedure Rejected_Service(Resource : in Manager_Type;
                           Id        : in Service_Id)
    is abstract;
procedure Terminated_Service(Resource : in Manager_Type;
                             Id        : in Service_Id)
    is abstract;
```

Fig. 10. *Resource Manager* tagged type

Attributes must implement the abstract function for difference, in order to support the evaluation of proposals of [4]. An attribute list is also provided for service requests to be able to specify a set (in decreasing importance order) of attribute values.

Managers themselves are extensions of a tagged type (Figure 10), and must implement the abstract primitive subprograms that are used by the Local Provider to request the evaluation of a service, and to inform of service acceptance, rejection and termination. The implementation of a particular resource manager must ensure the consistency of the resource, guaranteeing that after a request is evaluated, it is considered as granted for other resource requests performed until rejected or terminated. Note that several resource requests may coexist for the same service request, due to the layering of resources presented in Figure 3.

As an example of attribute and manager instantiation, Figure 11 presents a *User_Quality* resource manager, which maps to the high-level user perception manager of Figure 3. A single attribute is defined, which is must be mapped by the *User_Quality_Manager* to actual values in other Dimensions (such as Video and Audio quality).

```
package User_Quality is

    -- Attributes

    type Possible_Values is (High, Medium, Low);

    type User_Value is new Attribute_Value with record
        Value : Possible_Values;
    end record;

    -- Implementation of Difference


    -- Manager

    type User_Quality_Manager is new Manager_Type with record
        -- mapping between User and Audio/Video
    end record;


    -- Implementation of Manager_Type abstract services
    -- This Resource manager will use the managers for
    -- Video Quality and Audio Quality

    Manager : aliased User_Quality_Manager(User);

end User_Quality;
```

Fig. 11. User perception quality manager

Figure 12 presents an example of how this manager could be used by an application to request for High quality in what concerns the overall service (in annex, another example is provided, for the dimensions of Video and Audio quality). Note that if a service is accepted, it is possible to get the actual obtained QoS values, not only for the requested dimension, but also in lower-layer dimensions. For instance in Figure 12, upon acceptance, the procedure call

```
Attr_List.Get_First(QoS_Accepted(Video).Attributes, User_Accepted);
```

will provide in User_Accepted an access value to the first video attribute.

```
procedure Create_QoS_Request is

    QoS_Values, QoS_Accepted : QoS_Values_Type;
    Accepted                 : Boolean;
    Id                       : Service_Id;
    User_Perception          : Attribute_Value_Access;
    User_Accepted            : Attribute_Value_Access;

    Quality_Value            : QoS_Dimension_Access;

begin

    User_Perception := new User_Value;
    User_Value(User_Perception.all).Value := High;

    Quality_Value := new QoS_Dimension_Values;
    Quality_Value.Importance := 1;

    Attr_List.Insert_First(Quality_Value.Attributes,
                           User_Perception);

    QoS_Values := (User => Quality_Value,
                   others => null);

    Application_Interface.Request_Service( QoS_Values,
                                           QoS_Accepted,
                                           Accepted,
                                           Id);

    if Accepted = true then
          Attr_List.Get_First(
              QoS_Accepted(Video).Attributes,
              User_Accepted);
    else
          -- if not accepted
    end if;
end Create_QoS_Request;
```

Fig. 12. Example of requesting service with User Perception value

6   Conclusions

In this paper we presented an overview of a framework which is being implemented for managing QoS-aware applications in a dynamic, ad-hoc, distributed environment. This framework is being used both for validating the group formation and processing approach of [4], but also to assess the suitability of the Ada language to be used in the context of dynamic, QoS-aware systems.

Currently, the resource managing support, the service negotiation and proposal processing is already implemented, allowing us to demonstrate that Ada provides the required mechanisms for the framework purposes. Nevertheless, work must still be done on the management of the collaborative system as a whole, and on real experience on actual systems.

Acknowledgements

The authors would like to thank the anonymous reviewers for their helpful comments and suggestions. This work was partially supported by FCT, through the CISTER Research Unit (FCT UI 608) and the Reflect project (POSI/EIA/60797/2004).

References

1. Clemens C. Wust, Liesbeth Steffens, Reinder J. Bril, and Wim F.J.Verhaegh. Qos control strategies for high-quality video processing. In Proceedings of the 16th Euromicro Conference on Real-Time Systems, Catany, Italy, June 2004.
2. Christina Aurrecoechea, Andrew T. Campbell, and Linda Hauw. A survey of qos architectures. Multimedia Systems, 6(3):138{151, 1998.
3. ARTIST (IST-2001-34820). Selected topics in Embedded Systems Design: Roadmaps for Research. Part III Adaptive Real-Time Systems for Quality of Service Management, May 2004. Available at http://www.artist-embedded.org/.
4. Luis Nogueira, Luis Miguel Pinho. Dynamic QoS-Aware Coalition Formation. In 13th International Workshop on Parallel and Distributed Real-Time Systems, Denver, Colorado, USA, April 2005.
5. Michael Ditze, Berta Batista, Eduardo Tovar, Peter Altenbernd, and Filipe Pacheco. Workload balancing in distributed virtual reality environments. In 1st Intl. Workshop on Real-Time LANs in the Internet Age, Satellite Event to the 14th Euromicro Conference on Real- Time Systems, 2002.
6. V. Hadzilacos and S. Toueg. Fault-Tolerant Broadcasts and Related Problems. In Distributed Systems, Mullender, S. (Ed.), 2nd Ed., Addison-Wesley. 1993.
7. T. F. Abdelzaher, E. M. Atkins, and K. G. Shin. Qos negotiation in real-time systems and its application to automated flight control. IEEE Transactions on Computers, Best of RTAS'97 Special Issue, 49(11):1170{1183, November 2000.
8. Ricardo Barbosa, Luis Miguel Pinho. Mechanisms for Reflection-based Monitoring of Real-Time Systems. Work-In-Progress Session of the 16th Euromicro Conference on Real-Time Systems. Catany, Italy, June 2004.

Annex. Video and Audio Quality Managers

```ada
package Audio_Quality is

   -- Attributes
   type Audio_Attributes is (Sampling_Rate, Sample_Bits);

   type Sampling_Rate_Values is (rate_8, rate_16, rate_24, rate_44);

   type Sample_Bits_Values is (bits_8, bits_16, bits_24);


   type Sampling_Rate_Value is new Attribute_Value with record
      Value : Sampling_Rate_Values;
   end record;
   -- Implementation of Difference

   type Sample_Bits_Value is new RM.Attribute_Value with record
      Value : Sample_Bits_Values;
   end record;
   -- Implementation of Difference


   -- Manager
   type Audio_Quality_Manager is new Manager_Type with record
      -- mapping between Audio and CPU/Memory
   end record;

   -- Implementation of Manager_Type abstract services
   -- This Resource manager will use the managers for CPU and Memory

   Manager: aliased Audio_Quality_Manager(Audio);

end Audio_Quality;



package Video_Quality is

   -- Attributes
   type Video_Attributes is (Color_Depth, Frame_Rate);

   type Color_Depth_Values is (bits_1, bits_8, bits_16, bits_24);

   type Frame_Rate_Values is range 1 .. 30;


   type Color_Depth_Value is new Attribute_Value with record
      Value : Color_Depth_Values;
   end record;
   -- Implementation of Difference

   type Frame_Rate_Value is new Attribute_Value with record
      Value : Frame_Rate_Values;
   end record;
   -- Implementation of Difference

   type Frame_Rate_Range is new Attribute_Value with record
      Low: Frame_Rate_Values;
      High: Frame_Rate_Values;
   end record;
   -- Implementation of Difference


   -- Manager
   type Video_Quality_Manager is new Manager_Type with record
      -- mapping between Video and CPU/Memory
   end record;

   -- Implementation of Manager_Type abstract services
   -- This Resource manager will use the managers for CPU and Memory

   Manager: aliased Video_Quality_Manager(Video);

end Video_Quality;
```

```
-- Example of use of the Video and Audio Quality Managers

procedure Audio_Video_Managers_Request is

    QoS_Values, QoS_Accepted: QoS_Values_Type;
    Accepted:               Boolean;
    Id:                     Service_Id;
    Attribute_Value:        Attribute_Value_Access;
    Video_Values,
    Audio_Values:           QoS_Dimension_Access;

begin

    -- Video First

    Video_Values := new QoS_Dimension_Values;
    Video_Values.Importance := 1;


    -- video frame rate
    Attribute_Value := new Frame_Rate_Value;
    Frame_Rate_Value(Attribute_Value.all).Value := 15;

    Attr_List.Insert_First(Video_Values.Attributes, Attribute_Value);

    Attribute_Value := new Frame_Rate_Range;
    Frame_Rate_Range(Attribute_Value.all).Low := 5;
    Frame_Rate_Range(Attribute_Value.all).High := 10;

    Attr_List.Insert_Last(Video_Values.Attributes, Attribute_Value);


    -- video color
    Attribute_Value := new Color_Depth_Value;
    Color_Depth_Value(Attribute_Value.all).Value := bits_8;

    Attr_List.Insert_Last(Video_Values.Attributes, Attribute_Value);

    Attribute_Value := new Color_Depth_Value;
    Color_Depth_Value(Attribute_Value.all).Value := bits_1;

    Attr_List.Insert_Last(Video_Values.Attributes, Attribute_Value);


    -- Audio Second

    Audio_Values := new QoS_Dimension_Values;
    Audio_Values.Importance := 2;


    -- Sampling rate
    Attribute_Value := new Sampling_Rate_Value;
    Sampling_Rate_Value(Attribute_Value.all).Value := rate_8;

    Attr_List.Insert_First(Audio_Values.Attributes, Attribute_Value);


    -- Sample bits
    Attribute_Value := new Sample_Bits_Value;
    Sample_Bits_Value(Attribute_Value.all).Value := bits_8;

    Attr_List.Insert_Last(Audio_Values.Attributes, Attribute_Value);


    -- QoS Values to request

    QoS_Values := (Video => Video_Values,
                   Audio => Audio_Values,
                   others => null);


    Application_Interface.Request_Service(QoS_Values,
                                          QoS_Accepted,
                                          Accepted,
                                          Id);

end Audio_Video_Managers_Request;
```

Efficient Alternatives for Implementing Fixed-Priority Schedulers*

Sergio Sáez, Vicent Lorente, Silvia Terrasa, and Alfons Crespo

Universidad Politécnica de Valencia,
Camino de Vera s/n, Valencia, Spain
{ssaez, vlorente, sterrasa, alfons}@disca.upv.es

Abstract. Fixed-priority schedulers received a lot of attention from the real-time community, and a big effort has been performed to develop accurate and more general schedulability analysis that can ensure the correct execution of the system. Nevertheless, only few works analysed the overhead and blocking intervals introduced by the scheduler and the associated kernel routines, modifying the schedulability tests to take into account these overheads. However, all these works assume a very simple scheduler that uses trivial data structures to stores the tasks information. This work analyses data structures used in several open real-time kernels that supports Ada language. Additionally, a new data structure, the *Cartesian trees*, is proposed. As a conclusion, the preliminary studies show that alternative data structures, as proposed Cartesian trees, can improve the scalability of the system strongly reducing the scheduling overheads.

1 Introduction

In a real-time computing system, tasks have timing constraints that must be met for correct operation. These timing constraints are usually represented by a deadline and a task period. To guarantee such constraints, extensive research has been performed on schedulability analysis of real-time systems [1, 2, 3, 4]. Schedulability tests are designed to take into account the system workload characteristics and the kind of scheduler that is used by the real-time operating system. Fixed-priority scheduler is one of the most popular and widely accepted real-time schedulers, and therefore it is present in almost all the commercial real-time operating systems [5]. However, a wide gap still exists between scheduling theory and its implementation in operating system kernels. The scheduler is usually assumed to be executed without any kind of overhead. Very few works have analysed the side effects introduced by the scheduler and the associated operating systems routines [6, 7, 8].

As presented in [6], the kernel can introduce several computational costs that can be classified in: **overhead**, the time spent in the kernel performing a

---

* This work is partially supported by European Project IST-35102.

T. Vardanega and A. Wellings (Eds.): Ada-Europe 2005, LNCS 3555, pp. 39–50, 2005.

given service on behalf of a specific task, and **blocking**, the time spent in the kernel or in an application task, while a higher priority task is prevented from running. These costs have been incorporated to schedulability tests under different assumptions [6, 8]. While Katcher *et al.* analysed a wide range of possible fixed-priority scheduler implementations, Burns *et al.* only study the tick-based scheduler but in a deeper and more accurate manner.

Overhead Influencing Factors. Fixed-priority scheduler implementations can be classified into two categories [6]: *event-driven* and *timer-driven*. Event-driven schedulers rely on an external hardware device to generate interrupts on periodic task arrivals. These schedulers can be further classified into *integrated interrupt schedulers*, that only receive an interrupt when this is associated with a higher priority task, and *non-integrated interrupt schedulers*, that receive an interrupt on every task arrival. The former ones require a more sophisticated support inside the processor that stores the active task priority and allows only higher priority interrupts to be processed. On the other hand, the timer-driven approach only use periodic timer interrupts from a programmable timer to execute scheduler at fixed intervals.

The kind of implementation used in the scheduler determines the number of times the scheduler is executed and the overhead introduced by the clock interrupt handling. Taken these features into account, the integrated event-driven approach is stated in [6] to be the implementation that introduces less scheduling overhead. Although the hardware support required by this approach is not widely present on nowadays processors, a software alternative can emulate this behaviour. In this case, the scheduler has to look for the *next preemptor* before the timer interrupt is programmed and the current task starts to execute. The next preemptor is the suspended task with the closest activation instant among the suspended tasks with a higher priority than the current one. Finding out which is the next preemptor task gives rise to additional overheads in the software-based integrated interrupt schedulers. This is the approach used in RTLinux/GPL executive [9].

Another important factor that determines the worst execution time of a given scheduler are data structures used to organise the active and suspended tasks. These data structures have strong influence on the search methods used to find the next active task or the next activation instant. Previous works accurately incorporate scheduling overheads in the schedulability test, but they only consider schedulers based on a two queue implementation: the *run or dispatch queue* and the *start or delay queue*. This is a very common approach but requires to move a task from the delay queue to the dispatch queue when its activation interrupt arrives. In the worst case scenario, also known as *critical instant*, all the tasks have to be removed from the delay queue. Although this situation can be accounted in the schedulability test, it gives rise to important task release delays. As these delays are not fixed on all possible scenarios, the application tasks can suffer an undesirable release jitter, including the high priority ones.

Considered Schedulers. This work deals only with schedulers that follows the event-driven approach, since it is stated in [6] that introduces less kernel overhead. Furthermore, several data structures to store Task Control Blocks (TCB) have been considered.

Open real-time kernels that support Ada language has been analysed to determine which kind of scheduler and data structures they use. Considered kernels are Open Ravenscar Kernel [10], MaRTE OS [11] and RTLinux/GPL [9].

This work evaluates different alternatives to implement a real-time scheduler in Ada, giving several criteria to compare them. As a result of this evaluation, the use of a new data structure to organise the TCBs is proposed. This new data structure allows to minimise the activation jitter, the next preemptor search and the response time of the scheduler in general. The proposed data structure is based on Cartesian trees, also known as *treaps*[1].

The rest of the paper is organised as follows. Next section presents the system model used in this work. Section 3 presents different data structures commonly used to store task control blocks. Next, the evaluation framework and the simulation tool is described. Section 5 evaluates event-driven implementation approaches and section 6 presents a new data structure to implement integrated interrupt schedulers. Finally, section 7 compares different alternatives to implement a integrated scheduler and section 8 presents some conclusions and future work.

2   System Definitions

System Load. The task sets considered in this study are composed by n periodic tasks, $\tau_1 \ .. \ \tau_n$. Each task τ_i is defined by its period T_i, its deadline D_i, where $D_i < T_i$, its worst case execution time, C_i, its initial offset O_i and a fixed priority P_i. For any two tasks τ_i, τ_j, with priorities P_i, P_j, if $i \neq j$, then $P_i \neq P_j$.

The state of a periodic task is defined as follows: *active*, when the task can be selected for execution, *suspended*, when the task is waiting for some event and it cannot be selected for execution until the event occurs, *delayed*, when the task has finished its execution and it has programmed an alarm for its next activation. The last case is a specialisation of the suspended state.

System Overheads. As it has been explained bellow, Katcher *et al.* present a complete analysis of the times involved during the scheduling process [6]. The more important ones are:

- C_{int} time to handle an interrupt. This includes saving a minimal register context necessary to process the interrupt and then invoking the scheduler.
- C_{sched} time to execute the scheduling code to: Update the state of the delayed tasks that should be currently active, determine the next task to run, and program the timer to produce the next interrupt.

---

[1] This is the first time this structure is used to implement a real-time scheduler, as far as authors know.

All this actions, depending on the scheduler implementation, may involve: C_{insert}^{active}, the time to insert a new active task in the corresponding task queue, C_{select}^{active}, the time to select the active task with the highest priority, C_{delete}^{active}, the time to delete an old active task from the corresponding task queue, $C_{insert}^{delayed}$, the time to insert a new task/alarm in the delayed queue, $C_{select}^{delayed}$, the time to select the next clock to be programmed in the timer hardware (it usually includes the time to find the next preemptor), and $C_{delete}^{delayed}$, the time to remove a recently active task from the delayed queue.

- C_{resume} time to return to the previously active task when a preemption does not occur.
- C_{ctxt} time to save the state of the active task to TCB and to load the new active task state from its TCB.

As some implementations only use one queue to store TCBs, some of these times have been joined in a more simpler ones. In these cases, the particular scheduling times are detailed for such implementation.

3   Scheduling Data Structures

A kernel scheduler have to maintain several data structures used to know which tasks has the highest priority among the active tasks and, in a event-driven scheduler, which is the value used to program the timer hardware to trigger a new clock interrupt. There are several alternatives to store this data that varies in complexity and efficiency in retrieving a given information about task set state.

A Unique Task Queue. The simplest way to implement a scheduler is to have a unique unsorted list of tasks where all the TCBs are linked together. To determine which is the highest priority task the scheduler has to walk through the entire list checking only for the priority of the active tasks. Once next task has been found, the search for the next preemptor is quite similar. It has to walk through the entire list looking for the delayed task with the closest activation instant that has a priority greater than the next task to be executed.

C_{insert} and C_{delete} have a computational cost of $\Theta(1)$ and it is only accounted on task creation and deletion. However, to look for the highest priority task, C_{select}^{active}, or to find out the next preemptor, $C_{select}^{delayed}$, has a cost of $\Theta(n)$, where n is the number of tasks in the system.

Although it is a very simple and predictable scheduler, it is also the most inefficient one and it does not scale well with respect to the number of tasks. Despite of these inconveniences it is not a bad option for very small task sets.

Several optimisations can be performed to improve the behaviour of this scheduler. One modification is to divide the tasks list into two unsorted lists for active and delayed tasks. This change reduces the cost of looking for the next task or the next preemptor, because the number of examined tasks are reduced to the number of active tasks and delayed tasks respectively. However this modification implies to move task from one queue to another when the task state changes, introducing additional costs without improving the worst case execution time of the scheduler.

On the other hand, another optimisation is to maintain a unique queue but sorted by decreasing priorities [12]. In this case, the scheduler only needs to look for the first active task, that is the highest priority one by construction. The next preemptor is a delayed task with a higher priority than the next task, and therefore, it is located before the next task in the queue. In fact, using this sorted list, the next preemptor is the delayed task with the closest arrival time that is located before the first active task. With this optimisation select operation, C_{select}, has a computational costs of $O(n_{hp})$, where n_{hp} is the number of tasks with a priority higher that the implied task. This offers better isolation for higher priority tasks which are not affected by the number of total tasks in the system.

Two Sorted Queues Schedulers. The implementation of fixed-priority scheduler based on two sorted queues is the most used one. If the scheduler is a software-based integrated interrupt scheduler, it must be able to search in the delay queue to look for the next preemptor, limiting the kind structures that can be used to implement that queue.

As both queues are sorted, the time to select the highest priority task, C_{select}^{active}, is constant ($\Theta(1)$). To find out which is the next instant to be programmed in the system timer, i.e. the next activation, depends on the approach followed to implement the scheduler. If the scheduler is a non-integrated one, the time to select the next activation instant, $C_{select}^{delayed}$, is also constant ($\Theta(1)$). However, the time required to look for the next preemptor in an integrated interrupt scheduler depends directly on the number of delayed tasks ($O(n)$).

As it was commented above, the main drawback of this approach is that it requires to move a task from the delay queue to active queue on its arrival interrupt and back to the delay queue when the tasks finishes. In the worst case scenario, an interrupt may have to move all the tasks from the delay queue to the active queue. This has a computational cost of $O(n \cdot C_{delete}^{delayed} + n \cdot C_{insert}^{active})$, where n is the number of tasks in the system.

Then, the unique difference between implementations is located on the data structure used to implement the sorted queues and its associated computational cost. Next some common alternatives are presented.

Sorted Linked Lists. If the queues are implemented as simple sorted lists, time to insert a task in the active queue, C_{insert}^{active}, has a computational cost of $O(n_{hp})$, while inserting a task in the delayed queue, $C_{insert}^{delayed}$, has a computational cost of $O(n)$, where n is the number of tasks with an activation instant closest than the new delayed task. Although both times has linear computational cost, the scheduler code is very simple and, therefore, the time to process each element can be quite low.

Balanced Binary Trees. If a balanced binary tree is used to implement the sorted queues, the computational costs, C_{delete} and C_{insert}, can be bounded to $O(log(n))$, where n is the number of tasks in the corresponding queue. However, a careful selection must be performed to select a binary tree that allows efficient in-order traversal to find the next preemptor on the delay queue. In this work, the proposed structure is the AVL trees. This kind of trees allows to maintain a sorted list of nodes without disturbing the normal operation and computational cost of the tree. In this case, the computational cost of finding the next preemptor, $C_{select}^{delayed}$, is also $O(n)$.

Bitmap-Based Arrays. A possible optimisation of the two queues approach consists in replacing the active queue by a fixed size array that stores the pointers to the first active task of each priority and a bitmap that stores the priorities of the active tasks. This implementation usually takes advantage of architectural capabilities of modern processors to perform fast searching on small bitmaps. In such a way, the cost of inserting a new task in the active queue, C_{insert}^{active}, is drastically reduced. However, C_{select}^{active} is not constant any more, but its computational cost can be bounded by $O(log_{32}(n))$, where the base of the logarithm depends on the number of bits of the processor registers.

4   Evaluation Framework

In order to properly evaluate the different alternatives to implement a real-time scheduler, a simulation tool has been implemented using the Ada language. This tool allows to evaluate any scheduler implementation using the real scheduler code by simulating the behaviour of the real-time application tasks.

To achieve an execution environment for tested schedulers as real as possible, the simulation tool takes into account the following:

- The simulation clock and execution time measurements of the tested schedulers use a common time unit: the CPU cycle.
- The simulation tool uses time stamp counters available on several nowadays processors to measure the CPU time consumed by each scheduler function. These counters return the elapsed time in cycles.
- The simulation clock includes the application tasks execution times, system overheads and scheduler execution times.
- The instruction and data caches are enabled during the simulation, but both are flushed before each execution of the tested scheduler to simulate the interference introduced by the execution of the application tasks.

The tested schedulers are organised in two main functions, *run* and *wait*. These two functions are invoked each time the highest priority task must be selected and at the end of every periodic task activation, respectively.

Execution Platform and Tool Capabilities. The simulation tool has been executed over a x86 platform based on an AMD processor. The AMD architecture offers a time-stamp counter (TSC) available on x86 architectures from

the Pentium processor family and four configurable Performance Counters as
well. These Performance Counters are used by the simulation tool to study some
interesting behavioural aspects of the scheduler implementations. Some of the
events the tool is able to count are: the number of retired instructions, number
of instructions cache misses, number of data cache misses, number of retired
branches misspredicted, etc.

Hardware and Non-scheduling Times. In addition to the time consumed
by the scheduler execution and the application real-time tasks, the simulation
tool also takes into account the overhead introduced by the execution platform
and the pieces of the operating system that are independent from the scheduler
implementation. Independently of the selected scheduler implementation, the
overhead produced by the interrupt management (C_{int}), program the timer for
the next task activation and the context switch (C_{ctxt}) will always be found
due to the way the scheduler is invoked. This overhead depends mainly on the
platform in which the real-time operating system is running.

The simulation tool allows to configure these overheads that must be by
other means. In the studies performed in this work, these overheads have been
extracted and measured from an AMD XP 1500+ processor at 1.3GHz executing
an stand-alone version of the RTLinux/GPL. For interrupt management and
timer interrupts, the Advanced Programmable Interrupt Controller (local APIC)
and the APIC timer are used. Both are implemented inside the AMD processor.

5   Evaluation of the Implementation Approach

The kind of interrupt scheme that is used in the real-time scheduler implementation can have a strong influence in the performance of the whole system. This
section presents a preliminary simulation study that evaluates the differences
between interrupt integrated and non-integrated schedulers.

The simulation study presented in this section compares several of the proposed fixed-priority scheduler implementations: *TQ-LIN*, Two sorted Queues
using Linked lists to store the tasks. This approach is similar to the one used
at Open Ravenscar Kernel [10]. *TQ-AVL*, Two sorted Queues using an AVL
tree for both. *PM-AVL*, Priority-bitMap implementation using an AVL tree as
the delayed queue. The MaRTE OS [11] uses similar structures for the system
scheduler, but it uses a heap instead of an AVL tree for the delayed queue.

These schedulers can be implemented following both approaches, integrated
and non-integrated interrupts. So, they can be used to compare the suitability
of each approach to implement real-time schedulers.

Figure 1.a shows the worst case execution times occurred during the simulation studies. It can be observed that the maximum response time of the scheduling algorithm are almost identical for both approaches. This is due to the main
drawback of the schedulers based on two queue. If the system is synchronous,
there are instants in which all the tasks are suspended and become active simultaneously. This requires to move all the tasks from delayed queue to the active

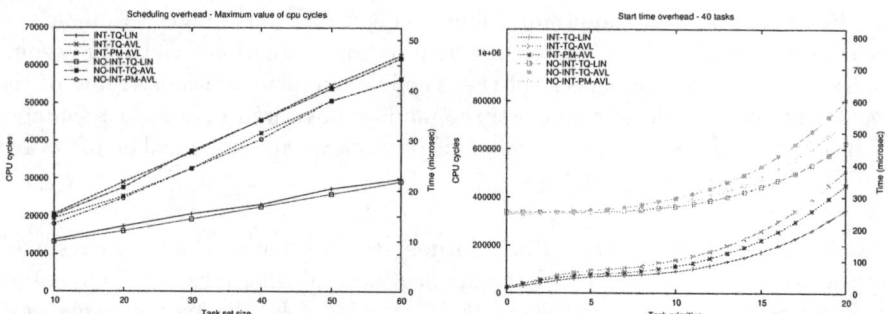

Fig. 1. Integrated vs Non-integrated: a) Scheduling overhead. b) Release time overhead

queue, and the computational cost of this operation is $O(n \cdot C_{delete}^{delayed} + n \cdot C_{insert}^{active})$. Moreover, in this scenario, the delayed queue becomes empty and therefore integrated schedulers have no additional work to do. As mentioned before, between the implementation based on AVL trees, the scheduler based on a priority map for the active tasks behaves better in the worst case scenario due to the lower value of C_{insert}^{active}.

Although the non-integrated versions of the schedulers run normally faster and have a worst case execution time quite similar, it must be taken into account that schedulers following the non-integrated approach can suffer a high number of unnecessary interrupts due to the activation of lower priority tasks. These interrupts can interfere in the release time and response time of higher priority tasks, giving rise to high input and output jitters. Figure 1.b shows how much is delayed a task release time due to the system overhead (ISR, scheduling and context switching). Due to these delays, the response time of the highest priority task can be 25 times greater than the WCRT calculated without taking into account any overhead.

These overheads can be taken into account to avoid jeopardising the off-line assured deadlines. However, the results point towards integrated schedulers as the more suitable approach to implement hard real-time execution platforms.

6   Schedulers Based on Cartesian Trees

Above proposed schedulers show several desirable characteristics to be present in a good real-time scheduler. Although the main one, predictability, is present in all the implementations, there are additional behaviours that a good scheduler should have. The desired characteristics are fast searching of next active task, low cost insert and delete operations in both queues and fast searching of next preemptor.

Taking this characteristics into account, this work proposes a new structure to stores the TCBs. The proposal is to use a Cartesian tree to store both, active and delayed tasks. A Cartesian tree, also known as a treap, is a binary tree that uses a Cartesian pair as a key. The first key is used to maintain sorted the

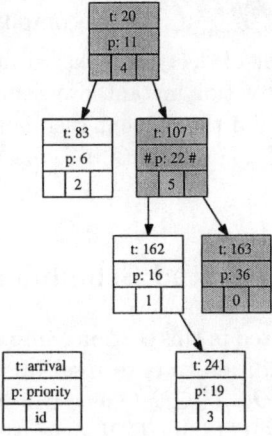

Fig. 2. A scheduler treap example

in-order sequence of the binary tree, and the second key is used to maintain the heap property between parent and child nodes: a parent node has a lower value in the second key that all its descendants. The proposed keys to be used by the scheduler are the priority as the first key and the activation time as the second key. In this way, the treap has as a root the oldest task or the task with the closest release time. On the right subtree are stored all the tasks that can preempt this one. On the left subtree are stored the rest of tasks which have equal or lower priorities than the root. This property can be applied to each node of the treap.

The figure 2 shows the example of a treap with 6 tasks. Each task τ_i, is represented by three parameters: its identifier, i, activation instant, t, and priority, p. In this example, current time is 120. Then, active tasks are τ_2, τ_5 and τ_4. τ_5 is the active task with the highest priority, and therefore, τ_5 is the current task. Delayed tasks are τ_0, τ_1 and τ_3. Among these inactive tasks, the next preemptor of the current task is τ_0, because it has a higher priority than the current one and also the closest activation instant. If the current task τ_5 does not finish before 163, the right child, task τ_0, has to preempt it and start its execution. If the task τ_5 finishes before 163, it is deleted and re-inserted with its new release time, and its parent node, task τ_4, becomes the current task. As it can be observed in this example, the right-most branch is an important part of the scheduling treap.

Some of the most important characteristics of the scheduling treap are: The structure of the treap only changes when a task finishes. When a task becomes active there are no actions to perform. Time to determine the next preemptor, $C_{select}^{delayed}$, has a constant computational cost ($O(1)$). When a preemption occur, to select the next running task is trivial, because the task to be selected is the preemptor of the current task (right child), and therefore, C_{select}^{active} is constant. When the preempting task finishes, the task that must be resumed is the task located at the parent node, and again the C_{select}^{active} is constant. Therefore, only the time to delete and re-inserting the preempting task is significant in the preemption process. This time $C^{delayed}_{delete+insert}$ has a computational cost of $O(n^{delayed}_{lp})$, where $n^{delayed}_{lp}$ is the number of delayed tasks with a priority lower to the preempting task that has an activation instant lower than the new activation instant of the preempting task. Only if the current task is at the root node, the cost of finding the next task, C^{active}_{select}, could be $O(n)$, where n is the number of task in the system.

7   Evaluation of Integrated Scheduler Implementations

The simulation study presented in this section compares several integrated scheduler implementations. In addition to ones used in section 5, the following algorithm have been compared: *OQ-U*, One Queue Unsorted implementation. This is the current scheduler for the RTLinux/GPL executive [9]. This scheduler follows the software-based integrated interrupts approach. *OQ-DP*, One Queue implementation sorted by Decreasing Priorities. This scheduler has been proposed by McGuire [12] as the new scheduler for the RTLinux/GPL executive. Until now, this is the unique integrated scheduler that tries to reduce the time to find the next preemptor. *S-Treap*, the new proposed scheduler based on a scheduling treap.

The main goal is to determine if the preemptor searching and the one queue model of the new S-Treap scheduler have a significant influence in the scheduler execution time, taking into account that Cartesian trees are not balanced. To achieve that goal the best integrated schedulers based on two queues jointly with the above proposed scheduler are compared.

Figure 3 shows the simulation results for a set of 50 tasks. Data is presented as the accumulated frequency of scheduling overhead, i.e, the Y-axis shows the precentage of cases that have an overhead equal or lower to the corresponding X-value. This plot shows that the new scheduling algorithm (S-Treap) clearly outperforms the rest of integrated schedulers. These is mainly due to the preemp-

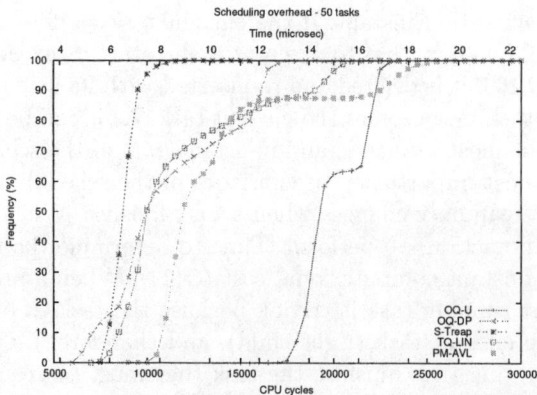

Fig. 3. Integrated schedulers: Accumulated frequency of scheduling overhead

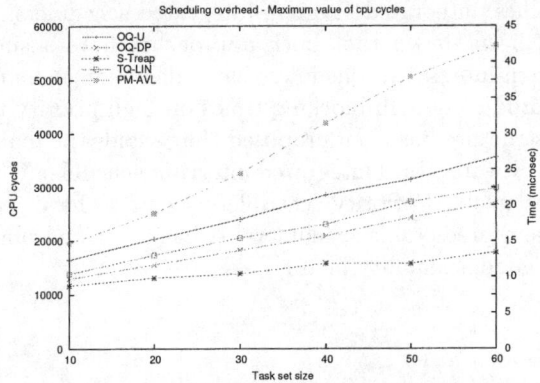

Fig. 4. Integrated schedulers: Maximum scheduling overhead

tor searching algorithm. The schedulers TQ-LIN and PM-AVL have a preemptor searching algorithm with a linear computational cost, i.e., the higher the priority of the current task, the higher the execution time of the searching algorithm. The OQ-U scheduler is always linear and the OQ-DP scheduler has an execution time that inversely proportional to the priority of the next task: the lower the priority of the current task, the higher the execution time of the scheduler.

As it is shown in figure 4, the worst case execution time of the S-Treap scheduler is also clearly lower than the rest of the integrated schedulers, and it shows a good scalability factor as task set size is increased.

Table 1. Instruction cache misses

Scheduler	Min	Mean	Max
OQ-U	33	38	46
OQ-DP	31	35	42
S-Treap	36	39	43
TQ-LIN	36	41	44
PM-AVL	43	50	61

In order to evaluate the complexity of the evaluated algorithms, table 1 summaries the *instruction cache misses* produced by integrated schedulers. The maximum value of instruction cache misses offers a good approximation of the instruction cache footprint of the different schedulers.

8   Conclusions and Future Work

A set of possible data structures to implement fixed-priority schedulers have been presented. The computational cost of each alternative have been analysed and a new data structure proposed that reduces the main drawbacks for implementing an integrated interrupt scheduler.

Both approaches, integrated and non-integrated schedulers, have been analysed and it has been shown that both approaches have a similar worst case behaviour, but non-integrated schedulers can suffer a great number of unnecessary interrupts producing high blocking times on high priority tasks.

A new data structure has been proposed that avoids the main drawbacks for implementing a software-based integrated interrupt scheduler. The new structure proposed to develop fixed-priority schedulers seems to have great potential to implement fast and predictable schedulers. It has short and bounded execution times and has a good scalability factor.

References

1. Liu, C., Layland, J.: Scheduling algorithms for multiprogramming in a hard real-time environment. Journal of the ACM **20** (1973) 40–61
2. Joseph, M., Pandya, P.: Finding response times in real-time systems. The Computer Journal **29** (1986) 390–395
3. Lehoczky, J., Sha, L., Ding, Y.: The rate-monotonic scheduling algorithm: Exact characterization and average behavior. In: Proceedings of the Real-Time Systems Symposium. (1989) 166–171
4. Audsley, N., Burns, A., David, R., Tindell, K., Wellings, A.: Fixed priority preemptive scheduling: An historical prespective. Real-Time Systems **8** (1995) 173–189
5. POSIX.13: IEEE Std. 1003.13-1998. Information Technology -Standardized Application Environment Profile- POSIX Realtime Application Support (AEP). The Institute of Electrical and Electronics Engineers. (1998)
6. Katcher, D., Arakawa, H., Strosnider, J.: Engineering and analysis of fixed priority schedulers. IEEE Transactions on Software Engineering **19** (1993) 920–934
7. Jeffay, K., Stone, D.L.: Accounting for interrupt handling costs in dynamic priority task systems. In: Proceedings of Real-Time Systems Symposium. (1993) 212–221
8. Burns, A., Tindell, K., Wellings, A.: Effective analysis for engineering real-time fixed priority schedulers. IEEE Transactions on Software Engineering **21** (1995) 475–480
9. Barabanov, M.: A Linux-based real time operating system. Master's thesis, New Mexico Institute of Mining and Technology (1997)
10. Puente, J., Zamorano, J., Ruiz, J.F., Fernández, R., García, R.: The design and implementation of the Open Ravenscar Kernel. ACM SIGAda Ada Letters **XXI** (2001) 85–90
11. Aldea-Rivas, M., González-Harbour, M.: Marte OS: An Ada kernel for real-time embedded applications. International Conference on Reliable Software Technologies, Ada-Europe (2001)
12. McGuire, N.: A sorted queue scheduler for RTLinux/GPL. (Personal communication)

A New Strategy for the HRT-HOOD to Ada Mapping

Matteo Bordin and Tullio Vardanega

Department of Pure and Applied Mathematics,
University of Padua,
via G. Belzoni 7, I-35131 Padova, Italy
mbordin@studenti.math.unipd.it, tullio.vardanega@math.unipd.it

Abstract. The original mapping of HRT-HOOD diagrams to Ada code dates back to the late stages of the Ada 9X project. Since then, considerably deeper insight has been gained into the practical use of Ada 95 for high-integrity applications, of which the Ravenscar Profile is a notable emanation. In this paper we present a new HRT-HOOD to Ada mapping strategy, which aims to overcome the shortcomings we noted in the original one, by leveraging on the better understanding of the language power and of the user requirements that has been generally achieved in the meanwhile.

1   Introduction

The ability to map graphical design diagram languages like HRT-HOOD [1] effectively onto a programming language is one of the inroads of generative programming [2], while it is also being pursued by the Model-Driven Architecture initiative of the OMG [3]. By and large, automated code generation from model diagrams can be viewed as a considerable aid to software correctness, all the more important where integrity requirements are at stake.

Automated code generation leverages on warranting the *a priori* correctness of an important proportion of the software code (the part that maps the structural element of the software design; in a word, the software architecture) and allows the design authority to concentrate on the verification of the functional element of the code.

Furthermore, the ability to generate compilable code directly from design diagrams boosts productivity in so far as it compresses the turn around time of early prototyping phases, where the designer may wish to explore design alternatives and also perform representative code measurements and executions.

Unfortunately, very few code generation engines have attained acceptable performance (cf. e.g.: [4, 5] for the specific domain of control applications), often because of an exceedingly general-purpose nature, scarce attention to the quality, expressiveness and efficiency of the produced code, perhaps compounded by inappropriate or thoughtless choice of programming languages and use paradigms.

This very failure however suggests that there may be better fortune for domain-specific automated code generators, which could, to the user's best advantage, shed loose generality for the adoption of programming paradigms that fit the needs and the idioms (a.k.a the restrictions) of the target application domain. One domain of particular

T. Vardanega and A. Wellings (Eds.): Ada-Europe 2005, LNCS 3555, pp. 51–66, 2005.

interest in this regard certainly is that of hard real-time systems, where Ada [6] has unquestionable value to deliver, also in view of its fitness for embedded computing.

The recent advent of the Ravenscar Profile [7], a subset of the Ada 95 tasking model especially tailored for real-time high-integrity systems and now being included in the revised version of the language standard [8], calls for an adaptation of the HRT-HOOD to Ada mapping originally proposed in [1], almost a decade ago.

The undisputed strength of the HRT-HOOD method is to enable the designer to use concurrency in a manner that fits the typical needs of real-time systems [9], while warranting the static analysability of the system since the early stage of design. In order that this value was not washed out by the mounting surge of tools, methods and profiles spawned by the UML wave [10], a recent project has undertaken to transpose the HRT-HOOD platform onto the admittedly greater expressive power of the UML meta-model, thus giving rise to the HRT-UML method [11]. As part of this effort we have also undertaken to design a new set of mapping rules suited for automated generation of Ravenscar Ada code from HRT-UML object diagrams. In this paper we highlight some aspects of the new code generation rules and compare them to the ones proposed in [1].

2   A Critical Review of the Original Mapping

Any reflection on the HRT-HOOD or -UML to Ada mapping must necessarily depart from a critical assessment of the pros and cons of the original approach described in [1]. The cited mapping strategy rests on architectural principles that reflect the HRT-HOOD meta-model semantics and that we can summarise as follows: (i) the ontological and structural separation between the OPCS and the OBCS: the former, termed the *operation control structure*, describes the implementation of the object's operation; the latter, called the *object control structure*, acts as the synchronisation agent between the external client of the object's provided interface and the object's internal flow of control; (ii) the rendering of design objects as Ada packages whose public interface delegates the handling of inbound requests to the internal — hence private — interface of the object's OBCS; (iii) the rendering of the OBCS itself as an Ada protected object, which allows the control flow of the callee to proceed concurrently with that of the called object itself.

We contend, though, that some of the original mapping choices can be challenged and better alternatives can be offered by leveraging on the expressive power of Ada 95 [6] more extensively. In fact, as we shall briefly see at the end of this paper, further considerable benefits can be expected from exploiting some of the new features of the 2005 revision of the language. However, the latter strand of work is best pursued upon the forthcoming availability of language implementations.

As part of our exercise, we have spotted and addressed four main arguable shortcomings:

1. the lack of code factoring;
2. the excessive use of anonymous objects;
3. the omission of mapping for non-terminal objects; and
4. the lack of a "Ravenscar-compliant" capability of the mapping.

(In full fairness, to call the latter a shortcoming we have the privilege of hindsight, which the original authors could not have, since the Ravenscar Profile definition was some way down the road at that time yet!)

Correcting each such defect should provide important benefits for the user:

- better code factoring would considerably reduce the amount of generated code, making it more easily understandable (hence more robust) and less onerous for embedded applications where program memory is a precious resource;
- rigorous use of typed objects (especially tasks and protected objects) would bridge the gap currently in place between HRT-HOOD generated code and the code accepted by such tools as the SPARK Examiner [12], with attractive prospects for the integrity of the project product;
- providing low-overhead mapping for the entire hierarchy of objects as it appears in the user design, including non-terminal (i.e. parent) objects would maintain exact design-to-code correspondence without incurring performance penalties, as in the premises of generative programming [2], and also preserve the extent of information hiding warranted by the strictly hierarchical nature of HOOD design;
- the ability to generate Ravenscar-compliant code would result from crafting a profile into the (HRT-UML or HRT-HOOD) method semantics that would avoid all conflicts with the Ravenscar restrictions [7]; should the method profile prove expressive enough (as current evidence suggests), then the user would have the compound value of a consolidated method and code generation into a language subset expressly intended for high-integrity systems.

In the remainder of this paper, we first illustrate the proposed strategy for the mapping of terminal objects (section 3), then outline the approach we take to code factoring (section 4), and further show the way we map the entire design hierarchy (section 5). Finally, we conclude by providing some quantitative and qualitative assessment of the comparative advantages of our solution.

3   Mapping Terminal Objects

3.1   PROTECTED Terminal Objects: Mapping PAER and PSER Operations

In HRT-HOOD, PROTECTED terminal objects[1] may provide two types of constrained operations: (i) PAER (protected asynchronous execution request); and (ii) PSER (protected synchronous execution request). The notion of synchronous operation descends from the HOOD heritage of HRT-HOOD, where it originally mapped to the Ada *rendezvous*, whose semantics cannot be rendered by the intermission of a protected object in the inter-task communication. HRT-HOOD intentionally sheds synchronous communication between tasks, which obstructs static timing analysis, and offers PRO-

---

[1] The PROTECTED object is a specific object type in HRT-HOOD, which is meant for data-oriented synchronisation among threaded objects and which directly maps to the protected type in Ada [6]. Furthermore, HRT-HOOD breaks the HOOD notion of ACTIVE (i.e. threaded) object into CYCLIC and SPORADIC based on the type of their activation.

```
for each protected object <Obj>
  with System;
  generic
for each OPCS of operation <OPn>
    with procedure OPCS_<OPn>(<Param>);
end for each
    package <Obj>_Template is
    protected type OBCS_T
      (OBCS_Priority : System.Priority) is
      pragma Priority(OBCS_Priority);
for each PAER operation <OPn>
      procedure <OPn>(<Param>);
end for each
for each PSER operation <OPn>
      entry <OPn>(<Param>);
end for each
      private
for each PSER operation <OPn>
      procedure <OPn>_Set_Barrier
        (V : Boolean);
      <OPn>_Barrier : Boolean := False;
end for each
    end OBCS_T;
  end <Obj>_Template;
end for each
```

```
package body <Obj>_Template is
  protected body OBCS_T is
for each PAER operation <OPn>
    procedure <OPn>(<Param>) is
    V : Boolean;
    begin
      OPCS_<OPn>(<Param>, V);
      <OPn>_Set_Barrier(V);
    end <OPn>;
end for each
for each PSER operation <OPn>
    entry <OPn>(<Param>)
      when <OPn>_Barrier is
    V : Boolean;
    begin
      OPCS_<OPn>(<Param>, V);
      <OPn>_Set_Barrier(V);
    end <OPn>;
end for each
    procedure <Opn>_Set_Barrier
      (V : Boolean) is
    begin
      <Opn>_Barrier := V;
    end <Opn>_Set_Barrier;
  end OBCS_T;
end <Obj>_Template;
```

Fig. 1. Code generation rules for the generic unit that factors the mapping of PROTECTED terminal objects. In order for the object's OPCS operations to affect the corresponding PSER barrier as the application logic requires, an **out** Boolean parameter is added to the corresponding signature and the resulting value is passed to the appropriate Set_Barrier procedure

TECTED objects for data oriented synchronisation among tasks instead. The "synchronous" flavour of PSER does therefore correspond to protected operations with functional activation constraints (essentially, protected entries). In contrast, PAER maps to unconstrained protected subprograms (functions and / or procedures).

Our mapping strategy strove to make systematic use of typed objects and to attain increased code factoring. To this end, to map PROTECTED objects we provide a generic unit whose formal generic parameters factor out the implementation of the operations delegated to the object, i.e. its OPCS. Figure 1 shows the corresponding code generation rules, including those required for the factoring of the PAER and PSER <OPn> operations.

The presence of PSER operations (at most 1 per protected object for the Ravenscar-mode generation) requires that one simple boolean barrier per PSER be placed in the private part of the template, along with as many (<OPn>_Set_Barrier) factored private operations that set the corresponding barrier value. The functional code attributed to each OPCS_<OPn> operation by the public interface of the <Obj> parent object resides in the <Obj>.Types package unit, along with all other types and internal op-

```
for each protected object  <Obj>
   package <Obj>_Template is
for each provided operation  <OPn>
      type <OPn>_A is access procedure (<Param>);
end for each
      protected type OBCS_T is
         (OBCS_Priority : System.Priority;
for each provided operation  <OPn>
         OPCS_<Opn> : <Opn>_A
end for each
         ) is
         pragma Priority(OBCS_Priority);
for each PAER operation  <OPn>
         procedure <OPn>(<Param>);
end for each
for each PSER operation  <OPn>
         entry <OPn>(<Param>);
end for each
         private
for each PSER operation  <OPn>
         procedure <OPn>_Set_Barrier(V : Boolean);
         <OPn>_Barrier : Boolean := False;
end for each
      end OBCS_T;
   end <Obj>_Template;
```

Fig. 2. An alternative strategy for generating code for protected objects without use of generic units and yet providing a type for each singleton protected object

erations required by the object implementation. The signature of each such operation is automatically added an **out** Boolean parameter, whose value will be conveyed to the corresponding Set_Barrier operation to update the barrier as the application logic requires.

Recalling that HRT-HOOD only allows singleton objects, the reader might consider it an oddity that we provide a generic unit for every single protected object to be generated, and thus take very little benefit from such an object factory mechanism. In fact, the bottom line of what we want is that there be *no* anonymous objects in the system, irrespective of whether they may be singleton or not. Encapsulating the protected object type in a generic unit was then chosen for uniformity with the mapping rules that we used for the other object types, as illustrated in the remainder of this paper.

Figure 2 illustrates the obvious alternative mapping to the one shown earlier. In this case we would do away with the generic unit and augment the protected type discriminant with one access procedure for each OPCS operation attributed to the object. The change would only concern the specification part, leaving the body unaffected.

Figure 3 shows the little code generation rules that it takes to make up the body of a PROTECTED object instance with each of the above strategies.

```
with <Obj>_Template;                  with <Obj>_Template;
with <Obj>.Types;                     with <Obj>.Types;
with <Obj>.RTATT;                     with <Obj>.RTATT;
package body <Obj> is                 package body <Obj> is
  package OBCS_P is new                 OBCS : <Obj>_Template.OBCS_T(
    <Obj>_Template(                       <Obj>.RTATT.OBCS_Priority,
for each operation  <OPn>             for each operation  <OPn>
    OPCS_<OPn> =>                         <Obj>.Types.OPCS_<Opn>'Access,
      <Obj>.Types.OPCS_<OPn>,         end for each;
end for each                            );
  );                                  for each operation  <OPn>
  OBCS : OBCS_P.OBCS_T                   procedure <Opn>(<Param>) is
    (<Obj>.RTATT.OBCS_Priority);        begin
for each operation  <OPn>                 OBCS.<Opn>(<Param>);
  procedure <OPn>(<Param>) is           end <Opn>;
  begin                               end for each;
    OBCS.<OPn> (<Param>);             end <Obj>;
  end <OPn>;
end for each;
end <Obj>;
```

Fig. 3. Code generation rules for the instantiation of the body of PROTECTED terminal object following each of the two alternate factory strategies shown in figures 1 (left) and 2 (right)

3.2   CYCLIC Terminal Objects: Mapping ATC Operations

HRT-HOOD CYCLIC terminal objects are not allowed to include service operations in their provided interface, except for ATC (Asynchronous Transfer of Control) operations. Each ATC operation maps to a protected subprogram (procedure or function) exported by the OBCS operating as the object's synchronisation agent. This agent, in turn, is meant to asynchronously affects the control flow of the periodic task that represents the cyclic concurrent behaviour of the object [1].

We expressly set out to extend and simplify the original mapping of this category of operations. The extension aimed at allowing CYCLIC terminal objects to export multiple ATC services (with possibly distinct parameters and semantics). The simplification aimed at devising mapping rules capable of producing considerably streamlined code, yet easy to understand and, most importantly, abiding by the Ravenscar constraints, which prohibit the use of select statements and therefore of language-level ATC. The reader will note that this decision makes genuine asynchronous transfer of control impossible (actually illegal) and provides for deferred handling of the corresponding requests.

HRT-HOOD originally distinguished among three variants of ATC requests, in accord with the extent of synchronisation incurred in the interaction between the caller and the callee's OBCS: (a) asynchronous, ASATC, whereby the caller simply posts its request in the OBCS buffer and continues its execution; (b) loosely synchronous, LSATC, whereby the caller is held synchronised with the callee's OBCS until the callee's thread has commenced to serve the request; and (c) highly synchronous, HSATC, whereby the callee's OBCS releases the caller only upon completion of the relevant service. It is obvious from this description that ASATC and LSATC requests do not allow **out** parameters, while only HSATC requests do. In the following, in the interest of brevity, we only present the mapping of ASATC requests.

We map ASATC operations to "deferred mode change" requests, whose service is attended to at the start of the first activation of the object's thread subsequent to the request reception at the object's OBCS. To this end, we use a single toggle buffer to store all of the incoming ATC requests (irrespective of their type) and a modular index to point at the read and write positions on it. Reading a request consumes it and advances the read index to the next position. Writing a request operates on the current position, thus overwriting unattended requests. We assume in fact that, there being a single thread of control that is the target of ATC requests, those that were still unattended become obsolete by the arrival of a fresher one.

Each ATC request is represented by a descriptor that holds the parameters the request may bring along. Differing ASATC types may give rise to different request types. In effect, such requests materially differ by the parameters that they carry. In order that the buffer can hold ATC requests with parameters of heterogeneous types, we allow for an extensible hierarchy of parameter types to be defined, as shown in figure 4, and place the root of it in the predefined environment library of the HRT-HOOD project.

Figure 4 shows the enumeration type that we have defined to cater for the allowable execution requests, including the notional START request that delivers the activation event to SPORADIC objects and a No_Req null value.

The ATC request parameters are held in a tagged value whose type is derived from the abstract type Param_T and the request descriptor type is a record with a field that points to request parameters of any type in the class (cf. figure 4). Each CYCLIC object will therefore possess: (i) one buffer for holding request descriptors; (ii) one index for reading and writing from the buffer; (iii) one counter of pending requests.

```
-- in global unit Types.ads
type Request_T is
     (No_Req, ATC_Req, Start_Req);
type Param_T is abstract tagged
   with null record;
type Param_T_Ref is access all Param_T;
type Request_Descriptor_T is
   record
      Req : Request_T;
      Par : Param_T_Ref;
   end record;
type Request_Buffer_Index_T is mod 2;
type Request_Buffer_T is
   array(Request_Buffer_Index_T'Range) of
      Request_Descriptor_T;
```

```
for each <Obj> object
   place in <Obj>.Types child unit
for each ATC operation
   type <OPn>_Param_T is new Param_T with
      record
   for each ATC operation parameter
         <PARAMn> : <PARAMn_Type>;
   end for each
      end record;
end for each
end for each
```

Fig. 4. Code generation rules for the hierarchy of request types

```
—— task body for CYCLIC object
task body Thread is
   use Ada.Real_Time;
   Period : constant Time_Span :=
      Milliseconds (Thread_Period);
   Next_Time : Time :=
      RTA.System_Start_Up_Time;
   Req_Desc : Request_Descriptor_T;
begin
   delay until Next_Time;
   loop
      C_OBCS.Get_ATC_Request (Req_Desc);
      case Req_Desc.Req is
         when ATC_Req =>
            Dispatcher (Req_Desc);
         when No_Req =>
            Thread_Action;
         when others =>
            —— error handling
      end case;
      Next_Time := Next_Time + Period;
      delay until Next_Time;
   end loop;
end Thread;
```

```
—— task body for SPORADIC object
task body Thread is
   use Ada.Real_Time;
   Interval : constant Time_Span :=
      Milliseconds (MIAT);
   Next_Time : Time :=
      RTA.System_Start_Up_Time;
   Req_Desc : Request_Descriptor_T;
begin
   delay until Next_Time;
   loop
      C_OBCS.Get_Request (Req_Desc);
      case Req_Desc.Req is
         when ATC_Req =>
            Dispatcher (Req_Desc);
         when Start_Req =>
            Start_Action (Req_Desc.Par);
         when others =>
            —— error handling
      end case;
      —— update barrier on Get_Request
      Update_Barrier;
      Next_Time := Next_Time + Interval;
      delay until Next_Time;
   end loop;
end Thread;
```

Fig. 5. Factored code for task bodies of CYCLIC terminal object and SPORADIC terminal object

Figure 5 shows the control flow within a CYCLIC object that provides ASATC operations, side by side with that for a standard SPORADIC object (which we discuss in section 3.3). At every periodic activation, the periodic task invokes the Get_ATC_Request procedure shown in figure 6, to check the buffer out for any pending request descriptors. If a new request has come in, it must be an ATC request. The task fetches the descriptor from the buffer, retrieves the parameters from their pointer in the descriptor and carries the request out. If no ATC request was pending, the procedure returns the default No_Req null descriptor, and the periodic control flow proceeds normally.

If the public interface of the object provides multiple ASATC operations, the code that handles the corresponding request descriptor must dispatch to the OPCS of the designated <OPn> procedure. To this end, the automatically generated code of the Dispatcher procedure shown in figure 6 performs explicit dispatching on the basis of the Tag attribute of the Par field of the incoming request descriptor. The type of that field will in fact be an object specific specialisation of the root Param_T type shown in figure 4.

```
procedure Get_ATC_Request
   (Req_Desc : out Request_Descriptor_T) is
begin
   -- prepare the default descriptor
   Req_Desc := (No_Req, null);
   if ATC_Pending > 0 then
      Req_Desc := Req_Buf(Req_Buf_Index);
      Req_Buf_Index := Req_Buf_Index + 1;
      ATC_Pending := ATC_Pending - 1;
   end if;
end Get_ATC_Request;
```

```
procedure Dispatcher
   (Req_Desc : in Request_Descriptor_T) is
   T : Tag := Req_Desc.Par'Tag;
begin
   -- explicit dispatching based on tag value
   if T = <Obj>.Types.<OPn>_Param_T'Tag then
      <Obj>.Types.OPCS_<OPn>
         (Req_Desc.Par);
      return;
   elsif T = -- for every other <OPn>, if any
   end if;
      -- error handling
end Dispatcher;
```

Fig. 6. Factored procedure bodies for Get_ATC_Request, for use by CYCLIC object task only, and Dispatcher, for use by CYCLIC and SPORADIC object tasks. The invocation of these procedures is shown in figure 5

3.3   SPORADIC Terminal Objects: Mapping ASATC Operations

Our mapping rules for the ASATC operations of SPORADIC terminal objects are much alike those we just illustrated for CYCLIC objects. We need to add one separate buffer for holding nominal START request descriptors, along with the relevant read and write indices and request counter, which we handle in exactly the same way as shown for ASATC requests. Furthermore, the OBCS of the object must provide a Get_Request entry whose barrier is opened by the invocation of either the Start procedure or any allowable ASATC request, all of which appear in the object public interface. Get_Request returns ATC requests in precedence to normal ones.

4   Factoring Out Common Parts

The CYCLIC and SPORADIC objects of HRT-HOOD specialise the archetypal ACTIVE object of HOOD. This common origin is the cause of a great deal of structural commonality in the code generation rules for both types of objects. It is one of our goals to factor out as much of such commonality as practical. In fact, the only differences between the two set of rules concern the realisation of the respective provided interface and the initialisation parameters. With this in mind, we have built the needed abstractions using a two-layered hierarchy of units. At the bottom layer we have placed the basic types that cover the whole spectrum of OBCS variants needed for the objects of interest. At the upper layer, we have defined the generic units that represent the basic types for the objects and embed the appropriate OBCS type.

In general, the START operation that appears in the provided interface of SPORADIC objects may have any parameter profile, including an empty one. By collecting all of the operation parameters into a single request descriptor of the type shown in figure 4, we streamline this variance to just two alternate signatures: one with a single

```
with System;                               with System;
with Types; use Types;                     with OBCS_C;
package OBCS_C is                          with Types; use Types;
   protected type OBCS_T                   generic
      (OBCS_Priority : System.Any_Priority) is   OBCS_Priority : System.Any_Priority;
      pragma Priority (OBCS_Priority);     with procedure Thread_Action;
      procedure Get_ATC_Request            with procedure Dispatcher
         (Req_Desc : out Request_Descriptor_T);   (Req_Desc : Request_Descriptor_T);
      procedure Put_ATC_Request            package Cyclic_A is
         (Req_Desc : in Request_Descriptor_T);   OBCS : OBCS_C.OBCS_T
   private                                       (OBCS_Priority);
      Req_Buf : Request_Buffer_T;          procedure Put_ATC_Request
      Req_Buf_Index : Request_Buffer_Index_T   (Req_Desc : in Request_Descriptor_T)
         := Request_Buffer_Index_T'First;     renames OBCS.Put_ATC_Request;
      ATC_Pending : Natural := 0;          task type Thread
   end OBCS_T;                                (Thread_Priority : System.Any_Priority;
end OBCS_C;                                    Thread_Period    : Integer) is
                                              pragma Priority (Thread_Priority);
                                           end Thread;
                                        end Cyclic_A;
```

Fig. 7. Factored template code for the OBCS of CYCLIC objects with ATC and for the CYCLIC object itself. The corresponding instantiation for the mapping of a CYCLIC terminal object is shown in figure 9

parameter and one parameterless. As the generic formal parameter profile of the generic unit in Ada must be strongly typed, we are compelled to use two distinct generic units to cater for SPORADIC objects with either kind of START operation.

The code generation rules for CYCLIC objects differentiates according to the presence, respectively the absence of ATC operations in the provided interface of the object. The full range of variants is as follows:

CYCLIC Terminal Objects with ASATC. The CYCLIC objects whose provided interface features ASATC operation(s) must include an OBCS equipped for handling the relevant requests. Figure 7 shows the factored code for the corresponding templates. (The data structures required for holding ATC requests were discussed earlier and shown in figure 4, while the Get_ATC_Request procedure has been outlined in figure 6.)

CYCLIC Terminal Objects Without ASATC. The CYCLIC objects that do not feature ASATC operations in their provided interface do not need an OBCS. All we need to map them is a generic unit parametric in the implementation of the periodic operation of the object.

SPORADIC Terminal Objects with Parameterless START Operation. Factoring code for this category of objects brings us very close to CYCLIC objects with ASATC. Figure 8 shows the corresponding code.

SPORADIC Terminal Objects with Parametric START Operation. This category of objects can easily be served by adapting the signature of the Start_Action formal generic

```
with System;                              with System;
with Types; use Types;                    with OBCS_S;
package OBCS_S is                         with Types; use Types;
  protected type OBCS_T                   generic
    (OBCS_Priority : System.Any_Priority) is   OBCS_Priority : System.Any_Priority;
    pragma Priority (OBCS_Priority);       with procedure Start_Action;
    entry Get_Request                      with procedure Dispatcher
      (Req_Desc : out Request_Descripto fT);   (Req_Desc : in Request_Descriptor_T);
    procedure Put Request                 package Sporadic is
      (Req_Desc : in Request_Descriptor T);   OBCS : OBCS_S.OBCS_T
  private                                      (OBCS_Priority);
    Start_Pending : Natural := 0;          procedure Put_Request
    ATC_Req_Buf : Request_Buffer_T;          (Req_Desc : in Request_Descriptor_T)
    ATC_Req_Buf_Index :                      renames OBCS.Put_Request;
      Request_Buffer_Index_T :=            task type Thread
      Request_Buffer_Index_T'First;          (Thread_Priority : System.Any_Priority;
    ATC_Pending : Natural := 0;             MIAT : Integer) is
    -- entry barrier:                        pragma Priority (Thread_Priority);
    --+ (Start_Pending+ATC_Pending)>0       end Thread;
    Req_Pending : Boolean := False;       end Sporadic;
  end OBCS_T;
end OBCS_S;
```

Fig. 8. Factored template code for the OBCS of SPORADIC objects with ATC and parameterless START and for the SPORADIC object itself. In the instantiation, the public interface of the SPORADIC terminal object will effectively provide a Start procedure, the body of which will be realised in the same style as that of the <OPn> provided operation of the CYCLIC terminal object shown in figure 9

profile to accept parameters of a type in the hierarchy of Param_T (cf. figure 4) and by equipping the OBCS with the appropriate buffering capabilities.

SPORADIC Terminal Objects with ASATC. This category of objects is taken care of in exactly the same way as described for CYCLIC terminal objects with ASATC.

4.1   Overall Structure of Terminal Objects

One of the principles that informed our strategy was to strive to map the user objects to very compact and cohesive units. The factoring effort we discussed above served the compactness objective well. The quest for cohesion resulted in mapping each user object into a hierarchy of three units, as follows:

- unit <Obj>, placed at the root the object's hierarchy, is generated in full automation and provides the instantiation of the appropriate object template, the implementation of the operations that appear in the object's provided interface, and the code of the Dispatcher procedure shown in figure 6; figure 9 shows the code generation rules for the body of the <Obj> unit of a CYCLIC object with an ASATC operation in its provided interface

- private child unit <Obj>.Types gathers the declaration of all the types that are local to the object and of the operations associated to them, including the required specialisations of the Param_T root type (cf. figure 4), the bodies for Thread_Action or Start_Action as appropriate, and the OPCS_<OPn> procedures that implement the object's provided interface
- private child unit <Obj>.RTATT provides values for the real-time attributes that are specific to the object.

In addition to easing automatic code generation, this structure also keeps the user modifiable code, placed in the *.Types child unit, apart from the one that the user need not touch, which is placed in the <Obj> unit. (The *.RTATT child unit only contains parameters and no functional code.)

Each operation that appears in the provided interface of a threaded terminal object maps to an automatically generated <OPn> procedure that wraps the inbound parame-

```
with Types;
with <Obj>.RTATT;
with <Obj>.Types;
with Cyclic_A;    pragma Elaborate_All(Cyclic_A);
package body <Obj> is
    procedure Dispatcher (Req_Desc :    in Request_Descriptor_T) is ... cf. figure 6
    package <Obj>_T is new Cyclic_A
      (OBCS_Priority => <Obj>.RTATT.Ceiling(RTA.Start_Mode),
       Thread_Action => <Obj>.Types.Thread_Action,
       Dispatcher => Dispatcher);
    <Obj>_Thread : <Obj>_T.Thread
      (Thread_Priority => <Obj>.RTATT.Thread_Priority (RTA.Start_Mode),
       Thread_Period => <Obj>.RTATT.Thread_Period (RTA.Start_Mode));
    procedure Put_ATC_Request (Req_Desc :   in Request_Descriptor_T)
      renames <Obj>_T.Put_ATC_Request;
    <OPn>_Par : Types.Param_T_Ref := new <Obj>.Types.<OPn>_Param_T;
    -- implementation of object's provided interface
    -- for each <OPn> operation
    procedure <OPn>(<Param_Part>) is
    begin
        <OPn>_Par.<Field> := <Param>; -- for each inbound parameter
        Put_ATC_Request
          (<Obj>.Types.Build_Request(Types.ATC_Req, <OPn>_Par));
    end <OPn>;
end <Obj>;
```

Fig. 9. Code generation rules for the instantiation body of CYCLIC terminal object with ATC. The client of this object need *not* know the structure of the object's request descriptor and simply supplies the parameter part of its call with no imposed structure. It is the automatically-generated code of the body of the object's provided operation (<OPn>) that places each inbound parameter in the internal request descriptor, invokes the automatically-generated function Build_Request as the required constructor and stores the result into the object's OBCS. The package specification for this object just needs to declare the object's provided interface

ters into a request descriptor of the object-specific type and passes it along to the object's
OBCS using the designated Put_ATC_Request protected procedure.

Eventually, the control flow in the CYCLIC thread will query the OBCS for a pending request (cf. Get_ATC_Request in figure 6) and will invoke the actual Dispatcher
procedure on it. Yet again, the code generation for the Dispatcher procedure (cf. figure 6) is fully automated off the object's provided interface as specified in the diagram
editor.

For any operation in the object provided interface, we allocate a static value of
the appropriate <OPn>_Param_T type in the corresponding unit, and we use it to hold
the single incoming parameter structure that the object will fetch from the OBCS at
any single activation. In this way we stay within the confines of the Ravenscar Profile,
which prohibits the use of dynamic memory allocation outside elaboration.

Arguably, the factored code that maps a CYCLIC object instance shown in figure
9 is very compact and easy to understand. Furthermore, the resulting code need not
include any implementation detail on the handling of the operation requests, which
is all taken care of by standard code generation rules, whose execution attributes can
easily be determined once and for all for any given target platform. All that is left for the
designer to do for the CYCLIC object is to supply the functional code for Thread_Action
and for its provided interface.

5   Mapping Non-terminal Objects

The mapping strategy described in [1] intentionally refrained from generating code for
non-terminal objects, thus deflecting from the hierarchical nature of HOOD design.
The latter is based on the principle of *delegation*: the client of a non-terminal object
may only request the operations that are published in the object's provided interface,
but their realisation is effectively delegated to operations provided by a range of child
objects fully invisible to the client. In Ada terms, the client would only need to "with"
the non-terminal object, and nothing further, to gain access to the requests of interest,
much in keeping with good old information hiding.

Limiting code generation to terminal objects only provides some ill-based expectation of performance gain, at the cost of breaking all encapsulation and causing clients
to explicitly "with" every single one of the child objects that happen to be the provider
of the client's required operation.

Generating code for non-terminal objects must however preserve the intended HRT-
HOOD meaning of them, which is just that of name space with no run-time identity.

In fact, Ada 95 [6] offers child units as the means for direct representation of design
hierarchies, and equips them with rather comprehensive support for user control of visibility. De la Puente et al. [13] propose a mapping strategy for HRT-HOOD non-terminal
objects, which uses child packages. The authors do not investigate the feasibility of applying their proposal to the original HRT-HOOD to Ada mapping in [1], which we
believe would not be warranted. Luckily instead, the ideas expressed in [13] do make a
very natural fit for our code generation strategy. Experimenting with Ada 95 compilation systems of different makes and for a variety of platforms we have noted that the use
of child units does not seem to incur any noticeable size or time performance penalties.

The strategy of de la Puente et al. is based on the following principles:

- the generated tree of Ada packages must match exactly the hierarchical architecture of the HRT-HOOD design
- the root object, i.e. the one that publishes the provided interface of an entire hierarchy must be represented by a public package; a client module that needs any of the corresponding services must simply "with" that public package
- any child of that object, irrespectively of whether being a parent or a terminal object itself, must be represented by a **private** child package
- any package, whether public or private, must "with" all the packages that represent the internal child hierarchy of the corresponding object
- the provided operations of a non-terminal object simply amount to the renaming of (and thus to the delegation to) the corresponding operation provided by one specific child in the non-terminal object's child hierarchy.

It is immediate to see that this strategy can directly fit our code generation rules by prefixing each package specification corresponding to a terminal object with the keyword **private** and by having the package body of every parent object include one **with** clause for each of its child objects.

6   Conclusions

At the end of our project we have attempted to quantitatively compare the performance of our novel code generation strategy with that achieved by the original mapping. To this end, we generated source code for an HRT-HOOD system comprised of a variable number of CYCLIC terminal objects, each equipped with a public interface providing two operations, each of which with two parameters in the signature. The comparative results we obtained were rather satisfactory. With as few as 6 objects in the system, our code generation strategy already produces 20% less source code than the original one, while the need for cater for factored templates incurs a little penalty for the generation of code for a single terminal object. Indeed, the gain grows linearly with the number of objects in the system and would be even greater in the face of more complex provided interfaces.

On the qualitative side, instead, we contend that we have also achieved the other objectives stated at the start of this paper. We have attained rigorous and systematic use of typed objects. Following on from the work described in [13], we have been able to produce very cohesive code units, and ensured that the generated code be in full match with the decomposition hierarchy of the original HRT-HOOD system. Finally, at the cost of placing some constraints on the original semantics of the HRT-HOOD execution requests (such as turning the original ATC requests for CYCLIC objects into "deferred mode change request") we have been able to yield code fully compliant with the Ravenscar Profile.

As a notable by-product, we have greatly simplified the code generation engine itself. The most frequently used source code generation technology consists in applying XSL transformations [14] on XML [15] representations of the design diagrams. Our intensive use of code factoring and template instantiations eases the production and the verification of the XSL transformation programs, making them considerably smaller in size and less complex to write and validate.

The HRT-HOOD to Ada 95 mapping strategy discussed in this paper sees the light only months ahead of the issue of the freshest revision of the Ada language standard, expectedly due in the fall of 2005. A number of interesting language features loom on the horizon, among which: the **limited with** clause for mutually dependent types; execution time clocks and time budgeting for better control of real-time computing (cf. [8]); **interface** types as a means for multiple inheritance.

In the way of an appetizer, it is immediate to see that the latter feature in particular would provide for a considerable extent of factoring of the various OBCS variants that our present strategy had to single out. All such variants would in fact become specific descendants of a single synchronized interface providing the two common procedures Put_Request and Get_Request shown in figures 7 and 8. The relevant hierarchy would thus look like as follows:

```
-- the root type
type OBCS_I is synchronized interface;
procedure Get_Request
  (Obj : in out OBCS_I;
   Req_Desc : out Request_Descriptor_T) is abstract;
procedure Put_Request
  (Obj : in out OBCS_I;
   Req_Desc : in Request_Descriptor_T) is abstract;

-- an instance of a descendant type
protected type OBCS_C (...) is new OBCS_I with
  procedure Put_Request (Req_Desc : in Request_Descriptor_T);
  entry Get_Request (Req_Desc : out Request_Descriptor_T);
end OBCS_C;
```

Fig. 10. The root of the OBCS type hierarchy using the **synchronized interface** facility of Ada 2005 and one instance of a descendant type

We eagerly look forward to experimenting with these new features to further the product of our mapping endeavour.

References

1. Burns, A., Wellings, A.: HRT-HOOD: A Structured Design Method for Hard Real-Time Systems. Elsevier Science, Amsterdam, NL (1995) ISBN 0-444-82164-3.
2. Czarnecki, K., Eisenecker, U.: Generative Programming: Methods, Tools and Applications. Addison-Wesley (2000) ISBN: 0201309777.
3. OMG: Model Driven Architecture. http://www.omg.org/mda (2004)
4. Halbwachs, N.: Synchronous Programming of Reactive Systems. Kluwer International Series in Engineering and Computer Science, 215. Kluwer Academic Publishers (1993) ISBN: 0792393112.

5. ESTEREL Technologies: Safety-, Mission- and Business-Critical Embedded Software. http://www.esterel-technologies.com/v3/?id=39425 (2005)
6. Taft, T., Duff, R., Brukard, R., Ploedereder, E., eds.: Consolidated Ada Reference Manual — International Standard ISO/IEC-8652:1995(E) with Technical Corrigendum 1. Volume 2219 of LNCS. Springer (2000) ISO/IEC 8652:1995.
7. Burns, A., Dobbing, B., Vardanega, T.: Guide for the Use of the Ada Ravenscar Profile in High Integrity Systems. Technical Report YCS-2003-348, University of York (UK) (2003) Approved as ISO/IEC JTC1/SC22 TR 42718.
8. Ada Conformity Assessment Authority: International Standard ISO/IEC 8652:1995 - Information Technology - Programming Languages - Ada - Amendment 1 (Draft 8). (2004) http://www.ada-auth.org/amendment.html.
9. Liu, J.W.S.: Real-Time Systems. Prentice-Hall (2000)
10. OMG: UML 1.5 Specification. (2001) http://www.uml.org/\#UML1.5.
11. Mazzini, S., D'Alessandro, M., Di Natale, M., Domenici, A., Lipari, G., Vardanega, T.: HRT-UML: Taking HRT-HOOD onto UML. In Rosen, J.P., Strohmeier, A., eds.: Reliable Software Technologies - Ada-Europe. Number 2655 in LNCS, Springer (2003) 405–416
12. Praxis High Integrity Systems: The SPARK Examiner. (2005) http://www.praxis-cs.co.uk/sparkada/examiner.asp.
13. de la Puente, J.A., Alonso, A., Alvarez, A.: Mapping HRT-HOOD Designs to Ada 95 Hierarchical Libraries. In Strohmeier, A., ed.: Reliable Software Technologies - Ada-Europe. Number 1088 in LNCS, Springer (1996) 78–88
14. W3C: XSL Transformations (XSLT). http://www.w3.org/TR/xslt (2005)
15. W3C: Extensible Markup Language (XML). http://www.w3.org/XML/ (2005)

Using the AADL to Describe Distributed Applications from Middleware to Software Components

Thomas Vergnaud[1], Laurent Pautet[1], and Fabrice Kordon[2]

[1] GET-Télécom Paris – LTCI-UMR 5141 CNRS,
46, rue Barrault, F-75634 Paris Cedex 13, France
{thomas.vergnaud, laurent.pautet}@enst.fr
[2] Université Pierre & Marie Curie, Laboratoire d'Informatique de Paris 6/SRC,
4, place Jussieu, F-75252 Paris Cedex 05, France
fabrice.kordon@lip6.fr

Abstract. Distributed Real-Time (DRE) systems require the verification of their properties to ensure both reliability and conformance to initial requirements. Architecture description languages (ADLs) such as the AADL provide adequate syntax and semantics to express all those properties on each component of a system. DRE systems rely on a key component, the middleware, to address distribution issues. In order to build efficient and verifiable systems, the middleware has to be tailorable to meet the application needs, and to be easily modeled to support a verification process. We propose the schizophrenic architecture as a canonical solution to these concerns. We study how to describe the middleware architecture using the AADL. We also study how the AADL can be used to aggregate the different aspects of the modeling of a complete system: architecture, behavioral descriptions, deployment, etc.

1 Introduction

Distributed systems are widely used in various application domains such as embedded systems, business applications or web applications. Distribution has to address different requirements, either related to system constraints (execution time, memory footprint, limited bandwidth...) or related to the application design (reuse of legacy components, programming languages heterogeneity...).

An application can take advantage by the reuse of COTS to cut down development costs. Besides, architecture description languages (ADL) can capture the design of a complete application and of its key components. As they allow for a more abstract view of the application than programming languages, they help in identifying the structural components, and eventually expressing properties on the whole architecture. Large projects rely on an ADL to design embedded systems. In addition to architectural considerations, attention is focused on property verification to assess system reliability.

The ASSERT project[1], coordinated by the European Space Agency and the European Union, chose the Architecture Analysis & Design Language (AADL) as a support

---

[1] http://www.assert-online.org

T. Vardanega and A. Wellings (Eds.): Ada-Europe 2005, LNCS 3555, pp. 67–78, 2005.
© Springer-Verlag Berlin Heidelberg 2005

for modeling. The AADL is targeted to the description of real-time embedded systems. It is based on component composition and provides very convenient facilities to specify properties on the architecture. AADL descriptions are tightly related to the implemented systems they represent, and the AADL provides support for system generation.

Distributed systems rely heavily on middleware to handle a large part of the distribution issues [1]. Compliance to constraints can only be verified once the system has been completely designed; in order to ensure property verification, the middleware has to be modelled as well as the other system components.

As a middleware is a complex piece of software, modelling it with an ADL may be a very tedious task. Moreover, middleware usually implements a given distribution model like CORBA [2], DSA [3] or Web Services [4]. Middleware may have a very different architecture depending on the distribution model it implements. To overcome these issues, we propose to focus on a middleware architecture which would be representative of most middlewares.

Schizophrenic middleware allows to instantiate a generic middleware for one or more distribution models. In other words, such a highly tailorable middleware can be adapted to meet the exact application requirements. In [5], we presented PolyORB, an implementation of the schizophrenic architecture.

The schizophrenic architecture can be decomposed into several well identified components that can be analyzed. Thus it eases the modeling of middleware; its clear structure facilitates its description using an ADL. This can ease property verification, configuration and deployment of an application.

Our long-term objective consists of extracting general properties from distributed real-time embedded (DRE) systems. In this paper, we aim at studying the ability of the AADL to describe such systems from middleware to application components. As a case study, we especially focus on the middleware, which represents the core component of a DRE system. Because of its clear structure and its versatility, the schizophrenic middleware architecture is a good candidate to evaluate AADL modelling capabilities.

This paper is structured as follows. We first give an overview of the AADL and its main features. We then describe the schizophrenic architecture and explain why it is a viable choice to model middleware. We give some elements on how to describe the architecture of a system based on a schizophrenic middleware using AADL. We finally study how the AADL can be used to federate all the aspects of a system description.

2   Modeling the Architecture Using the AADL

The AADL is an evolution of MetaH, [6] and thus they share many common features. The AADL aims at allowing for the description of DRE systems by assembling blocks developed separately. Thus, it focuses on the definition of clear block interfaces [7], and separates the implementations from those interfaces.

The AADL standard [8] is based on a textual syntax. It also provides a graphical notation. An XML notation [9] is also defined to ease interoperability between tools. It also defines a run-time and how to translate AADL constructions into programming languages [10]. Hence, the structure of an application can be automatically generated.

An AADL description consists of *components*. Each component has an interface providing *features* (e.g. communication ports), and zero, one or several implementations. The implementations give the internals of the component. Most component implementations can have *subcomponents*, so that an AADL description is hierarchical. The components communicate one with another by *connecting* their features. The AADL defines a set of standard *properties* that can be attached to most elements (components, connections, ports, etc.). In addition, it is possible to add user-defined properties, to specify specific description information.

2.1   Components

Basically, an AADL description is a set of components that represent the different elements of the whole architecture. The AADL standard defines software and hardware components; so it is possible to model a complete system.

Execution platform components represent all the components related to the computers and networks that are part of the whole system.

- *buses* are used to describe all kinds of networks, buses, etc;
- *memories* are used to represent any storage device: RAM, hard disk,...;
- *processors* model micro-processors with schedulers: they are the general representation of a computer shipped with a basic operating system;
- *devices* represent components whose internals are not precisely known. Typical examples of such black boxes are sensors: the knowledge is limited to their external behavior and their interface. We do not control their structure.

Execution platform components are mostly hardware components. Yet, components like *devices* or *processors* may have software parts.

Software components allow for the description of pure software elements (no hardware is involved).

- *data* components are used to describe data structures that are stored in *memory* or exchanged between components;
- *threads* are the active components of a software application;
- *thread groups* gather several *threads*, thus allowing to describe a hierarchy among the *threads* of an application;
- *processes* correspond to memory spaces used to execute *threads*. A *thread* must execute within a *process*, and a *process* must have at least one *thread*;
- *subprograms* correspond to procedure calls in imperative programing languages such as Ada or C. They allow to model an entry point in a *thread* or a *data* component (which can be viewed as a class for object oriented languages) or can simply be used to model normal subprograms.

Systems are either used to make high-level descriptions or to add hierarchy in the description. They contain other components, and thus are neither pure software nor pure hardware components. *Systems* describe self-sufficient components. For instance, a *thread* cannot be directly put into a *system*, since a *thread* must be contained in a process.

The AADL introduces the notion of *component types* and *component implementations*. A *component type* corresponds to what is visible from the outside of the component, such as its interface (basically its inputs and outputs); a *component implementation* describes the internals of a component: its sub-components, the connections between them, etc. There can be several different *implementations* of a given *type*. The AADL also allows for the inheritance of *component types* and *component implementations*: a *type* or an *implementation* can extend another one.

Subcomponents are instantiations of component types or implementations, the same way as objects are instances of classes in object oriented languages.

2.2   Ports, Subprograms and Connections

Components communicate through *ports* and *subprogram calls*, that are provided as features of the component type.

Ports are used to model asynchronous communications:

- *data ports* are associated to a data component. They can be compared to the state of a port in an integrated circuit: the destination component may or may not listen to the data. If not, the information is lost;
- *event ports* can be seen like the signals of an operating system. Compared to *data ports*, they can trigger events in components, but do not carry data. Unlike data ports, a queue is associated with each event port;
- *data event ports* have the characteristics of the two former ports: they can trigger events and carry data. They are typically used to model the communications with message oriented middleware.

Event data ports can be used to model communications based on message passing. *Ports* can be declared *in*, *out* or *in out*.

Subprograms correspond to synchronous calls, like Remote Procedure Calls (RPC) or direct procedure call (as defined in programming languages) and accept *in*, *out* and *in out* parameters; *parameters* are comparable to *data* ports or *event data* ports, but are synchronous and dedicated to *subprograms*.

2.3   Properties and Property Sets

The AADL defines a set of standard properties. These are used to specify execution deadlines for *threads*, bindings between software and execution platform components, protocols for *connections*, transmission times for *buses*, etc. They can describe all the information required to check the validity of the system, or to complete the description of its architecture.

Property types can be integers, floats, strings or booleans, *component* references or enumerations. Complex data structures such as Ada records or C structures do not exist.

Each *property* name is meant to be applied to some (or all) elements of a description: processors, connections, ports, etc.

Properties can be specified inside elements (e.g. component *types* or *implementations*). They can also be associated to instances of subcomponents. This allows for great flexibility, as a given component implementation can be characterized when instantiated; it is not necessary to specify another implementation.

If a given characteristic does not correspond to a property of the standard set of properties, it is possible to define specific properties, using *property sets*. A *property set* defines a namespace that contains *property types* and *property names*.

2.4   Packages

By default, all elements of an AADL description are declared in a global namespace. To avoid possible name conflicts in the case of a large description, it is possible to gather components within *packages*.

A *package* can have a public part and a private part; the private part is only visible to elements of the same package.

Packages can contain *component* declarations. So, they can be used to structure the description from a logical point of view – unlike systems, they do not impact the architecture.

3   Architecture Concerns for Distributed Applications

Middleware is a fundamental element of a distributed application, as it addresses several distribution issues. Some of them are related to the distributed nature of the application, like the location of the physical nodes. Others are related to each local node, like the execution of the whole application. Some other considerations are related to both local configuration and deployment, like the communication protocol used between the nodes. All these issues can be separated, as shown on figure 1. In this paper, we focus on the local node concerns.

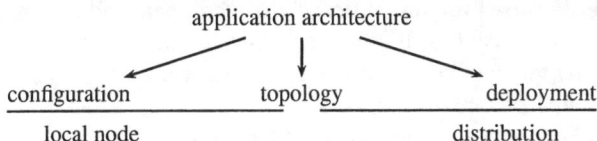

Fig. 1. Principles of distributed application description

3.1   Tailorable Middleware Architectures

There are two main reasons to design a highly tailorable middleware. First, such a middleware would fit exactly with the application requirements with a reasonable development cost. Second, it could meet the requirements of several system families by being configured for a specific distribution model. Some middleware architectures have been proposed to provide tailorability; for example configurable and generic middlewares.

The main limitation of configurable architectures (e.g. TAO [11]) is that they focus on a given distribution model (CORBA in the case of TAO). They are not efficient enough with applications that do not fit well into this model: An application designed in a Message Oriented Middleware (MOM) approach will not be as efficient if implemented with a Distributed Object Computing (DOC) middleware such as TAO.

The main drawback of generic architectures (e.g. Jonathan [12]) is that the development of a new personality implies the engineering of a significant amount of code.

For instance, since Jonathan is mostly based on abstract interfaces, personalities like David (for CORBA applications) and Jeremie (for RMI applications) reuse only 10% of the generic code. Despite the fact that such an architecture could be a good solution to adapt the middleware to application needs, the cost of this adaptation is too high in most cases.

3.2   The Schizophrenic Architecture

Configurable and generic architectures ease middleware adaptation; they are one step towards middleware modularity. However, they do not provide complete solutions, as they are either restricted to a distribution model, or too expensive. A middleware architecture combining configurability, genericity but also addressing interoperability with other middlewares is needed to support a distribution infrastructure that can be fully tailorable and built from reused components.

This requires an architecture that provides a synthesis of different middleware architectures, and emphasizes the separation of concerns. Such an architecture should be compared to the one adopted in classical compilers: compiler theory describes a flexible architecture, separating machine code generation from source code analysis: a front-end module analyzes source code; a back-end assembles machine code; both of them interact using different neutral representations. Projects like GCC[2] clearly demonstrates component reuse capabilities while providing support for multiple languages and targets.

Similarly, we proposed an original middleware architecture which separates concerns between distribution model API and protocol, and their implementation related mechanisms.

Decoupling Middleware Functionalities. A schizophrenic middleware refines the definition and role of personalities. It introduces *application-level* and *protocol-level* personalities and a *neutral* core layer which are to middleware what front-ends, back-ends and an intermediate layer are to compilers.

Application Personalities constitute the adaptation layer between application components and middleware through a dedicated API or code generator; they provide services similar to those provided by a compiler front-end: translation of high-level constructs into simpler ones. They provide APIs to plug application components with the core middleware; they interact with the core layer in order to allow the exchange of requests between entities.

- On the client side, they map requests made by client components from their personality-dependent representation to a personality-independent one. This neutral representation is then processed by the neutral core layer; results are translated back from neutral to personality-dependent form.
- On the server side, they receive requests for local objects from the core middleware, assign them to actual application components for evaluation, and return results.

Application personalities can instantiate middleware implementations such as CORBA, the Distributed System Annex of Ada 95 (DSA), the Java Message Service (JMS), etc.

---

[2] Free software compiler front-ends and back-ends available at http://gcc.gnu.org

Protocol personalities handle the mapping of personality-neutral requests (representing interactions between application entities) onto messages exchanged using a chosen communication network and protocol; similar to a compiler back-end which transforms intermediate code representation into low level mnemonics. Requests can be received either from application entities (through an application personality and the neutral core layer) or from another node of the distributed application. They can also be received from another protocol personality: in this case the application node acts as a proxy performing protocol translation between third-party nodes. Protocol personalities can instantiate middleware protocols such as IIOP (for CORBA), SOAP (for Web Services), etc.

The neutral core layer acts as an adaptation layer between application and protocol personalities. It manages execution resources and provides the necessary abstractions to transparently pass requests between protocol and application personalities in a neutral way. It is completely independent from both application and protocol personalities. This enables the selection of any combination of application and/or protocol personalities; as the GCC compiler allows the selection of any given front-end/back-end pair.

Fundamental Services. A schizophrenic middleware requires a flexible implementation and the identification of the functionalities involved in request processing to ease the prototyping of new personalities and their interactions.

Figure 2 describes the main elements of the schizophrenic architecture.

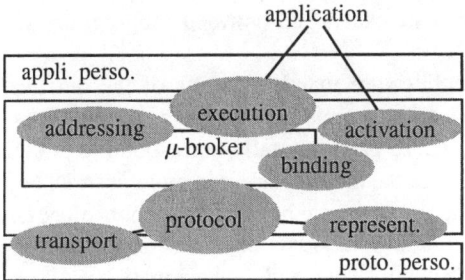

Fig. 2. The schizophrenic architecture

The personalities and the neutral core layer are built on top of seven fundamental services embodying client/server interactions found in the distribution models.

A client personality invokes the **addressing** service to get the reference of the server entity (e.g. an object). The **binding** service then associates a binding object to this reference; a gateway is created between the actual server entity and the surrogate entity on the client side. The **protocol** service calls the **representation** service to format the request data and sends them through the **transport** service. Upon reception on the server side, the **activation** service ensures the targeted entity is available. The **execution** service is then invoked so that the targeted entity actually processes the request. The response is returned using the same mechanism.

The composition of these fundamental services allows for the implementation of different distribution models. The inner part of the middleware core is controlled by a central element named μ-broker, on which the services rely. It is formally described, and supports verification facilities to ensure real-time properties [13].

A distributed application is made of several components, an important one being the middleware. The schizophrenic middleware architecture provides a canonical architecture, made of fundamental services that provide well identified functions. Schizophrenic middleware is versatile enough to instantiate middleware supporting different distribution models. The architecture of the neutral core layer remains unchanged from one instantiation to another. It can ensure various properties regarding real-time requirements. The schizophrenic architecture helps model middleware using a component-based language such as an ADL.

4   Using the AADL to Describe a DRE System

We now present elements on the description of the server node of a simple mono-task application. We first describe the middleware architecture. This description is based on PolyORB, our implementation of the schizophrenic architecture, presented in 2. We then describe how the middleware part integrates with the other parts of the whole server application: the application itself and the operating system.

4.1   Describing the Schizophrenic Architecture

Middleware is made of active components (i.e. *threads*) that call reactive components (i.e. *subprograms*). The data exchanged between subprograms or threads are modeled by *data* components.

The middleware architecture mainly consists of the reactive components. Those components model the different middleware parts: personalities and the internals of the neutral core layer. Those parts naturally correspond to AADL *packages*. We cannot use *systems* to structure the architecture into more abstract components: the AADL syntax does not allow *subprograms* to be subcomponents of *systems*.

A middleware configuration consists of a selection of the appropriate component implementations for the neutral layer and the personalities.

The seven services of the neutral layer and the μ-broker are represented by distinct packages. Thus we can isolate the different fundamental functions of the neutral layer. The public part of each package should only contain the subprograms that are required for the interconnection with the other elements of the middleware. The auxiliary subprograms are to be placed in the private part of the packages. So the public parts of the packages will contain the data components and the entry points for the services.

Protocol and applicative personalities are not modeled the same way. An application personality can be modeled as a subprogram. This subprogram is to be called by the execution service, which transmits the neutral request. This neutral request has to be translated into the particular data format used by the application. This translation is typically handled by auxiliary subprograms of the personality. The main subprogram of the personality is to be placed in the public part of the personality package, while the translation subprograms should be in the private part.

A protocol personality is actually a combination of three services: protocol, transport and representation. Consequently, a protocol personality may just correspond to a selection of given service implementations. However, in practice, protocol personalities often require specific service implementations. So a protocol personality is typically modeled by a package which contains the required service implementations.

The active part of the middleware is an execution *thread*. The thread receives requests and returns responses using *sockets*. *sockets* are modeled as event data ports, since at the lowest network level, data frames can be actually compared to messages.

Upon the reception of a request, this thread calls the subprograms of the μ-broker. Then the μ-broker will invoke the appropriate services to process the request. The response returned by the μ-broker will be sent back by the thread.

4.2   Describing a Complete Node

We gave the outline of the description of a schizophrenic middleware architecture using the AADL. In order to be able to perform analysis related to memory footprint or schedulability, we have to completely describe each node of the distributed system. A node is constituted by the application executed on the node, the middleware and the operating system components (cf. figure 3). The hardware part of the system could also be of some interest, but we will not discuss this here, as we focus on the software architecture.

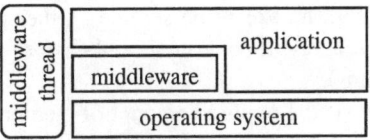

Fig. 3. A server application

The application relies on the middleware and operating system components. Since the application consists of purely software components (i.e. mainly subprograms), it should be described as a package, like the middleware application personalities.

The operating system can be modeled by a set of subprograms. Since a processor component is meant to model both a hardware micro-processor and a minimalist operating system, the entry point subprograms of the operating system may be integrated in a processor component, while the auxiliary subprograms could be located in a package.

The middleware and application subprograms and the threads are instantiated as subcomponents of a process. This process must be bound to the processor which contains the operating system.

5   Discussion

We gave the main lines of the modeling of the server part of a PolyORB-based DRE system using the AADL.

We isolated three main parts: the operating system, the middleware and the application itself. These three parts are independent enough to be treated as separated issues, provided that the interfaces are clearly defined. This allows the separate development of the different parts of the system. For example, in the ASSERT project, PolyORB is to be used on the real-time kernel ORK [14], separately developed. The middleware itself is not represented as a component, but as a set of components defined in packages; this illustrates the fact that the middleware is part of the application, not an independent component. The services of the schizophrenic architecture remain easily identified.

A noticeable aspect of this description is that all AADL packages and components have clearly identifiable Ada counterparts: AADL packages correspond to Ada packages, same thing for subprograms; threads can be compared to Ada tasks. The AADL allows the specification of additional properties, such as execution time, etc. In addition, the AADL allows for the description of hardware components; it provides a unified notation to describe the whole system.

We can see that a software description made with the AADL leads mainly to define *subprograms*. Therefore, a too much detailed description would nearly lead to a direct mapping between Ada procedures and AADL subprograms, which would be useless. The AADL *subprograms* should rather correspond to sets of Ada procedures.

Component implementation should not necessarily be described using programming language: as it is the control part of the middleware, the μ-broker is likely to be modeled using formal methods in order to ensure the reliability of the application.

So, the generation of the whole system shall require intermediate code generation: some components are described using formal methods; others are purely related to the middleware configuration (e.g. the execution service). Other parts of the middleware, such as the personalities, are likely to be written in plain Ada (or any language chosen to implement the subprograms).

Relevant properties, such as the required amount of memory or the processing time could be associated to each component of the description. This would facilitate the verification or the simulation of the whole system.

Besides node generation or analysis, the AADL could also be used to describe the deployment of the whole distributed system. GLADE, an implementation of the Distributed System Annex (DSA), provides a configuration language to partition a distributed system. We are currently working on an AADL model to generalize such an approach for any distribution model and to express the deployment of a distributed system using AADL properties.

Tools are required to process AADL descriptions: perform analysis on the description (schedulability of the whole system, compliance to system constraints...); or to instantiate an executable system, by generating the code for the components, and then linking them to an AADL execution runtime; or to configure and deploy a system, according to its description; or simply to check the syntax and the completeness of the description.

OSATE[3], an open source tool, has been developed for this purpose. OSATE is written in Java and is bound to the Eclipse platform. OSATE is meant to receive *plug-ins* that perform analysis, code generation, etc.

Since we are developing PolyORB in Ada, the fact that OSATE is a Java oriented tool is a drawback for us. As we are experimenting with the AADL, we need complete control on the tools, so that we can study some extensions to the AADL syn-

---

[3] Available at http://www.aadl.info

tax, etc. Thus we are developing our own multi-purpose free software tool in Ada 95: Ocarina[4].

Ocarina is a set of libraries built around a central core. The core provides an API to manipulate and check the semantics of AADL models. We developed a parser/printer for the AADL syntax as described in the revision 1.0 of the standard. Other modules are under development, such as an XML parser/printer to ease the interoperability with other tools (e.g. OSATE). Ocarina will be used for the configuration and deployment tools associated with PolyORB.

6   Conclusion

In this paper, we focused on the modeling of DRE applications. Building DRE applications requires verifications on the architecture. Such verifications are related to quantitative properties like timeliness or memory footprint, as well as properties of reliability (no deadlocks, no starvation, etc.).

We first presented the Architecture Analysis & Design Language. The AADL aims at describing systems as an integration of separate components. Information can be associated to the architectural description, using properties.

We outlined the fact that distributed applications have different and specific requirements. As designing specific middleware to a specific application would cost too much, therefore, adaptable middleware is required that can meet many different requirements. There is a need for fully tailorable middleware which can be verified.

We introduced the schizophrenic architecture as a good solution to middleware tailorability. It relies on a clear separation of middleware functions and can then be structured into different modules; thus it eases modeling using languages such as the AADL. As a large part of a schizophrenic middleware implementation remains unchanged, verification can be performed.

We showed how to describe the architecture of a node of a distributed application. We first described the middleware part and then its integration into the application node. The AADL allows for a clear modeling structure. Architectural description and properties provide all the required information to configure a local application node. In addition, the AADL can integrate behavioral descriptions of the components, using either programming languages or formal methods. As additional properties can be defined, the AADL can also be used to describe the deployment of the whole distributed system. Consequently, the AADL can be used as a unification language to aggregate all that is required to entirely describe a DRE system.

References

1. Bernstein, P.A.: Middleware: An archictecture: for distributed system services. Technical Report CRL 93/6, Cambridge MA (USA) (1993)
2. OMG: The Common Object Request Broker: Architecture and Specification, revision 2.2. OMG (1998) OMG Technical Document formal/98-07-01.

---

[4] Available at http://eve.enst.fr/ocarina

3. Pautet, L., Tardieu, S.: GLADE: a Framework for Building Large Object-Oriented Real-Time Distributed Systems. In: Proceedings of the 3rd IEEE International Symposium on Object-Oriented Real-Time Distributed Computing (ISORC'00), Newport Beach, California, USA, IEEE Computer Society Press (2000)
4. W3C: Simple Object Access Protocol (SOAP) 1.1. (2000) http://www.w3.org/TR/SOAP/.
5. Vergnaud, T., Hugues, J., Pautet, L., Kordon, F.: PolyORB: a schizophrenic middleware to build versatile reliable distributed applications. In: Proceedings of the 9th International Conference on Reliable Software Techologies Ada-Europe 2004 (RST'04). Volume LNCS 3063., Palma de Mallorca, Spain, Springer Verlag (2004) 106 – 119
6. Vestal, S.: Technical and historical overview of MetaH. Technical report, Honeywell (2000) available at http://la.sei.cmu.edu/aadlinfosite/MetaHPublications.html.
7. Lewis, B.: architecture based model driven software and system development for real-time embedded systems (2003) avilable at http://la.sei.cmu.edu/aadlinfosite/AADLPublications.html.
8. SAE: Architecture Analysis & Design Language (AS5506). (2004) available at http://www.sae.org.
9. Feiler, P.: Annex A: AADL Model interchange formats. (2004) Part of the AADL standard, available from SAE.
10. Tokar, J.: Annex D: Language compliance and application program interface. (2004) Part of the AADL standard, available from SAE.
11. Schmidt, D., Cleeland, C.: Applying patterns to develop extensible and maintainable ORB middleware. Communications of the ACM, CACM **40** (1997)
12. Dumant, B., Horn, F., Tran, F.D., Stefani, J.B.: Jonathan: an open distributed processing environment in java. In: Proceedings of the IFIP International Conference on Distributed Systems Platforms and Open Distributed Processing, Londres, Springer Verlag (1998) 175–190
13. Hugues, J., Thierry-Mieg, Y., Kordon, F., Pautet, L., Baarir, S., Vergnaud, T.: On the Formal Verification of Middleware Behavioral Properties. In: Proceedings of the 9th International Workshop on Formal Methods for Industrial Critical Systems (FMICS'04), Linz, Austria (2004) To be published.
14. de la Puente, J.A., Zamorano, J., Ruiz, J., Fernández, R., García, R.: The design and implementation of the Open Ravenscar Kernel. In: Proceedings of the 10th international workshop on Real-time Ada workshop, ACM Press (2001) 85–90

Extending Ravenscar with CSP Channels

Diyaa-Addein Atiya and Steve King

Department of Computer Science, University of York,
Heslington, York, YO10 5DD, UK
{diyaa, king}@cs.york.ac.uk

Abstract. The Ravenscar Profile is a restricted subset of the Ada tasking model, designed to meet the requirements of producing analysable and deterministic code. A central feature of Ravenscar is the use of protected objects to ensure mutually exclusive access to shared data. This paper uses Ravenscar protected objects to implement CSP channels in Ada – the proposed implementation is formally verified using model checking. The advantage of these *Ravenscar channels* is transforming the data-oriented asynchronous tasking model of Ravenscar into the cleaner message-passing synchronous model of CSP. Thus, formal proofs and techniques for model-checking CSP specifications can be applied to Ravenscar programs. In turn, this increases confidence in these programs and their reliability. Indeed, elsewhere, we use the proposed Ravenscar channels as the basis for a cost-effective technique for verifying concurrent safety-critical system.

1 Introduction

Ada's model for concurrent programming is powerful and extensive, but it is also complex, making it difficult to reason about the properties of real-time systems. Indeed, analysis of programs that make unrestricted use of Ada run-time features like rendezvous, select statements, and abort is currently infeasible [4]. With predictability and verifiability as design objectives, the Ravenscar Profile [3,4] has been proposed as a greatly simplified subset of the Ada tasking model.

In Ravenscar, there is no task-to-task communication as that of Ada's rendezvous constructs. Instead, data communications between tasks are indirect, through the use of *protected objects*. This makes protected objects central and fundamental building blocks in Ravenscar programs. We use Ravenscar protected objects to implement CSP [6] channels in Ada. This allows us to transform the data-oriented asynchronous tasking model of Ravenscar into the synchronous message-passing model of CSP. The advantages of doing this are manifold. For example, the CSP model eliminates the need for the programmer to worry about synchronization and physical data transfer between communicating tasks; all of these are now embedded into the channel construct. Also, synchronous Ravenscar programs are more amenable to formal proof and model checking. In turn, this contributes to the production of more reliable and trustworthy systems.

The rest of this paper is organised as follows. Section 2 provides a brief account of Ravenscar protected objects. Section 3 presents an implementation

T. Vardanega and A. Wellings (Eds.): Ada-Europe 2005, LNCS 3555, pp. 79–90, 2005.

of CSP channels in Ravenscar. Section 4 describes a CSP model for the Ravenscar implementation. Using that CSP model, Section 5 shows that the implemented Ravenscar channels have the same semantics as CSP channels. Finally, Section 6 draws conclusions and discusses related work.

2   Ravenscar Protected Objects

Simply, Ravenscar protected objects are Ada protected objects with extra restrictions imposed to meet various design requirements such as determinism and schedulability analysis. Thus, as in Ada, a Ravenscar protected object ensures mutually exclusive access to its encapsulated data, through a provided interface of *protected functions, protected procedures,* and/or *protected entries*. However, to meet the design requirements, the Profile imposes a number of restrictions on protected objects. Many of these restrictions are syntactic; for example, the Ravenscar Profile does not permit declaration of protected objects local to subprograms, tasks, or other protected objects. The discussion of such restrictions is not relevant to this work; rather, we are interested in the restrictions imposed on the functional aspects of protected objects, which can be summarised as follows:

R1 A protected object can have at most one entry.
R2 No more than one task may queue on an entry at any time.
R3 The barrier must be either static or the value of a state variable.
R4 As in Ada, potentially blocking operations are not allowed inside the body of a protected object.

An application could further restrict **R2** so that only one task is able to call each protected entry. This paper adopts the stronger version of **R2**, as a static check could be provided for it.

Figure 1 represents a Ravenscar protected object, *Data*, which comprises: a protected entry *Get*, a protected procedure *Put*, and two variables. The first variable, *d*, represents the encapulated data, which can be of any valid Ada type *T*. The second variable, *ReadyToRead*, is of type *Boolean* and is used as a barrier for *Get*. The definition of *Data* guarantees that every call to the protected entry *Get* has to be followed by a call to the protected procedure *Put* before the next entry call can execute. This protected object is used as part of the implementation of CSP channels in Ravenscar, see Section 3.

3   Implementing CSP Channels in Ravenscar

In CSP, communication between concurrent processes occurs by passing values on channels. Two types of events can happen on a channel: input and output. An input receives a value from a channel and assigns that value to a variable. An output event, on the other hand, sends out a value to a channel. Respectively, the CSP notation for input and output is $c?x : T$ and $c!v$ – where c is the channel name, x is the variable to which the input value is assigned, v is the

```
protected Data is
    entry Get(var: out T);
    procedure Put(var: in T);
Private
    d : T;
    ReadyToRead : Boolean := False;
end Data;

protected body  Data is
    entry Get(var: out T) when ReadyToRead is
    begin
      var := d;
      ReadyToRead := False;
    end Get;

    procedure Put(var: in T) is
    begin
      d := var;
      ReadyToRead := True;
    end Put;
end Data;
```

Fig. 1. Protected object *Data*

value output through the channel, and T is the type of values communicated on the channel c.

CSP channels are synchronous; that is, both the input and the output processes have to be ready for a communication to proceed, and whoever gets to the communication point first has to wait for the other party. In this section we consider two Ada tasks, *Producer* and *Consumer*, and provide an implementation of a CSP channel for communicating values from *Producer* to *Consumer*.

We need two protected objects:

1. **Data** (Figure 1): encapsulates the data communicated between the tasks, and ensures that every *read* by *Consumer* is followed with a *write* by *Producer*. The protected object comprises a protected entry *Get*, a protected procedure *Put*, and two variables. Only the task *Consumer* can call *Get* and only the task *Producer* can call *Put*.
2. **Sync** (Figure 2): ensures that whoever reads/writes first has to wait for synchronisation with the other party before leaving the channel. The protected object comprises a protected entry *Stay*, a protected procedure *Proceed*, and a boolean variable *HasRead* which is used as a barrier for *Stay*. Only the task *Producer* can call *Stay* and only the task *Consumer* can call *Proceed*.

The two protected objects conform to the restrictions of Ravenscar. However, *Data* and *Sync* can simulate the behaviour of a CSP channel only if calls by *Producer* and *Consumer* are made according to the following protocols. To write

```
protected Sync is
   entry Stay;
   procedure Proceed;
Private
   HasRead : Boolean := False;
end Sync;

protected body Sync is
   entry Stay when HasRead is
   begin
     HasRead := False;
   end Stay;

   procedure Proceed is
   begin
     HasRead := True;
   end Proceed;
end Sync;
```

Fig. 2. Protected object *Sync*

a value *v* to the channel, the *Producer* task has to make the following two calls:
`Data.Put(v); Sync.Stay;`
And, to read a value *v* from the channel, the *Consumer* task has to make the
following two calls: `Data.Get(v); Sync.Proceed;`
The *Read* and *Write* protocols are depicted in Figure 3, and are implemented
as the interface procedures to the Ada package representing Ravenscar channels,
see [1–Appendix C].

To show how the two protected objects can simulate a CSP channel, consider
the initial state. When *Producer* and *Consumer* reach the protected object *Data*,
only *Producer* can execute the procedure *Data.Put(v)* – if *Consumer* gets there
first, it will wait at the entry barrier until *Producer* finishes writing the data to
the protected object. When *Producer* finishes writing the data to *Data* it changes

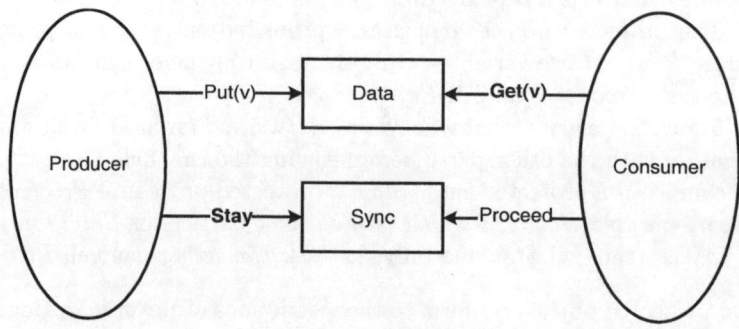

Fig. 3. Write/Read protocols; entry calls are shown in **bold**

the entry barrier *ReadyToRead* into True, giving *Consumer* the chance to proceed and read the data just written. However, leaving *Data*, the *Producer* will wait at the entry barrier of *Sync* until *Consumer* finishes its reading operation. Now, when *Consumer* reaches the protected object *Sync*, it changes the entry barrier *HasRead* to True, enabling *Producer* to proceed. Thus, the two tasks move on to carry their own computations.

4   The Formal Model of Ravenscar Channels

From the discussion above, one can see that the correctness of our implementation depends on which task calls which protected entry/procedure. Nonetheless, the behaviour of the two protected objects and the "read" and "write" protocols is independent of the communicated data, which could be of any type. Thus, the correctness of Ravenscar channels depends on the communicating tasks, and *not* on the communicated data – this remark will become more evident in the formal model presented below. As in occam [7] our implementation provides a One-To-One CSP channel; that is, only two tasks can communicate over a single channel. This small number of tasks suggests that model-checking is a good approach for verification. Therefore, we provide a CSP model of the implementation and verify it using the FDR [5] tool.

4.1   Ravenscar Protected Objects in CSP

Let *PO* be a Ravenscar protected object that has an entry task[1]. Also, let the tasks communicating on *PO* be drawn from the non-empty[2] set *ValidTaskId*.

There are six components that determine the state of *PO*.

– The data encapsulated, *data*, of type T.
– The entry task's identifier, *entry_task*, which determines the one task that can call the protected entry of the object.
– The current value of the boolean entry barrier, *barrier*.
– A boolean flag (*waiting*) that is true exactly when the entry task is waiting on the entry queue.
– The set of *writers* ($\subseteq$ *ValidTaskId*), those tasks currently actively executing a procedure or an entry call.
– The set of *readers* ($\subseteq$ *ValidTaskId*), those tasks currently actively executing a function call.

We model *PO* as a CSP process with nine channels, each corresponding to some interaction between the protected object and its environment.

---

[1] Since both *Data* and *Sync* has an entry task, we here limit the CSP model to that restricted form of protected objects. A full formal model of Ravenscar protected objects is presented and verified in [1, 2].

[2] *ValidTaskId* is not empty since it contains the entry task associated with *PO*.

channel $read, write, enter, wait, start, leave : ValidTaskId$
channel $update\_bar : ValidTaskId \times Boolean$
channel $[\,T\,]\ get, put : ValidTaskId \times T$

The channel $read$ ($write$) is used to communicate the events where a task issues a call to a protected function (procedure). If the entry task issues a call to the protected-object entry, and the barrier is true and no other task is accessing the object, then the entry task can gain access; this is modelled by a communication over the $enter$ channel. Otherwise, the entry task must $wait$. If at some later point, the barrier becomes true and there are no tasks accessing the object, then the waiting entry task may $start$. An event on the channel $leave$ corresponds to a task leaving the protected object. Changes in the state of the barrier are signalled through the $update\_bar$ channel, after the execution of a protected procedure or the protected entry. Finally, the channels get and put are used for accessing and updating the protected object's data.

There are nine processes that control the external behaviour of PO.

1. When a task issues a function call, it may become a reader within the protected object; this is signalled by the communication of the task's identifier over the $read$ channel. This event is permitted if there are no writers, and no waiting entry task with an open barrier

$$BecomeReader(data, entry\_task, barrier, waiting, writers, readers) =$$
$$writers = \emptyset \wedge \neg\,(barrier \wedge waiting)\ \&$$
$$read?t : ValidTaskId \setminus (\{entry\_task\} \lhd waiting \rhd \emptyset) \rightarrow$$
$$PO(data, entry\_task, barrier, waiting, writers, readers \cup \{t\})$$

If the entry task is waiting, then it cannot also become a reader[3].

2. When a task issues a procedure call, it may become a writer within the protected object; this is signalled by the communication of the task's identifier over the $write$ channel. This event is permitted if there are no writers, and no waiting entry task with an open barrier. Also, if the entry task is waiting, then it cannot become a writer.

$$Become Writer(data, entry\_task, barrier, waiting, writers, readers) =$$
$$writers = \emptyset \wedge \neg\,(barrier \wedge waiting)\ \&$$
$$write?t : ValidTaskId \setminus (\{entry\_task\} \lhd waiting \rhd \emptyset) \rightarrow$$
$$PO(data, entry\_task, barrier, waiting, \{t\}, readers)$$

3. When the entry task issues the protected entry call, it may become a writer or it may have to wait, depending on the $barrier$. In both cases, there must be no writers, and the entry task must not be already waiting.
   (a) If the barrier is open, then the entry task may enter the object; this is signalled by the event $enter.entry\_task$.

---

[3] $A \lhd B \rhd C\ =\ If\ B\ then\ A\ else\ C.$

$$ETEnter(data, entry\_task, barrier, waiting, writers, readers) =$$
$$writers = \emptyset \land barrier \land \neg \ waiting \ \&$$
$$enter.entry\_task \rightarrow$$
$$PO(data, entry\_task, barrier, waiting, \{entry\_task\}, readers)$$

The entry task becomes the sole writer.

(b) If the barrier is closed, then the entry task must wait on the entry queue; this is signalled by the event *wait.entry_task*.

$$ETWait(data, entry\_task, barrier, waiting, writers, readers) =$$
$$writers = \emptyset \land \neg \ barrier \land \neg \ waiting \ \&$$
$$wait.entry\_task \rightarrow$$
$$PO(data, entry\_task, barrier, \mathsf{True}, writers, readers)$$

The next process describes how the waiting entry task can proceed.

4. If the barrier is open, there are no writers, and there is a waiting entry task, then it may become a writer.

$$ETStart(data, entry\_task, barrier, waiting, writers, readers) =$$
$$writers = \emptyset \land barrier \land waiting \ \&$$
$$start.entry\_task \rightarrow$$
$$PO(data, entry\_task, barrier, \mathsf{False}, \{entry\_task\}, readers)$$

When the waiting task starts, it leaves the entry queue.

5. When a reading task completes its function call, it leaves the protected object; this is signalled by the communication of the task's identifier over the *leave* channel.

$$ReaderLeave(data, entry\_task, barrier, waiting, writers, readers) =$$
$$leave?t : readers \rightarrow$$
$$ReaderLeave(data, entry\_task, barrier, waiting, writers, readers \setminus \{t\})$$

6. When a writing task completes its procedure or entry call, it leaves the protected object; this is signalled by the communication of the task's identifier over the *leave* channel.

$$WriterLeave(data, entry\_task, barrier, waiting, writers, readers) =$$
$$leave?t : writers \rightarrow$$
$$update\_bar.t?b \rightarrow PO(data, entry\_task, b, waiting, \emptyset, readers)$$

The barrier may have changed as a result of the actions of the writer, so it must be updated – the leaving task updates the barrier.

7. Any of the tasks currently reading or writing may read the protected data; this is signalled by a communication on the *get* channel.

$$GetData(data, entry\_task, barrier, waiting, writers, readers) =$$
$$get?t : (readers \cup writers)!data \rightarrow$$
$$GetData(data, entry\_task, barrier, waiting, writers, readers)$$

8. Any of the tasks currently writing may write to the protected object; this is signalled by a communication on the *put* channel.

$PutData(data, entry\_task, barrier, waiting, writers, readers) =$
$\quad put?t : writers?d : T \rightarrow$
$\qquad PO(d, entry\_task, barrier, waiting, writers, readers)$

The process *PO* repeatedly offers the choice between the above processes.

$PO(data, entry\_task, barrier, waiting, writers, readers) =$
$\qquad (\quad BecomeReader(data, entry\_task, barrier, waiting, writers, readers)$
$\qquad \square\ BecomeWriter(data, entry\_task, barrier, waiting, writers, readers)$
$\qquad \square\ ETEnter(data, entry\_task, barrier, waiting, writers, readers)$
$\qquad \square\ ETWait(data, entry\_task, barrier, waiting, writers, readers)$
$\qquad \square\ ETStart(data, entry\_task, barrier, waiting, writers, readers)$
$\qquad \square\ ReaderLeave(data, entry\_task, barrier, waiting, writers, readers)$
$\qquad \square\ WriterLeave(data, entry\_task, barrier, waiting, writers, readers)$
$\qquad \square\ GetData(data, entry\_task, barrier, waiting, writers, readers)$
$\qquad \square\ PutData(data, entry\_task, barrier, waiting, writers, readers)\quad)$

Now, we will use this CSP model of Ravenscar protected objects to provide a formal semantics for Ravenscar channels.

4.2   The Two Protected Objects

The two protected objects can be defined as instantiations of the above *PO* process through *renaming*. Let the set *channels*, and the two bijective relations *D* and *S* be defined as follows:

$channels ::= read \mid write \mid enter \mid wait \mid start \mid leave \mid update\_bar \mid get \mid put$

$D = \{x : channels \bullet (x, D\_x)\}$
$S = \{x : channels \bullet (x, S\_x)\}$

That is, the relation D (S) add the suffix $D\_$ ($S\_$) to each channel of the process *PO*. Now, using the CSP renaming operator, the protected objects *Data* and *Sync* can be defined as:

$Data = PO[\![D]\!]$
$Sync = PO[\![S]\!]$

Data is the process that can perform the event $D(e)$ whenever *PO* can perform the event e. Similarly, *Sync* is the one that can perform the event $S(e)$ whenever *PO* can perform the event e. Since they are both defined in terms of the renaming operator, both *Data* and *Sync* are guaranteed to preserve the properties of Ravenscar protected object exhibited by *PO*. In particular, the behaviour of *Data* and *Sync* is independent of the data they encapsulate.

4.3   The Protocols

As well as the two protected objects, the implementation of the Ravenscar channel requires two protocols to regulate how the tasks can write to or read from the protected objects. To write a *value* to the channel, the *Producer* task has to make the following two calls: `Data.Put(v); Sync.Stay;`
We model this protocol by the following CSP process, $REC(\_)$.

> **channel** $obtain : ValidTaskId \times T$; $ack : ValidTaskId$
> $REC(t) = obtain.t?value \rightarrow Write(t, value); \; ack.t \rightarrow REC(t)$
> $Write(t, value) = PutData(t, value); \; WSynchronise(t)$

That is, the process $REC(\_)$ repeatedly waits to receive an event (comprising the identification of writing task and the value to be written) on the channel *obtain*. When the value to be written is obtained, the process then executes the $Write(\_,\_)$ protocol to write the received value to the Ravenscar channel. Finally, a successful *Write* is acknowledged by an event on the channel *ack*.

The *PutData* process stands for the call *Data.Put*. First, the task has to gain a write access to the protected object *Data*. Then, the task executes the procedure *Put*; this is signalled by communicating the task's identifier and the *value* over the channel *D_put*. Finally, the task leaves the protected object, updating the entry barrier as it leaves.

> $PutData(t, value) =$
> $\quad D\_write!t \rightarrow D\_put!t!value \rightarrow D\_leave!t \rightarrow D\_update\_bar.t!\mathsf{True} \rightarrow Skip$

The *WSynchronise* process stands for the call *Sync.Stay*. First, the task has to gain write access as the entry task of the protected object *Sync*. Then, the task executes the entry *Stay*; this is signalled by communicating the task's identifier over the channel *S_put*. Finally, the task leaves the protected object, updating the entry barrier as it leaves.

> $WSynchronise(t) =$
> $\quad (\; S\_enter.t \rightarrow Skip \;\square\; S\_wait.t \rightarrow S\_start.t \rightarrow Skip \;);$
> $\quad S\_put!t \rightarrow S\_leave!t \rightarrow S\_update\_bar.t!\mathsf{False} \rightarrow Skip$

An important remark here is that the communicated *value* does not determine the subsequent behaviour of the $REC(\_)$ process. The reading protocol, $SEND(\_)$, is defined similarly [1–Appendix C]. As $REC(\_)$, the behaviour of $SEND(\_)$ is independent of the communicated data.

4.4   Ravenscar Channels

The process representing a Ravenscar One-To-One channel is the parallel composition of the two protected objects, the write protocol, and the read protocol.

> $RavenChannel(t_1, t_2) = REC(t_1)$
> $\qquad \lVert WriterEvents \rVert$
> $\qquad (\; Data(0, t_2, \mathsf{False}, \mathsf{False}, \emptyset, \emptyset) \; \lVert\lVert$
> $\qquad\quad Sync(\mathsf{False}, t_1, \mathsf{False}, \mathsf{False}, \emptyset, \emptyset) \;)$
> $\qquad \lVert ReaderEvents \rVert \; SEND(t_2)$

The two protected objects run independently of each other, hence the interleaving operator. The protocols for writing and reading synchronise with the two protected objects on the events described by the sets *WriterEvents* and *ReaderEvents*, respectively.

$$WriterEvents = \{\!|\ D\_read.t_1, D\_write.t_1, D\_enter.t_1, D\_wait.t_1, D\_start.t_1,$$
$$D\_leave.t_1, D\_update\_bar.t_1.true, D\_put.t_1, D\_get.t_1,$$
$$S\_read.t_1, S\_write.t_1, S\_enter.t_1, S\_wait.t_1, S\_start.t_1,$$
$$S\_leave.t_1, S\_update\_bar.t_1.false, S\_put.t_1, S\_get.t_1\ |\!\}$$

$$ReaderEvents = \{\!|\ D\_read.t_2, D\_write.t_2, D\_enter.t_2, D\_wait.t_2, D\_start.t_2,$$
$$D\_leave.t_2, D\_update\_bar.t_2.false, D\_put.t_2, D\_get.t_2,$$
$$S\_read.t_2, S\_write.t_2, S\_enter.t_2, S\_wait.t_2, S\_start.t_2,$$
$$S\_leave.t_2, S\_update\_bar.t_2.true, S\_put.t_2, S\_get.t_2\ |\!\}$$

The behaviour of *Data*, *Sync*, *REC*, and *SEND* does not depend on the data communicated. Thus, the behaviour of *RavenChannel*(_) is also independent of the communicated data.

5   Correctness of Ravenscar Channels

Consider a CSP network of parallel processes ($Net = P_1 \parallel P_2 \parallel .. \parallel P_n$). If our Ravenscar channel is correct, we should be able to replace all CSP channels in *Net* with the *RavenChannel* processes, without affecting the external behaviour of the network. We will show that this is possible if *Net* satisfies the following two conditions:

1. *Net* is free from the external choice operator ($\Box$).
2. The channels used by *Net* are One-To-One; that is, each channel c is used by exactly one process P_i for input and exactly one process P_j ($i \neq j$) for output.

Consider the following CSP process

channel *transmit* : T

$$Left(t) = obtain.t?value \rightarrow transmit!value \rightarrow ack.t \rightarrow Left(t)$$
$$Right(t) = ready.t \rightarrow transmit?value \rightarrow deliver.t!value \rightarrow Right(t)$$

$$JCSPCHANNEL(t_1, t_2) = Left(t_1) \parallel \{\!| \ transmit \ |\!\} \parallel Right(t_2) \setminus \{\!| \ transmit \ |\!\}$$

In their work [8] on implementing CSP channels for Java, P. Welsh and J. Martin have given a proof-by-hand that *JCSPCHANNEL*, shown in figure 4, can be used as CSP channels for any network *Net* satisfying the two conditions above. The replacement of the CSP channels with the *JCSPCHANNEL* happens by transforming each process P_i as follows:

– replace all occurrences of "$c!x \rightarrow$" by "$obtain.i!x \rightarrow ack.i \rightarrow$"
– replace all occurrences of "$c?x \rightarrow$" by "$ready.i \rightarrow deliver?x \rightarrow$"

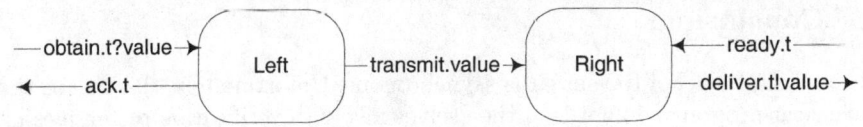

Fig. 4. JCSP Channel

This result is of special interest to us as now the problem of proving the correctness of Ravenscar channel can be reduced to proving that our process *RavenChannel* is equivalent to *JCSPCHANNEL*.

Theorem 1 (Implementation is Correct). *Let Net = $P_1 \parallel P_2 \parallel .. \parallel P_n$ be a network of parallel processes. Assume that Net satisfies the following two conditions:*

- *Net is free from the external choice operator ($\Box$).*
- *Each channel c in Net is One-To-One, i.e. c is used by exactly one process P_i for input and exactly one process P_j ($i \neq j$) for output.*

Then, we can replace the channels in Net with RavenChannel processes while preserving the external behaviour of Net.

Proof.   *It is sufficient to prove that the processes JCSPCHANNEL and RavenChannel are equivalent. We used FDR to prove this equivalence and successfully discharged the two assertions:*

  1. *SimpleRavenChannel(prod, cons) $\sqsubseteq$ JCSPCHANNEL(prod, cons)*

  2. *JCSPCHANNEL(prod, cons) $\sqsubseteq$ SimpleRavenChannel(prod, cons)*

  Where

  ValidTaskId = {prod, cons}
  SimpleRavenChannel(t_1, t_2) = RavenChannel(t_1, t_2) \ Internal
  Internal = {| D_read, D_write, D_enter, D_wait, D_start, D_leave,
              D_update_bar, D_put, D_get, S_read, S_write, S_enter,
              S_wait, S_start, S_leave, S_update_bar, S_put, S_get |}   □

Actually, this proof-by-equivalence approach gives us more than just the correctness of our implementation. Since *SimpleRavenChannel* and *JCSP CHANNEL* are equivalent, we know that our channel implementation inherits all the properties satisfied by the Java implementation of One-to-One CSP channels, as described in [8]. For example, as in Java channels, we can tell that our Ravenscar implementation works fine as long as there are at most two concurrent threads in existence (one is writing and one is reading). Indeed, a simple check with FDR (increasing the number of elements in ValidTaskId beyond two) reveals that *RavenChannel* can deadlock. This is a positive result in its own right, as now the equivalence between *SimpleRavenChannel* and *JCSPCHANNEL* not only increases the confidence about our implementation but also informs us about possible limitations.

6   Conclusions

The tasking model of Ravenscar is asynchronous. Unfortunately, this means that Ravenscar programs do not lend themselves nicely to verification techniques like model checking. In this paper we have implemented One-to-One CSP channels in Ravenscar. As a consequence, we can now transform the asynchronous tasking model of Ravenscar into the synchronous message passing model of CSP.

Like in CSP, using channels in Ravenscar programs eliminates the need to worry about issues of synchronisation and physical transfer of data between tasks. Also, synchronous Ravenscar programs are more amenable to formal proofs and techniques for model checking. For example, we can now use tools like FDR to check Ravenscar programs for properties like deadlock/livelock freedom. This all contributes to the production of more reliable and trustworthy systems.

To verify our implementation, we showed that the CSP semantics of our Ravenscar channels is equivalent to the semantics of the one-to-one channels in the JCSP library [8] for Java. This is a valuable result, as it allows arguments of correctness and proofs about properties of JCSP channels to be automatically deployed in favour of our Ravenscar channels.

Elsewhere, we have used Ravenscar channels as a key element in developing a cost-effective technique for verifying Ravenscar programs: more details of that work are available in [1].

References

1. D. Atiya. *Verification of Concurrent Safety–critical Systems: The Compliance Notation Approach.* PhD thesis, University of York. Submitted in October 2004.
2. D. M. Atiya, S. King, and J. C. P. Woodcock. A *Circus* semantics for Ravenscar protected objects. In *FME 2003*, volume 2805 of *Lecture Notes in Computer Science*, pages 617–635. Springer-Verlag, 2003.
3. A. Burns, B. Dobbing, and G. Romanski. The Ravenscar tasking profile for high integrity real-time programs. In L. Asplund, editor, *Ada-Europe 98*, volume 1411 of *Lecture Notes in Computer Science*, pages 263–275. Springer-Verlag, 1998.
4. A. Burns, B. Dobbing, and T. Vardanega. Guide for the use of the Ada Ravenscar Profile in high integrity systems. Technical Report YCS-2003-348, Department of Computer Science, University of York, UK, January 2003.
5. Formal Systems (Europe) Ltd. *Failures-divergences refinement: FDR2 user manual.* May, 2000.
6. A. W. Roscoe. *The Theory and Practice of Concurrency.* Prentice Hall International Series in Computer Science. Prentice Hall, 1998.
7. SGS-THOMSON Microelectronics Limited. *occam 2.1 reference manual.* May, 1995.
8. P. H. Welch and J. M. R. Martin. A CSP Model for Java Multithreading. In P. Nixon and I. Ritchie, editors, *Software Engineering for Parallel and Distributed Systems*, pages 114–122. ICSE 2000, IEEE Computer Society Press, June 2000.

Dynamic Tasks Verification with QUASAR

Sami Evangelista, Claude Kaiser, Christophe Pajault,
Jean Francois Pradat-Peyre, and Pierre Rousseau

CEDRIC - CNAM Paris,292, rue St Martin, 75003 Paris
{evangeli, kaiser, pajault, peyre, rousseau}@cnam.fr

Abstract. The inclusion of dynamic tasks modelisation in QUASAR, a tool for automatic analysis of concurrent programs, extends its applicative usefulness. However this extension leads to large size models whose processing has to face combinatory explosion of modeling states. This paper presents briefly Ada dynamic tasks semantic and dependences and then it explains the choice of an efficient generic modeling pattern. This implies to consider the naming, the hierarchy, the master retrieval, the termination of dynamic tasks and their synchronization dependences successively. The adequacy of both this modeling and the QUASAR techniques is highlighted by the analysis of two non-trivial Ada programs. The large reduction factor between the initial and final state numbers of these program models shows that the state explosion can be limited, making automatic validation of dynamic concurrent programs feasible.

1 Introduction

As a program structuring entity as well as a distribution support, multi-threading is becoming significantly important in application programs design. Its use is thus being developed in applications which need a high level of integrity and which have to be verified and validated. Nevertheless, interleaving and indeterminism induced by multi-threading introduce a high degree of combinatory that human brain cannot always master. Moreover, concurrent programs are more sensitive to this phenomenon when objects are dynamically created at run time. Using automatic analysis and validation tools is becoming mandatory to obtain reliable concurrent software.

Two years ago, we proposed a tool named QUASAR [EKPPR03] meant to analyze concurrent Ada programs automatically. This first version of QUASAR is relevant to validate critical applications which take care of safety by using a fixed number of tasks and banishing dynamic allocation. This cautious design strategy avoids the explosion of state number and eases certification as well as validation. For this use, QUASAR provides a lot of language constructions related to concurrency such as static tasks declaration, interaction between tasks by means of rendez-vous, protected objects or shared variables.

As an increasing number of concurrent applications programs use dynamic task allocation and object-oriented-programming (which relies on object dynamic allocation), we decided to augment QUASAR usability by allowing it modeling dynamic task allocation, even if this extension may involve the risk to generate a large number of application states and to have to face combinatory explosion. However we were confident in

T. Vardanega and A. Wellings (Eds.): Ada-Europe 2005, LNCS 3555, pp. 91–104, 2005.
© Springer-Verlag Berlin Heidelberg 2005

the QUASAR approach in so far as it reduces the application state numbers as soon as possible in the verification process.

Compared to other works in the domain [MSS89], [SMBT90], [BW99], [BWB+00], [BBS00], our approach is fully automatic. The analysis of concurrent programs is performed in four steps.

First, the original source code of the program is automatically sliced in order to extract the part of the program that is relevant to the property the user wants to check. Safety properties of concurrent programs concern the absence of deadlock or of livelock, the coherence of shared variable, the respect of mutual exclusion when using some shared resource. Liveness properties concern the absence of starvation, the guarantee that some service will eventually be done for a given client.

Second, the sliced program is translated into a coloured Petri net using a library of patterns. A pattern is a meta-net corresponding to a declaration, a statement or an expression. Each pattern definition is recursive in the way that its definition may contain one or several others patterns. For example, the loop pattern contains a meta-net corresponding to the pattern of sequence of statements. The target model mapping the whole sliced program is obtained by replacing each meta-net by its corresponding concrete sub-nets and by merging all sub-nets.

In the third step QUASAR checks the required property on the Petri net, using successively graph reduction and structural techniques or state based enumeration techniques (model-checking).

At last, if the required property is not verified, the user is provided with a report demonstrating a sequence invalidating the property.

A detailed description of this process can be found in [EKPPR03], [EKPPR04] or at the url quasar.cnam.fr.

This paper describes the new feature that makes QUASAR suitable for automatic analysis of dynamic concurrent programs and is organized as follows.

Section 2 presents briefly Ada dynamic tasks semantic and their synchronization constraints at elaboration and completion stages.

Section 3 presents the choices that we made to model the dynamic tasks together with the static tasks in QUASAR and describes the Petri nets library patterns corresponding to dynamic allocation and to operations on pointers. We justify our choices regarding the solution by evaluating the consequences on the analysis step.

At last, Section 4 highlights this new feature by analyzing two significant Ada programs that use dynamic tasks, and by displaying the state number of each model. This shows that the state explosion has been limited by our design choices and that automatically validating significant concurrent programs using dynamic allocation is a feasible enterprise.

2   Ada Tasks

In Ada the unit of parallelism, the sequential process, is named a task. Concurrency between tasks may be achieved via task rendez-vous, via protected objects or via global variables (possibly further qualified with volatile and atomic pragmas). As these features belong to the language, and have a precise semantic definition, the tasks behavior control is not dependent on compiler or operating system choices as it is the case with application programmer's interfaces (even if standardized as POSIX API).

In order to analyze concurrent programs, QUASAR models the tasks behavior and their interactions. As we assume that the concurrent programs have been designed following the Ada 95 Reference Manual [TD97] and are free of compiling errors, QUASAR can focus on the regular states reached by Ada tasks during their lifetime.

In this section, we will briefly describe task declaration and task lifetime. A more detailed description can be found in [BW95], [Dil93], [Dil97], and naturally in the Ada Reference Manual [TD97].

2.1   Task Declaration

A task declaration has two parts : the interface (or specification part) and the body.

The body corresponds to the code executed by the task at run-time. The interface is the visible part of a task and is used to specify the *entries* of the task.

A task entry can be remotely called by other tasks to synchronize, to send informations, or to communicate with the task owning the called entry. The calling task and the called task cooperate by rendez-vous.

2.2   Task Creation

Tasks can be created in two ways. The first way is static creation : one can declare a task type describing the task and then declare a variable of this type. The other way is dynamic creation : it uses *access types* (pointers).

The program Figure 1 illustrates the two ways of creating tasks :

- line 2 shows a task type declaration ;
- line 20 shows a static instance declaration; such a task is called a **static** or an **elaborated** task ;

```
 1 procedure ALLOC is
 2    task type TT;
 3    type OUTT is access TT;
 4
 5    procedure P is
 6       type INTT is access TT;
 7       O : OUTT;
 8       I : INTT;
 9    begin — body of P
10       O := new TT; — allocated / dynamic task
11       I := new TT; — allocated / dynamic task
12       ...
13       — procedure P completion
14    end P;
15
16    task body TT is
17       ...
18    end TT;
19
20    T : TT; — elaborate / static task
21
22 begin — body of ALLOC
23    P; — call P
24    ...
25    — ALLOC completion
26 end ALLOC;
```

Fig. 1. Ada program with task declarations and creations

– line 10 shows a dynamic instance creation of a given type ; the access type is declared at line 3 and the pointer is declared at line 7 ; such a task is called a **dynamic**
or an **allocated** task ; the *new* clause refers to a generic storage allocator used for
the creation of the task.

This paper discusses how QUASAR copes with dynamic task instantiation.

2.3   Task Hierarchy

Ada is a block structured language in which blocks may be nested within blocks. Ada
distinguishes between declarations and statements. At compile time, the declaration
of an entity declares the entity. At run time, the declarations are elaborated and this
elaboration creates the declared entities.

A task can be declared in any block and this creates a task hierarchy. A task which
is directly responsible for creating another task is the *parent* of the task and the created
task is called the *child*.

The creation and termination of tasks within a hierarchy affect the behavior of other
tasks in the hierarchy.

The parent of a child task is responsible for the creation of that task. The *master* of
a *dependant* task must wait for that task to terminate before it can itself terminate. The
parent of a task is often the master of that task, however with dynamic task creation the
master is not the parent task but the task that contains the declaration of the access type.

More precisely [Dil97], every task instance in program state, except the root instance
created for the main procedure, has exactly one direct master and possible indirect masters, as described by the three following rules:

[Master 1.] The parent of an elaborated task instance is also the direct master of the
   elaborated task instance.
[Master 2.] The instance that declares the access type of an allocator expression is
   the direct master of all allocated tasks instances that are created by evaluating the
   expression.
[Indirect Master.] An instance is an indirect master of a task instance if either (1) it
   invokes (directly or indirectly) a master of the task instance, or (2) it is a master of
   a master of the task instance.

To illustrate this notion, let's consider Figure 1. The first rule implies that the parent
of task T elaborated at line 20 is also its master. As the parent of this task is the procedure ALLOC, it is also its master. The second rule implies that, even if the pointer O
is allocated by the procedure P at line 10, since the access type OUTT is declared by
the procedure ALLOC, this procedure is the master of the task created line 10. The third
rule implies that ALLOC is an indirect master of the task I, since it invokes P which is
a direct master of I.

2.4   Task Activation, Execution, Finalization and Termination

Using these rules we can now present the synchronizations induced by these dependences at each stage of a task lifetime.

- *Activation*. This state corresponds to the elaboration of the declarative part of a task, the creation and initialization of the local variables of the task. A task cannot achieve its activation phase as long as all tasks declared in its declarative part have not finished their own activation phase. This is the first synchronization point. A child activation starts at the end of its parent task elaboration and proceeds concurrently with its parent task.

  Note that in the case of a dynamic task, this task is activated as the last step of its creation and the parent of an allocated instance is blocked during the call of the task allocator until the instance finishes activating.

  Note that a task entry can be called before the task has been activated.

- *Execution*. This state corresponds to the execution of the task body. No synchronization is induced by task dependences.

- *Completion*. This state corresponds to the state of a task in which all the statements of its body have been executed. A task cannot leave this state and start its termination step if the tasks depending on it have not yet finished their termination. This is the second and last synchronization point.

  Note that during completion, entries of the task can be called.

- *Termination*. This state corresponds to the destruction process of the task. No synchronization is induced by task dependences. According to the second and last synchronization point defined above, a task instance enters this state when it is completed and all of its dependent tasks are terminated.

We have presented the definitions of Master and of different dependence rules for tasks, but they apply also for procedures, functions and any kind of blocks.

3   Modeling Tasks

We consider now how to map an Ada task into a coloured Petri net. The generic pattern modeling a component that includes both declarations and statements (e.g. a subprogram, a task, or a block statements) is composed of four "meta-transitions" (i.e. abstract transitions that will be replaced by more concrete ones) and by five intermediate states (places C.Begin, C.Ready, ..., C.End). It is depicted Fig. 2.

In order to analyze concurrent programs including dynamic tasks we have to take into account the dependences existing between a "spawned" task and its master. Several difficulties have to be solved: the dynamic naming of a task, the dynamic referencing of the master, the dependence synchronizations modeling.

3.1   Dynamic *id* Computation

Each task of a program analyzed by QUASAR is assigned a unique model *id* that is used to synchronize tasks. When all tasks are elaborated in the main procedure we can assign statically a unique *id* to each of them at compile time. However, when tasks are elaborated or allocated dynamically we have to generate models that can compute new *ids* at model run time.

Three solutions are possible: first we can manage a "global *id* server" such that each created task (elaborated or allocated) is given an *id* by the "*id* server". The main

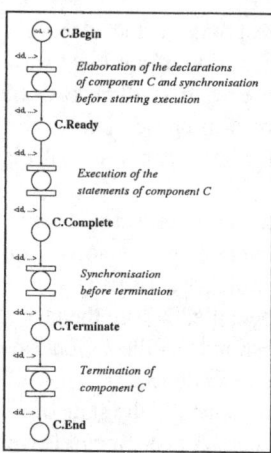

Fig. 2. Component model in QUASAR

drawback of this solution is the combinatory implied by the global server. Indeed, for different executions of a program, a task can get different ids. As all the possible executions are considered at the verification step, this leads to combinatory explosion.

A second possibility is to use "local id servers" associated with each statement that may spawn tasks. This local server has a statically determined id and assigns a new id to the task. Task identification is therefore done with two values : the id of the local server and the value this server gives to the task. This solution allows to consider the combinations at a local level and highly reduces combinatory as compared to the global server. This is a solution similar to the known "divide and conquer" strategy for program complexity reduction.

A third choice is to use a one-to-one mapping. For each task, we keep a local value n that is modified at each task creation (using for instance the number of created tasks, or the id of the last created task). The id of a spawned task is then computed using a hash made the id of the father, the local value and eventually a third constant value (for instance the maximum number of tasks spawned by the program).Each id assigned to a new task is then not dependent of the interleaving, and thus, no combinatory is induced by the dynamic task internal naming. An example of one-to-one function is thus:

$$f : \mathbb{N}^* \times \mathbb{N} \to \mathbb{N}$$
$$f(id,n) = id + n + max$$

where id is the id of the parent task, n is the id of the last created task by the parent and max is the maximum number of tasks that may be spawned by the program ($max \in \mathbb{N}$). When the maximum number of tasks that may be spawned by the program is not known, we cannot use a generic one-to-one function. In that case, a specific one-to-one function must be found for the program. More details and an appraisal based on case studies are given in [Paj05].

We have chosen to implement this last solution since it is the one that minimizes combinatory in practice.

3.2   Referencing the Master of a Task

For the sake of simplicity we have decided to implement differently allocated and elaborated tasks and to generate one net for the task type and one net for each access type. For instance, the model corresponding to the program depicted Figure 1 will contain three different nets issued from type TT : one for the type itself, one for the type INTT and one for the type OUTTT.

In order to retrieve the master of a task we have to store partially the task hierarchy. This hierarchy is specific to every block that declares an access task type. Two different ways of modeling this hierarchy may be used, either using specific places or using a more complex token for the task.

Modeling a Part of the Task Hierarchy with Places.   First, we can store the master of an allocated task in a specific place for each block declaring an access task type. This place will contain tokens $\langle id, id\_master \rangle$ where id is the identifier of an allocated or an elaborated task and id_master is the identifier of the master of the corresponding block. Then, each time an allocated task ends it can use this place to retrieve its master id.

For the program Figure 1 we have to define two places: one for the block Alloc (we denote it p_A) and one for the procedure P (we denote it p_P). When a task id_0 (may be the main task) calls procedure Alloc it puts a token $\langle id_0, id_0 \rangle$ in p_A. The declaration of T leads to put a token $\langle id\_T, id_0 \rangle$ in the place p_A (where id_T is the id assigned to T); so T may allocate tasks of type OUTT and give them the correct master. When id_0 calls P, it puts a token $\langle id_0, id_0 \rangle$ in p_P. The allocation of O puts the token $\langle id\_O, id_0 \rangle$ in both places p_A and p_P since these two blocks declare access task type visible from O. The same operation occurs when allocating I.

The advantage of this solution is to simplify the task token and this may optimize the firing rule and the memory used to store the state space when the model is analyzed. The drawback is that this solution may complicate synchronization patterns and then may result in a less efficient reduction ratio in the reduction step (occurring before the analysis).

Modeling a Part of the Task Hierarchy in the Task Token.   The second solution consists in adding an id table in task tokens and in giving a part of the execution history to created tasks so that they can find their master. The table size is fixed at compile time and is set to the number of blocks that declares access types on task types. For each one of these blocks which is a possible master of some allocated tasks, a specific entry is added in the table.

In the net, when a block declares an access type, it puts its id in the corresponding entry of the table. When a block spawns a new task or calls a new block, it gives it its id table. The idea is to propagate the table so that when an allocated task has to find its master, it just has to catch the id at the corresponding entry of the table.

To illustrate this, let's consider the example presented on Figure 1. Procedure ALLOC declares the access type OUTT, so an entry is added to the table. Procedure P declares the access type INTT, so a second entry is added. As there is no more access type declaration in the program, table size is two: the first entry is for procedure ALLOC id and the second one for procedure P id. In the generated net, when procedure

ALLOC calls procedure P at line 27, it gives it its table value (that is, [*alloc_id,null*]).
Then, when P declares its access type at line 6, it adds its *id* in the corresponding entry.
When P spawns O and I, it gives them its table ([*alloc_id,p_id*]). As the master of O is
procedure ALLOC, O has just to catch the right *id* in the corresponding entry of the table
(that is, the first entry) and as the master of I is procedure P, I just has to catch the *id*
in the corresponding entry (that is, the second one).

The main drawback of this solution is that all tokens have to keep this table even
if they will not use it. Moreover, if many access types are declared in many different
blocks, the size of the table will be large and state representation will need more memory. A good way to limit this increase is to group the access type declaration in a single
block as much as possible. By this way, the table size will remain small, leading to a
better efficiency of QUASAR.

3.3   Tasks Management Patterns with Hierarchy in Task Token

We now define the patterns that we use to generate coloured nets for Ada programs
that contain dynamic tasks creation. The first pattern concerns the elaboration of a
block containing a definition of an access task type and is depicted Figure 3. It acts
as follows: when a task *id* (may be the main one) elaborates a component containing the definition of an access task type, a token ⟨ *id*, 0 ⟩ is produced in the place
Task_Type_Name.Dependences where Task_Type_Name is the name of the
type. This transition initializes the counter associated with this type by noting that, at
this state, C does not depend of any task. The task that has elaborated the component *C*
cannot reach the state C.Terminate until the number of active task depending on it
equals zero (transition t2).

For the allocation of a new task we use the pattern depicted Figure 4. First we
increment the number of tasks on which the block that elaborated the type of the allocated task depends and therefore modify the token ⟨ *id_master*, *cpt* ⟩ into the token
⟨ *id_master*, *cpt* + 1 ⟩ in the place Task.Dependence.

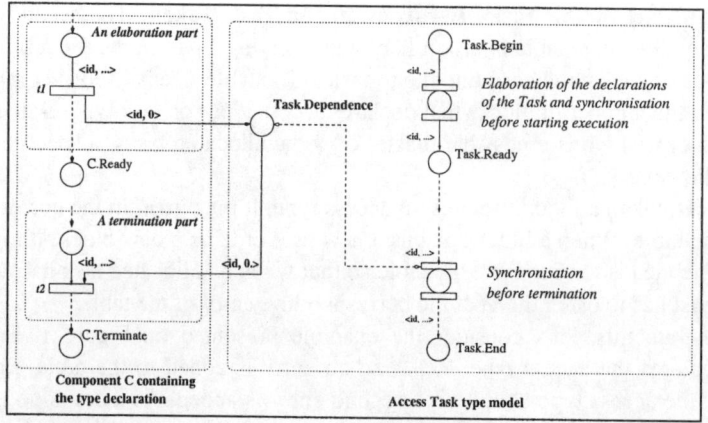

Fig. 3. Elaboration of a component containing an access task type definition

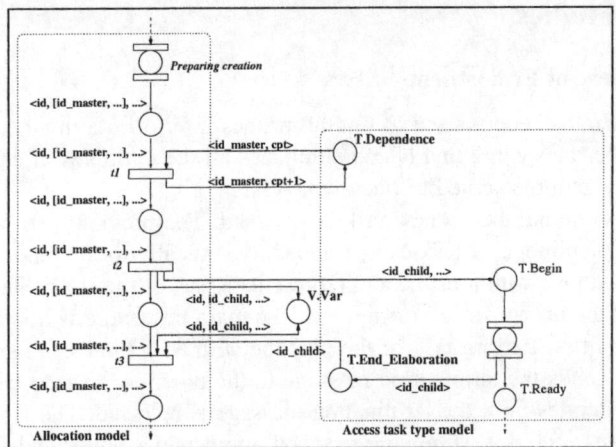

Fig. 4. Evaluation of a task allocator

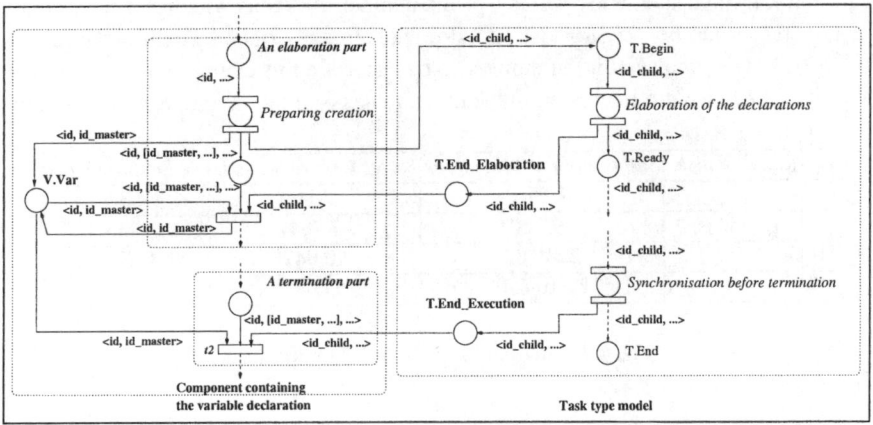

Fig. 5. Creation of a task by the evaluation of a declaration

Then, with transition t2, we start the new task by putting a token $\langle\, id, id\_child\,\rangle$ in the place T.Begin (the identifier of this new task is computed as described in a previous section). At last, at transition t3, the task waits until the allocated task has finished its elaboration. The place $V.Var$ is used to store that task id allocate task id_child and to synchronize the termination of a task with its father.

The creation of a task by the evaluation of a declaration is done according to the pattern depicted Figure 5. The created task is activated and the father waits until the end of its elaboration. At the end of the created task, this one signals that it has finished by putting a token in the place T.End_Execution. This token allows the task that declared it to continue (transition t2).

4   Cases Studies

4.1   The Sieve of Eratosthene

The sieve of Eratosthene is used to find all primes inferior to a number N. It considers each number between 2 and N and eliminates all the multiples of each considered number. We have implemented a concurrent version of it.

For each prime number, a new task is spawned. The program can be viewed as a dynamic task pipeline, as a task can be added dynamically to the pipe. Each stage of the pipeline is a task with a prime and represents a part of the sieve. The source code is available at the url `quasar.cnam.fr`. The main procedure is a loop which calls the entry of the first `Prime` task of the pipeline with each number to sift. At the end of the loop, it sends the termination message to the pipeline. `Prime` task program is a loop which iterates until the termination message is received. The task waits on its entry `Test_Primality`, stores the received number in a buffer and ends the entry call. Then, it checks the primality of the received number; if the task has not stored any prime number yet, it keeps the received number as its prime and waits for another call on its entry. If the task already stores a prime number, it checks whether it can divide it, if not, it creates another `Prime` task (if it does not already exists) by calling the function `Create_Prime` and send it the number to be tested. In this example, we don't collect the primes since we are interested in the dynamic tasks creation and termination only.

N	Running tasks	States without reductions	States with reductions	Reduction factor
3	3	1 556	294	5
6	4	19 160	1 784	11
10	5	224 102	10 047	22
12	6	2 810 870	65 645	43

Fig. 6. Evaluation for the sieve of Eratosthene

We made experimentations with our new model-checker Helena ([Eva05]) and results are presented Figure 6. Given N, we indicate the number of running tasks and we calculate the number of states generated by the model both with and without reductions.

4.2   A Client/Server Example

The program presented Fig.8 in the Appendix is a simple client/server program example. The main loop spawns clients of the task server. For each calling client, the task server creates a `Thread` task by allocating an `Access_Thread` pointer and by returning the pointer to the client. The client thus calls the entry of this `Thread` task which accesses the protected object managing the data. For different numbers of clients, we calculate the number of generated states both with and without reductions and also the number of states relevant to the deadlock free property after slicing and reductions. Results (presented Fig.7) show that even when the integration of dynamic tasks and synchronization mechanisms implies a great combinatory, QUASAR is able to reduce highly the generated model via slicing mechanisms [Rou05] and structural reductions of the Petri net.

Clients	Running tasks	States without reductions	States with reductions	Slicing & reductions
1	4	2 549	247	221
2	6	438 913	9 499	5 939
3	8	–	735 767	239 723
4	10	–	–	12 847 017

Fig. 7. Evaluation for the Client/Server program

4.3   Further Remarks

Let us now modify the previous program so that it contains run time errors and let us show that these errors can be easily detected by QUASAR. In an execution without deadlocks, each task token reaches the place END of its Petri net model. So, if in a terminal state, a task token is in another place, this means that there exists an execution leading to a terminal state which corresponds either to a deadlock or to a run-time error.

In QUASAR, when a task calls an entry, it puts a token with its *id* and the *id* of the "server" task in an entry call place and gets the results from an entry return place. The "server" task takes the token in the call place, gets the client's *id* and notifies it in the return place when it has finished the call. Then the client can continue its execution and reach its place END.

Suppose that the task Task_Server loops from 1 to MAX_CLIENT-1 only, the server task will never take the token of the last client in the call place. So, this client will be blocked and will never reach the place END. The detection of such a deadlock is very easy in QUASAR.

Imagine now a second case of error when the variable The_Task_Server is of access type. Suppose that this access variable is allocated by the main procedure. When a client calls the entry of this dynamic task, two cases are possible: in the first one, the client calls the entry of The_Task_Server before this dynamic task has been allocated and it is blocked; this leads to a deadlock. In the second case, the client calls the entry after the allocation and the entry call is accepted.

The behavior of such a program depends on the order in which allocations are performed and this kind of error is not detected by the compiler. As QUASAR enumerates each possible execution, it points out this kind of behavior. When an access variable is declared, it gets a special initialization value set to the null value. Then, if the client calls the entry before the variable has been allocated, it is blocked in the entry call place because of a wrong *id* for the variable The_Task_Server. Its entry call is never accepted and it never reaches its END place. This causes a deadlock which is detected by QUASAR.

5   Conclusion and Future Works

This paper shows that dynamic allocation can be modeled by tools that make use of Petri nets. The use of both this modeling and the QUASAR techniques allow to limit the model states explosion, making automatic validation of dynamic concurrent programs feasible. Moreover it has been shown that QUASAR is able to detect synchronization errors which occurrence depends on the dynamic task allocation order and which is not detected at compile time.

The scope of application programs that can be verified by QUASAR can still be extended, and in particular to object oriented programming as it is approached for Java programs in [NAC99], [CDH+00], [BR01], [FLL+02], or for other concurrent languages as in [AQR+04] or in [HRD04].

Integrating these concepts involves a high level of combinatory. We are now considering this problem : on the one hand, we are already working on Helena [Eva05], a new model checker which allows coloured Petri nets reductions and on the other hand we will further increase the analysis power by studying parallel and distributed model checking algorithms.

References

[AQR+04]   T. Andrews, S. Qadeer, J. Rehof, S.K. Rajamani, and Y. Xie. Zing: Exploiting program structure for model checking concurrent software. In *Proc. of the 15th International Conference on Concurrency Theory*, 2004.

[BBS00]   J. Blieberger, B. Burgstaller, and B. Scholz. Symbolic Data Flow Analysis for Detecting Deadlocks in Ada Tasking Programs. In *Proc. of the Ada-Europe International Conference on Reliable Software Technologies*, Potsdam, Germany, 2000.

[BR01]   Chandrasekhar Boyapati and Martin Rinard. A parameterized type system for race-free java programs. *SIGPLAN Not.*, 36(11):56–69, 2001.

[BW95]   A. Burns and A. Wellings. *Concurrency in Ada*, chapter 6.11, pages 134–137. Cambridge University Press, 1995.

[BW99]   A. Burns and A. J. Wellings. How to verify concurrent Ada programs: the application of model checking. *ACM SIGADA Ada Letters*, 19(2), 1999.

[BWB+00]   A. Burns, A. J. Wellings, F. Burns, A. M. Koelmans, M. Koutny, A. Romanovsky, and A. Yakovlev. Towards modelling and verification of concurrent ada programs using petri nets. In Pezzé, M. and Shatz, M., editors, *DAIMI PB: Workshop Proceedings Software Engineering and Petri Nets*, pages 115–134, 2000.

[CDH+00]   James C. Corbett, Matthew B. Dwyer, John Hatcliff, Shawn Laubach, Corina S. Pasareanu, Robby, and Hongjun Zheng. Bandera: extracting finite-state models from java source code. In *International Conference on Software Engineering*, pages 439–448, 2000.

[Dil93]   Laura K. Dillon. A visual execution model for ada tasking. *ACM Trans. Softw. Eng. Methodol.*, 2(4):311–345, 1993.

[Dil97]   Laura K. Dillon. Task dependence and termination in ada. *ACM Trans. Softw. Eng. Methodol.*, 6(1):80–110, 1997.

[EKPPR03]   S. Evangelista, C. Kaiser, J. F. Pradat-Peyre, and P. Rousseau. Quasar: a new tool for analysing concurrent programs. In *Reliable Software Technologies - Ada-Europe 2003*, volume 2655 of *LNCS*. Springer-Verlag, 2003.

[EKPPR04]   S. Evangelista, C. Kaiser, J. F. Pradat-Peyre, and P. Rousseau. Verifying linear time temporal logic properties of concurrent ada programs with quasar. *Ada Lett.*, XXIV(1):17–24, 2004.

[Eva05]   S. Evangelista. High level Petri nets analysis with Helena. In *26th International Conference On Application and Theory of Petri Nets and Other Models of Concurrency, ICAPTN*, 2005.

[FLL+02]   Cormac Flanagan, K. Rustan M. Leino, Mark Lillibridge, Greg Nelson, James B. Saxe, and Raymie Stata. Extended static checking for java. In *Proceedings of the ACM SIGPLAN 2002 Conference on Programming language design and implementation*, pages 234–245. ACM Press, 2002.

[HRD04]   John Hatcliff, Robby, and Matthew B. Dwyer. Verifying atomicity specifications for concurrent object-oriented software using model-checking. In *Proceedings of the International Conference on Verification, Model Checking and Abstract Interpretation*, 2004.

[MSS89]   T. Murata, B. Shenker, and S.M. Shatz. Detection of Ada static deadlocks using Petri nets invariants. *IEEE Transactions on Software Engineering*, Vol. 15(No. 3):314–326, March 1989.

[NAC99]   Gleb Naumovich, George S. Avrunin, and Lori A. Clarke. Data flow analysis for checking properties of concurrent java programs. In *Proceedings of the 21st international conference on Software engineering*, pages 399–410. IEEE Computer Society Press, 1999.

[Paj05]   C. Pajault. Extending Quasar with dynamic tasks computation. Technical Report 695, CNAM, CEDRIC, Paris, 2005.

[Rou05]   P. Rousseau. Concurrent ada program slicing for source code understanding and formal analysis. Technical Report 708, CNAM, CEDRIC, 2005.

[SMBT90]   S.M. Shatz, K. Mai, C. Black, and S. Tu. Design and implementation of a petri net based toolkit for ada tasking analysis. *IEEE Transactions on Parallel and Distributed Systems*, Vol. 1(No. 4):424–441, 1990.

[TD97]   S. Tucker Taft and Robert A. Duff, editors. *Ada 95 Reference Manual, Language and Standard Libraries, Int. Standard ISO/IEC 8652: 1995(E)*, volume 1246 of *Lecture Notes in Computer Science*. Springer, 1997.

Appendix

```
 1  procedure Server is
 2     Max_Client : Integer := 5;
 3     protected Data is              — The accessed data
 4        procedure Get_Value (Value : out Integer);
 5     private
 6        Data_Value : Integer := 0;
 7     end Data;
 8     protected body Data is
 9        procedure Get_Value (Value : out Integer)is
10        begin
11           Data_Value := Data_Value + 1;
12           Value := Data_Value;
13        end Get_Value;
14     end Data;
15     task type Thread is            — Only the threads can access the data
16        entry Get_Value (Param : out Integer);
17     end Thread;
18     type Access_Thread is access Thread;
19     task body Thread is
20     begin
21        accept Get_Value (Param : out Integer) do
22           Data.Get_Value(Param);
23        end Get_Value;
24     end Thread;
25     task type Task_Server is — Creates a thread for each client's request
26        entry Get_Thread(Id : out Access_Thread);
27     end Task_Server;
28     task body Task_Server is
29     begin
30        for I in 1..Max_Client loop
31           accept Get_Thread (Id : out Access_Thread) do
32              Id := new Thread;
33           end Get_Thread;
34        end loop;
35     end Task_Server;
36     The_Task_Server : Task_Server;   — The task server
37     task type Client;                — Client of the task server
38     type Access_Client is access Client;
39     task body Client is
40        Id    : Access_Thread;
41        Value : Integer;
42     begin
43        The_Task_Server.Get_Thread(Id); — Get the thread
44        Id.Get_Value(Value);            — Get the value of the data
45     end;
46     A_Client : Access_Client;
47  begin
48     for I in 1..Max_Client loop       — main loop, creates clients
49        A_Client := new Client;
50     end loop;
51  end Server;
```

Fig. 8. A client/Server program

Proving Functional Equivalence
for Program Slicing in SPARK™

Ricky E. Sward and Leemon C. Baird III

Department of Computer Science,
U.S. Air Force Academy, CO 80840
719-333-7664 / 8321
{ricky.sward, leemon.baird}@usafa.af.mil

Abstract. Recent trends in software re-engineering have included tools to extract program slices from existing Ada procedures. This paper presents another such tool that extracts program slices from SPARK procedures and proves that the functionality of the original procedure is equivalent to the functionality of the collection of resulting slices. By showing that the effects of the SPARK statements in the collection of slices has the same effect on the input and output parameters of the procedure, we show that the SPARK program slicer, SPARKSlicer produces functionally equivalent program slices from SPARK procedures.

1 Introduction

In recent years, the technique known as program slicing has been applied to several areas of software engineering including program understanding, software maintenance, re-engineering, testing, debugging, and reuse [12, 9, 6]. *Program slicing* is a well defined process that extracts the statements from an existing program that are required to produce a value from the program [11]. As program slicing is used more and more in software engineering it becomes pertinent to answer the question of whether or not the collection of program slices maintain the functionality of the original program. Specifically, given the same inputs, will the collection of program slices produce the same outputs as the original code? In this paper, we show that for one such program slicer based on the SPARK programming language, the collection of program slices are functionally equivalent to the original code.

Previous work in the area of program slicing includes slicers for various languages such as C [10, 12], Java [3], Oberon-2 [4], and others. A program slicing tool called AdaSlicer has also been developed for the Ada programming language [7]. The slicing tool presented in this paper builds on the AdaSlicer tool producing slices for programs written in the SPARK programming language [2], which finds its roots in Ada. Our program slicer for SPARK called SPARKSlicer is written using the Ada Semantic Interface Specification (ASIS) [1].

2 Program Slicing

This paper assumes that the reader already has an understanding of *program slicing*. For more detailed descriptions see Weiser [11] or Sward and Chamillard [7]. In gen-

T. Vardanega and A. Wellings (Eds.): Ada-Europe 2005, LNCS 3555, pp. 105–114, 2005.

eral, program slicing is a projection of behavior from an original program into a new program called a *program slice* [11]. Program slicing is a static analysis process that relies on information about which variables and, consequently, program statements are required to produce a single variable called the slice variable. For each statement, the variables that are defined by that statement are collected into a definition set or *DEF* set and the variables referenced in the statement are collected into a reference or *REF* set. A variable V is *defined* in a statement S if V is assigned a new value in S. For example, variables on the left-hand-side of an assignment statement are defined by the statement. A variable V is referenced in a statement S if any part of S includes V. For example, any variables on the right-hand-side of an assignment statement are referenced in that statement and, by definition, appear in the *REF* set for the statement.

To produce a program slice for a procedure P, the statements S_1 to S_n included in P are analyzed. The analysis begins with S_n and proceeds up to S_1 since variables in statements that appear after a statement S_i can be affected by S_i. The slice variable V_s is placed in a relevant set R that includes any variables relevant to the program slice. If the *DEF* set for statement S_i includes any variables in R, then S_i is added to the program slice. All variables in the *REF* set for S_i are added to R since the definition of V_s is derived from the variables contained in S_i. This process continues until all statements S_1 to S_n are analyzed. The resulting collection of statements S_j to S_k is a subset of S_1 to S_n that preserves the sequential ordering of the statements from P. Weiser [11] defines the program slice S_j to S_k as a *projection $Pr(V_s)$* of the behavior from P required to produce V_s. The definition of program slicing given here is taken from the more complete, formal algorithm provided by Weiser [11].

The program slices produced by SPARKSlicer are considered to be conservative slices because they may include more than the minimal statements required to produce V_s. More extensive data flow analysis could be used to remove statements that are overshadowed by later statements that redefine variables in R. For simplicity, the data flow analysis in SPARKSlicer is not this extensive, but the slices are guaranteed to produce the correct value of V_s as required by the definition of a program slice.

3   A SPARK Program Slicer

We have developed a prototype tool called SPARKSlicer that produces program slices from SPARK code. Given a package specification and body that includes at least one procedure P, we can produce a program slice $Pr(V_s)$ from P. Program slices are produced only for output parameters of P, so the user indicates which procedure and parameter to slice on. The result is the program slice $Pr(V_s)$ built as a new procedure that includes those statements needed to produce V_s. The name of the new procedure is built by appending the name of the parameter to the name of the procedure. Only those parameters needed for the new procedure are included in the parameter list for the program slice. Similarly, only those variables needed for the new procedure are included as local variables of the new procedure.

```
package Gather_Summary_Info_Pkg is
   type Integer_Array is array (1 .. 100) of Integer;
   procedure Gather_Summary_Info (
         Num_Students  : in      Integer;
         Min_Choice    : in      Integer_Array;
         Max_Choice    : in      Integer_Array;
         Lowest_Min    :      out Integer;
         Highest_Max   :      out Integer;
         Increment     : in out Integer              );
   --# derives Lowest_Min from Min_Choice, Num_Students &
               Highest_Max from Max_Choice, Num_Students;
   --# pre (Num_Students >= 0)
   --# post for all E in range 1..Num_Students =>
              Lowest_Min <= Min_Choice(E) &
           for all E in range 1..Num_Students =>
              Highest_Max >= Max_Choice(E);
end Gather_Summary_Info_Pkg;
```

Fig. 1. Package specification for SPARK code example

Figure 1 shows the specification file for an example SPARK program.

```
package body Gather_Summary_Info_Pkg is

   procedure Gather_Summary_Info (
         Num_Students  : in      Integer;
         Min_Choice    : in      Integer_Array;
         Max_Choice    : in      Integer_Array;
         Lowest_Min    :      out Integer;
         Highest_Max   :      out Integer;
         Increment     : in out Integer        ) is
   begin
      Increment := Increment + 1;
      Lowest_Min:= 1000;
      Highest_Max:= 0;
      for Student in 1 .. Num_Students loop
         if ( Min_Choice(Student) < Lowest_Min) then
            Lowest_Min:= Min_Choice(Student);
         end if;
         if ( Max_Choice(Student) > Highest_Max) then
            Highest_Max:= Max_Choice(Student);
         end if;
      end loop;
   end Gather_Summary_Info;

end Gather_Summary_Info_Pkg;
```

Fig. 2. Package body for SPARK code example

Figure 2 shows the package body for this example SPARK code. This example includes a package that contains one procedure Gather_Summary_Info. This procedure contains three input parameters, two output parameters, and one input/output parameter. Since slicing is done on the values produced from a procedure, we can slice on the Lowest_Min parameter, the Highest_Max parameter, and the Increment parameter.

```
procedure Gather_Summary_Info_Lowest_Min (
      Num_Students : in       Integer;
      Min_Choice   : in       Integer_Array;
      Lowest_Min   :     out Integer          ) is
begin
   Lowest_Min:= 1000;
   for Student in 1 .. Num_Students loop
      if ( Min_Choice(Student) < Lowest_Min) then
         Lowest_Min:= Min_Choice(Student);
      end if;
   end loop;
end Gather_Summary_Info_Lowest_Min;
```

Fig. 3. Slice produced for Lowest_Min

Figure 3 shows the slice built for the Lowest_Min parameter. This new procedure contains only those statements from Gather_Summary_Info that are needed to produce the parameter Lowest_Min. Only the Num_Students and Min_Choice input parameters are needed to produce the output parameter Lowest_Min.

```
procedure Gather_Summary_Info_Highest_Max (
      Num_Students : in       Integer;
      Max_Choice   : in       Integer_Array;
      Highest_Max  :     out Integer          ) is
begin
   Highest_Max:= 0;
   for Student in 1 .. Num_Students loop
      if ( Max_Choice(Student) > Highest_Max) then
         Highest_Max:= Max_Choice(Student);
      end if;
   end loop;
end Gather_Summary_Info_Highest_Max;
```

Fig. 4. Slice produced for Highest_Max

Figure 4 shows the slice built for the Highest_Max parameter. This new procedure contains only those statements from Gather_Summary_Info that are needed to produce the parameter Highest_Max. Only the Num_Students and Max_Choice input parameters are needed to produce the output parameter Highest_Max.

```
procedure Gather_Summary_Info_Increment (
      Increment_In  : in       Integer;
      Increment_Out :     out Integer          ) is
   Increment_Local : Integer := Increment_In;
begin
   Increment_Local := Increment_Local + 1;
   Increment_Out := Increment_Local;
end Gather_Summary_Info_Increment;
```

Fig. 5. Slice produced for Increment

Figure 5 shows the slice built for the Increment parameter. This new procedure contains only those statements from Gather_Summary_Info that are needed to produce the parameter Increment. Notice that a different approach has been taken for this parameter since it is an input/output parameter. In this case, the input/output parameter is replaced with one input parameter, Increment_In, and one output parameter, Increment_Out. This is done to enforce the copy-in, copy-out semantics for the slice, which is needed for our proof of functional equivalence as explained below. Each occurrence of Increment in the statements of the procedure is replaced with a local variable, Increment_Local, which is initialized to the value of Increment_In. After all processing has been completed in the procedure, the value of Increment_Local is copied into the output parameter, Increment_Out, thus enforcing copy-in, copy-out semantics. Note that this will preserve correctness when using arrays and records, but may be inefficient.

```
procedure Gather_Summary_Info_Glue (
      Num_Students : in      Integer;
      Max_Choice   : in      Integer_Array;
      Highest_Max  :     out Integer;
      Min_Choice   : in      Integer_Array;
      Lowest_Min   :     out Integer;
      Increment    : in out Integer          ) is
   Increment_Local : Integer := Increment;
begin
   Gather_Summary_Info_Highest_Max (
      Num_Students, Max_Choice, Highest_Max);
   Gather_Summary_Info_Lowest_Min (
      Num_Students, Min_Choice, Lowest_Min);
   Gather_Summary_Info_Increment (
      Increment_Local, Increment);
end Gather_Summary_Info_Glue;
```

Fig. 6. Example of glue code

Now that the original procedure has been sliced into three new procedures, it is useful to have some standard way of calling the three procedures to perform the same operation as the original, unsliced procedure. Figure 6 shows a short procedure consisting of *glue code* which calls the three slices and which will behave identically to the original procedure (except perhaps for the time and memory required). In this glue code procedure, the three slices are called one after the other with the proper actual parameters to match the formal parameters of the slices. The parameters needed for these calls to the slices are included as formal parameters to the glue code procedure.

Note that the parameters for the Gather_Summary_Info_Increment slice are handled in a unique way. The original parameters to the glue code procedure are identical to the original procedure. The value of the input/output parameter, Increment, is stored in the local variable, Increment_Local. This variable is passed to any of the slices that have been built with Increment_In as an input formal parameter. Notice this local variable is passed to Gather_Summary_Info_Increment as the input actual parameter. For any slices that have been built with Increment_Out as an output formal parameter, the parameter Increment is passed as the actual parameter. Gather_Summary_Info_Increment includes Increment as an output actual parameter.

All this special processing for the input/output parameters, such as Increment, is needed to ensure that the other slices do not interfere with the original value of Increment and that there is only one value of Increment produced from the procedure Gather_Summary_Info_Glue. This special handling of input/output parameters is needed for the proof of functional equivalence as explained below.

4 SPARK Features

There are many features of the SPARK language that make proving functional equivalence possible. We will not go into great depth about the exact nature of these features, but instead discuss how these features are useful for proving functional equivalence. The reader is referred to Barnes [2] for a thorough discussion of these features and the rationale for excluding them from the SPARK language.

The most critical limitations of the SPARK language that benefit our proof limit the *dynamic storage allocation* features of Ada. For example, access types, i.e. pointers, and dynamic allocation of memory from the heap are not allowed in SPARK. Excluding pointers benefits our proof of functional equivalence in two ways. First, it eliminates the difficulty in determining whether or not a pointer variable is defined and hence a member of the DEF set for a particular statement. Second, it eliminates the problem of aliasing of variables. In general, SPARK does not allow aliasing of variables or parameters to procedures. This benefits our proof by clearly defining the inputs and outputs of a program to be sliced.

Recursion is another dynamic storage allocation feature of Ada that is not allowed in SPARK. The algorithm for slicing a recursive program is not yet defined. SPARK's exclusion of recursion allows us to limit our proofs to slices of programs that do not include recursive calls.

Certain statements in Ada complicate the formal definition of programs and are not allowed in SPARK. Goto statements are not allowed in SPARK. As with recursion, the algorithm for slicing a program with goto statements is not defined. This limitation in SPARK allows us to limit our slicer to programs that do not include goto statements. Similar statement restrictions in SPARK, such as limiting procedure subprograms from including return statements, allow us to slice programs that are well defined, structured programs.

Tasking in Ada allows interactions between two independent processes. There is currently no formal model of these interactions, so tasking is not allowed in the SPARK language [5]. This limits our proof of functional equivalence to slices extracted from a single, deterministic program executing as a single process.

Exceptions in Ada allow a program to jump from its sequential execution of a program to an exception handler. Since exception handling seriously complicates the formal definition of the Ada code, exceptions are not allowed in SPARK [5]. Instead, the approach in SPARK is to write code that can be proven to be exception free. This exclusion of exceptions limits our proof of functional equivalence to code that does not jump to an exception handler but instead is limited to normal, sequential execution.

Generic units in Ada are meant to aid in code reuse but also complicate the formal definition of Ada code. Proofs of SPARK code that rely on generics are required to build a proof for each instantiation of the generic. We impose the same restriction for program slicing in that a program that relies on a generic unit would be sliced using the instantiation of the generic unit. This limits the dynamic nature of the generic unit and allows for static program slicing.

5 Proving Functional Equivalence

In order to prove functional equivalence, we rely on several of the SPARK language limitations. Since we are working with SPARK programs, we assume that there is no tasking or use of threads in the code. We assume there are no exceptions or exception handling. We assume there are no pointers and no dynamic heap allocation. We assume there is no recursive code in the program. We assume no aliasing of procedure parameter, i.e. a single variable cannot be passed as an actual parameter for both an input and output parameter in the same procedure call.

We also assume that there are no global variables in the code. Sward and Chamillard [8] have shown that any global variables in Ada code can be converted to parameters in the calling sub-programs. This can easily be extended to the SPARK language. We also assume no non-determinism in the code. For example, when we say a transformed procedure gives the same result as the untransformed, we'll ignore the possibility of the procedures reading the system clock and returning different times, or calling a true random number generator and return different random numbers. We also assume that all procedures eventually return, for all possible inputs.

For the SPARKSlicer program, we assume that the slicer produces one procedure for each of the "out" or "in out" parameters in the original function, and that the created procedure will also have that parameter as part of its signature. We assume that each slice procedure created will have only a single "out" or "in out" parameter. We also assume that the slice procedure created for that output parameter is a correct projection of the behavior of the original procedure required to produce that parameter.

5.1 Algorithm for Creating the Glue Procedure

A SPARK procedure P with n "out" or "in out" parameters is transformed into $n+1$ procedures named P_0 through P_n. This is done by first transforming P into a procedure P', then running the slicer n times on P' to create P_1 through P_n, and finally creating the procedure P_0 which is functionally equivalent to P as shown in Figure 7.

The procedure P' is identical to P except for the following modifications. Replace each "in out" parameter X with an "in" parameter X_in and an out parameter X_out. Inside the procedure, create a local variable X_local which is assigned the value of X_in when it is declared. Note that this copies the entire contents of the parameter, even if it is a large array. A global substitution should replace X with X_local throughout the procedure. At the end of the procedure, insert an assignment from X_local to X_out. This would need to be done just before each return from the procedure, but in SPARK there are no explicit return statements allowed in procedures and no exceptions, so this only needs to be done once at the end of the procedure.

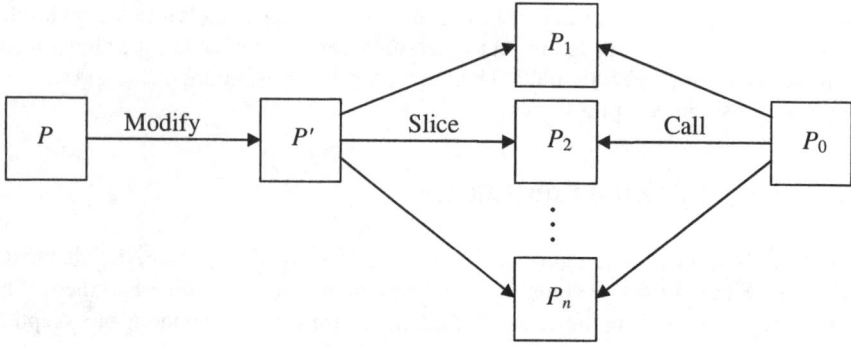

Fig. 7. Slicing and Glue Code

Then slice the procedure P' once for each "out" parameter, creating the procedures P_1 through P_n. None of the P_i procedures will have "in out" variables, since P' had none.

Finally, create the procedure P_0 with the same parameters as P. For each "in out" parameter X, this procedure will have a local variable X_local. It should then call each of the procedures P_1 through P_n, in an arbitrary order. When a procedure P_i has a formal parameter that matches a formal parameter of P_0, that parameter from P_0 should be passed in as the actual parameter. If the formal parameter in P_i is an X_in created as described above, then the actual parameter should be X_local. When the formal parameter is an X_out created as described above, then the actual parameter should be X. Note that the local variables in this procedure are only needed because SPARK forbids the same parameter being passed to a procedure as both an input and output.

5.2 Definitions

The inputs to a procedure are those parameters that are either "in" or "in out". The outputs are those that are "out" or "in out". Two procedures are functionally equivalent if they both yield the same outputs whenever they are passed the same inputs. Weiser [11] defines a *program slice* as a subset of a program that preserves a specified projection of its behavior. We assume here that the slicer generates slices of a procedure that preserve one particular output as a function of its inputs.

$$P_0 \text{ is functionally equivalent to } P \qquad\qquad \text{Theorem (1)}$$

Theorem 1 states that the procedure P_0, which calls procedures P_1 through P_n, is functionally equivalent to the original procedure P.

5.3 Proof

The procedures P' and P will always return the same outputs when given the same inputs. This is guaranteed because SPARK is designed to make aliasing impossible, so procedures have identical behavior whether the compiler implements them as pass-by-reference or as copy-in-copy-out. The procedure P' is simply P with the copy-in-copy-out semantics implemented directly. Therefore it must return the same outputs when given the same inputs.

Since we are assuming that the slicer works correctly, then the procedures P_0 and P' will return the same outputs when given the same inputs. This can be seen by considering the three types of parameters. The "in" parameters in P_0 are the same as in P' and are not changed while it is running because they are "in" parameters in the P_i functions. Each "out" parameter of P_0 is only used by one of the P_i calls, because each P_i was formed by slicing on a different output. Each "in out" parameter in P_0 is first copied into a local variable in P_0, then this value is passed unchanged to each of the P_i procedures that need it. The "in out" parameter itself will be changed by exactly one of the P_i functions (it will be the one that sliced on it).

In other words, P_0 is designed to prevent the P_i calls from interfering with each other. The calls can occur in any order, and each one will set one of the outputs from P_0. This ensures that P_0 returns the same values as P', which returns the same values as P. Therefore P_0 and P must always return the same values when given the same inputs, and are therefore functionally equivalent.

6 Summary

In conclusion, given the features provided in the SPARK language, we have shown that the collection of slices produced from a procedure is functionally equivalent to the original procedure. If the glue code is built as described in this paper, then, as we have shown, functional equivalence is maintained. The prototype implementation of the SPARKSlicer has been built using the Ada Semantic Interface Specification (ASIS) interface [1]. Future research could rewrite this tool using the SPARK language and annotations. This future research would verify that the slicer is a correct implementation of Weiser's algorithm.

As program slicing is used in more and more software engineering applications, it is becoming more desirable to prove that these tools preserve functional equivalence. This paper provides an example of one such proof which shows that the collection of slices produced from our SPARKSlicer tool is functionally equivalent to the original procedure.

References

[1] *ASIS Basic Concepts*. Retrieved June 3, 2003, from www.acm.org/sigada/wg/asiswg/basics.html, 1998.

[2] Barnes, J. High Integrity Software, The SPARK Approach to Safety and Security. c2003 Praxis Critical Systems, Addison-Wesley, London, England.

[3] Dwyer, M. B., Corbett, J.C., Hatcliff, J., Sokolowski, S., and Zheng, H. *Slicing Multi-Threaded Java Programs: A Case Study*. Tech Report KSU CIS TR 99-7.

[4] *Program Slicing*. Retrieved June 4, 2003 from www.ssw.unilinz.ac.at/Research/Projects/ProgramSlicing.

[5] *SPARK 95 – The SPADE Ada 95 Kernel*, copyright Praxis Critical Systems. Edition 4.1, Oct 2003.

[6] Sward, R.E. Extracting Functionally Equivalent Object-Oriented Designs from Legacy Imperative Code. PhD Thesis, Air Force Institute of Technology, Wright-Patterson AFB, OH, Sep 1997.

[7] Sward, R.E. and A.T. Chamillard, AdaSlicer: A Program Slicer for Ada. *Proceedings of the ACM International SIGAda 2003 Conference*, Dec 2003, San Diego, CA.

[8] Sward, R.E. and A.T. Chamillard, Re-engineering Global Variables in Ada, *Proceedings of the ACM International SIGAda 2004 Conference*, Nov 2004, Atlanta, GA.

[9] Sward, R.E. and Hartrum, T.C. Extracting objects from legacy imperative code. In *Proceedings of the 12th IEEE International Conference on Automated Software Engineering*, Incline Village, Nevada, November 1997, pp. 98-106.

[10] *The Unravel Project*. Retrieved June 4, 2003, from http://hissa.nist.gov/unravel/, 1998.

[11] Weiser, M. Program slicing. *IEEE Transactions on Software Engineering*, SE-10(4):352-357, July 1984.

[12] *The Wisconsin Program-Slicing Tool, Version 1.1.* Retrieved June 4, 2003, from www.cs.wisc.edu/wpis/slicing_tool/, 2000.

Teaching Software Engineering with Ada 95

Daniel Simon, Gunther Vogel, and Erhard Plödereder

Universität Stuttgart, Institut für Softwaretechnologie,
Universitätsstraße 38, 70569 Stuttgart, Germany
{simon, vogel, ploedere}@informatik.uni-stuttgart.de

Abstract. At the University of Stuttgart we performed five major software projects using Ada95 in groups of six to nine third-year students. Since the year 2000, the students have produced more than 180'000 effective lines of Ada95 source code in total and delivered five different graphical tools for the navigation and manipulation of complex data structures.

In this paper, we report on our experience with these projects. First, we give a short overview, describe the software engineering curriculum, and introduce the Bauhaus reengineering project as the context of the projects. We summarise the characteristics of the projects and the applied development processes in terms of statistics. Finally, we report on the lessons we learnt when supervising the students and give recommendations for successful software projects with Ada95 in education.

1 Introduction

At the University of Stuttgart, students of software engineering get to know Ada95 as their first language. In the third year of their curriculum they have to take part in a one-year software project that is organised and managed within the computer science department. The project has an identified customer within the department and there are tutors who help the students in following the principles of software engineering when developing the software.

The department of compiler construction offers such software projects in the context of the Bauhaus reengineering project [1]. The Bauhaus project aims at the research and development of means, methods, and tools to analyse and recover facts from legacy software written in Ada, C, C++, COBOL, and Java. For the analysis of these languages, advanced data flow and control flow technology from the compiler domain are used. An important aspect for program understanding is the visualisation of software and this has been the main focus of the student projects.

Since 2000 we have run five software projects addressing the development of software tools for the navigation and manipulation of the data structures that are defined and used in the Bauhaus project. The projects were quite successful: the delivered tools are actually used for documentation and debugging purposes or have become the basis for core assets of the Bauhaus system.

T. Vardanega and A. Wellings (Eds.): Ada-Europe 2005, LNCS 3555, pp. 115–128, 2005.

This paper is organised as follows. In Section 2 we give a short introduction to the background of the student projects. We outline the administrative set-up of the projects, summarise the research project that is the context of the students' implementations, and describe the tasks and goals of the student projects. Section 3 documents the facts and figures of the projects in terms of statistics. The lessons learnt and the recommendations are provided in Section 4. Finally, we draw our conclusions in Section 5.

2   Background

This section presents the background of the student projects. First, we outline the curriculum with respect to the software projects, then, we report on the Bauhaus project at our department that serves as the implementation environment of the software projects. Finally, the tasks of the software projects are described.

2.1   The Projects

The software projects that we report on are a part of the "software engineering" curriculum at the University of Stuttgart. As a mandatory program element, third- and forth-year students take part in two large software projects, each lasting for one year. The first of these student projects is in the sheltered environment of the computer science department, whereas the second software project takes place in and is supervised by some other department or by industry in need of software for their application area. For each project, the allotted working time is 750 to 800 hours per student. Of that time, 180 hours are dedicated to a lecture in the application field and 100 hours to a seminar. The remaining 500 working hours are devoted to the software development. Assuming eight students per project, the total of 4'000 hours for the project work allows the realistic simulation of industry projects of similar scope.

All our projects are habitually divided into a pre-project and a main project. The pre-projects are conducted by teams of four students and a customer (who is represented by one of the Bauhaus team members). The goal of the pre-project is to generate a proposal for the software to be implemented in the main project. This includes a project plan, cost estimates, and other relevant documents. We usually demand some prototype implementation to be built by the small teams to prove their technical skills. The duration of the pre-projects is about four to six weeks.

The pre-projects are competitive: after four to six weeks, the students have to submit a project bid and give a sales presentation. The customer then selects the winners among the pre-project teams, based on the promised functionality, the solidity of the proposal, and the quality of the presentation. Only half of the pre-projects win. The winning teams can (or better: have to) implement their proposal whereas the losing teams are disbanded and the team members are reassigned to the winning teams. Hence, the winning teams become twice as large for the main project, usually anywhere from 6 to 9 persons.

The main project is tasked to fulfil the bid, i.e., implement the proposal. The teams have to organise autonomously. Staff members of the Bauhaus project serve as external controllers and give technical support and advice upon request. The main projects last for the remainder of a full year (and sometimes longer if the product cannot be delivered in a state satisfactory to the customer). The details of the study program for software engineering at the University of Stuttgart can be found in [2, 3, 4].

2.2   Bauhaus

The Bauhaus project at the University of Stuttgart [1] is a research project that aims at the development of means to describe software architectures and to provide methods and tools to analyse and recover the software architecture of legacy systems written in Ada, C, C++, COBOL, or Java. Bauhaus is implemented in Ada95 to a large extent and has interfaces to both C and C++ software. Figure 1 provides basic data about the composition of the Bauhaus system. While not all code in Bauhaus is relevant to the student projects, a reasonable overall familiarity and very detailed knowledge in some parts is necessary to perform the projects.

Language	Handwritten	Generated	Total
Ada95	368'198	391'918	760'116
C	73'166	0	73'166
C++	35'070	13'109	48'179
...	...	...	...
Total	500'590	406'556	907'146

Fig. 1. The Bauhaus project: number of non-commented source lines of code, categorised by programming language

As the Bauhaus project applies compiler technology to analyse software, there are two important intermediate graph structures for the representation of source code. The low-level attributed abstract syntax tree format is called *InterMediate Language* (IML). There is a second format that is used for modelling knowledge about the software on a higher level named *Resource Flow Graph* (RFG). Both representations are suitable for all analysed languages. While IML can be used for control- and data-flow analyses, RFG is used for the analysis of the architecture of the software.

These two rich graph formats need debugging and visualisation. Therefore, it was a natural idea to have the students implement graphical user interfaces for the navigation and manipulation of the graph data.

2.3   Tasks of the Student Projects

All of the student projects were tasked to produce some kind of graphical user interface to the internal data formats IML or RFG of the Bauhaus project.

In 2000, we had the idea of replacing the reengineering GUI Rigi [5] (which increasingly caused performance and interfacing problems) by a new GUI in Ada95 using the GtkAda [6, 7] binding for GTK (Gimp Toolkit). After the pre-projects, the two projects *OpenCAGE* (Open Computer Aided Graph Editor) and *GraVis* (Graph Visualiser) survived the customer's selection. These projects aimed at producing a navigation and manipulation tool for the RFG format. There were 17 students participating in the two projects.

In 2002, we decided to set up two projects, *Dracula* (in German, this is a play on words) and *GIANT* (Graphical IML Analysis and Navigation Tool), for the navigation of the IML format. As in 2000, there were four pre-projects and two main projects. Again, GtkAda was used for the GUI. Since we wanted to have a scripting language built into the tools, we recommended the usage of AFlex and AYacc [8] to implement the scanners and parsers. The number of students totalled only twelve; the team size was at the minimum that we accept for these projects.

All four of these projects were successful: the students delivered software products that were ready for working with the Bauhaus data structures. The first two projects surprised us very pleasantly: The new GUI outperformed our old GUI by orders of magnitude and, as we are displaying and navigating in huge graphs, performance mattered to us. (The same can be said for the following projects, but by then we were already used to nearly instantaneous displays of large graphs.)

Since then, the GraVis project has served as a starting base for the implementation of a powerful GUI for the Bauhaus reengineering tools. OpenCAGE is no longer used, partly because we did not have the manpower to maintain two such systems at the same time and GraVis seemed easier to understand.

Both Dracula and GIANT are in use for the debugging of the IML data structures. There is no active maintenance for the tools, but because the IML format is relatively stable (and the tools abstract away those parts of IML that still change) both tools are still in useable shape. The graphical representation of the IML graphs is very useful for other students who have to implement tools that operate on IML.

The recently completed fifth Ada95 project *PLAM* (Product Line Asset Manager) was based on the RFG format. The Java competitor of PLAM is called the *Kobold* project: this project implemented a similar functionality as a plug-in extension for the Eclipse platform [9]. The goal of the PLAM and Kobold tools was to provide interactive support for the management of software product lines.

3   Statistics

This section summarises the characteristics of the six software projects. The first subsection reports the basic data on the scope of the projects and the chosen development processes. In the next subsection, we compare the estimated project efforts with the actual performances. Finally, we describe the current state and the maintenance of the project results.

3.1   Overall Data

Figure 2 shows the academic year in which the projects took place, the number of students involved in each of the projects, the total working hours, and the development model used. All projects started in the winter semester and ended after the summer semester of the ensuing year, so each project lasted one year.

In each period two projects were running in competition with the same overall goal, but based on different winning proposals.

Based on fixed budgets, the students had to work out a realistic proposal and project plan.

The development processes that were applied in the specific projects were all different. Figure 2 summarises the most apparent similarities and differences. In principle, all models were derived from either the waterfall model [10, 11] or the iterative spiral model [12] by Boehm. Four projects (GraVis, Dracula, GIANT, and PLAM) adopted the waterfall model with one or more stages. Each stage (S) produced an executable application which was presented to and discussed with the customer. GIANT was the only project using one stage and one remedy phase. All other projects with a waterfall model had at least two stages. The first stage was used to implement an initial version which contained most but not all of the functionality of the final product. In the remaining phases, this version was improved and completed. The main parts of the analysis and specification were done before the first code was implemented and only small changes were applied to the resulting documents. The effort estimates assigned most of the working time to the first stage, the allocation for the later stages was considerably smaller.

The other two groups (OpenCAGE and Kobold) used an iterative model with three or more iterations (I), in which a prototype produced in the first iteration was extended and completed. In contrast to the staged model, the iterations were planned to use the same amount of working time. Significant parts of the analysis and specification were realised in the later iterations. The OpenCAGE group originally planned five iterations. Because of timing problems, only two iterations could finally be accomplished.

Since 2002, all project plans also contained a remedy phase (denoted by $+1$) that took place after the delivery to the customer. The purpose of this phase is to give the customer the opportunity to intensively test the software and report defects. These defects were immediately fixed by the students. After the first two projects, it became obvious that such an additional phase was necessary because many problems were only noticed by the customer after the delivery.

	GraVis	O'CAGE	Dracula	GIANT	Kobold	PLAM
Year	00/01	00/01	02/03	02/03	03/04	03/04
Nr. of students	8	9	6	6	9	9
Working hours	4'000	4'500	3'000	3'000	4'500	4'500
Development	2 S	5 I	3 S + 1	1 S + 1	4 I + 1	2 S + 1

Fig. 2. Overall project data

Estimated effort in working hours

Project Name	GraVis	OpenCAGE	Dracula	GIANT	Kobold	PLAM	Total
Administration	100 (2%)	280 (8%)	140 (5%)	485 (21%)	300 (7%)	705 (16%)	2'010 (9%)
Analysis	2'300 (43%)	1'050 (31%)	630 (24%)	805 (35%)	900 (21%)	1'520 (35%)	7'205 (32%)
Implementation	1'800 (34%)	1'620 (48%)	1'600 (62%)	645 (28%)	1'700 (40%)	1'000 (23%)	8'365 (37%)
Test	1'000 (19%)	180 (5%)	80 (3%)	160 (7%)	300 (7%)	420 (10%)	2'140 (10%)
Manual	150 (3%)	120 (4%)	150 (6%)	115 (5%)	300 (7%)	215 (5%)	1'050 (5%)
Other	0 (0%)	150 (4%)	0 (0%)	90 (4%)	800 (19%)	500 (11%)	1'540 (7%)
Overall	5'350	3'400	2'600	2'300	4'300	4'360	22'310

Actual effort in working hours

Project Name	GraVis	OpenCAGE	Dracula	GIANT	Kobold	PLAM	Total
Administration	90 (1%)	1'055 (19%)	74 (3%)	453 (20%)	930 (19%)	335 (8%)	2'937 (11%)
Analysis	3'787 (46%)	1'669 (30%)	684 (29%)	655 (29%)	1238 (26%)	1'512 (36%)	9'545 (35%)
Implementation	3'170 (39%)	2'504 (45%)	1'441 (62%)	818 (36%)	2'079 (43%)	1'760 (42%)	11'772 (43%)
Test	1'100 (13%)	278 (5%)	106 (5%)	106 (5%)	410 (9%)	354 (8%)	2'354 (9%)
Manual	9 (0%)	89 (2%)	36 (2%)	155 (7%)	160 (3%)	133 (3%)	582 (2%)
Other	0 (0%)	0 (0%)	0 (0%)	108 (5%)	0 (0%)	88 (2%)	196 (1%)
Overall	8'156	5'595	2'341	2'295	4'817	4'182	27'386

Actual effort vs. estimated effort

Project Name	GraVis	OpenCAGE	Dracula	GIANT	Kobold	PLAM	Total
Administration	90%	377%	53%	93%	310%	48%	146%
Analysis	165%	159%	109%	81%	138%	99%	132%
Implementation	176%	155%	90%	127%	122%	176%	141%
Test	110%	154%	133%	66%	137%	84%	110%
Manual	6%	74%	24%	135%	53%	62%	55%
Other	n/a	0	n/a	120%	0%	18%	13%
Overall	152%	165%	90%	100%	112%	96%	123%

Fig. 3. Estimated and actual project effort in working hours and the accuracy of the estimations

3.2   Estimates and Reality

Fig. 3 reports the effort attributed to the major activities of the projects. The first table shows the estimated effort in working hours. The estimates are the result of the students' cost estimations during project planning in the pre-projects. The second table presents the actual effort in working hours that was measured during the software development process. The third table compares the estimated and actual costs of the projects.

In each of the tables, the effort is divided into six categories. The first category *Administration* covers group administration, planning, and organisation. The category *Analysis* contains requirement analysis, specification, and design. *Implementation* comprises the writing of the code for the software. The category *Test* sums up the time for unit and module testing. The category *Manual* is dedicated to the writing of the user manual for the customer. Finally, all other tasks that did not fit in any of the previous categories, e.g. customer support and time buffers are accumulated in the category *Other*. The *Overall* effort for each project is shown in the last line of each column. The last column of the tables titled *Total* for estimated and actual effort shows the sum of each category. The percentage of each category with respect to the overall effort is shown in parentheses in the first two tables. In the third table, we divide the actual effort by the estimated effort to illustrate the degree of misestimation for each category.

The overall estimates of the projects Dracula and GIANT, Kobold and PLAM correspond remarkably well to the actual costs and have been recorded with the help of tools. The projects GraVis and OpenCAGE had significant budget overruns. In both cases (being one of the first of these projects), the tutors had overestimated the students' skills. The OpenCAGE project had spent far too much time building up a generic administrative framework — this framework has been reused by subsequent projects (except Kobold) and drastically reduced their effort for administration.

3.3   Delivery and Maintenance

For each project, Fig. 4 shows the total development effort, the delivered lines of source code, and the productivity in lines of code per hour. Additionally, the current lines of source code for each project are shown as they have evolved over time within the integrated Bauhaus system.

A number of problems has only been observed after the final delivery. For example, not all of the students are experienced programmers. In part, the readability of the delivered source code was poor; the code had to be re-factored during the maintenance phase. The results of the Java project suffer from high resource usage: the tool uses about forty Java threads running in parallel and the memory requirements quickly exceed 512 megabytes of RAM. This renders the tool useless on most of the computers in our department.

	GraVis	O'CAGE	Dracula	GIANT	Kobold	PLAM	Total	Avg.
Man hours	8'156	5'595	2'341	2'295	4'817	4'182	27'386	4'564
Deliv. LOC	47'520	43'856	23'097	38'777	20'983	33'673	207'906	34'651
LOC/hour	5.83	7.84	9.87	16.90	4.36	8.05	7.59	
Curr. LOC	60'968	33'841	24'623	38'784	20'983	33'673	212'872	35'479

Fig. 4. The produced source code in lines of non-commented code and productivity in lines of non-commented code per hour

4 Lessons Learnt

This section describes the most important lessons that we have learnt in the course of the software projects. First, we report on our general experiences we made when tutoring the software projects. Then we give an overview of the development environment. Finally, we give recommendations on how to make the software projects more challenging.

4.1 Project Administration

Pre-projects and Competition. The students neither have any experience with large software projects nor do they know the application domain of software reengineering. Therefore, the pre-projects also serve for initial training purposes. These early weeks are extremely intense for the students, since they also need to generate a realistic and convincing proposal to ultimately achieve the acceptance of their bid by the customer in preference over their competitors.

This way of organising the projects proved to be successful: the small team size at the beginning of the projects ensures that all of the students acquire the necessary domain knowledge. The competition between the pre-projects and later the main projects leads to high motivation and a great team spirit, e.g., the teams designed team logos and produced their distinguishing T-shirts. However, there is one drawback: by necessity, there are students that will be on the losing side when it comes down to choosing the "better" project proposals. The customer (backed by the tutors) must give convincing technical arguments for the choice so that the losing teams are not discouraged.

Motivating the Students. In our experience, the main stimulus for the motivation of the students lies in the chance of creating *useful* software, not student prototypes rapidly forgotten after completion of the project. Building up a team spirit, in part by running several competing projects, is crucial for the willingness to contribute and the commitment to the software project. The development of a graphical application has the benefit of giving the software developers early visual feedback on their work. The students reported a rise in motivation when the first widgets of the application appeared on their screens. The project work receives a grade as a whole, with grades for the team members centered around the project grade. Thus, the team creates its own mechanisms to bring members in line by motivation or peer pressure.

Prototyping. The customer should request a prototype GUI as part of the sales presentation by the pre-project teams. This puts the students in contact with a number of tools and the tutors can verify that the students gained sufficient domain knowledge to master the implementation challenges.

Monitoring. The projects are organised autonomously by the students and the tutors do not continuously monitor or supervise the work. We only request time sheets and activity protocols on a monthly basis from each of the students. Further, the tutors are informed about internal project meetings and request copies of the minutes of meetings. In this way, the tutors can survey the progress of the projects. The tutors should consult, but not dictate to the project team. It is the role of the customer to get nasty when deadlines visible to him are missed.

Simulating Reality. The projects take place in the sheltered environment of the university. It is nevertheless a goal to simulate the reality of industrial projects, in particular for the role of the customer. To be a realistic customer, one needs to pay attention to the dress code: customers do not dress in T-shirts and shorts. If the customer wears business clothing he appears more important and credible: the students show completely different behaviour with respect to the kind of questions that come up. The customer should not be the grading professor or else each requirement uttered might be taken as gospel.

In the pre-projects, the customer presents an unordered vision about the software. Note that this vision need and should not be consistent or realistic. It is the task of the students to filter this input and to come up with a concise specification of the requirements and of the software. They quickly learn that, unless one writes requirement and design documents, confusion can easily become rampant in the team and in talking with the customer.

4.2 Infrastructure

Because the software projects aimed at creating GUIs for the Bauhaus project, some parts of the infrastructure were pre-determined. The implementation language was Ada95, the compiler for Ada95 was the public version of the GNAT compiler [13], and the GUI toolkit was GtkAda [6, 7]. The students used Glade[14] for building the GUI of the prototype implementations for the pre-projects. The code generated by Glade is only useful for interface prototypes and should not be used for the main projects because it is very difficult to maintain.

The availability of a reuse library with the most fundamental data structures is a sine qua non. We provided the students with our own packages from the Bauhaus project, but one could also use a library like Charles [15]. For the scanning and parsing tasks that occurred during the projects, AFlex and AYacc [8] were sufficient.

In some of the projects, the students defined configuration files in various XML formats. First we used Xml/Ada [16], then we developed XML4Ada95 [17] to read and write XML. At the time we used Xml/Ada, the library was in an unstable state and was not able to validate XML documents. Therefore, subsequent projects make use of the XML4Ada95 library that is a binding to the Xerces C++ XML parser [18].

Testing the produced systems proved difficult. While unit testing is supported by AUnit [19], the interactive GUI has to be tested manually. For installation tests on various operating systems, we recently introduced VMWare [20] that allows for running a number of virtual machines on a single computer. The operating systems installed on these virtual machines are independent from the development environment and allow for secure testing in a sand box.

4.3   Experiences with UML

In the beginning of the projects, the students had a severe infection by several of the UML fevers [21]. They tried to make use of UML use-case diagrams for the purpose of communication with the customer and for specifying the application. Firstly, the students produced numerous use-case diagrams without appropriate textual descriptions in order to analyse the application domain of the tool they should develop. This has been diagnosed by Bell as an occurrence of "curator fever".

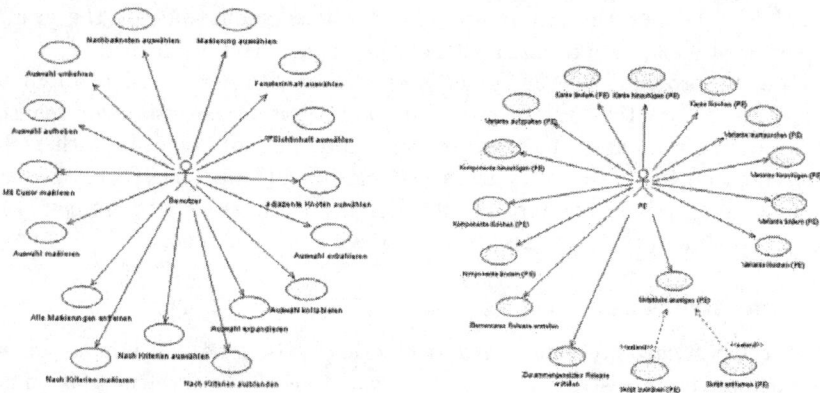

Fig. 5. Excerpt from one of the student project's specifications showing the symptoms of the circled wagon fever

Further, they obviously were infected with the "circled wagon fever", where the students draw wonderful (but rather meaningless) UML use-case diagrams as shown in Fig. 5. The discussion with the customer about the application on the basis of these drawings was difficult and tedious. Eventually, the students used a different method for the description of the software, e.g. textual and tabular descriptions. They learned that UML — like any other formalism — is insufficient for communication with a customer unless the application semantics are described in adequate detail and understood by the customer and the contractor.

4.4   Experiences with Ada95

At the start of the projects, the students often had reservations about the usage of Ada95 as the implementation language and most would have preferred Java or C++ over Ada95. In retrospective (and after having worked on Java or C++ projects), Ada95 often seems to have become their language of choice.

However, the object-oriented features of Ada95 proved to be a challenge for the students. In particular, the students of the OpenCAGE project had severe problems. Their way of object-oriented design was in effect a Java-oriented design, which they tried to map one-to-one onto an Ada implementation, an exercise that was doomed to fail, partly because of conceptual and type system mismatches, partly due to their lack of experience with object-oriented programming in Ada95.

The lack of support for cyclic dependencies among tagged records in different packages led to an architecturally unsound agglomeration of many tagged records in a single package. In other projects that separated tagged types into different packages, it was quite annoying to the students familiar with other languages that visibility of primitive operations needed to be established by context clauses for the respective packages.

The OpenCAGE design was based on design patterns that assumed re-dispatching in dispatching calls, which in Ada (intentionally and for good reasons) requires explicit conversion to the class-wide type within the body of the primitive operation. The lack of polymorphic named access types caused a highly annoying need for many access type conversions in the code. 97% of a total of about 800 explicit conversions in roughly 14'000 lines of OpenCAGE code served these purposes, as a subsequent study of the OpenCAGE code established.

This study also examined five other Ada95 systems with significant use of tagged types. It showed that the bad effects of the lack of polymorphic access types in Ada95 were not singular to OpenCAGE: four out of the six systems contained one type conversion per 12–70 lines of primitive operation code. At least 25–60% of these conversions were conversions "up" the hierarchy and, hence, a mere nuisance to the programmers and confusing to the readers of the code. None of the other systems exhibited a significant number of conversions for the sake of causing re-dispatching.

For these reasons we discouraged the heavy use of object-oriented Ada features in the subsequent projects.

Ada05 solves some of these problems. It allows circular dependencies and solves the visibility issues by the new object prefix notation. The expanded use of anonymous access types in Ada05 may provide partial solutions to the problem of polymorphic access variables. However, it remains to be seen whether intuitive programming patterns can be developed that do not fall prey to the associated accessibility level checks.

4.5   Sabotage

The purpose of running the software projects is to train the students to enrich their experience in a realistic project setting. One way of gaining experience is to make mistakes and learn from them. Dawson [22] mentions a number of tricks how to sabotage software projects for the purpose of training software engineers. It is our experience that in most cases the students will sabotage their projects unintentionally on their own if you just let them. The perennial configuration management issues in projects of that size are a prime example. To ensure that the students gain experience from mistakes, the following additional interventions are successful.

Always Change a Running System. During the software projects, there were several upgrades for development tools that were used by the students. For example, the GNAT compiler changed from version 3.13p via 3.14p to 3.15p and the GtkAda binding upgraded from version 1.2.12 to version 2.2 (while Dracula and GIANT were being developed). It is easy for the customer to argue that the software should be upgraded. In the case of the compiler upgrades, even the students wanted the more recent versions. The students experienced that no software upgrade is *really* backward compatible. In particular the upgrade of the GUI toolkit had a severe impact on the application software.

Withdrawal of Resources. Software development often takes place in front of a computer. For the projects Dracula and GIANT, we had the unique opportunity to refuse access to university equipment because the computer science department was closed to students for about four weeks of relocation. The relocation plans were known to the students and were considered in their project plans so that negative effects were largely avoided.

Application Environment. The customer should always request the program to run on at least two different platforms. We usually want a Linux, Solaris, and a Windows version to be developed. Furthermore, we specify "low-end" hardware requirements such as available in our department (a part of our hardware is more than five years old) thereby forcing the students to carefully design an efficient implementation. So, they learn that they have to consider the differences in the hardware and operating systems and that they should not expect that the next generation of desktops solves all the speed and space problems that the application still has.

5   Conclusions

Dawson suggests a number of dirty tricks to train software engineers in [22]. We believe that we arranged for all of these tricks during the software projects. Most tricks, however, are played on the students by themselves.

Using Ada95 in challenging student software development projects is certainly feasible. There is sufficient support for programming tools and GUI tool kits that are available free of charge.

Most of these tools and libraries, be it for Ada, C++ or Java, are not fully mature. During the software projects there were a number of annoying technical problems, e.g., malfunctions in libraries or internal compiler errors, posing a serious problem for novice software engineers and requiring consulting by experienced tutors.

In all the Ada-based projects, the final product was of decent quality and exhibited good or very good performance characteristics. The students realised that part of their success was due to the programming language. For some, it has become the language of choice.

In terms of the final product, the Java-based project failed the performance criterion by a huge margin. One can and should not generalise from a single data point, though. Nevertheless, it is disturbing that two competing developments focused on meeting the same user requirements and applying two different implementation technologies, yielded such diverging results.

As a final remark, it can be said that each of the projects was successful in the sense that the students gained much experience. The results of most of our Ada95 projects are still in actual use whereas those of other projects within the computer science department usually disappear soon after the student projects are completed.

References

1. Eisenbarth, T., Koschke, R., Plödereder, E., Girard, J.F., Würthner, M.: Projekt Bauhaus: Interaktive und inkrementelle Wiedergewinnung von SW-Architekturen. In: 1. Workshop Software-Reengineering, Bad Honnef, Germany, Universität Koblenz-Landau (1999) 17–26 Fachberichte Informatik, Nr. 7/99.
2. Universität Stuttgart: Studienplan Diplomstudiengang Informatik und Diplomstudiengang Softwaretechnik. Available at
   http://www.informatik.uni-stuttgart.de/fakultaet/lehre/softwaretechnik/studium/studienplan.html (2000)
3. Ludewig, J., Reißing, R.: Teaching what they need instead of teaching what we like – the new software engineering curriculum at the University of Stuttgart. Information and Software Technology 40 (1998) 239–244
4. Ludewig, J.: Softwaretechnik in Stuttgart – ein konstruktiver Informatik-Studiengang. Informatik-Spektrum 22 (1999)
5. Storey, M.A.D., Wong, K., Müller, H.A.: Rigi: a visualization environment for reverse engineering. In: Proc. 19th International Conference on Software Engineering, ACM Press (1997) 606–607
6. Briot, E., Brobecker, J., Charlet, A.: GtkAda: Design and Implementation of a High Level Binding in Ada. In: Proc. 5th Ada-Europe Conference, Potsdam, Germany. Volume 1845 of LNCS, Springer (2000) 112–124
7. Briot, E., Brobecker, J., Charlet, A., Setton, N.: GtkAda: a complete Ada95 graphical toolkit. Available at http://libre.act-europe.fr/GtkAda/ (2003)
8. Self, J.: Aflex and ayacc. Available at http://www.ics.uci.edu/~self/ (1996)
9. Eclipse Consortium: Eclipse IDE. Available at http://www.eclipse.org/ (2004)
10. IEEE Standards Board: IEEE Standard Glossary of Software Engineering Terminology—IEEE Std 610.12 (1991)
11. Royce, W.W.: Managing the development of large software systems: concepts and techniques. In: Proc. 9th International Conference on Software Engineering, IEEE Press (1987) 328–338
12. Boehm, B.W.: A Spiral Model of Software Development and Enhancement. IEEE Computer 21 (1988) 61–72
13. Ada Core Technologies: GNAT Ada 95 Compiler. Available at
    http://libre.act-europe.fr/GNAT/ (2003)
14. Chaplin, D.: Glade: GTK User Interface Builder. Available at
    http://glade.gnome.org/ (2004)
15. Heaney, M.: Charles: A Data Structure Library for Ada95. In: Proc. 8th Ada-Europe Conference, Toulouse, France. Volume 2655 of LNCS, Springer (2003) 217–282
16. Briot, E.: XML/Ada: a full XML suite. Available at
    http://libre.act-europe.fr/xmlada/ (2003)
17. Vrandečić, Z., Simon, D.: XML4Ada95: Accessing XML using the DOM in Ada95. In: Proc. 9th Ada-Europe Conference, Palma de Mallorca, Spain. Volume 3063 of LNCS, Springer (2004) 178–189

18. Apache Software Foundation: Xerces C++ Parser. Available at
    `http://xml.apache.org/xerces-c/` (2003)
19. Falis, E.: Aunit: Ada unit testing framework. Available at
    `http://libre.act-europe.fr/aunit/` (2003)
20. VMware, Inc.: VMWare Virtual Infrastructure. Available at
    `http://www.vmware.com/` (2004)
21. Bell, A.E.: Death by UML Fever. ACM Queue **2** (2004)
22. Dawson, R.: Twenty Dirty Tricks to Train Software Engineers. In: Proc. International Conference on Software Maintenance, Limerick, Ireland, ACM Press (2000) 209–218

A Comparison of the Mutual Exclusion Features in Ada and the Real-Time Specification for Java™

Benjamin M. Brosgol

AdaCore,
Belmont, Massachusetts USA
brosgol@adacore.com

Abstract. A concurrent program generally comprises a collection of threads[1] that interact cooperatively, either directly or through shared data objects. In the latter case the sharing needs to be implemented by some mechanism that ensures mutually exclusive access, or possibly "concurrent read / exclusive write". Ada and the Real-Time Specification for Java have taken different approaches to mutual exclusion. This paper analyzes and compares them with respect to programming style (clarity, encapsulation, avoidance of errors such as deadlock), priority inversion management, expressibility/generality, and efficiency. It also looks at interactions with exceptions and asynchronous transfer of control.

1 Introduction

Mutual exclusion is a fundamental requirement in a concurrent program, and over the years a number of different approaches have been proposed, studied, and implemented, ranging from low-level primitives to higher-level features. This paper shows how Ada [1] and the Real-Time Specification for Java ("RTSJ")[2] [2] [3] approach this issue. The basic problem that each must address, especially with respect to meeting real-time requirements, is how to provide mutual exclusion in a way that offers sufficient generality, supports sound software engineering practice, prevents unbounded priority inversion, and allows efficient implementations.

In brief, mutual exclusion in Ada is obtainable via three mechanisms, listed in order of increasing generality:

- Atomically accessible data objects, so designated via a pragma
- Protected objects, with an associated locking policy
- "Passive tasks" sequentializing accesses via rendezvous

---

[1] We use the term "thread" generically to refer to a concurrent activity. When discussing a particular language's mechanism we use that language's terminology (e.g., "task" in Ada).

[2] The RTSJ is the product of the Java Community Process's Java Specification Request 00001. It adds real-time functionality to the Java platform through the javax.realtime class library together with constraints on certain behaviors that are implementation dependent in Java.

T. Vardanega and A. Wellings (Eds.): Ada-Europe 2005, LNCS 3555, pp. 129–143, 2005.

The RTSJ captures mutual exclusion in two ways:

- Atomically accessible variables so marked via the `volatile` modifier
- Methods or blocks that are "synchronized" on an object, with priority inversion management based on the object's "monitor control policy"

The second mechanism basically extends and makes more deterministic the semantics of Java's "synchronized" facility.

It is also possible to simulate Ada's passive task style in Java (and thus in the RTSJ), but this is not a typical idiom.

The following sections discuss and contrast the Ada and RTSJ approaches, with a particular focus on priority inversion management. Given the context for this paper, it is assumed that the reader is more familiar with Ada than with Java or the RTSJ. Thus more background information and technical detail are provided for Java and especially the RTSJ than for Ada.

2   Mutual Exclusion in Java

Since the RTSJ builds directly on the Java [4] mechanisms, this section summarizes and evaluates Java's facilities for mutual exclusion. A more comprehensive analysis of Java's concurrency model may be found in [5], [6], and [7].

2.1   `Volatile` Variables

In simple cases two threads may need to communicate via a shared variable, but Java's memory model [8] allows the compiler to cache the value of the variable in each thread's local memory. To prevent this unwanted optimization, the programmer can declare the variable as `volatile`. Because of Java's pointer-based semantics, `volatile` never applies to an entire object, but only to either a scalar variable or a reference to an object. The intent is that any access to the variable is atomic with respect to thread context switches. Indeed, when `volatile` is specified then atomicity is required, but with two exceptions: variables of type `long` or `double`, which take 64 bits. In these cases the language rules encourage but do not require atomic accesses. Further, `volatile` can not be specified for array components. It can be specified for an array variable, but then it applies only to the array reference and not to the components.

2.2   `Synchronized` Code

Java's mutual exclusion facility is based on the concept of "object locks". Conceptually, each object (including class objects[3]) has an associated lock. The program can attempt to acquire a lock on an object referenced by a variable `ref` either by executing a statement `synchronized(ref){...}` or by invoking an instance method `ref.func(...)` where `func` is declared as `synchronized`. (A static method may

---

[3] A *class object* is an instance of class `Class` and serves as a run-time manifestation of a Java class.

also be declared as `synchronized`, in which case the lock in question applies to the corresponding class object.)

When a thread holds a lock on an object, any other thread attempting to synchronize on that object will be prevented from running[4] until the lock has been released, at which point it becomes ready and competes with other threads that were similarly stalled. Java does not dictate how the stalling is to be implemented.

An object lock is not simply a boolean, it needs to have a non-negative count associated with it to handle situations when a thread acquires a lock on an object for which it already holds the lock. When a thread exits from synchronized code, either normally or through exception propagation, the count is decreased. If/when it becomes zero, the lock is released.

The `synchronized` mechanism is rather general; there are no restrictions on the statements that can be executed inside synchronized code. In particular, a thread can block (e.g., via the `sleep()` method) while holding the lock. Some blocking methods (specifically `wait`) release the lock; others do not.

Java's `synchronized` mechanism has several problems:

- It is susceptible to the "nested monitors" problem: if two threads attempt to synchronize on different objects in different orders, they may deadlock.
- The language semantics do not specify how priorities affect lock acquisition. If low- and high-priority threads are competing for the same object lock, there is no guarantee that preference is given to the high-priority thread. If a low-priority thread owns a lock that is needed by a high-priority thread, there is no requirement for priority inheritance, and thus unbounded priority inversion may result.
- Java's `synchronized` construct is not fully integrated with state-based mutual exclusion (i.e., when a thread not only needs mutually exclusive access to an object but also needs to wait until the object is in a particular state). The `wait`/`notify`/`notifyAll` mechanism basically supports just one condition variable per object, which makes it somewhat error-prone to express classical idioms such as the bounded buffer. Further, there is a run-time check to ensure that when one of these methods is invoked, the calling thread holds the lock on the object.
- Methodologically, the presence of synchronized methods in a class does not mean that uses of objects in that class are "thread safe". For example, even though one thread has "locked" an object through a synchronized method, another thread can corrupt the object by invoking a non-synchronized method or by directly accessing the object's fields.

These last two issues imply that Java's use of the term "monitor" to denote the object lock mechanism is somewhat of a misnomer, since the classical monitor construct includes condition variables and data encapsulation. Indeed, Brinch Hansen's rather scathing critique of Java's thread model [9] was due to a large extent to Java's failure to provide a safe mutual exclusion mechanism as the basis for its concurrency model.

---

[4] We use the term *stalled* to denote the state of a thread that has attempted to synchronize on an object that has been locked by some other thread. It is useful to differentiate the stalled state from the *blocked* state that results from invocation of methods such as `sleep` and `wait`.

Java has no notion of synchronized code being immune to asynchronous interruption. This caused some anomalous interactions with several methods in the `Thread` class:

- If `t.stop()` is invoked while `t` is inside code that is synchronized on some object `obj`, then `t` will suffer the throwing of a `ThreadDeath` exception. If not handled inside the synchronized code, the exception will be propagated and the lock on `obj` will be released, possibly leaving `obj` in an inconsistent state.
- If `t.destroy()` is invoked while `t` is inside code that is synchronized on some object `obj`, then `t` is terminated "immediately" without propagating any exceptions or releasing the lock on `obj`. Thus threads that later attempt to synchronize on `obj` will be deadlocked.

Because of such anomalies, the `Thread.stop` and `Thread.destroy` methods have been deprecated.

In summary, Java's `synchronized` mechanism can best be regarded as a low-level building block. It is a flexible construct that offers quite a bit of generality, but needs to be used with care. The Java designers made no pretext of attempting to support real-time requirements, and indeed the semantics are too loose to be depended upon.

More recently, an attempt has been made to enhance the basic facilities with higher-level constructs: the concurrency utilities from JSR-166 [10]. Their development was in parallel with the RTSJ and had different objectives; JSR-166 did not attempt to address real-time requirements but rather sought to define a common set of idioms for general-purpose concurrent programming. In the interest of minimizing its assumptions about the underlying Java platform, the RTSJ makes no use of the JSR-166 facilities, and thus they will not be further considered in this paper.

3   A Note on Priority Inversion

A *priority inversion*[5] occurs when a ready or stalled thread is prevented from running while a lower priority thread is running. Some priority inversions are necessary and desirable; for example, stalling a high priority thread that attempts to acquire a lock owned by a lower priority thread. A major issue for real-time programming, which is affected by both language semantics and programming style, is to ensure that priority inversions are anticipated and that their durations are predictable and sufficiently short / bounded.

4   RTSJ Summary

The RTSJ needed to address several major issues that make Java unsuitable for real-time applications:

- The implementation-dependent nature of the thread semantics, making it impossible to write portable code that manages priority inversions and ensures that deadlines will be met

---

[5] See [11] for further background information.

- The reliance on heap allocation and garbage collection for storage reclamation, resulting in unpredictable space and/or time behavior
- Inadequate functionality in areas such as low-level programming and asynchrony

The RTSJ provides a class library, together with implementation constraints, that are designed to overcome these problems.

It offers a flexible scheduling framework based on the `Schedulable` interface and the `Thread` subclass `RealtimeThread` that implements this interface. The latter class overrides various `Thread` methods with versions that add real-time functionality, and supplies new methods for operations such as periodic scheduling. The `Schedulable` interface is introduced because certain schedulable entities (in particular, handlers for asynchronous events) might not be implemented as dedicated threads.

The RTSJ mandates a default POSIX-compliant preemptive priority-based scheduler – the so-called *base scheduler* – that supports at least 28 distinct priority levels beyond the 10 that are defined by Java's thread model. The implementation can provide other schedulers (e.g., Earliest Deadline First). For priority inversion management the RTSJ provides Priority Inheritance (required) and Priority Ceiling Emulation (optional).

To deal with Garbage Collection issues, the RTSJ defines various "memory areas" that are not subject to Garbage Collection: *immortal memory*, which persists for the duration of the application; and *scoped memory*, which is a generalization of the run-time stack. Restrictions on assignment, enforced in general at run time, prevent dangling references. The RTSJ also provides a `NoHeapRealtimeThread` class; instances of this class never reference the heap, may preempt the Garbage Collector at any time (even when the heap is in an inconsistent state), and thus do not incur Garbage Collector latency except in specialized circumstances as described below. A `NoHeapRealtime-Thread` can reference objects in memory areas not subject to garbage collection (immortal or scoped memory).

Java's asynchrony issues are addressed through two main features. First, the RTSJ allows the definition of asynchronous events and asynchronous event handlers – these are basically a high-level mechanism for handling hardware interrupts or software signals. Secondly, the RTSJ extends the effect of `Thread.interrupt()` to apply not only to blocked threads, but also to real-time threads and asynchronous event handlers whether blocked or not.

The RTSJ supports absolute and relative high-resolution time, as well as one-shot and periodic timers. It also provides several classes for low-level programming. "Peek" and "poke" facilities for integral and floating-point data are available for *raw memory*, and *physical memory* may be defined with particular characteristics (such as flash memory) and used for general object allocation.

The RTSJ does not provide any specialized support for multiprocessor architectures.

5   Mutual Exclusion in the RTSJ

It would have been outside the scope of the RTSJ to introduce a new mutual exclusion facility, so the approach was to make the standard Java mechanism suitable for real-time applications. This entailed addressing two main issues:

- Managing priority inversions
- Dealing with asynchronous interruptibility

5.1   Managing Priority Inversions

The RTSJ offers a general, extensible, and somewhat ambitious approach to solving the priority inversion problem. It provides an abstract class MonitorControl and non-abstract subclasses PriorityInheritance and PriorityCeiling Emulation. PriorityInheritance is a singleton class; PriorityCeiling Emulation has distinct instances, one per ceiling level. The program can assign a MonitorControl instance (referred to as a *monitor control policy*) to any object, and can dynamically change the assignment. (Thus dynamic ceiling changes are allowed.) A default policy can also be established system-wide, so that it governs all objects subsequently constructed. The initial default policy is Priority Inheritance, but this can be overridden at system startup.

At any point in time a thread has a set of *priority sources*, namely its *base priority* (which reflects explicitly-invoked dynamic priority changes) and also other values depending on the monitor control policies governing the objects that the thread has locked. For example the ceiling of a PriorityCeilingEmulation instance is a priority source for any thread that has locked an object governed by this policy. A thread's *active priority* is the maximum of the values of its priority sources. Entering synchronized code adds a priority source; leaving synchronized code removes a priority source. Thus both actions affect the thread's active priority. Priority sources may be added/removed either synchronously or asynchronously.

The integration of both Priority Inheritance and Priority Ceiling Emulation into a common framework, with well-defined semantics, is new. (Posix includes both mechanisms but in an underspecified manner.) As will be pointed out below, the interactions between the two protocols led to an interesting formalization of the Priority Ceiling Emulation policy.

Under the base scheduler, access to synchronization locks is controlled by priority ordered queues, FIFO within priority. Thus a thread attempting to acquire a lock that is in use goes to the tail of the "stalled" queue associated with that lock.

Priority Inheritance. If an object obj is governed by the Priority Inheritance instance and is currently locked by a thread t1, and a thread t2 attempts to synchronize on obj, then t2 becomes a priority source for t1. If t1 has an active priority less than t2's, then t1's active priority will be boosted to that of t2. When t1 releases the lock on obj, t2 ceases serving as a priority source for t1, and t1's active priority is adjusted accordingly.

Full (recursive) priority inheritance is required by the RTSJ. In the above description, if t1 is stalled, waiting for an object locked by thread t0, then t0's active priority will be boosted to that of t2 as a result of t2 attempting to synchronize on obj.

An interesting issue arises when a NoHeapRealtimeThread t2 at high-priority p2 attempts to synchronize on a Priority Inheritance-governed object (in immortal or scoped memory) locked by a heap-using thread t1 at low priority p1 while the Garbage Collector ("GC") is in progress. (We assume that the GC is running at a priority higher than p1 but lower than p2). Ordinarily, t1 would have its priority boosted to p2, but if this were the sole effect then t1 would preempt the GC, thus leaving the heap inconsistent. The solution is to postulate a Priority Inheritance-governed lock on the heap. When t1, executing at inherited priority p2, attempts to access the heap, it fails because the lock on the heap is in use by the GC. The GC inherits t1's active priority p2 and then runs until it reaches a safe preemption point, at which time it relinquishes the lock, allowing t1 to continue. The effect is to induce a GC-induced latency for t2 (and also for NoHeapRealtimeThreads executing at priorities higher than the GC's base priority and lower than p2). Since this somewhat defeats the purpose of NoHeapRealtimeThreads, the RTSJ provides "wait-free queues" as the recommended mechanism for communication between heap-using threads and NoHeapRealtimeThreads.

A *wait-free queue* is a data structure that allows concurrent "writers" and "readers" to store / retrieve items without interference but without blocking (on one side). The RTSJ supplies two classes to obtain this effect:

- A WaitFreeWriteQueue is intended for access by a single writer (generally a NoHeapRealtimeThread) and multiple readers (arbitrary threads). The write operations are non-synchronized and non-blocking (one method returns a status value, another method overwrites an existing element when the queue is full). The read operation is synchronized and will block when the queue is empty.
- A WaitFreeReadQueue is intended for access by a single reader (generally a NoHeapRealtimeThread) and multiple writers (arbitrary threads). The read operation is non-synchronized and non-blocking (if the queue is empty a special value is returned). The write operation is synchronized and will block when the queue is full.

Priority Ceiling Emulation. Informally, Priority Ceiling Emulation (also known as *Highest Lockers Protocol*) is a technique in which a thread holding a lock executes at a *ceiling priority* associated with the lock. The ceiling value, which the application must define for the lock, is the highest priority of any thread that could hold that lock. The benefits of Priority Ceiling Emulation, compared with Priority Inheritance, are that it reduces the blocking time from priority inversions, and it prevents "nested monitor" deadlocks. Moreover, as exemplified by protected objects in Ada, in specialized circumstances (when blocking cannot occur while holding a lock) an especially efficient implementation is possible; this point will be further addressed below.

In order for Priority Ceiling Emulation to have the desired effect in terms of avoiding unbounded priority inversion, the priority of the locking thread must be no higher than the lock's ceiling, a condition that in general requires a run-time check. (On the other hand, once a lock is acquired, increasing the priority of the locker above the ceiling does not risk priority inversion, and indeed nested locking where the ceiling of the inner lock exceeds the ceiling of the outer lock will result in the thread's executing the inner code at a priority higher than the ceiling of the outer lock.)

This informal description omits an important detail: when an application assigns a ceiling value to a lock (and when the implementation checks that a thread's priority does not exceed the ceiling), which priority should be used: the *active priority*, or the *base priority*? Historically, and in fact in the initial release of the RTSJ, it is the active priority. However, this led to some subtle interactions between Priority Inheritance and Priority Ceiling Emulation. As an example, suppose low-priority thread t holds a Priority Inheritance lock and (asynchronously) inherits priority p from another thread that attempts to acquire that lock. If t then attempts to lock an object governed by Priority Ceiling Emulation with ceiling c, and p exceeds c, then t will suffer a ceiling violation exception. If t does not provide a handler, then synchronized code (for the lock governed by Priority Inheritance) will be abruptly terminated, possibly leaving the object in an inconsistent state. This may be regarded as a design error – the programmer needs to understand the global locking behavior and assign priority ceilings accordingly – but the asynchronous nature of priority inheritance makes this difficult to solve in practice.

The RTSJ is being updated (in early 2005) to address such issues. The likely approach, inspired by suggestions from [12], consists of several main points:[6]

1. In the ceiling violation check, use the thread's base priority (or the ceiling of the most recently acquired Priority Ceiling Emulation lock, if there is such a lock) rather than the active priority
2. Treat a busy Priority Ceiling Emulation lock with Priority Inheritance semantics when a thread that owns a Priority Inheritance lock attempts to acquire it

Here's an example that shows the effect of these rules. Suppose thread t1 at priority 10 locks an object objPI governed by Priority Inheritance. It then locks an object objPCE15 governed by Priority Ceiling Emulation, with ceiling 15. The active priority for t1 is 15. Another thread t2, at priority 20, attempts to lock objPI. This causes t1's active priority to be boosted to 20. Suppose t1 then attempts to lock object objPCE17, governed by Priority Ceiling Emulation with ceiling 17. Since t1's base priority is used in the ceiling check, t1 is allowed to obtain the lock, and it is still running at priority 20. If it then attempted to acquire a Priority Ceiling Emulation lock with ceiling 16 it would fail, since it is currently holding a lock at a higher ceiling.

Now suppose thread t3 at base priority 11 and active priority 30 (via Priority Inheritance) preempts t1 and attempts to acquire the lock on objPCE15. Since t3's base priority is less than the ceiling, there is no ceiling violation. If the rules simply provided for enqueueing t3 on objPCE15's lock, then we could have an unbounded priority inversion, since threads at priorities in the range 21 through 29 could preempt t1 and run to completion while t3 is waiting for the lock on objPCE15. This is where the 2nd rule above comes in. Since a thread that holds a Priority Inheritance lock is attempting to obtain the lock on objPCE15, the latter lock has Priority Inheritance semantics. In particular, the active priority of the thread t1 that owns the Priority Ceiling Emulation lock is boosted to 30, thus avoiding the priority inversion.

Dynamic ceiling changes are permitted – this is a special case of the general principle that an object's monitor control policy may be updated – by assigning to the object

---

[6] These are captured more formally in the rules for a thread's priority sources and in the semantics for the PriorityCeilingEmulation class.

a monitor control policy with a different ceiling value. This is only permitted for the thread that currently owns the lock on the object. There are some subtleties lurking in the details – for example, a thread may acquire a lock at ceiling c1, block on a call of wait(), and then be awakened to reacquire the lock after the ceiling has been lowered to c2. Should the ceiling violation check be performed? This issue is currently under discussion.

Support for the PriorityCeilingEmulation class is optional. The RTSJ designers felt that it was not as prevalent as Priority Inheritance in existing RTOSes or in real-time practice.

Example. The following fragment illustrates several concepts:

- Defining a class's constructor to provide a Priority Ceiling Emulation policy for the new object, with the ceiling value passed as a constructor parameter
- Changing an object's monitor control policy dynamically, to be Priority Inheritance

```
public class Resource{
   public Resource( int ceiling ){
      synchronized(this){
         MonitorControl.setMonitorControl(
            this,
            PriorityCeilingEmulation.instance(ceiling) );
      }
   }
   ...
}

class MyRealtimeThread extends RealtimeThread{
   public void run(){
      Resource r = new Resource(20);
      // r is governed by Priority Ceiling Emulation with ceiling 20
      ...
      synchronized(r){
         MonitorControl.setMonitorControl(
                     r,
                     PriorityInheritance.instance() );
      }
      // r is now governed by Priority Inheritance
      ...
   }
}
```

Note that the invocation of setMonitorControl needs to be in code that is synchronized on the target object.

"Lock-Free" Priority Ceiling Emulation. During the maintenance phase of the RTSJ, the Technical Interpretations Committee[7] considered adding support for "lock free" (queueless) Priority Ceiling Emulation, along the lines of the Ada 95 model. The main idea was that a thread that was synchronized on an object governed by a lock-free Priority Ceiling Emulation policy would not be allowed to block. Several designs were considered. The simplest scheme was to introduce a `PriorityCeilingEmulation` subclass, say `LockOptimizedPCE`. A thread that blocks while holding such a lock would suffer the throwing of an exception. However, this scheme interacts poorly with the dynamic nature of the RTSJ's monitor control policies. An object of a class with synchronized code that was not written under the lock-free assumption (i.e., which could block) might be assigned a `LockOptimizedPCE` policy. The consequential exception propagation could leave the object in an inconsistent state; this was considered unacceptable.

An alternative approach was also contemplated: a "marker interface"[8] `LockOptimizable`. A class that implemented this interface would need to ensure that all synchronized methods were non-blocking; if it blocked, an exception would be thrown. (This is different from the situation above, since here the author of the lock optimizable class knows in advance that synchronized code should not block.) An implementation could optimize such a class, Ada style, by using priority instead of actual locks / mutexes to enforce mutual exclusion. However, this raises several issues:

- An implementation that did not want to bother with the lock-free optimization could not simply ignore the fact that a class implemented the `LockOptimizable` interface, since the semantics required throwing an exception on blocking in synchronized code.
- Capturing the optimization on a class-wide basis was judged too coarse; in practice, it might be desirable to specify the lock-free optimization on a per-instance basis.

Since there was no consensus on how to best model lock-free Priority Ceiling Emulation, it was omitted from the RTSJ.

5.2   Interactions with Asynchronous Transfer of Control

A complete discussion of asynchronous transfer of control ("ATC") in the RTSJ and Ada is given in [13]. Here we consider only the issues related to mutual exclusion.

The RTSJ solves the problem of ATC out of synchronized code by defining it out of existence: synchronized code is simply not asynchronously interruptible ("AI"). If `t.interrupt()` is invoked while t is (lexically) inside synchronized code, the interrupt stays pending until the next time t attempts to execute AI code. This may occur during a later invocation of an AI method from within the synchronized code. This invocation will throw an `AsynchronouslyInterruptedException` ("AIE"), but

---

[7] After the RTSJ was approved, it went into a maintenance phase administered by a group known as the Technical Interpretations Committee.

[8] A *marker interface* is an empty interface. A common style in Java is to use a marker interface to define a boolean property for a class: a class has the property if and only if it implements the interface.

such an exception occurrence is considered to be synchronous in this context, since in general a method invoked from synchronized code may throw any exception identified in its throws clause. Indeed, it would be good RTSJ style for a synchronized block to provide a handler for AIE if it calls any AI methods, since that will explicitly show that it anticipates such situations and will provide the necessary cleanup. (Such style is required if the synchronized code is the body of a synchronized method, since AIE is a checked[9] exception.)

6   Mutual Exclusion in Ada

This section discusses Ada's approach to managing priority inversions and also summarizes its handling of the interaction between mutual exclusion and asynchronous transfer of control.

6.1   Managing Priority Inversions

Ada has a mixed approach to priority inversion, depending on whether protected objects or passive tasks are used. In the former situation, the Ceiling_Locking policy prevents unbounded priority inversions; indeed, a task attempting to invoke a protected operation is deferred at most once by a lower-priority task. The assumption that blocking does not occur within a protected operation allows an extremely efficient ("lock free") implementation.

The situation with rendezvous is different, however. The rule that an accept statement is executed at the higher of the priorities of the calling and the called tasks is only part of what would be required for priority inheritance. This was a well-known issue in Ada 83, but the solution (full, recursive priority inheritance) was judged to impose too high an overhead and was intentionally omitted from Ada 95 [14]. As a result, it is possible to incur unbounded priority inversions. For example, if a high-priority task T2 calls an entry of a low-priority server task S while S is serving a task T1 at priority lower than T2's, then T2's priority is not required to be inherited by the server task. Thus T2 can suffer an unbounded priority inversion from intermediate-priority tasks (higher than T1's but lower than T2's). The typical programming style to deal with this issue is to assign to each server task a priority at least as high as that of any of its callers, which effectively simulates the Priority Ceiling Emulation policy.

6.2   Interactions with Asynchronous Transfer of Control

The Ada model for ATC in code that is executed with mutual exclusion is similar in its basic approach to the RTSJ's – not surprising, since the RTSJ model was directly inspired by Ada's – but differs in detail. The similarity is that protected operations and accept statements are defined to be "abort deferred". The difference is that in Ada the abort deferral is "inherited" by invoked subprograms. In principle, this results in lower latency for RTSJ programs, since asynchronous interruptions are detected earlier. In

---

[9] Recall that a "checked" exception in Java is one for which the throwing method must explicitly provide either a handler or a throws clause.

practice this will likely not be an issue with protected objects, since protected operations are generally short.

7   Comparison

In the area of mutual exclusion it is useful to regard Ada 95 and the RTSJ as each addressing real-time issues that arose in the languages they were based on / extending, Ada 83 and Java, respectively. Ada 83 semantics were not strong enough to avoid unbounded priority inversions, and the "passive task" idiom was widely criticized by users as being inefficient and stylistically clumsy. The protected object / locking policy mechanism was basically a completely new feature, though designed to fit in smoothly with existing Ada syntax. In contrast, the RTSJ introduced an API rather than a new language feature, constraining the Java semantics for synchronized code to help realize real-time behavior. In fact, such an approach was mandated by the Java Community Process, which prohibited syntactic extensions.

7.1   Generality

The RTSJ offers more generality than Ada's protected objects:

- There are no restrictions on what can be executed from synchronized code, whereas an Ada implementation may assume that potentially blocking operations are absent from protected operations.
- Both Priority Inheritance and Priority Ceiling Emulation are provided; Ada defines only the latter policy.

The RTSJ model is highly dynamic. Some objects may be governed by Priority Inheritance, others by Priority Ceiling Inheritance; indeed, the same object may be governed by different monitor control policies at different times. Ada's model is much more static; the object locking policy is established on a per-partition basis. An implementation may (but is not required to) provide locking control at a finer granularity.

In Ada 95, priority ceilings are constant. This is an inconvenient restriction, and one of the proposed revisions for Ada 2005 [15] provides additional generality by allowing a ceiling to be modified as a protected action on the affected object.

Both the RTSJ and Ada are extensible: the RTSJ through an API (subclassing MonitorControl) and Ada through pragmas.

Ada offers more generality in the area of volatile / atomic data, for example by allowing array components to be so specified and also by allowing whole arrays and records to be marked as volatile.

7.2   Software Engineering

Ada's approach enforces encapsulation: accesses to protected data are only permitted inside the implementation of protected operations. In contrast, the synchronized mechanism in Java and the RTSJ is independent of the encapsulation facility, and it is certainly possible to have unsynchronized access to an object's data even when all of the methods are synchronized.

The low-level nature of synchronized code and the `wait` / `notify` / `notifyAll` mechanism makes the expression of state-based mutual exclusion rather error prone in Java and thus also in the RTSJ. Ada's protected object/type model is a more reliable basis for mutual exclusion, with state notification automatic in the entry barrier evaluation semantics.

A drawback to Ada is that the error of executing a potentially blocking operation from protected code is a bounded error, not guaranteed to be caught at either compile time or run time. The looseness of the language standard thus results in implementation-dependent effects, although restricted profiles for high-integrity systems define deterministic behavior. For example, the Ravenscar profile [16] requires that `Program_Error` be raised.

A portability issue in the RTSJ is that Priority Ceiling Emulation is an optional feature.

7.3   Management of Priority Inversion

Both the RTSJ and Ada deal effectively with Priority Inversion, although some subtleties arise in both approaches. In the case of the RTSJ, an interaction between a `NoHeapRealtimeThread` and a heap-using thread attempting to synchronize on a shared object can result in GC-induced latencies for `NoHeapRealtimeThreads`. Further, the provision of both Priority Inheritance and Priority Ceiling Emulation, with specific semantics on their interactions, is an ambitious undertaking; some rules (for example the definition of priority inheritance semantics for priority ceiling emulation locks under some circumstances) may seem surprising. In Ada, the uses of server tasks may lead to priority inversion for callers unless a specific programming style is used (assigning high priorities to servers).

7.4   Efficiency

Comparing the performance of a specific feature in different languages is a challenge, since it is difficult to separate the implementation of that feature from other elements. Nevertheless it is possible to offer a qualitative analysis based on the anticipated runtime cost of the features and the practicality of optimizations.

Several factors give an efficiency advantage to Ada:

– Its static (per partition) approach to locking policies
– Its potential for lock-free priority ceiling emulation
– Its ability to specify that array components are atomically accessible
– Its efficiency in accessing protected data, which are always declared in protected specifications rather than bodies and thus can be referenced without a level of indirection

The much more dynamic Java model makes optimizations difficult, as evidenced by the problems in trying to capture lock-free priority ceiling emulation.

8   Conclusions

Both Ada and the RTSJ can be regarded as solving the underlying issues with mutual exclusion: arranging safe accesses, providing well defined semantics, and allowing priority inversion management and predictable performance. They achieve these goals rather differently, however, with both languages consistent with their respective underlying philosophies. Ada, especially through its protected type mechanism, offers encapsulation, freedom from certain kinds of deadlock, and the opportunity for efficient implementation; it achieves these at the expense of generality. The RTSJ trades off in the other direction. It reflects Java's highly dynamic nature by providing complete flexibility (for example, dynamic replacement of monitor control policies). On the other hand, optimization will likely be more difficult. Further, the low-level nature of the RTSJ approach (defined in terms of lock acquisition and release) comes somewhat at the expense of program understandability.

Interestingly, both the RTSJ and Ada approaches to mutual exclusion have benefited from "cross fertilization". This is perhaps more evident in the case of the RTSJ design, which has directly borrowed some Ada ideas such as abort deferral in synchronized code. Also, the success of the Priority Ceiling Emulation policy in Ada was one of the reasons that it has been included in the RTSJ. The influence in the other direction has been more subtle, but several facilities proposed for Ada 2005 (such as dynamic ceiling priorities) may be due to the realization that flexibility and generality are often important in real-time systems, a fact that is one of the underpinnings of the RTSJ.

Acknowledgements

Anonymous referees provided many useful suggestions that helped improve this paper. I am also grateful to my colleagues on the RTSJ Technical Interpretations Committee for their many stimulating discussions of priority inversion management issues in the RTSJ: Rudy Belliardi, Greg Bollella, Peter Dibble, David Holmes, Doug Locke, and Andy Wellings.

References

1. S.T. Taft, R.A.Duff, R.L. Brukardt, and E. Ploedereder; *Consolidated Ada Reference Manual, Language and Standard Libraries, International Standard ISO/IEC 8652/1995(E) with Technical Corrigendum 1*; Springer LNCS 2219; 2000
2. Java Community Process; *JSR-001: Real-Time Specification for Java*; March 2004; www.jcp.org/en/jsr/detail?id=1
3. G. Bollella, J. Gosling, B. Brosgol, P. Dibble, S. Furr, D. Hardin, and M. Turnbull; *The Real-Time Specification for Java*, Addison-Wesley, 2000
4. J. Gosling, B. Joy, G. Steele, G. Bracha; *The Java Language Specification (2nd ed.)*; Addison Wesley, 2000
5. B. Brosgol; *A Comparison of the Concurrency and Real-Time Features of Ada 95 and Java*; Ada UK Conference; Bristol, UK; 1998.
6. S. Oaks and H. Wong; *Java Threads (3rd Edition)*; O'Reilly, 2004.

7. A. Wellings; *Concurrent and Real-Time Programming in Java*; John Wiley & Sons; 2004.
8. Java Community Process; *JSR-133: Java Memory Model and Thread Specification*; March 2004; www.jcp.org/aboutJava/communityprocess/review/jsr133/
9. P. Brinch Hansen; "Java's Insecure Parallelism"; *ACM SIGPLAN Notices*, V.34(4), April 1999.
10. Java Community Process; *JSR-166: Java Concurrency Utilities*; December 2003; www.jcp.org/aboutJava/communityprocess/review/jsr166/
11. L. Sha, R. Rajkumar, and J. Lehoczky; "Priority Inheritance Protocols: An Approach to Real-Time Synchronization", *IEEE Transaction on Computers*; Vol.39, pp.1175-1185; 1990.
12. A. Wellings and A. Burns; Informal communication; December 2004.
13. B. Brosgol and A. Wellings; "A Comparison of the Asynchronous Transfer of Control Facilities in Ada and the Real-Time Specification for Java", *Proc. Ada Europe 2003*, June 2003, Toulouse, France.
14. Intermetrics, Inc.; *Ada 95 Rationale*; January 1995.
15. ISO/IEC JTC1 / SC22 / WG9; *AI-327, Dynamic Ceiling Priorities*; November 2004; www.ada-auth.org/cgi-bin/cvsweb.cgi/AIs/AI-00327.TXT?rev=1.13
16. A. Burns; "The Ravenscar Profile", *Ada Letters*, XIX (4), pp.49-52, 1999.

Smart Certification of Mixed Criticality Systems

Peter Amey, Rod Chapman, and Neil White

Praxis High Integrity Systems, 20 Manvers St., Bath BA1 1PX, UK
{peter.amey, rod.chapman, neil.white}@praxis-his.com

Abstract. High integrity applications, such as those performing safety or security critical functions, are usually built to conform to standards such RTCA DO-
178B [1] or UK Def Stan 00-55 [2]. Typically such standards define ascending
levels of criticality each of which requires a different and increasingly onerous
level of verification. It is very common to find that real systems contain code of
multiple criticality levels. For example, a critical control system may generate
a non-critical usage log. Unless segregation can be demonstrated to a very high
degree of confidence, there is usually no alternative to verifying all the software
components to the standard required by the most critical element, leading to an
increase in overall cost. This paper describes the novel use of static analysis to
provide a robust segregation of differing criticality levels, thus allowing appropriate verification techniques to be applied at the subprogram level. We call this
fine-grained matching of verification level to subprogram criticality *smart certification*.

1   Introduction

Many systems are composed of mixed criticality code. A military system being developed to DEF-STAN 00-55 [2] may contain SIL0, SIL2 and a small amount of SIL4
code. A civil aviation application being developed to EUROCAE ED12B/DO-178B [1]
may contain Level C and Level A code. The same applies to almost any system you
pick, compliant with almost any standard, from any sector of industry. Even if your application is not business-, mission- or safety-critical, there are almost certainly functions
that are considered "core", and thus worthy of a more rigorous validation phase.

The premise behind Smart Certification is to allow a mathematically rigorous partitioning of the source code into the different criticalities within an application. Criticalities could mean SIL level, DO-178B level, or a user-defined distinction between core
and non-core.

This partitioning, which operates at a subprogram granularity, allows verification
and validation techniques to be focused on specific areas, rather than spread over large
swathes of the system. For example, EUROCAE ED12B/DO-178B sets the goal of
full MCDC (Multiple Condition Multiple Decision) coverage for all Level A code. By
partitioning the code we can ensure we do not spend time and money achieving this
goal for non-Level A subprograms.

This focussed approach reduces costs and development time without impacting code
quality or integrity.

T. Vardanega and A. Wellings (Eds.): Ada-Europe 2005, LNCS 3555, pp. 144–155, 2005.

2   Requirements for Segregation

Showing that two software components, running on the same processor, in shared memory space, do not interfere with one another is a non-trivial task. The principal causes of interference between two software components are as follows:

- unintended data and information flow from one component to another;
- misbehaviour by one component, such as a writing outside an array boundary, such that data or code used by the other component is corrupted;
- preventing one component from running because the other has halted the processor by, for example, dividing by zero;
- resource hogging by one component such as consumption of all free memory or all available clock cycles; and,
- in concurrent systems, one component blocking the timely scheduling of another.

Furthermore, demonstrating that there are no malign effects present by use of source code static analysis requires an unambiguous mapping from source code to its compiled behaviour.

3   The Role of SPARK

SPARK [3, 4] is an annotated subset of Ada with some specific properties that are designed to make static analysis both deep and fast. The annotations take the form of special comments which are ignored by an Ada compiler but have semantic meaning for SPARK's support tool, the SPARK Examiner.

For the purposes of this paper, the key properties of SPARK are:

Lack of Ambiguity. The language rules of SPARK, enhanced by its annotations, ensure that a source text can only be interpreted in one way by a legal Ada compiler. Compiler implementation freedoms such as sub-expression evaluation order, cannot affect the way object code generated from a SPARK source behaves. For example, a complete detection of parameter and global variable aliasing ensures that SPARK parameters have pass-by-copy semantics even if the compiler actually passes them by reference.

Bounded Resources. SPARK language rules prohibit both direct and indirect recursion. They also prevent direct use of dynamically allocated heap memory and avoid constructs, such as functions returning unconstrained arrays, where implicit heap use may be required. The result of these rules is that it is possible to know statically, prior to execution, what the worst case memory usage for a SPARK program will be.

Freedom from Run-Time Exceptions. SPARK programs are amenable to proof-based forms of formal verification. The Examiner toolset includes provisions for the automatic generation of proof obligations that correspond to each predefined run-time exception check defined by the Ada language. Discharging these proof obligations is sufficient to guarantee that the associated exception can never be raised. The process is described in [5].

Well-Behaved Concurrency. SPARK has recently been extended to include a subset of Ada 95 concurrency constructs compatible with the Ravenscar profile, see [6]. A combination of language rules and additional annotations allows the static elimination of exceptional behaviour defined by the Ravenscar profile. A RavenSPARK program can therefore be shown to be free from problems of blocking or priority inversion.

Facilitates Information Flow Analysis. Many of SPARK's language rule were motivated by the desire to provide an analytical framework in which mathematically rigorous data and information flow analyses can be conducted. The principles of such analyses are described in the seminal ACM paper [7]. Flow analysis is important for two reasons:

1. Elimination of undefined variable values by data flow analysis is an essential step in providing a sound environment for program proof. Clearly such proofs are complicated if we have to allow for unknown and potentially invalid data items.
2. Information flow analysis, which establishes the *influence* of variability of one data item on another, provides the main foundation on which we can build segregation arguments.

We can see that these properties have a significant bearing on the requirements for segregation described in Section 2.

Lack of ambiguity is a straightforward prerequisite for any reliance on source code static analysis. We cannot *trust* such analysis if there is the possibility that our analysis tool and compiler may be making different interpretations of the source code. (We may of course still *use* static analysis in such circumstances but only in the hope of finding some errors rather than proving their absence).

Bounded resource usage is a necessary precondition for ensuring that low-criticality code cannot prevent operation of high-criticality code by, for example, consuming all the system's memory. There remains an outstanding issue here, proof of loop termination, which is discussed in Section 5.3.

The ability, by static means, to prove that a SPARK program will never raise a predefined exception provides the support necessary to ensure that low-criticality code cannot corrupt the memory space or unexpectedly halt processing.

Well-behaved, Ravenscar-compliant, concurrency ensures that critical tasks are not blocked by less critical ones.

That leaves only the flow of data and information from one subprogram to another as a potential source of influence of less critical on more critical code. Our final SPARK property, a detailed and precise data and information flow analysis, provides a starting point for addressing this remaining source of potential corruption. The rest of this paper is concerned with improved methods for showing freedom from incorrect data coupling between units.

4   Case Studies

Before we go on to address incorrect data coupling we present two historical case studies. These are real systems where software segregation has been demonstrated manually. Both systems would have benefited from the tool-supported segregation we are describing.

4.1   SHOLIS

The SHOLIS system, described in [8], provides safety-critical guidance on the safe operating of ship-borne helicopters. In particular, it defines safe operating envelopes for prevailing wind conditions and sea states. SHOLIS was the first project ever to attempt to meet the requirements of UK Defence Standard 00-55 [2] which placed a significant emphasis on formal methods and program proof.

A novel aspect of the SHOLIS implementation was the mixing of different criticality levels of software in a single memory space and running on a single processor. The primary application was fully safety critical, SIL 4 in 00-55 terms, but other software components concerned with data logging for example, were much less critical. The Standard requires the generation of a safety case and as part of this, a rigorous justification for the mixing of SIL level was required.

We did a *manual* allocation of criticality to package-level state, and then did a *manual* verification of the derives annotation on every procedure to show that that no lower-criticality state was used to update higher-criticality state. Obviously this justification needs to be laboriously maintained for every small code change.

4.2   Engine Monitoring Unit

The Engine Monitoring Unit (EMU) is a health monitoring system for a large civil jet engine. The system was developed to DO-178B [1], with some system functions assessed to be Level C, and the remaining functionality assessed to be Level E.

The application software was a multi-tasked SPARK95 program running on the GreenHills INTEGRITY real-time operating system. The INTEGRITY RTOS is designed for use in mission-critical embedded systems. Task groups run in hardware isolated memory spaces to minimise the impact of errors, and resource requirements can be analysed to guarantee availability. Extra INTEGRITY modules build on the basic RTOS functionality, providing Ethernet drivers, file systems, and much more. The core INTEGRITY RTOS can be certified to DO-178B Level A, but some of the additional INTEGRITY modules (for example, the Ethernet driver) can only be certified to lower levels.

In project EMU, the option to build and certify the entire system to DO-178B Level C - the highest common denominator - was not available. The software implementing one of the Level E functions used an INTEGRITY module which could only be certified to Level E. A re-implementation of the module in question was prohibitively expensive.

The solution was to partition the functionality so that individual tasks were either level C or Level E. No task had mixed level functionality. Communication between tasks was only allowed via semaphore protected, uni-directional shared data. The term uni-directional is simply used to mean that one task produced data, and one task consumed the data. This enabled us to use SPARK information flow to show that no level E task could influence a level C task. We were then able to certify the code for distinct tasks to the level applicable for that task. The troublesome Level E module, used only by a Level E task, was separated from all the Level C code.

The disadvantage of this design-time architecture constraint was that we ended up with a task structure that was not optimal and not particularly intuitive. This caused an increase in implementation cost, and looms over all future maintenance work. (Since certification there have been zero reported application software faults, but we assume that somebody will want to maintain the software at some point in the future.)

Using the techniques described in this paper, we would not have required the architecture constraint, and would have been in a position to produce a system with a more optimal assignment of system functionality to tasks. We would also have reduced implementation costs, and been able to provide an easily repeatable, tool supported argument of the partitioning.

5   Extensions to SPARK

From the case studies it is clear that information flow analysis provides an approach to demonstrating code segregation but that better support is required to both simplify and automate the arguments used so as to make them easily repeatable.

5.1   Foundation Work

The first steps to exploiting information flow analysis to show separation of concerns exploits the SPARK *own variable* annotation. An own variable annotation provides a name for one or more items of static, package-level data or for a point where the program interacts with its external environment. The rationale for and use of own variables is described in [9]. The foundation work for the developments described in this paper is to allocate criticality levels to each own variable by means of a new annotation. Information flow analysis is then used to show that no critical output is dependent on a non-critical input or a non-critical intermediate state variable. The process is described fully in [10] and is applicable to both safety and security critical applications.

Clearly this approach moves us closer to our goal of demonstrable separation of criticality levels at the subprogram level but does not get us there for reasons described in the next section.

5.2   New Developments

The SPARK language extensions outlined in the previous section allow us to ensure that critical outputs are not tainted by untrusted data; however, they are not sufficient to identify each critical code *statement sequence*. Further extensions to the analysis are needed because of the parameterisation of subprograms. Where a subprogram directly updates an own variable of a particular criticality then it is clear that that subprogram is at least as critical as the data it is processing. Such global dependencies are revealed by SPARK annotations.

Consider a trivial example, a package that maintains a highly critical counter variable.

```
package Counter
--# own State (Integrity => SIL4);
--# initializes State;
is
    procedure Increment;
    --# global in out State;
    --# derives State from State;

    function Read return Integer;
    --# global in State;
end Counter;
```

From the annotation of procedure Increment it is clear that it *updates* own variable State which is marked as being of integrity level "SIL4" (a suitably-defined numeric constant). From this we can conclude that procedure Increment must be considered a SIL4 subprogram and verified in a manner appropriate to that level.

Note that there is no similar assumption to be made about function Read. Although this *references* own variable State that does not impose any criticality considerations on it; it is the way in which the function is *used* that matters. For example, if we only called Read in order to pass the current counter value to some low-level data logging routine then the integrity of the function would not be important.

Things are less clear, however, when we consider the following implementation.

```
package body Counter
is
    State : Integer := 0;

    procedure Inc (X : in out Integer)
    --# derives X from X;
    is
    begin
       X := X + 1;
    end Inc;

    procedure Increment
    is
    begin
       Inc (State);
    end Increment;

    function Read return Integer
    is
    begin
       return State;
    end Read;
end Counter;
```

Here the annotations give us no indication that local procedure `Inc` is being used to update the critical data item `Counter.State` and should therefore be regarded as critical code.

We could certainly determine the criticality of such data flows given a complete program from which we could determine the whole call tree and hence know the use to which each subprogram was being put. However, an important SPARK principle is the desire to be able to analyse programs incrementally before they are complete. Interactive analysis during development is a prime means by which SPARK has been shown to both improve quality *and* reduce cost. We can achieve the goal of detecting critical code segments while still doing partial program analysis by annotating subprograms with the level of data they are permitted to handle and performing an analysis to detect cases where there is a mismatch between subprogram and data criticality levels.

Mathematical Details

In this section we will look at the mathematical model which underpins both the rigorous partition, and the static analysis which enforces the partition. Each subprogram, S, is annotated with its proposed level of criticality, S_C. This is the developer stating the level of criticality that the subprogram will be developed to. Every own variable, G, already has an associated criticality, G_C. By analysing the global and derives annotations for S we can calculate S's highest criticality exported own variable, which we denote S_{GC}. Condition 1 follows immediately.

Condition 1. *We need $S_{GC} \leq S_C$ for a useful subprogram.*

If condition 1 is violated, so if S_{GC} is larger than S_C, then we have a subprogram directly or in-directly updating an item of state with a higher criticality. This is not allowed. Now our subprogram is internally consistent, we can look at calls to S.

Condition 2. *Every call to S from a distinct[1] subprogram D must satisfy $S_{GC} \leq D_C$.*

To violate condition 2 would allow a lower criticality subprogram to indirectly update a higher criticality state element. Note that a low criticality subprogram is not banned from calling a higher criticality subprogram[2].

As we saw in the earlier example, actual parameters used in calls to S are a complication. In a call to S list the actual parameters for `out` and `in out` formal parameters as $P^1, P^2, \ldots P^n$. These each have a criticality P_C^i.

Condition 3. *For each call to S, we require $\forall i \in 1..n \cdot P_C^i \leq S_C$.*

To violate condition 3 would allow S to update a higher integrity state element via a parameter[3].

---

[1] Since SPARK does not allow recursion, D must be distinct from S.

[2] For a well formed SPARK program Condition 2 actually follows from Condition 1. If D calls S, then D must export own variables of at least the same criticality as S, so $S_{GC} \leq D_{GC} \leq D_C$. We state the condition separately for clarity.

[3] The `in` parameters must be of suitable criticality for the state they are used to derive. This is handled by the existing functionality described in section 5.1 and [10].

Functions in SPARK are pure, so they update no global data and have only in parameters. This means that the criticality of a function is bounded only by its calling environment. Consider a call to function F, where the return result is assigned to a variable R of criticality R_C.

Condition 4. *For each call to F, we require $R_C \leq F_C$.*

In other words, a function must be at least as critical as the most critical state item ever used to capture the return value.

The last question we must address is the criticality of local variables. This is essential if we are to be able to check the validity of our subprogram calls. Each local variable is used to derive one or more own variables, otherwise the local variable is ineffective[4]. Local variables inherit the criticality of the *most* critical own variable they are used to derive. So for a local variable L, used to derive own variables $G^1, G^2, \ldots G^n$, we have $L_C = max\{\forall i \in 1..n \cdot G_C^i\}$. This concludes our look at the underlying mathematical model.

In the previous example, Increment must be annotated with a criticality of *at least* SIL4 because it exports the global State, which is SIL4 (See condition 1). Inc exports no globals, so condition 1 gives us no lower bound for the criticality, allowing any subprogram to call Inc. Increment calls Inc with a SIL4 actual parameter for X. If Inc is annotated as anything less than SIL4, then the actual parameter is more critical than the called routine, which is a violation of condition 3. Inc can only be legally annotated as SIL4. Note that we could still call Inc from a lower SIL subprogram with a lower SIL parameter. The criticality of the function Read has no lower bound, and the upper bound cannot be deduced in isolation. (See condition 4.)

The only extension to the SPARK language is an annotation to allow a specific subprogram to be given a criticality by the developer. We propose the following notation, which nicely complements the notation for state criticality:

```
package Counter
--# own State (Integrity => SIL4);
--# initializes State;
is
   procedure Increment;
   --# global in out State;
   --# derives State from State;
   --# declare Integrity => SIL4;

   function Read return Integer;
   --# global in State;
   --# declare Integrity => SIL2;
end Counter;
```

---

[4] The Examiner will identify any ineffective variables and issue suitable warnings.

5.3   Possible Future Work

There is a single remaining way in which interference can occur: the non-termination of a loop in non-critical code such that execution of critical code is blocked. The proof facilities of the SPARK Examiner currently allow *partial proof*, ie a proof the the code is correct *if it terminates*. Work is underway to extend the proof model to include a proof of loop termination[11].

In the interim, one option is to force a proof of loop termination through the proof of absence of run-time errors. We can declare a fresh numeric variable, initialise it, and then increment it on each trip round the loop. In order to show the variable does not exceed its upper bound, we are forced to construct a rigorous argument about the maximum number of times the loop can iterate.

6   Smart Certification Example

This section presents an example, loosely based on real life, showing the detection of the misuse of a subprogram above its authorised criticality level. The example centres around a brake-by-wire system. First we give a specification for package Brake.

```
package Brake
--# own in     Pedal                (Integrity => SIL4);
--#        out HydraulicPressure (Integrity => SIL4);
is
   type BrakeLevel is range 0 .. 100;

   procedure Operate(Amount : out BrakeLevel);
   --# global HydraulicPressure, Pedal;
   --# derives HydraulicPressure, Amount from Pedal;
   --# declare Integrity => SIL4;
end Brake;
```

The procedure Operate reads the variable Pedal to ascertain the users current braking request. The operation updates HydraulicPressure accordingly, and returns the current retardation (as a percentage of the maximum retardation available) to the calling environment. Note that both state items and the procedure are all annotated as SIL4 state. We omit the body of package Brake. The package Log is a simple non-critical record of the vehicle's braking history.

```
package Log
--# own Data (Integrity => SIL0);
--# initializes Data;
is
   procedure Enter(IsBraking : in Boolean);
   --# global Data;
   --# derives Data from Data, IsBraking;
   --# declare Integrity => SIL0;
end Log;
```

```
package body Log
--# own Data is Pointer, Queue;
--  Both SIL0, inherited from abstract own.
is
   type HistoryIndex is mod 256;
   type History is array(HistoryIndex) of Boolean;

   Pointer : HistoryIndex := 0;
   Queue   : History      := History'(others => False);

   procedure Enter(IsBraking : in Boolean);
   --# global Pointer, Queue;
   --# derives Queue    from Queue, Pointer, IsBraking &
   --#         Pointer from Pointer;
   --  No new SIL declaration allowed.
   is
   begin
      Queue(Pointer) := IsBraking;
      Pointer := Pointer + 1;
   end Enter;
end Log;
```

We simply build up an buffer of Booleans to indicate if we were breaking at a particular time. The buffer is circular, with new overwriting old as required. All we need now is a controlling procedure to pull everything together.

```
with Brake, Log;
use type Brake.BrakeLevel;
--# inherit Brake, Log;
package Controller
is
   procedure Run;
   --# global Brake.Pedal, Brake.HydraulicPressure, Log.Data;
   --# derives Brake.HydraulicPressure from Brake.Pedal &
   --#         Log.Data                from Log.Data, Brake.Pedal;
   --# declare Integrity => SIL4;
end Controller;

package body Controller
is
   procedure Run
   is
      LogIt   : constant Brake.BrakeLevel := 20;
      CurrentAmount : Brake.BrakeLevel;
   begin
      Brake.Operate(CurrentAmount);
      Log.Enter(CurrentAmount > LogIt);
   end Run;
end Controller;
```

`Controller.Run` is called at a suitable frequency by the overall vehicle software scheduler (not shown). The procedure `Run` is SIL4 because it calls into `Brake` and updates SIL4 state. Just as we finish, we get a change in requirements - we need a stop light. Consider the specification of package `Lamp`.

```
package Lamp
--# own out Stop (Integrity => SIL3);
is
   procedure Light(On : in Boolean);
   --# global Stop;
   --# derives Stop from On;
   --# declare Integrity => SIL3;
end Lamp;
```

All we need to decide is how to call `Lamp.Light`. The obvious location is the body of `Log.Enter`, as this has the Boolean parameter `IsBraking` which can be used in the call to `Lamp.Light`. If we do this, the Examiner immediately points out that any caller of `Lamp.Light` must be SIL3. `Log.Enter` is only SIL0. We need to increase the criticality of the `Log.Enter` procedure to SIL3 before the system can be considered sound. But the `Log` package is *not* critical code. We are corrupting our design. A preferable solution is to modify the procedure `Controller.Run`.

```
procedure Run
is
   LogIt   : constant Brake.BrakeLevel := 20;
   LampOn  : constant Brake.BrakeLevel := 20;
   CurrentAmount : Brake.BrakeLevel;
begin
   Brake.Operate(CurrentAmount);
   Lamp.Light(CurrentAmount > LampOn);
   Log.Enter(CurrentAmount > LogIt);
end Run;
```

This option is sound, as `Run` is SIL4 already. Furthermore, this option provides greater future proofing as the "lamp on" and "log it" conditions are de-coupled. We could in future choose to log braking at a different retardation percentage than that which triggers the lamp.

This example is small, and the punch line can be seen coming from a significant distance, but it provides an indication of how the process works. With 150 packages, 10 levels of subprogram calling, and 5 distinct criticality levels, it become a distinctly non-trivial activity to "see the punch line coming".

7   Conclusions

We have shown that a simple static analysis extension to the SPARK Examiner allows the confident development of mixed criticality code in a cost effective manner. With the mathematically rigorous partitioning of criticalities we can construct simple, tool-supported, arguments about the scope of required certification. By applying verification and validation techniques to specific areas we reduce both development cost and development time without impacting quality.

During the maintenance phase we can easily see the impact of changes, and construct equally simple arguments about the scope of re-certification. This allows us to minimise the cost of re-certification by doing only what is necessary.

This approach is equally suitable for security critical systems. The rigorous partitioning allows us to show that the data we wish to remain secure is not used to derive insecure outputs. Furthermore, we can easily see the sequences of code that are manipulating secure data.

References

1. *RTCA-EUROCAE: Software Considerations in Airborne Systems and Equipment Certification*. DO-178B/ED-12B. 1992.
2. Ministry of Defence: *Requirements for Safety Related Software in Defence Equipment, Defence Standard 00-55*. August 1997.
3. Barnes, John: *High Integrity Software - the SPARK Approach to Safety and Security*. Addison Wesley Longman, ISBN 0-321-13616-0. 2003.
4. Finnie, Gavin et al: *SPARK 95 - The SPADE Ada 95 Kernel — Edition 3.1*. 2002, Praxis Critical Systems[5].
5. Chapman, Rod; Amey, Peter: *Industrial Strength Exception Freedom*. Proceedings of ACM SIGAda 2002[6].
6. Amey, Peter: *High Integrity Ravenscar*. Proceedings of Reliable Software Technologies - Ada Europe 2003. Lecture Notes in Computer Science Volume 2655[6].
7. Bergeretti, Jean-Francois; Carré, Bernard: *Information-flow and data-flow analysis of while-programs*. ACM Transactions on Programming Languages and Systems 1985[5], pp37-61.
8. King, Steve; Hammond, Jonathan; Chapman, Rod; Pryor, Andy: *Is Proof More Cost Effective Than Testing?*. IEEE Transactions on Software Engineering Vol 26, No 8, August 2000, pp 675-686[6].
9. Amey, Peter: *A Language for Systems not just Software*. Proceedings of ACM SIGAda 2001[6].
10. Chapman, Rod; Hilton, Adrian: *Enforcing Security and Safety Models with an Information Flow Analysis Tool*. Proceedings of ACM SIGAda 2004.
11. Hammond, Jonathan: *Specification of SPARK Total Correctness Proofs*. Praxis HIS, S.P0468.41.5. October 2004.

---

[5] Also available from Praxis High Integrity Systems.

[6] Also downloadable from www.sparkada.com

Non-intrusive System Level Fault-Tolerance

Kristina Lundqvist, Jayakanth Srinivasan, and Sébastien Gorelov

Embedded Systems Laboratory, Department of Aeronautics and Astronautics,
Massachusetts Institute of Technology, Cambridge, MA 02139
{kristina, jksrini, gorelov}@mit.edu

Abstract. High-integrity embedded systems operate in multiple modes, in order to ensure system availability in the face of faults. Unanticipated state-dependent faults that remain in software after system design and development behave like hardware transient faults: they appear, do the damage and disappear. The conventional approach used for handling task overruns caused by transient faults is to use a single recovery task that implements minimal functionality. This approach provides limited availability and should be used as a last resort in order to keep the system online. Traditional fault detection approaches are often intrusive in that they consume processor resources in order to monitor system behavior. This paper presents a novel approach for fault-monitoring by leveraging the Ravenscar profile, model-checking and a system-on-chip implementation of both the kernel and an execution time monitor. System fault-tolerance is provided through a hierarchical set of operational modes that are based on timing behavior violations of individual tasks within the application. The approach is illustrated through a simple case study of a generic navigation system.

1 Introduction

Embedded systems are becoming permeating every facet of our daily lives, ranging from the control of toasters to managing complex flight control operations. A crucial segment of the embedded systems market addresses the needs of high-integrity systems, i.e., systems whose incorrect operation leads to significant losses in monetary terms, in terms of human lives or a combination thereof. High-integrity embedded real-time systems have to address the requirements imposed by the need for high-integrity as well as to satisfy the real-time nature of the system. By real-time, we mean the need to operate within the temporal constraints on system behavior. There are a number of well proven approaches for developing predictable real-time systems, in which the correctness of temporal behavior is assured in a systematic manner [11, 12]. A good example is fixed priority scheduling, which assumes that the system is formed by a fixed-set of tasks that provide system capabilities through periodic/aperiodic execution. This approach works extremely well when the system operates in a single mode, however, the class of systems, Figure 1., addressed in this paper display multi-moded behavior i.e. the system has a set of modes that involve overlapping sets of tasks providing different capabilities depending on the current state of the system, and the environment in which the system operates.

T. Vardanega and A. Wellings (Eds.): Ada-Europe 2005, LNCS 3555, pp. 156–166, 2005.

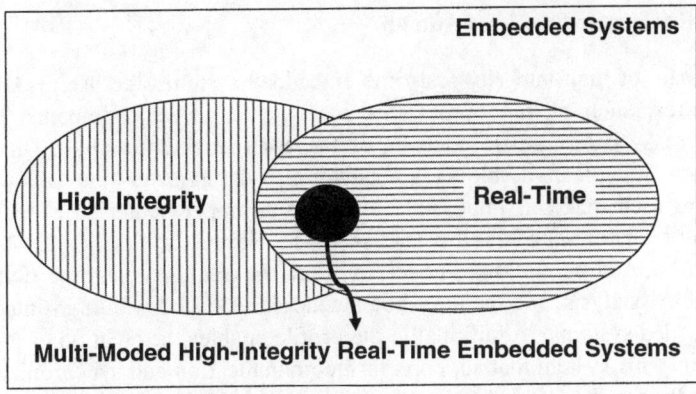

Fig. 1. Embedded Systems Problem Space

These systems undergo significant verification and validation activities prior to fielding. However, there are unanticipated state-dependent faults that remain in operational software after system design and development. These faults behave like hardware transient faults: they appear, do the damage and disappear [17]. In the context of real-time systems, the most visible manifestation of this class of faults is tasks missing their deadlines either through overruns or underruns. A multi-moded high-integrity real-time embedded system has to have the ability to detect the violation of timing bounds, and transition to the appropriate operational mode, while retaining predictable behavior and providing continued service. This paper presents a novel approach that leverages formal methods, System-on-chip design and the Ravenscar profile [2] to provide non-intrusive system level fault-tolerance.

The remainder of the paper is organized as follows: The *Technology* section discusses the three key areas that enable our approach for non-intrusive monitoring, and allow mode-transitions to provide continued service when tasks violate their timing bounds; the section on *Approach* provides an overview of the modeling, analysis and implementation adopted in this paper; the *Gurkh Generic Navigation System* section illustrates the approach using a simple case study of a navigation system; the *Conclusions* section documents the limitations of the current approach and charts the path forward in terms of future work.

2 Technology

Three key technologies have enabled us to reconsider and challenge the conventional approach of handling timing overruns of tasks. The first is the Ravenscar Profile [2, 4], a subset of the Ada 95 tasking model, which allows for analyzable deterministic concurrent tasking. The second is the emergence of low-cost system-on-chip technologies that contain embedded processors and Field-Programmable Gate Arrays (FPGAs). The third is the successful development and use of model-checking tools, e.g., UPPAAL [6], to automate the formal verification.

2.1 The Ravenscar Profile of Ada 95

In the domain of high-integrity real-time embedded systems, the use of Ada 83 run-time features, such as the rendezvous mechanism, select statements, and abort statement make deterministic analysis of the application infeasible [2]. The non-determinism and potentially blocking behavior of tasking or run-time calls when these features are used makes it impossible to derive an upper bound on execution time, which is critical for schedulability analysis. The Ravenscar Profile [2, 4] defines a subset of the Ada 95 tasking model to meet the requirements for determinism, schedulability analysis, and memory-boundedness associated with high-integrity real-time embedded systems. Additionally, the profile enables the creation of a small and efficient run-time system that supports task communication and synchronization. The Ravenscar Profile mandates the use of a static task set in the system and only allows inter-task communication to occur via protected objects. A static task set implies that the system has a fixed number of tasks at all time, hence the tasks cannot be created dynamically or terminate. Tasks have a single invocation event, but can have potentially unbounded number of invocations. Task invocations can either be time-triggered (tasks executing in response to a time event, such as delays) or event-triggered (executing in response to an event external to tasks). Task scheduling is carried out in a pre-emptive highest priority first manner. These restrictions imposed by the Ravenscar Profile allow systems to be analyzed for both functional and timing behavior.

2.2 Xilinx Virtex II Pro Platform

The Xilinx Virtex II Pro platform [18] contains an embedded PowerPC (PPC) core and an FPGA. The complete system architecture is shown in Figure 2. The software component of the system is implemented as a set of Ada 95 tasks that run on the PPC. A hardware implemented runtime kernel called RavenHaRT provides inter-task communication and scheduling services.

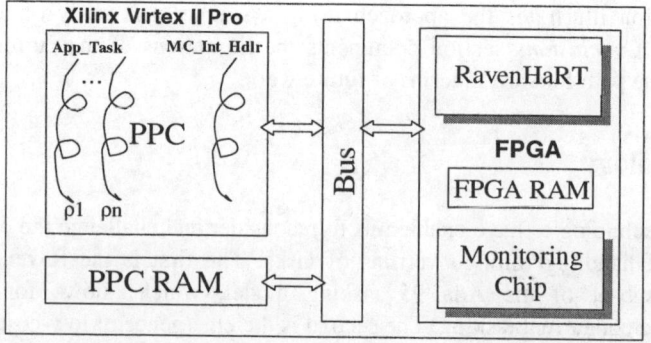

Fig. 2. System Architecture

RavenHaRT [16] is a formally verified, deterministic run-time system based on the Ravenscar Profile. The kernel specification enables the user to create a custom run-time system that can be synthesized onto the FPGA at the end of system design. The other critical component is the monitoring chip (MC). The MC contains a set of execution timers associated with application tasks, and is synthesized onto the FPGA. The MC monitors the timing behavior based on information from RavenHaRT, and informs RavenHaRT when a timing violation is detected.

2.3 Model Checking Using UPPAAL

The UPPAAL model-checking toolkit [4, 6] consists of three main parts: a description language, a simulator and a model checker. The idea behind the tool is to model a system using the graphical user interface and timed automata [1, 8], validate the system by simulation, and finally verify the system that it is correct with respect to a set of properties. UPPAAL uses a non-deterministic guarded command language to describe the system behavior as networks of automata extended with clock and data variables. The simulator is a validation tool, which can be used to examine a set of possible dynamic executions of the system as part of the design process. The model checker uses (directed) state space exploration to cover the dynamic behavior of the system and check invariant and bounded-liveness properties.

3 Approach

The intuitive principle behind implementing fault-tolerance in a system is to increase design robustness by adding redundant resources and the mechanisms necessary to make use of them when needed [10]. Fault-tolerance mechanisms can be broadly partitioned into fault detection and fault handling. Fault detection mechanisms identify the occurrence of the fault and determine when to initiate/trigger a recovery action. The fault handling mechanisms act on the signal provided by the fault detection mechanism to protect the system either by reconfiguration of resources or by transitioning to a safe mode.

Conventionally high-integrity real-time embedded systems are built using cyclic schedulers [4]. A task exceeding its budgeted execution time over a cyclic schedule can be easily detected, and necessary corrective action can be taken. This is carried out by checking if the current action was completed by the task when a minor cycle interrupt occurs. If the action has not been completed, then it is assumed that a task has overrun its budgeted time, and the necessary fault-handling mechanism is adopted. Preemptive multi-tasking schedulers make system design a lot simpler through the use of concurrency, but there are no comparable approaches for detecting and handling execution time overruns [7]. Classical overrun management schemes that use techniques such as dynamic priorities and aborts are not Ravenscar compliant. Work carried out by de la Puente and Zamorano proposes a Ravenscar compliant scheme that allows a supervisory task to detect overruns and preempt the faulty task [5]. Similar work carried out by Harbour et.al, [7], proposes an execution time clock library that can be used to monitor timing behavior of the executing application. Both approaches are constrained by the fact that the monitor itself alters the timing behavior of the total system. The approach proposed in this paper is to carry out non-intrusive fault detection by externally monitoring of execution time behavior of the application software running on the PPC by using a set of hardware implemented execution timers; and carry out fault handling though mode changes of the application, as shown in Figure 3.

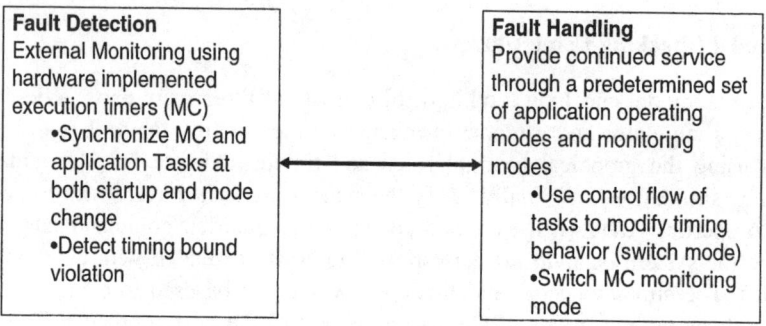

Fig. 3. Overarching Approach for Fault Detection and Handling

3.1 Fault Detection

The timing bounds of each of the application tasks are specified in terms of the worst case execution time (WCET) and the best case execution time (BCET). These bounds are implemented as timers in hardware, and the set of timers associated with the application is referred to as the Monitoring Chip (MC). The MC is implemented on the FPGA along with RavenHaRT as shown in Figure 4.

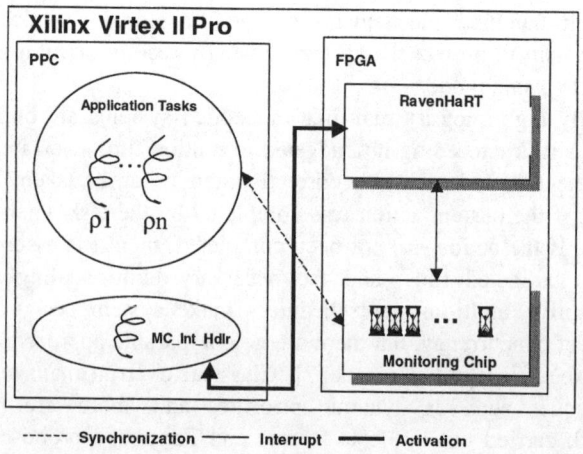

Fig. 4. Fault-Detection Using MC

When a timing bound violation is detected, MC informs RavenHaRT through an interrupt mechanism. The interrupt raised by MC is processed by RavenHaRT, which then activates the MC_Int_Hdlr task in order to switch the application's mode of operation. The timers within the MC are selected based on the application's mode of operation, and the timing bound violated (BCET/WCET). The application tasks on the PPC and the execution timers running in the MC are synchronized by RavenHaRT to ensure that there are no false alarms raised by the MC.

3.2 Mode Change

Real and Crespo [14] identify the four requirements for a successful mode change as schedulability, periodicity, promptness and consistency. Each requirement is addressed in the context of the proposed approach:

- *Schedulability* - In the uniprocessor environment provided by the Xilinx Virtex II Pro, at most one task violating its deadline is detected at any given time hence the mode switch is restricted to changing the control flow of a single task. All other tasks continue to operate in the previous mode. Hence the only task whose deadline changes is the aberrant task. The timing behavior of the application tasks are modeled in UPPAAL for the required operational modes and the schedulability is verified prior to system implementation.
- *Periodicity* –The periodicity requirement is satisfied by the RavenHaRT scheduler, which ensures the activation of periodic tasks.
- *Promptness* – The mode change handler receives the identity of the aberrant task, and the bound (BCET/WCET) that it violated. The mode change is carried out based on the priority of the task, and the impact on dependent tasks.
- *Consistency* – The use of protected objects for inter-task communication ensures that shared resources are used consistently.

Each application task follows the same template as shown in Figure 5. The first instruction that the task executes within the loop is a call to the Check_Mode function to read the MODE protected variable present in the SWITCH protected object. This MODE variable determines the control flow of the application task. The different paths through the program converge before the task delays itself or loops. The Change_Mode procedure of the SWITCH protected object is the only way to change the value of MODE, and is accessed by the MC_Int_Hdlr task to issue a mode change instruction. The MC has a state machine, which determines which set of timers to use in the new operating mode based on the current mode of operation and the bound that was violated. The mode switching mechanism is verified by model-checking the operational modes in UPPAAL to ensure that tasks meet their deadlines under degraded operations.

Switchback capability to nominal mode of operation uses the same functional pieces that operate the switch to the different operating modes. The task violating its

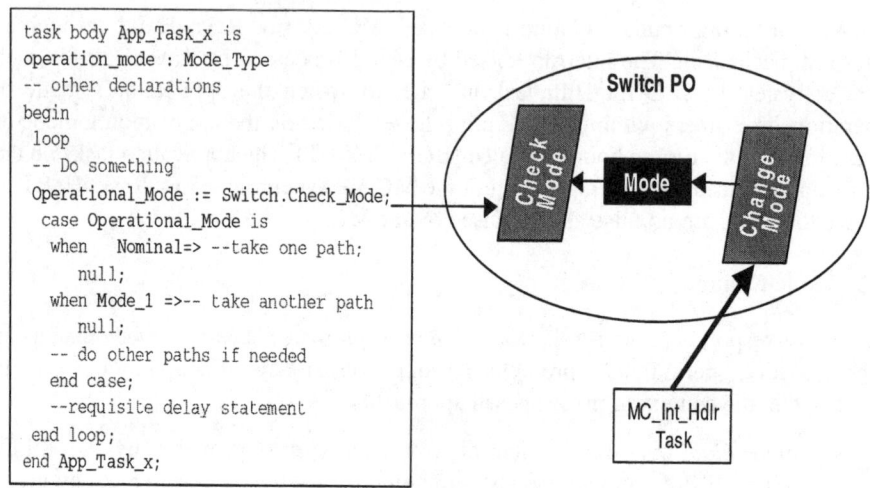

```
task body App_Task_x is
operation_mode : Mode_Type
-- other declarations
begin
 loop
 -- Do something
 Operational_Mode := Switch.Check_Mode;
  case Operational_Mode is
   when  Nominal=> --take one path;
    null;
   when Mode_1 =>-- take another path
    null;
   -- do other paths if needed
   end case;
   --requisite delay statement
 end loop;
end App_Task_x;
```

Fig. 5. Fault-Detection Using MC

bounds continues to run, and the rest of the system is configured to behave as if the faulty task does not exist; i.e., the faulty task is quarantined and the system does not rely on its services. The monitoring chip inspects the timing behavior of the quarantined task. If it runs and communicates with POs nominally then its timing should correspond to the nominal timing. One simple means of quarantining and monitoring task behavior is to modify the timing behavior such that the best case execution time of the quarantined task exceeds the worst case execution time when the task runs nominally, i.e., the MC sets the *BCET'* of the task equal to WCET (where the ' symbol indicates quarantined task). The MC detects the restoration of normal services if *BCET'* is now violated.

4   Gurkh Generic Navigation System

The Gurkh Generic Navigation System (GGNS) models the core real-time software architecture of a generic guidance and navigation system. The model provides enough functional complexity to be challenging and is small enough for the MC to be synthesized on the FPGA along with the hardware implemented run-time kernel. The GGNS model computes navigation information, such as position, velocity and acceleration, based on two sensors: the Inertial Measurement Unit (IMU) and the Global Positioning System (GPS). GPS data enters the system in the form of messages that are processed to yield Line-Of-Sight (LOS) data, which is fed into a Kalman Filter (KF). The KF estimates present and future navigation information and corrects these estimates according to incoming LOS navigation data. These estimates are fed to a high rate Sequencer task. The Sequencer acts as the central node, gathering all inputs and performs the actual navigation computations. The Sequencer can also request an immediate estimate from the KF if the data is not provided earlier.

4.1 GGNS Task Model

The GGNS task model is shown in Figure 6. The system consists of five tasks, three internal to GGNS and two external trigger tasks that simulate input data streams. The High_Rate_Nav task, acts as the overall sequencer, which provides navigation data to the external world. The Low_Rate_Nav task acts as the Kalman filter, carrying out estimation of navigation information by integrating information from both the GPS and IMU. The GPS_RCV task is an event triggered task that gathers LOS data from External_Trigger_Task_1.

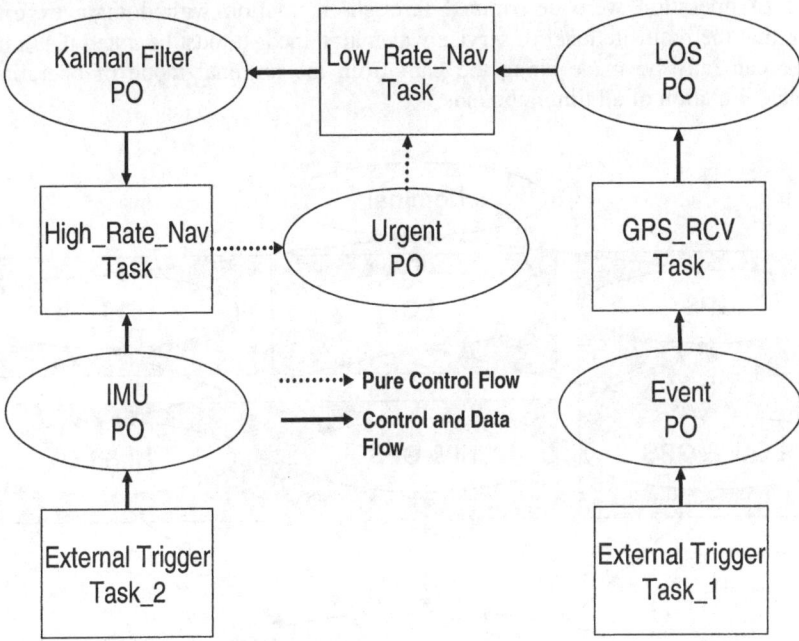

Fig. 6. Task Model of GGNS

The High_Rate_Nav task collects IMU data, KF data, and raises a flag if KF data is not available fast enough. The Low_Rate_Nav task has three activities: collect LOS data, send KF data, and responds to the flag raised by the High_Rate_Nav task by outputting KF data as soon as it becomes runnable. The GPS_Receive task is triggered by the arrival of a GPS message and has two activities: collect the GPS message, and send LOS data.

The data communications between these three main tasks are implemented with protected objects (POs). Three of the POs are the buffers containing LOS data, KF navigation data, and IMU data. The Urgent PO implements the signaling capability that needs to exist between the High_Rate_Nav and the Low_Rate_Nav Tasks. Event PO implements the event triggering capability of the GPS Receive Task. The External_Trigger_Task_1 simulates incoming GPS messages and interacts only with

Event PO. External_Trigger_Task_2 simulates incoming IMU data and interacts only with the IMU data buffer.

4.2 Monitoring and Mode Switching

Operational modes are organized hierarchically based on timing behavior violations of the three tasks: High_Rate_Nav, Low_Rate_Nav and GPS_Receive. There are eight possible combinations of task's violating their deadlines, as shown in Figure 7. The hierarchical organization serves to illustrate the different classes of degraded service in decreasing order of the quality of navigation information generated. The modes of operation were determined through interaction with domain experts to ensure that the requisite level of service was maintained. It must be noted that a mode change can only be made along the path from the nominal mode of operation to complete violation of all timing bounds.

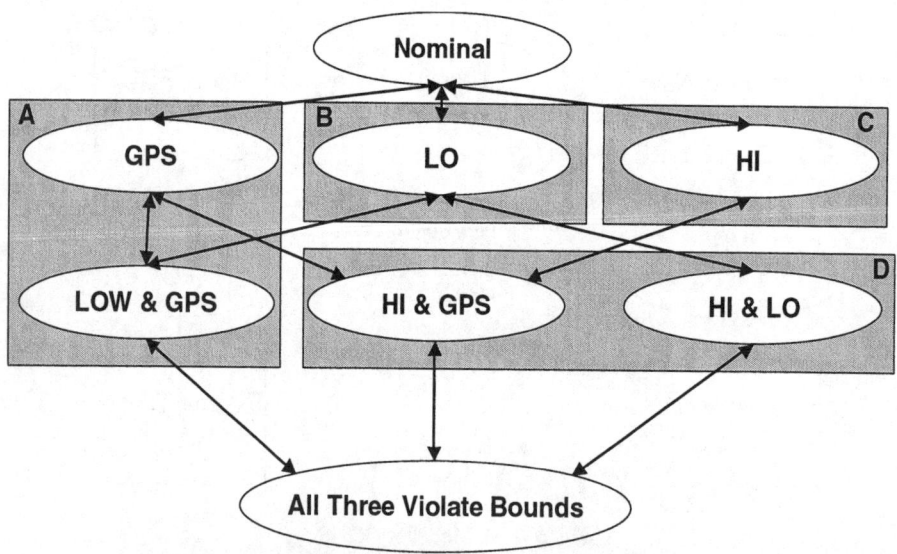

Fig. 7. GGNS Operational Modes

The High_Rate_Nav (HI) task receives input from both the Low_Rate_Nav task (LO), as well as the External_Trigger_Task_2 (which provides inertial measurement data. If the GPS_RCV task (GPS), or the LO violates their timing bounds, HI will not have access to reliable GPS information. The designer may however choose to completely ignore GPS data, switch to Mode A – which is the approach adopted in the implementation. If the system designer works under the assumption that some raw information is more useful than no information, the system bypasses LO temporarily and transitions to Mode B. The system switches to Mode C if HI violates its execution time bound while waiting for IMU data. If both HI and LO violate their deadlines, or both HI and GPS violate their deadlines, then it is essential to ensure that HI can fulfill its essential responsibilities without reliable GPS information, which yields the operating mode D. In the case in which all tasks violate their bounds, the system transitions into safety mode. The summary of the system fault modes is presented in Table 1.

Table 1. GGNS Modes of Operation

Operating Mode	High_Rate_Nav	Low_Rate_Nav	GPS_Receive_Task
A	Degraded GPS Mode	Holding Error States	Quarantined
B	Degraded LOS Mode	Quarantined	Nominal
C	Basic Mode and Quarantined	Nominal	Nominal
D	Basic IMU Mode Only	Quarantined	Quarantined
E	Survival	Survival	Survival

5   Conclusions

The Gurkh Generic Navigation System is used as a proof-of-concept demonstrator for monitoring the timing behavior of a system with multiple operating modes. The faults are detected based on violation of expected timing behavior, and degraded system performance is guaranteed by modeling system behavior in the presence of faults and formally verifying that the degraded system behavior is deterministic. The current system model and implementation assumes a static set of possible configurations of the system operation in the presence of faults. The operational mode is selected, and the mode transition is predetermined at system implementation time. It must be noted that the approach is currently limited to handling violations of timing behavior that are caused by non-replicable transient faults. This assumption is made to address the limited computational resources available for advanced fault-detection algorithms at the subsystem level. The mode change protocol used is based on the modifying the control flow of tasks that violate their deadlines, and thereby modifying their timing behavior independent of unaffected tasks. The analysis of mode change timing behavior is carried out offline, to ensure schedulability.

An alternative approach is to allow an external system master to determine the subsystem transition mode. This will provide the system the ability to reconfigure itself based on the complete system state (as opposed to the state of just the component such as GGNS). For example, the avionics system may be able to reconfigure position information based on an alternative sensor such as the radar subsystem or the star tracker, in which case the system may choose to transition to the suboptimal operational mode. Work is currently underway to provide reconfiguration support by using dual operating system: RavenHaRT for regular operation and a reconfiguration OS (implemented as an application task), which will determine how the application software running on the PowerPC changes mode, and which monitoring model is used for configuring the MC. Determining the operating mode externally introduces significant challenges in terms of scheduling the mode change, as the subsystem cannot be idle until the mode change request comes through. The system master has to have visibility in terms of affected and unaffected tasks in any given mode, in order to make an informed mode change request.

References

1. Alur, R., D.L. Dill., "Automata for modeling real-time systems", In Proc. of Int. Colloquium on Algorithms, Languages, and Programming, LNCS 443:322-335, 1990
2. Burns A., "The Ravenscar Profile". *ACM Ada Letters*, XIX, 4, 49–52, Dec 1999
3. Burns, A., "How to Verify a Safe Real-Time System: The Application of Model Checking and Timed Automata to the Production Cell Case Study", Real-Time Systems, 24, 135-151, 2003, Kluwer Academic Publishers, The Netherlands, 2003
4. Burns, A., B. Dobbing, T. Vardanega, "Guide for the Use of the Ada Ravenscar Profile in High Integrity Systems," University of York Technical Report YCS-2003-348, 2003
5. de la Puente, J.A., and J. Zamorano, "Execution-Time Clocks and Ravenscar Kernels", Ada Letters Vol.XXIII, No.4, December 2003
6. Behrmann, G., A. David, and K.G. Larsen, "A Tutorial on UPPAAL", In proceedings of the 4th International School on Formal Methods for the Design of Computer, Communication, and Software Systems (SFM-RT'04). LNCS 3185. 2004
7. Harbour M.G., M.A. Rivas, et.al., "Implementing and Using Execution Time Clocks in Ada Hard Real-Time Applications", Proceedings of the 1998 Ada-Europe International Conference on Reliable Software Technologies, pp 90-101, June 08-12, 1998
8. Hopcroft, J.E., J.D. Ullman, "Introduction of Automata Theory, Languages, and Computation", Addison Wesley, 2001
9. ISO/IEC Ada 95 Reference Manual, Language and Standard Libraries, Version 6.0
10. Lee, P.A. and Anderson, T., "Fault Tolerance: Principles and Practice (Second Revised Edition)", Springer-Verlag Wien-New York
11. Liu C.L., J.W. Layland, "Scheduling Algorithms for Multiprogramming in a Hard-Real-Time Environment", Journal of the ACM (JACM), 20(1): 46-61, Jan. 1973
12. Leung J. Y. T. and J. Whitehead, "On the complexity of fixed-priority scheduling of periodic real-time tasks. Performance Evaluation", 2(4):237--250, Dec 1982.
13. Pettersson, P., and K.G. Larsen, "UPPAAL2k", Bulletin of the European Association for Theoretical Computer Science, volume 70, pages 40-44, 2000
14. Real J., A. Crespo, "Mode Change Protocols for Real-Time Systems: A Survey and a New Proposal", Real-Time Systems , 4:161-197, 2004
15. Ram Murthy, C.S., G. Manimaran, "Resource Management in Real-Time Systems and Networks", The MIT Press, Cambridge, Massachusetts, 2001
16. Silbovitz, A., "RavenHaRT- A Hardware Implementation of a Ravenscar Compliant Kernel", SM Thesis, Aeronautics and Astronautics, MIT, 2003
17. Torres-Pomales W., "Software Fault-Tolerance: A Tutorial", NASA Technical Report, NASA-2000-tm210616, 2000.
18. "Virtex-II Pro Platform FPGA Handbook", v1.0, 2002, www.xilinx.com

Observing the Development of a Reliable Embedded System

Devaraj Ayavoo[1], Michael J. Pont[1], and Stephen Parker[2]

[1] Embedded Systems Laboratory, University of Leicester,
University Road, Leicester LE1 7RH, UK
http://www.le.ac.uk/eg/embedded/
[2] Pi Technology, Milton Hall, Ely Road, Milton,
Cambridge CB4 6WZ, UK
http://www.pitechnology.com/

Abstract. Distributed embedded systems are becoming ubiquitous and increasingly complex. It is frequently assumed that the use of simulation can support the design and implementation of such systems. However the contribution made by simulation towards the development process is rarely explored in depth and is incompletely understood. The pilot study described in this paper was intended to help identify techniques which may be used to provide a quantitative assessment of the contribution which simulation makes in this area. The study involved the observation of the "simulation first" development of a distributed embedded system. The results obtained in the study are described, and will form the basis for future investigations in this important area.

1 Introduction

Distributed embedded systems are becoming increasingly common and increasingly complex. For example, the designer of a modern passenger car may need to choose between the use of one (or more) network protocols based on CAN, TTCAN, LIN, FlexRay or TTP/C. The resulting network may be connected in, for example, a bus or star topology. The individual processor nodes in the network may use event-triggered or time-triggered software architectures, or some combination of the two. The clocks associated with these processors may be linked using, for example, shared-clock techniques or synchronization messages. These individual processors may, for example, be C167, ARM, MPC555 or 8051.

Overall, the number of possible system designs is enormous and prototyping even a small subset of these possibilities is impractical: an alternative approach is therefore required [22]. According to Karatza: "The most straightforward way to evaluate the performance without a full-scale implementation is through a modelling and simulation approach. Detailed simulation models help determine performance bottlenecks inherent in the architecture and provide the basis for refining the system configuration."([12], p. 183). Various other investigators have also argued for the use of simulation to support the development of this type of system [3, 4, 8, 14, 17, 24].

Intuitively, one might expect that use of an appropriate simulator may assist in the development process. However, there is very little empirical data available that can

T. Vardanega and A. Wellings (Eds.): Ada-Europe 2005, LNCS 3555, pp. 167–179, 2005.

demonstrate that - for example - simulation reduces the overall effort in a project. Similarly, even if use of a simulator does reduce the required effort, it is not clear exactly how such a tool should be employed. Should we, for example, simulate the whole system then build it, or should we simulate part of the system, build this, then simulate the next part, and so on?

The lack of empirical evidence is not, of course, a problem unique to the use of simulators and the software-engineering community is becoming increasingly aware of the need to seek evidence of the effectiveness of any form of new technology [10, 15], rather than relying on sweeping statements about its "obvious" effectiveness (e.g. see [9, 25]).

In light of the observations above, the pilot study described in this paper was intended to help identify techniques which can be used in future experiments in order to provide a quantitative assessment of the contribution which simulation makes in this area. The study involved the observation of the development of a non-trivial distributed embedded control system, first using a simulator and then developing "real code" for a network of suitable microcontrollers.

The paper is organised as follows. Section 2 describes in detail the case study used in the project described here. A comparison of the results from the simulation process and the hardware implementation is presented in Section 3. Section 4 then presents the raw results from the measures of "effort" for the two development processes. Synchronisation of the timescales for these processes is then discussed in Section 5. An analysis of the synchronised results is then presented in Section 6. Finally, the results are discussed and conclusions are presented in Section 7.

2 The Case Study

As outlined in the introduction, the study described in this paper involved the observation of the "simulation first" development of a distributed embedded control system.

We describe the study in this section.

2.1 The Testbed

The testbed used in this study was based on part of an X-by-Wire control system for a passenger car: it was adapted from a platform described by Castelpietra et al. (see [3]).

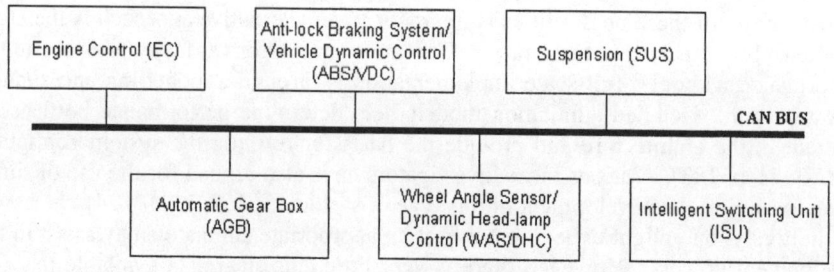

Fig. 1. Test bed used in this study (based on [3])

In our version of Castelpietra's system, six embedded nodes were connected using a CAN bus (see Fig. 1). Each node contained an Infineon "167" microcontroller: such devices are widely used in the automotive sector [19].

Table 1. Task and message characteristics of the six distributed nodes. The Initial Delay and Period values are in milliseconds. Each task on the node is associated with either sending or receiving a message on the CAN bus

Task Name	Node	Priority	Initial Delay	Period	Input Message	Output Message
EC Task1	EC	1	1	10		M1
EC Task2		2	2	20		M3
EC Task3		3	3	100		M10
EC Task4		4	4	7	M4	
EC Task5		5	5	7	M2	
EC Task6		6	6	25	M8	
EC Task7		7	7	20	M6	
AGB Task1	AGB	1	1	15		M4
AGB Task2		2	2	50		M11
AGB Task3		3	3	25	M8	
AGB Task4		4	4	7	M2	
ABS Task1	ABS/VDC	1	1	20		M5
ABS Task2		2	2	40		M6
ABS Task3		3	3	15		M7
ABS Task4		4	4	100		M12
ABS Task5		5	5	10	M3	
ABS Task6		6	6	10	M9	
WAS Task1	WAS/DHC	1	1	14		M2
WAS Task2		2	2	10	M9	
SUS Task1	SUS	1	1	20		M9
SUS Task2		2	2	10	M5	
SUS Task3		3	3	5	M1	
SUS Task4		4	4	7	M2	
SUS Task5		5	5	7	M7	
ISU Task1	ISU	1	1	50		M8
ISU Task2		2	2	25	M11	
ISU Task3		3	3	5	M1	
ISU Task4		4	4	50	M10	
ISU Task5		5	5	20	M6	
ISU Task6		6	6	10	M9	
ISU Task7		7	7	50	M12	

The case study was developed using a Shared-Clock CAN (SCC) architecture using a tick interval of 1ms and a CAN baudrate of 500Kbits/sec [16]. A FIFO buffer was designed to ensure that the messages were queued correctly.

2.2 Selecting a Suitable Simulator

To develop the system described in Section 0, a "simulation first" approach was employed. The simulation process was used to predict the response times of all the signals between the nodes, in order to avoid the expense of repeated prototyping at the implementation stage [17].

A number of simulation tools have been developed by different research groups and companies. For example, El-khoury and Törngren [8] described a toolset which integrates the modelling of schedulers and distributed systems with models of control system performance. This was later expanded to form a more versatile simulation tool called AIDA [17]. Another tool – RTSIM - was described by Palopoli et al. [14] to help engineers to develop real-time distributed embedded control systems. Similarly Eker and Cervin [7] described a Matlab toolbox simulating a real-time scheduler: this was later extended to develop the TrueTime Simulator [4].

In the present study, the TrueTime simulator was chosen to simulate the behaviour of the system for the following reasons:

- TrueTime is capable of simulating the system to be controlled (that is, the plant dynamics) and a wide range of software architectures and network protocols for the distributed control system.
- Many control engineers are familiar with Matlab and Simulink (e.g. see [5, 6]). Since TrueTime is a Matlab / Simulink package, this makes it easy to integrate the software and network design process with the development of the control system.
- TrueTime is an open-source package. This provides obvious advantages in terms of cost, and also provides flexibility: both are important considerations in a research project such as that described in this paper.

2.3 How Do We Measure (and Compare) the Effort Involved?

There has been comparatively little research into the measurement of effort involved in development of software-rich systems [1, 10, 20].

In the present study we first needed to understand the work involved in the development of both the "simulated" and "real" systems.

The work involved in the simulation phase included creating block diagrams (with the appropriate connections as shown in Fig. 2) for the system and subsequently writing Matlab codes for the TrueTime simulator. An example of a task in Matlab is shown in Listing 1.

All of the work involved in the implementation phase required coding in C. For example, the task specified in TrueTime in Listing 1 is shown in C in Listing 2.

Since both the simulation and implementation phases required coding, we used code-based metrics as the basis of the comparisons that were carried out. Please note that although the languages of the simulation and implementation are different, the structure and logic of the tasks are similar. In addition, for the simulation phase, we included the time required to build the block diagrams in the measures of effort required to develop the code since the code and diagrams are interdependent.

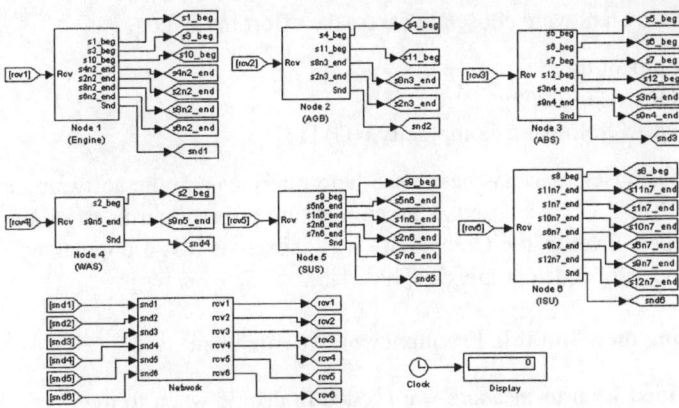

Fig. 2. The TrueTime block diagrams for the system described in Section 2.1

```
function [exectime, data] = N1_Task7(seg, data)
global N1_MSG_6;
switch seg,
   case 1,
       Sig_6 = N1_MSG_6(3);
       % Turn on the LED on and off
       if (Sig_6 == 1)
          data.Sig_out = 1;
       else
          data.Sig_out = 0;
       end

       exectime = 0.0001;
   case 2,
       ttAnalogOut(data.out7Chan, data.Sig_out);
       exectime = -1;
end
```

Listing 1. An example of a task specification created using the TrueTime simulator

```
void N1_Task7(void)
   {
   // Turn on the LED on and off (reverse logic)
   if (Msg_6)
      {
      Sig_pin_7 = 0;
      }
   else
      {
      Sig_pin_7 = 1;
      }
   }
```

Listing 2. The task specified in TrueTime in Listing 1 is shown in C here

Three parameters were chosen to assess the effort involved:

- Development time;
- Lines Of Code (LOC);
- McCabe's Cyclomatic Complexity $v(G)$ [13].

Time was chosen as it has been used before to measure the software development process [1, 20]. LOC was used as it can measure effort in terms of product size [21, 26]. McCabe's Cyclomatic Complexity was chosen as it is a popular way of assessing and comparing code complexity [13, 21].

2.4 Deciding on a Suitable Frequency of Measurement

Having decided what to measure, we needed to decide when to measure. In general, we wish to have as much data as possible: thus a continuous sampling technique would seem to be ideal. However, carrying out the measurements is likely to have an impact on the process under observation [18]: that is, the more frequently a measurement is taken, the more likely we are to influence the development process itself.

In this study, it was decided that measurements should be taken every time a "new version" of the software was developed: this technique is usually used to keep track of code development that is constantly evolving [23]. Copies of all the versions created were retained for subsequent analysis.

2.5 The Observer and Observee

Finding suitable test subjects to carry out an experiment is a common problem in empirical software engineering [15]. In this pilot study, we used one observee (one of the authors – DA): the same individual acted as the observer. This "one person" approach has previously been shown to be effective (see [2]).

3 Does the Simulator Work?

After the simulation and implementation processes were completed, the first verification test was to determine if the results obtained from the simulation matched those from the hardware implementation. To do this, measurements of the response time for each of the signals (19 in total) were made. Results for the TrueTime simulator were collected by running the experiment on Simulink and logging the response time in a .MAT file. The signals on the hardware implementation were measured using LabView via a National Instruments data acquisition card (NI PCI-6035E).

The results obtained showed that the response time of all the 19 signals from the simulation matched closely the measured results from the hardware (within 2 ms).

4 Raw Results

A new version of the software was saved every time the project reached a significant milestone. The versions produced are summarised in Table 2.

Table 2. Description of all the versions that were created for the software simulation and hardware implementation and their corresponding development time in hours[1]

Version	Description	Duration
SIM v1	Created one Master (M) and two slaves (S1 & S2) SCC configuration. S1 sends a signal to S2 and S2 sends a signal to S1.	5
SIM v2	Similar to SIM v1 but uses a basic message queue.	4
SIM v3	Increased to five slaves with basic message queue but couldn't work.	2
SIM v4	Reverted back to SIM v2 and gradually added another three slaves (S3, S4 & S5). S3, S4 & S5 only took part in the SCC, but not in the message queue.	2
SIM v5	Added another two signals, one from S3 and one from M. S4 & S5 acted as receivers.	2
SIM v6	Ported Castelpietra's testcase to the existing platform (SIM v5).	5
HW v1	Implemented the basic SCC architecture on all the six nodes.	7
HW v2	Developed the initial message queue. Works for only a single message sent out from slave.	4
HW v3	Code was modified to send multiple messages out from the slaves.	3
HW v4	Master node was modified to also have the capability to send multiple messages. Got a basic system working on three nodes, where a message is sent from S1–S2 through M.	4
HW v5	Tested the message transfer for master-to-slave, slave-to-master and slave-to-slave.	4
HW v6	Implemented five nodes message queue system with all nodes sending a signal out.	4
HW v7	Begin to port Castelpietra's testcase for M, S1, S2, S4 and S5.	3
HW v8	Continued porting Castelpietra's testcase for S3. Performed checks for all tasks, signals and message properties.	2
HW v9	Modified the receiving signal for LabView measurement purpose.	1

Please note that for the first version of the hardware implementation (HW v1) and software simulation (SIM v1), the number of nodes used in both processes were different. For the HW v1, all the six nodes were initially connected with the SCC approach to test the development boards for any potential faults. This check was not necessary on the simulator as there were no physical hardware component involved. Therefore, we decided to begin testing the SCC architecture with only three nodes.

5 Synchronising the Timescales

As can be seen from Table 2, there were six different simulation versions produced and nine versions of the hardware implementation. This makes comparison of the two development processes difficult. In order to be able to carry out a meaningful comparison of the two development processes, we needed to synchronise the two development processes.

The first step we took was to divide the development process into three stages:

- To develop the basic SCC
- To implement a message queue within the scheduler
- To port Castelpietra's testcase onto the existing platform

---

[1] There was one problem with the raw data obtained for HW v1. The raw data showed duration of seven hours. However, this included the time (five hours) taken to detect a hardware error on a faulty 167 board. Assuming no hardware error was present, the actual development time for HW v1 would have been two hours, and this figure will be used in the remainder of the paper.

These three stages were then mapped onto the various versions of the software development as illustrated in Table 3.

Table 3. Mapping of versions to development stages

Simulation		Hardware		Development
Version X	Duration	Version X	Duration	Stage
SIM v1	5	HW v1	2	Basic SCC (A)
SIM v2	4			
SIM v3	2	HW v2	4	Message Queue (B)
SIM v4	2	HW v3	3	
SIM v5	2	HW v4	4	
		HW v5	4	
		HW v6	4	
SIM v6	5	HW v7	3	Castelpietra (C)
		HW v8	2	
		HW v9	1	
Total	20	Total	27	

Based on Table 3, it can be seen that for the three stages (A, B and C), the number of versions produced during simulation and hardware implementation were different. In order to produce the same number of versions in each stage, two approaches were employed:

- Grouping 'similar' versions together
- Adding 'dummy' versions

5.1 Grouping Versions Together

Based on Table 3, it can be seen that Development Stage A and C seem to have only one version for the hardware and simulation respectively. On the simulator, there were two versions in Development Stage A. These two versions (SIM v1 and SIM v2) were grouped together into SIM v1. Note that the number of hours of the 'new' SIM v1 was the summation of SIM v1 and SIM v2. The similar process was also carried out for the hardware (Development Stage C). The resulting data are summarized in Table 4.

Table 4. Results after grouping versions together

Simulation		Hardware		Development
Version X	Duration	Version X	Duration	Stage
SIM v1	9	HW v1	2	Basic SCC (A)
SIM v2	2	HW v2	4	Message Queue (B)
SIM v3	2	HW v3	3	
SIM v4	2	HW v4	4	
		HW v5	4	
		HW v6	4	
SIM v5	5	HW v7	6	Castelpietra (C)
Total	20	Total	27	

5.2 Adding Dummy Versions

Dummy versions are added to a particular stage when we wish to retain the resolution of the results (grouping them would reduce the resolution). From Table 4, it can be seen that in Stage B the simulation process resulted in the creation of three versions while the hardware process generated five versions. Since Stage B showed significant development effort, it was decided that two dummy version will be added in the simulation results as shown in Table 5. The dummy versions were added such that they were evenly distributed in the designated development stages.

Table 5. Adding dummy task

Simulation		Hardware		Development Stage
Version X	Duration	Version X	Duration	
SIM v1	9	HW v1	2	Basic SCC (A)
SIM v2	2	HW v2	4	
Dummy	2	HW v3	3	
SIM v3	2	HW v4	4	Message Queue (B)
Dummy	2	HW v5	4	
SIM v4	2	HW v6	4	
SIM v5	5	HW v7	6	Castelpietra (C)
Total	20	Total	27	

Note that for the task duration, the previous value before the dummy version was inherited for the dummy version. This will have the effect of 'stretching' Development Stage B of the simulation such that the timescale is synchronised with the hardware implementation. However, notice that the total task duration has not been changed. This will preserve the actual time properties of the simulation process. The similar procedure was carried out for LOC and McCabe's Cyclomatic Complexity. The final results are shown in Table 6.

Table 6. Results for all attributes after performing the timeline synchronisation

Simulation				Hardware				Development Stage
Version X	Duration	LOC	$v(G)$	Version X	Duration	LOC	$v(G)$	
SIM v1	9	312	21	HW v1	2	6095	184	Basic SCC (A)
SIM v2	2	322	24	HW v2	4	2611	70	
Dummy	2	322	24	HW v3	3	2655	74	
SIM v3	2	649	52	HW v4	4	3954	109	Message Queue (B)
Dummy	2	649	52	HW v5	4	3997	116	
SIM v4	2	1025	91	HW v6	4	6612	218	
SIM v5	5	1190	101	HW v7	6	7752	250	Castelpietra (C)

6 Analysis of the Synchronised Results

Using the synchronised results (Table 6), the measured attributes for the simulation and hardware implementation were plotted. Fig. 3 compares the effort (in terms of working hours) for the simulation and the hardware.

Part I on the graph took longer for the simulation than on the hardware because the SCC architecture was already available on the hardware (as a software pattern [16]) but had to be built from scratch for the simulator. Part II was where the message queue was developed. Here, the simulation took less time than the hardware because a FIFO architecture was already available on the simulator (as a message box [11]) but not on the hardware. Part III was where testing and further enhancement of the message queue was carried out. Again, this part required more effort on the hardware than on the simulator due to the availability of a message queue.

Finally, Castelpietra's testcase was ported onto the two platforms (Part IV). In this part, both the hardware and simulator show an increase in effort. This is due to the manual work of porting all the tasks and message properties to the existing platform.

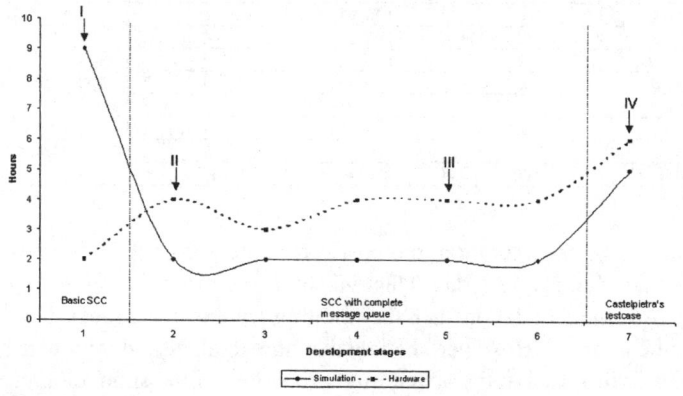

Fig. 3. Comparison of the effort (time) between the simulation and hardware

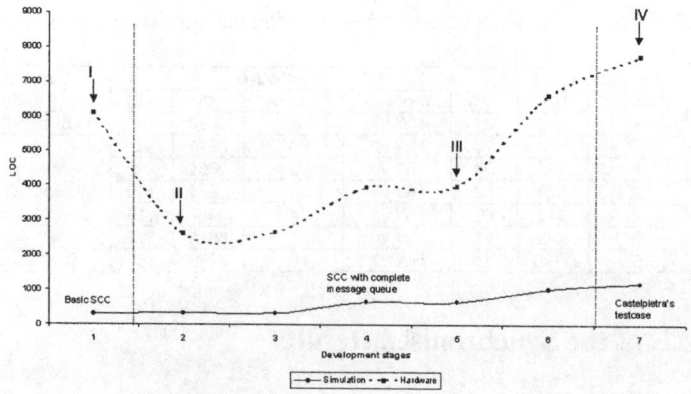

Fig. 4. Comparison of the effort (LOC) between the simulation and hardware

Looking at Fig. 4 and Fig. 5, it can be seen that LOC and v(G) follow a similar trend. Both the results indicate that more effort (in terms of LOC and v(G)) was needed on the hardware than on the simulator.

The difference in Part I was due to the number of nodes that were initially used to set up the SCC. The hardware used six nodes whereas the simulator only used three. As the development stage progressed, the growth rate of the LOC and v(G) was much more rapid on the hardware than on the software.

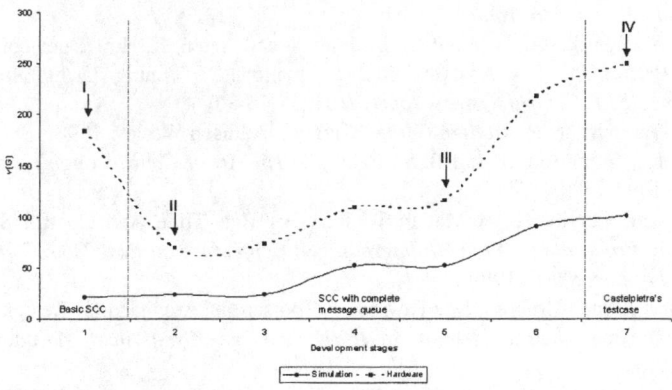

Fig. 5. Comparison of the effort (McCabe) between the simulation and hardware

7 Discussion and Conclusions

The pilot study described in this paper was intended to help identify techniques which can be used in future experiments in order to provide a quantitative assessment of the contribution which simulation makes in the development of distributed embedded systems. The study involved the observation of the development of a non-trivial distributed embedded control system, first using a simulator and then developing "real code" for a network of suitable microcontrollers.

The results presented here involved only a single study, involving one developer. It would be inappropriate to claim that the findings presented here provide solid evidence for (or against) the use of simulation in the development of distributed embedded control systems. However, the results from this study do suggest that the measurements made here, used in conjunction with techniques for timescale synchronisation, are worth pursuing in a future study involving larger numbers of test subjects.

Acknowledgements. This work is supported by an ORS award (to DA) from the UK Government (Department for Education and Skills), and by Pi Technology. Work on this paper was completed while MJP was on Study Leave from the University of Leicester.

References

1. Basili, V., Asgari, S., Carver, J., Hochstein, L., Hollingsworth, J.K., Shull, F. and Zelko-witz, M.V. A Pilot Study to Evaluate Development Effort for High Performance Comput-ing *Technical report CS-TR-4588*, University of Maryland, 2004.
2. Basili, V.R. and Turner, A.J. Iterative Enhancement: A practical Technique for Software Development. *IEEE Transaction on Software Engineering, 1* (4). 390-396.
3. Castelpietra, P., Song, Y.Q., Lion, F.S. and Attia, M. Analysis and Simulation Methods for Performance Evaluation of a Multiple Networks Embedded Architecture. *IEEE Transac-tions on Industrial Electronics, 49* (No. 6).
4. Cervin, A., Henriksson, D., Lincoln, B., Eker, J. and Årzén, K. How Does control Timing Affect Performance? - Analysis And Simulation Of Timing Using Jitterbug And TrueTime. *IEEE Control Systems Journal, 23* (3). 16-30.
5. Dorf, D. and Bishop, R. *Modern Control Systems*. Addison Wesley, 1998.
6. Dutton, K., Thompson, S. and Barraclough, B. *The Art of Control Engineering*. Addison Wesley, 1997.
7. Eker, J. and Cervin, A., A Matlab Toolbox For Real-Time And Control Systems Co-Design. in *Proceedings of the 6th International Conference on Real-Time Computing Sys-tems and Applications*, (1999).
8. El-khoury, J. and Törngren, M., Towards A Toolset For Architectural Design Of Distrib-uted Real-Time Control Systems. in *IEEE Real-Time Symposium*, (London, England, 2001), IEEE.
9. Fenton, N., Pfleeger, S.L. and Glass, R.L. Science and Substance: A Challenge to Soft-ware Engineers. *IEEE Software, 11* (4). 86-95.
10. Germain, E. and Robillard, P.N. Engineering-Based Processes and Agile Methodologies for Software Development: A Comparative Case Study. *Journal of Systems and Software, 75* (1-2). 17-27.
11. Henriksson, D. and Cervin, A. TrueTime 1.2—Reference Manual, Department of Auto-matic Control, Lund University, Sweden, 2004.
12. Karatza, H.D. Modelling and Simulation of Distributed Systems and Networks. *Simulation Modelling Practice and Theory, 12* (3-4). 183-185.
13. McCabe, T. A Software Complexity Measure. *IEEE Transactions on Software Engineer-ing, 2*. 308-320.
14. Palopoli, L., Lipari, G., Abeni, L., Abeni, M.D., P.Ancilotti and Conticelli, F., A Tool For Simulation And Fast Prototyping Of Embedded Control Systems. in *Proceedings of LCTES01*, (Snow Bird, Utah, United States, 2001), ACM Press.
15. Pickard, L.M., Kitchenham, B.A. and Jones, P.W. Combining Empirical Results in Soft-ware Engineering. *Information and Software Technology, 40* (14). 811-821.
16. Pont, M.J. *Patterns For Time Triggered Embedded Systems*. Addison Wesley, 2001.
17. Redell, O., El-khoury, J. and Törngren, M. The AIDA Toolset for Design and Implementa-tion Analysis of Distributed Real-time Control Systems. *Microprocessors and Microsys-tems, 28* (4). 163-182.
18. SEL. Software Measurement Guidebook *Software Engineering Laboratory Series*, NASA/GSFC, 1995.
19. Siemens. C167 Derivatives - User's manual *Version 2.0*, 1996.
20. Solingen, R.V. and Stalenhoef, P., Effort Measurement of Support to Software Products. in *Proceeding of the International Workshop on Empirical Studies of Software Maintenance*, (Bari, Italy, 1997).

21. Stark, G., Durst, R.C. and Vowell, C.W. Using Metrics in Management Decision Making. *IEEE Computer, 27* (9). 42-48.
22. Thane, H. Monitoring, Testing and Debugging of Distributed Real-Time Systems *Mechatronics Laboratory, Department of Machine Design*, Royal Institute of Technology, Sweden, 2000.
23. Tichy, W.F. RCS - A System for Version Control. *Software - Practice & Experience, 15* (7). 637-654.
24. Törngren, M., El-khoury, J., Sandfridson, M. and Redell, O. Modelling And Simulation Of Embedded Computer Control Systems: Problem Formulation, Mechatronics Laboratory, Department of Machine Design, Royal Institute of Technology, Sweden, 2001.
25. Turski, W.M., And no Philosophers' Stone Either. in *Information Processing 86*, (1986), Elsevier Science (Northern Holland), 1077-1080.
26. Weller, E.F. Using Metrics to Manage Software Projects. *IEEE Computer, 27* (9). 27-33.

RT-EP: A Fixed-Priority Real Time Communication Protocol over Standard Ethernet

José María Martínez and Michael González Harbour

Departamento de Electrónica y Computadores,
Universidad de Cantabria, 39005 - Santander, Spain
{martinjm, mgh}@unican.es

Abstract. This paper presents the design and implementation of RT-EP (Real-Time Ethernet Protocol), which is a software-based token-passing Ethernet protocol for multipoint communications in real-time applications, that does not require any modification to existing Ethernet hardware. The protocol allows a fixed priority to be assigned to each message, and consequently well-known schedulability analysis techniques can be applied. A precise model of its timing behavior has been obtained. Furthermore, this protocol provides the ability of recovering from some fault conditions. It has been ported to an implementation of the Minimal Real-Time POSIX standard called MaRTE OS [10], and is being used to support real-time communications in an implementation of Ada's Distributed Systems Annex (RT-GLADE). It has been successfully used to implement a distributed controlled for an industrial robot.

Keywords: Real-Time, Embedded Systems, Networks, Ethernet, Distributed Systems, Ada 95, Modelling, Schedulability.

1 Introduction[1]

Ethernet is by far the most widely used local area networking (LAN) technology in the world today, even though it has unpredictable transmission times because it uses a non-deterministic arbitration mechanism (CSMA/CD). Several approaches and techniques have been used to make Ethernet deterministic in order to take advantage of its low cost and higher speeds than those of real-time field buses available today (like the CAN bus [9], for example). Some of these approaches are the modification of the Medium Access Control [7], the addition of transmission control [2], a protocol using time-triggered traffic [14], or the usage of a switched Ethernet [3].

The objective of this work is to achieve a relatively high speed mechanism for real-time communications at a low cost, while keeping the predictable timing behaviour required in distributed hard real-time applications. The communication protocol

---

[1] This work has been funded in part by the *Comisión Interministerial de Ciencia y Tecnología* (CICYT) of the Spanish Government under grant number TIC2002-04123-C03-02 (TRECOM), and by the IST Programme of the European Commission under project IST-2001-34820 (FIRST).

T. Vardanega and A. Wellings (Eds.): Ada-Europe 2005, LNCS 3555, pp. 180–195, 2005.

proposed in this work is called RT-EP (Real-Time Ethernet Protocol), and can be classified as an addition of a transmission control layer over Ethernet, since it is basically a token-passing arbitration in a bus [6], capable of transmitting fixed-priority messages. It provides a Real-Time Ethernet communication without modifying the existing hardware, and has been designed to avoid collisions in Ethernet media.

In a previous work we presented a preliminary version of RT-EP [11] in which we discussed the fault-recovery mechanism and the way in which the protocol can be modelled using the MAST [12] Real-time Modelling and Analysis Suite. We also discussed the implementation, in C language, of RT-EP in MaRTE OS [10] and we also measured the overheads it introduces.

In this paper we present a complete description of the protocol and we propose the Ada language for its implementation, to ensure a smooth integration with DSA middleware such as RT-GLADE [8], or Polyorb [15] in the future. By porting the protocol to Ada we can also take advantage of the reliability and robustness that the Ada language provides, and we open the door to a possible future extension to support real-time distribution in the Ravescar profile [1]. We also have done a clean-up of the protocol, we have generalized the architecture to make it independent of the underlying communications network, and we have developed a more precise real-time model to be used with MAST, with measurements performed on a MaRTE OS platform. The RT-EP protocol is being used to support real-time communications in an implementation of Ada's Distributed Systems Annex (DSA) called RT-GLADE. It has also been successfully used to implement a distributed controller for an industrial robot.

The paper is organized as follows. Section 2 introduces how the protocol works. In Section 3 we describe the state diagram that controls the behaviour of the protocol. In Section 4 we explain the layout of the packets used in the protocol. Section 5 discusses some details of the current implementation. Section 6 gives some details about the MAST model that describes the timing behaviour of the protocol. In Section 7 we provide some results of the metrics taken in a particular platform. Section 8 briefly describes the robot system that has been implemented with RT-EP. Finally, Section 9 gives our conclusions.

2 Description of the Communication Protocol

RT-EP has been designed to avoid collisions in the Ethernet media by the use of a token. It implements an adaptation layer over the Medium Access Control in Ethernet. The protocol is used to transmit messages that have a fixed priority assigned to them. It works by dividing the message transmission process into two phases: a priority arbitration phase in which the highest priority message to be transmitted is determined, and the transmission of the message itself. With this mechanism, the protocol does not require any clock synchronization mechanism to keep a synchronized notion of time in all the nodes.

Messages size is limited by the parameter RT-EP_MTU (RT-EP Maximum Transmission Unit) which depends on the MTU of the underlying protocol (1492 bytes for Ethernet). Message packets are non preemptible, and therefore there is a bounded blocking time that has to be taken into account during the analysis. We do not provide fragmentation of messages at this layer, although it would be easy to add. In that case large messages would be partitioned into several packets, and preemption would be possible up to the packet-size limit.

Each station (processing node or CPU) has a transmission priority queue, in which all the packets to be transmitted are stored in priority order. Each station also has a set of reception priority queues that provide the equivalent of virtual separate channels for sending messages to the desired recipient. Packets with the same priority are stored in FIFO order. The number of reception queues can be configured depending on the number of application threads (or tasks) running in the system and requiring reception of messages. The common usage model is that each application task has its own channel or reception queue reserved for itself, and in that way the sender can send messages addressed to that specific task, through the desired channel. Channels are identified with a number called the channel ID.

The network is organized as a logical ring over a bus, as shown in Fig. 1. The ring is configured statically, and every station has access to the full ring configuration, including topological information with the successor of every station, so that the logical ring can be built. The protocol works by rotating a token in this logical ring. The token holds information about the station having the highest priority packet to be transmitted and its priority value.

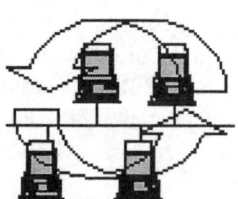

Fig. 1. Logical ring

For the transmission of one message, an arbitrary station is designated as the *token_master*. During the priority-arbitration phase the token travels through the whole ring, visiting all the nodes, in a type of packet called a *Regular Token*. Each station checks the information in the token to determine if one of its own packets has a priority higher than the priority carried by the token. In that case, it changes the highest priority station and associated priority in the token information; otherwise the token is left unchanged. Then, the token is sent to the successor station. This process is followed until the token arrives back at the *token_master* station, finishing the arbitration phase.

In the message-transmission phase the *token_master* station sends a packet with a token of a special type called a *Transmit Token*, addressed to the station with the highest priority message, which then sends its message in a packet of the type *Info Packet*. The receiving station becomes the new *token_master* station.

The actual behaviour of the protocol is a bit more complex because it is designed to tolerate some faults. Otherwise, the loss of a token, for example, would cause communications to be stopped. We have considered three possible faults to be handled by the protocol:

- *Failure of a Station:* A reconfiguration of the ring is performed to leave the failing station out of the ring.
- *Loss of a packet:* A retransmission takes place after a configurable timeout.
- *Busy station* (a station that takes too long to respond): A retransmission will occur, but if it was not caused by a packet loss a duplicate packet would be generated. We need to trash such duplicate packets.

The real-time behaviour is only guaranteed in case of the loss of a packet. A busy station error is a consequence of bad system design, and should be detected and corrected at system design time. The failure of a station is a major fault that would require fault-tolerant techniques with redundant software and/or hardware, which are outside the scope of our work. Therefore, we provide some level of recovery from this error, but real-time response is not guaranteed during the recovery process.

The recovery method for these errors is based on simultaneous listening to the media by all the stations, in a promiscuous mode. Each station, after sending a packet, listens to the media for an *acknowledge*, which is the correct transmission of the next frame by the receiving station. If no acknowledge is received after some specified *timeout*, the station assumes that the packet is lost and retransmits it. The station repeats this process until an acknowledge is received or a specified number or retransmissions is produced. In the latter case the receiving station is considered as a *failing station* and will be excluded from the logical ring. Because retransmission opens the door to duplicate packets if a station does not respond in time, a *sequence number* is used to discard duplicates at the receiving end.

3 RT-EP as a State Machine

RT-EP can be described as a state machine for each station, in order to understand its functionality and to identify operations involved in the timing model. Fig. 2. shows the states and the transitions among them using UML notation [13], which is based on Harel's statecharts [4]. The description of the different states is as follows:

- *Offline*. It is the initial state reached during configuration time. Each station reads the configuration describing the logical ring and gets configured as one of its stations. The station configured as the initial *token_master* (*isTokenMaster* = True) performs a *Send_Initial_Token* action and then enter the *Error_Check* state. The others are set to the *Idle* state.
- *Idle*. In this state, the station listens for the arrival of any packet, discarding possible duplicates. In addition, due to the promiscuous mode (every station listens to every packet), it discards all the packets not specifically addressed to this station. When a non-discarded packet is received, a check is made to determine its type: if it is an *Info_Packet* (*Message Reception* event) the station stores the message and performs a *Send_Initial_Token* action; if it is a *Token Packet* (either a *Token Reception* or a *Transmit Token Reception* event), three different actions can be performed: *Send_Info* (if a *Transmit Token* is received or if the *token_master* receives a regular token and it has the highest priority message to transmit), *Send_Token* (if a regular token is received and the station is

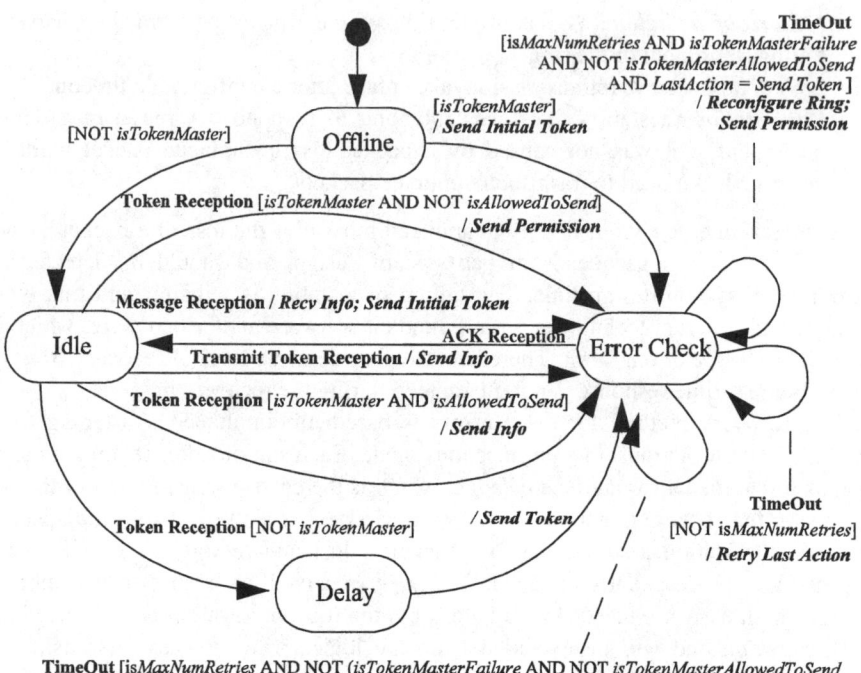

Fig. 2. RT-EP state machine

not the current *token_master*), or *Send_Permission* (when the *token_master* receives a regular token and is not the station with the highest priority message).

- *Error Check*. The station starts listening to the media after transmitting a frame. If a correct packet is detected the station switches to the *Idle* state. If not, after a configurable timeout, the station tries to recover from the error by resending the last packet. If the number of resent packets exceeds a configurable maximum, the successor station is considered to have failed. The failing station identifier is transmitted in the token and is erased from the ring in all the stations. No subsequent info message transmission is allowed for that station.
- *Delay*. This state represents a delay when sending the token. It is introduced to reduce the overhead incurred by the execution of the protocol operations in the different stations. Its interval is a configurable parameter inside the protocol, with which we can trade message latency against processor overhead.

The actions that appear in the state machine are:

- *Send_Initial_Token*. The station performing this action becomes the current *token_master*. A token is sent to the successor station with the highest of the priorities of the messages pending in the transmission queue, if any. Then, the station switches to the *Error_Check* state.

- *Send_Token*. The station compares the priority of the token with the highest priority element on its transmission queue, updates the token with its own priority if it is higher, and sends the token to next station. Then, it switches to the *Error_Check* state.
- *Send_Permission*. The *token_master* role is lost and a *Transmit Token* is built and sent to the *Station Address* recorded in the last received token, which is the station with the highest priority message. Then, the *Error_Check* state is reached.
- *Send_Info*. This is the action performed when a station has the highest priority packet in the ring and is allowed to transmit it. Then it switches to the *Error_Check* state.
- *Recv_Info*. The information received inside the *Info_Packet* is written into the appropriate reception queue and the station performs a *Send_Initial_Token* action, becoming the new *token_master*.

4   RT-EP Packets

RT-EP packets are carried inside the *Data* field of the lower-layer protocol. We are currently using Ethernet for the lower layer, but it can be easily replaced by another protocol. Ethernet II has the following structure [5]:

8 bytes	6 bytes	6 bytes	2 bytes	46-1500 bytes	4 bytes
Preamble	*Destination Address*	*Source Address*	*Type*	*Data*	*Frame Check Sequence*

The *Type* field identifies what type of high-level network protocol is being carried in the data field. We use a value of 0x1000 for the *Type* field, which represents an unused number protocol that could be changed if the protocol is registered in the future.

The mximum message size of Ethernet is 1500 bytes and therefore the RT-EP_MTU parameter is 1492 bytes (Ethernet MTU minus the RT-EP info packet header). The protocol packets are carried inside the *Data* field of the Ethernet frame, which must be at least 46 bytes long. Due to this restriction, if the packet to be sent is less than 46 bytes long, it is padded with zeros to build a 46 bytes packet. Our protocol has two types of packets:

- *Token Packet*: it is used to transmit the tokens and has the following structure:

1 byte	1 byte	2 bytes	2 bytes	2 bytes	2 bytes	2 bytes
Packet Identifier	*Priority*	*Packet Number*	*Token Master ID*	*Failing Station*	*Failing Station ID*	*Station ID*

The *Packet Identifier* field is present also in the *Info Packet* and is used to identify the type of the packet. It can hold two different values for this type of packet:

- *Regular Token*, used in the arbitration phase to find the highest priority packet
- *Transmit Token*, which grants permission to transmit a message

The *Priority* indicates the highest priority element in the ring, found during the rotation. The *Packet Number* is used as a sequence number to eliminate duplicate packets. Each station transmits the received *Packet Number* incremented by one. *Token Master ID* stores the identification of the current *token_master* station, which is needed to recover from a *token_master* failure. *Failing Station* indicates whether there is a failing station or not, and *Failing Station ID* specifies which station, if any. By including this information in the token it is possible for the stations in the ring to remove the failing station from their local configuration, discarding any further messages to this station. The *Station ID* stores the station with the highest priority packet.

- *Info Packet*: it is used to transmit data and has the following structure:

1 byte	1 byte	2 bytes	2 bytes	2 bytes	0-RT-EP_MTU bytes
Packet Identifier	Priority	Packet Number	Channel ID	Info Length	Info

The *Packet Identifier* has a value that identifies it as an *Info Packet*. The *Priority* field holds the priority of the packet being transmitted. As well as in the *Token Packet*, *Packet Number* is the sequence number. The *Channel ID* is used to identify the destination queue in the destination station. The *Info Length* is the size of the data stored in the *Info* field. In Ethernet, if the information to be transmitted is less than 38 bytes long, padding is performed in order to get the 46 data bytes required in an Ethernet frame.

5 RT-EP Implementation

The functionality and architecture of the communication protocol are shown in Fig. 3. This protocol offers four primitives to any application or middleware using the network: *Init_Comm* (to initialize the network), *Send_Info* (to send a message), *Receive_Info* (to receive a message), and *Try_Receive_Info* (a non-blocking version of receive message). To send a message it is necessary to encapsulate the information in a message type, which is used both for transmission and reception. This message type contains the destination station address, the destination channel ID, the priority of the message and the application data.

Inside RT-EP there is only one task, the *Main Communications Task,* that is responsible of reading the packets from the transmission queue and of writing the received packets into the reception queues. Usually this task executes at a priority level higher than that of the application tasks, and its overhead is modelled as extra load using the model described in Section 6. In addition, there is an interrupt service routine (ISR) that handles incoming packets, and awakens the internal task if necessary.

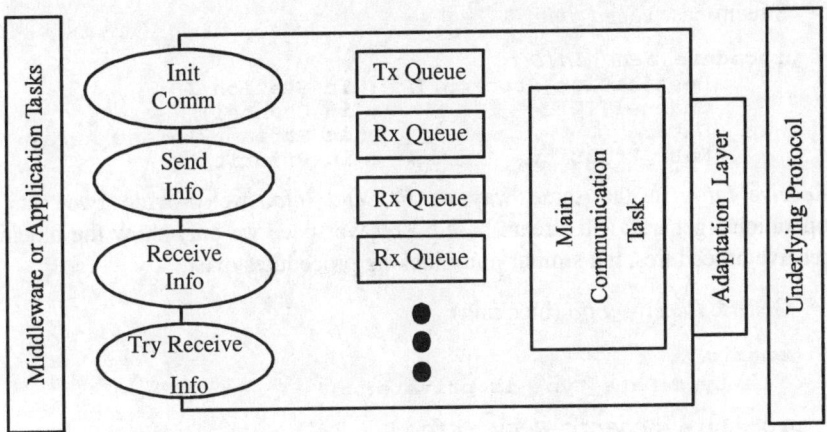

Fig. 3. Functionality and architecture of RT-EP

We have attempted to make the protocol as system independent as possible. To achieve this we have made separate modules that deal with the system, the Ethernet frames and the network drivers. If someone needs to port the protocol to another communications subsystem (for instance, on top of UDP), only the modules under the adaptation layer need to be changed. The protocol has a clear interface with functions to identify the stations and to construct the frame that is going to be sent through the network.

We have provided Ada and C interfaces to the protocol. We will now show the Ada interfaces for the application and the adaptation layer.

5.1 Ada Application Interface

The main primitives to be used by an Ada application or middleware are the following:

- *Init_Comm*: When initializing the protocol, the Main Communication Task is started. The priority of this special task has to be configured at compilation time and it has to be higher than that of the tasks that are communicating through the network:

  procedure *Init_Comm*;

- *Send_Info*: To implement this primitive two operations are provided:

  - Generic *Send_Info*:

  ```
  generic
        type Data_Type is private;

  procedure Generic_Send_Info
        (Destination_Station_ID      : in Station_ID;
         Channel_ID                  : in Channel;
         Data                        : in Data_Type;
         Data_Priority               : in Priority);
  ```

- Stream-based *Send_Info*:

```
procedure Send_Info
        (Destination_Station_ID  : in Station_ID;
        Channel_ID              : in Channel;
        Data                    : in Stream_Element_Array;
        Data_Priority           : in Priority);
```

- *Receive_Info*: In the same way as in *Send_Info*, we provide two sets of operations: generic, and stream-based. To save space we only show the blocking receive procedures, but similar non-blocking procedures exist.

  - Generic *Receive_Info* (blocking):

```
generic
        type Data_type is private;

procedure Generic_Recv_Info
        (Source_Address          : out Station_ID;
        Channel_ID              : in Channel;
        Data                    : out Data_Type;
        Data_Priority           : out Priority);
```

  - Stream-based *Receive_Info* (blocking):

```
procedure Recv_Info
        (Source_Address          : out Station_ID;
        Channel_ID              : in Channel;
        Data                    : out Stream_Element_Array;
        Last                    : out Stream_Element_Offset;
        Data_Priority           : out Priority);
```

5.2 Adaptation Layer

This API must be implemented for the specific underlying protocol:

- **Set_Promiscuous_Mode**: Sets the promiscuous mode in the system. The protocol has to be able to receive all the frames transmitted in the media.

```
procedure Set_Promiscuous_Mode;
```

- **Open_RTEP_Comm**: Makes the required initialization to be able to read/write from/to the media. Further calls to this function will have no effect.

```
procedure Open_RTEP_Comm;
```

- **Close_RTEP_Comm**: Closes the media.

```
procedure Close_RTEP_Comm;
```

- **Send_RTEP_Packet**: Sends the RT_EP_Packet to the Dest_Station

```
procedure Send_RTEP_Packet
        (Dest_Station            : in Station_ID;
        RT_EP_Packet            : in Stream_Element_Array);
```

- **Recv_RTEP_Packet**: Returns a packet addressed to Dest_Station.

```
procedure Recv_RTEP_Packet
       (Dest_Station            : out Station_ID;
        Source_Station          : out Station_ID;
        RT_EP_Packet            : out Stream_Element_Array;
        Last                    : out Stream_Element_Offset);
```

6 MAST Model of RT-EP

This subsection describes the modelling information of RT-EP according to MAST (Modelling and Analysis Suite for Real-Time Applications) [12]. This methodology provides an open-source set of tools that enables engineers developing real-time applications to check the timing behaviour of their application, including schedulability analysis for checking hard timing requirements.

We have built a MAST model to characterize a communications system based on RT-EP, so that the timing behaviour of the distributed hard real-time application can be analysed. The model is divided into three elements: network drivers, the network itself, and the network scheduler.

6.1 Network Drivers

In MAST, the overhead of the protocol in the different processors in the ring is modelled by a set of network drivers, one for each processor. The drivers previously available in MAST were not appropriate for modelling the complexity of the RT-EP protocol, and therefore we had to create a new driver called the *RTEP_Packet_Driver*. Its most important attributes are the following:

- *Packet Server*: the task executing the driver in the corresponding processor.
- *Packet Interrupt Server*: It represents the interrupt routine that stores the frames received from the net.
- *Packet ISR Operation (ISR)*: Code executed by the *Packet Interrupt Server*.
- *Packet Send Operation (PSO)*: Code executed for the *Send_Info* action.
- *Packet Receive Operation (PRxO)*: Code executed for the *Recv_Info* and *Send_Initial_Token* actions.
- *Number of Stations (N)*.
- *Token Manage Operation (TMO)*: Maximum of the times required to send the token in the *Send_Token* or the *Send_Permission* actions.
- *Token Check Operation (TCO)*. Code executed in the *Idle* state upon the *Token_Reception* event, that determines the following state.
- *Token Delay (TD)*. The configurable time of the *Delay* state.
- *Packet Discard Operation (PDO)*. Code executed when packets addressed to other stations are received, because of the network promiscuous mode used.
- *Token Transmission Retry (TR)*: Maximum number of faults (and their retransmissions) that we allow in each token arbitration.
- *Packet Transmission Retry (PR)*: Maximum number of retransmissions when transmitting an *Info Packet*.

- *Timeout (T)*: Timeout used to detect a message transmission failure.
- *Token Retransmission Operation (TRO)*: Time consumed in a token retransmission. It corresponds to *Retry_Last_Action* in the *Error_Check* state, when the retransmitted packet is a token.
- *Packet Retransmission Operation (PRO)*: Time consumed in an *Info_Packet* retransmission. It corresponds to *Retry_Last_Action* in the *Error_Check* state, when an info packet is retransmitted.

6.2 Network

For modelling the ethernet we use a model already built in MAST that is called the *Packet_Based_Network*. Its most important attributes for modelling the timing behaviour are the following:

- *Throughput (Rb)*: It is the bit rate of the media.
- *Max Packet Transmission Time (MaxPTT)*: $MaxPTT = (1492 \cdot 8)/Rb$
- *Min Packet Transmission Time (MinPTT)*. $MinPTT = (72 \cdot 8)/Rb$
- *Max Packet Size* and *Min Packet Size*: They are 1492 and 72 respectively.
- *Max Blocking*: The maximum blocking caused by the non preemptability of message packets. In RT-EP, it is calculated as:

$$(N)(MinPTT + ISR + TCO + TMO) + ((N-1) \cdot TD) +$$

$$\left(PSO + ISR + PRxO + MaxPTT + \frac{34 \cdot 8}{R_b} + PR \cdot (PRO + T)\right) + (TRO + T) \cdot TR$$

it represents a complete rotation of the token (*N-1* tokens sent), plus the blocking effect caused by the transmission of non preemptible packet considering the possible faults in the info packet (*PR*(PRO+T)*), and also in the tokens (*TR*(TRO+T)*).

6.3 Scheduler

Each network mush have a primary scheduler for its messages with a scheduling policy. For the latter we use the *FP_Packet_Based* policy that models fixed priority messages composed of non-preemptible packets. Its main attribute is:

- *Packet Overhead*. This is the overhead caused by the protocol information that needs to be sent before or after each packet. It is calculated as:

$$(N+1)(MinPTT + ISR + TCO + TMO) + (N \cdot TD) +$$

$$(TRO + T) \cdot TR + \frac{34 \cdot 8}{R_b}$$

which is the time spent to send a number of tokens equal to the number of stations, N, performing a complete circulation of the *Token*, plus one *Transmit Token*. The time needed to send a token is calculated as the sum of the *Min Packet Transmission Time*, *Min_PTT*, the time to get the packet from the media (*ISR*), the time of the *Token Check Operation*, and the time of the *Token Manage Operation*.

We also take into account the number of token retries (*TR*) and the cost of the associated *Token Retransmit Operation* (*TRO*) and the Timeouts (*T*). We also have to add the time to send the protocol bytes.

7 Evaluation Under MaRTE OS

We have obtained metrics of the worst, average, and best case response times of the different operations executed in the RT-EP protocol, measured in a minimum platform composed of two industrial PCs (Pentium III 750 MHz) running MaRTE OS and connected by a 100 Mbps Ethernet network. The application consisted of five tasks in each PC sending each other average-size messages through five different channels. The results are shown in Table 1.

Table 1. Measured execution times for the RTEP driver operations

RTEP driver operation	Worst (µs)	Best (µs)	Av (µs)
Packet ISR (ISR)	6.48	2.50	3.74
Packet Send (PSO)	60.39	47.98	49.72
Packet Receive (PRxO)	93.13	76.12	77.30
Token Manage (TMO)	41.86	34.70	35.10
Token Check (TCO)	15.65	8.673	9.515
Packet Discard (PDO)	6.169	1.545	1.685
Token Retransmit (TRO)	48.03	36.25	36.79
Packet Retransmit (PRO)	60.38	47.98	49.72

It is also interesting to show the parameters of the network overhead model, including the time it takes to perform a token rotation, the *Packet Overhead* parameter, and the *Max Blocking* parameter (see Table 2). The token rotation was measured with a protocol delay of 100 μs. The other two parameters were calculated using the data from Table 1 in the corresponding formulas.

Table 2. Main Parameters of the Network Overhead Model

Operation	Worst case (μs)	Best case (μs)	Avg. case (μs)
Token Rotation Time	297.56	287.01	288.83
Packet Overhead	411.97	357.62	365.06
Max Blocking	521.58	451.95	461.07

Due to the priority arbitration prior to sending the packet, the effective throughput of the media gets degraded. In order to calculate which is the effective bit rate achieved with the protocol we have extracted two different cases:

- *Synchronized Tx/Rx*: A "synchronized" communication occurs when the stations agree to transmit or receive by any method, producer-consumer, stop and wait, etc. In this case we don't have blocking and the attribute that influences the bit rate is the *Packet Overhead*:

$$R_{bT} = \frac{1492 \cdot 8}{PacketOverhead + MaxPTT}$$

In this case we have achieved an effective bit rate of 22.464 Mbps

- *General case*: The transmission of a packet in the network is totally asynchronous. In this case we have to consider the maximum blocking (521.58 μs with the measured values):

$$R_{bT} = \frac{1492 \cdot 8}{MaxBlocking + PacketOverhead + MaxPTT}$$

With this consideration the effective bit rate is 11.336 Mbps.

Another important factor of the protocol is how the delay introduced in the configuration influences the load introduced by the protocol. With the delay attribute we can control the protocol CPU utilization, as shown in Table 3.

As it can be seen from the table, the optimum values from the utilization point of view, are with a delay value between 30 and 100 μs. In this band we achieve a low utilization with a quick response from the protocol.

Table 3. Driver overhead as a function of the protocol delay

Delay (µs)	CPU Utilization
0	12 %
1	12 %
10	12 %
30	7.8 %
50	6.0 %
100	3.8 %
1.000	0.5 %

8 RT-EP Demonstrator

Once the protocol is designed, implemented and characterized, it is important to use it in a demonstrator in order to confirm its validity in hard real time communications. The chosen demonstrator is an industrial robot arm for maintenance in radioactive environments. A diagram of this platform is shown in Fig. 4.

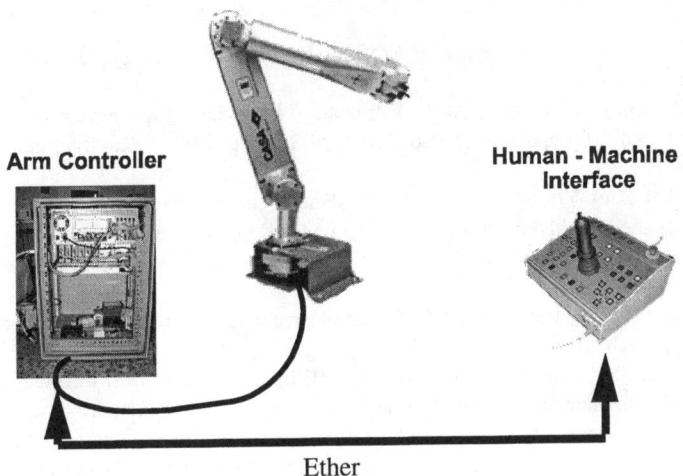

Fig. 4. Demonstrator platform

The control software is written in Ada and the distribution is done through RT-GLADE [8] implemented on top of RT-EP. Through this demonstrator we have confirmed the validity of the protocol.

9 Conclusions

We have presented an implementation of a software-based token-passing Ethernet protocol for multipoint communications in real-time applications, that does not require any modification to existing Ethernet hardware, and does not require any clock synchronization mechanism. The protocol is based on fixed priorities and thus common tools for fixed priority schedulability analysis can be used to analyse the timing behaviour of applications using it. For this purpose, a precise timing model of the protocol has been obtained.

In order to avoid collisions in the ethernet media the protocol uses a token passing mechanism that causes the utilization of the network to be rather low compared to the usual utilization level in standard ethernet. However, the bit rate obtained is still larger than in most field busses, so compared to them we can get the same predictability level at a very low cost and with high performance. The overhead caused by the network driver can be traded against the latency of message passing in the network by means of the protocol delay parameter. Consequently, RT-EP has proven to be an excellent choice for real-time communications for systems that do not have a large number of stations.

Although the current implementation is in MaRTE OS, it is important to say that the protocol is suitable for other Real-Time OSs and underlying protocols.

References

[1] Alan Burns. "The Ravenscar Profile". Department of Computer Science, University of York, UK
[2] Chiueh Tzi-Cker and C. Venkatramani. "Fault handling mechanisms in the RETHER protocol". Symposium on Fault-Tolerant Systems, Pacific Rim International, pp. 153-159, 1997.
[3] Choi Baek-Young, Song Sejun, N. Birch, and Huang Jim. "Probabilistic approach to switched Ethernet for real-time control applications". Proceedings of Seventh International Conference on Real-Time Computing Systems and Applications, pp. 384-388, 2000.
[4] Harel David, Politi Michael. "Modeling reactive systems with statecharts: the statemate approach". McGraw-Hill, 1998
[5] IEEE Std 802.3, 2000 Edition: "IEEE Standard for Information technology--Telecommunications and information exchange between systems--Local and metropolitan area networks--Common specifications--Part 3: Carrier sense multiple access with collision detection (CSMA/CD) access method and physical layer specifications"
[6] IEEE Std 802.4-1990. "IEEE Standard for Information technology--Telecommunications and information exchange between systems--Local and metropolitan area networks--Common specifications--Part 4: Token-Passing Bus Access Method and Physical Layer Specifications".

[7] Jae-Young Lee, Hong-Ju Moon, Sang Yong Moon, Wook Hyun Kwon, Sung Woo Lee, and Ik Soo Park. "Token-Passing bus access method on the IEEE 802.3 physical layer for distributed control networks". Distributed Computer Control Systems 1998 (DCCS'98), Proceedings volume from the 15th IFAC Workshop. Elsevier Science, Kidlington, UK, pp. 31-36, 1999.

[8] J. López Campos, J. J. Gutiérrez, and M. González Harbour, "The Chance for Ada to Support Distribution and Real-Time in Embedded Systems". 9th Proceedings of the International Conference on Reliable Software Technologies, Ada-Europe-2004.

[9] K. Tindell, A. Burns, and A.J. Wellings, "Calculating Controller Area Network (CAN) Message Response Times". Proceedings of the 1994 IFAC Workshop on Distributed Computer Control Systems (DCCS), Toledo, Spain, 1994.

[10] M. Aldea and M. González. "MaRTE OS: An Ada Kernel for Real-Time Embedded Applications". Proceedings of the International Conference on Reliable Software Technologies, Ada-Europe-2001, Leuven, Belgium, Lecture Notes in Computer Science, LNCS 2043, May, 2001

[11] Martínez, J.M. González Harbour, M. and Gutiérrez, J.J. "RT-EP: Real-Time Ethernet Protocol for Analyzable Distributed Applications on a Minimum Real-Time POSIX Kernel". Proceedings of the 2nd International Workshop on Real-Time LANs in the Internet Age, RTLIA 2003, Porto (Portugal), July 2003.

[12] M. González Harbour, J.J. Gutiérrez, J.C. Palencia and J.M. Drake: "MAST: Modelling and Analysis Suite for Real-Time Applications". Proceedings of the Euromicro Conference on Real-Time Systems, Delft, The Netherlands, June 2001

[13] Object Management Group (OMG). Unified Modeling Language (UML). http://www.uml.org

[14] Paulo Pedreiras, Luis Almeida, Paolo Gar. "The FTT-Ethernet protocol: Merging flexibility, timeliness and efficiency". Proceedings of the 14th Euromicro Conference on Real-Time Systems, Vienna, Austria, June 2002.

[15] Thomas Vergnaud, Jérome Hugues, Laurent Pautet, and Fabrice Kordon "PolyORB: A Schizophrenic Middleware to Build Versatile Reliable Distributed Applications". Proceedings of the 9th Ada-Europe International Conference on Reliable Software Technologies, Palma de Mallorca, Spain, June 14-18, 2004, in LNCS 3063, Springer Varlag.

Distributing Criticality Across Ada Partitions*

Miguel Masmano, Jorge Real, Alfons Crespo, and Ismael Ripoll

Department of Computer Engineering (DISCA),
Universidad Politécnica de Valencia, Spain
jorge@disca.upv.es

Abstract. A number of real-time systems combine strict (hard) and non strict (soft) timing requirements. In such systems, the hard timing requirements must be guaranteed, whereas tasks with soft requirements may miss some deadlines with no harmful consequences. One possibility to organise such systems is to run the critical tasks in the kernel space, at the highest priority available, while executing the soft tasks in user space, where they will use the remaining execution time after servicing the hard tasks. A recently produced porting of Ada to Real-Time Linux makes this architecture feasible.

In this paper we propose a method for splitting a hard/soft real-time application into criticality-based partitions: the hard partition will run on RTLinux and the soft partition (or partitions) will be placed in the user space of Linux. The use of the Distributed System Annex enables the programmer to automatically place each partition in the right space and allows to hide the communication details between partitions. We also outline a strategy to reduce the average response time of soft tasks.

1 Introduction

Real-Time applications often combine strict (hard) and non-strict (soft) real-time requirements. An example of this is a control and monitoring application, where the tasks in charge of implementing the control law have strict deadlines to achieve stability in the controlled process, but a task in charge of drawing a log diagram of the system state (values of the reference and controlled physical variables) may be occasionally delayed with no harmful consequences.

The main concern of this work is related to the architecture and execution environment of hard/soft real-time applications: running soft and hard tasks in the same memory space (when they form a single task set) is often a risk, since a failing soft task may affect hard tasks. To avoid this problem, it is possible to run the hard part in kernel space and the soft part in user space in a *dual kernel* real-time operating system [2] (approaches such as Real-Time Linux [3, 4] and others allow this choice to be implemented). In this case, the resources available for critical tasks (running in kernel mode) are scarce, but this can be worked around by limiting hard tasks to the very low-level, relatively simple input-output (e.g., A/D reading, D/A writing) and leaving the more

---

* This work has been partly funded by the European OCERA project [1] and by the Spanish *Comisión Interministerial de Ciencia y Tecnología* project number TIC-99-1043-C03-02.

T. Vardanega and A. Wellings (Eds.): Ada-Europe 2005, LNCS 3555, pp. 196–207, 2005.

intensive and complex input-output to soft tasks (e.g., text input-output, graphics, disk, etc.)

In [5], a porting of Ada to Real-Time Linux (RTLinux for short) is proposed, based on the GNAT Ada compiler and run-time support. This porting allows to map Ada tasks to RTLinux threads, therefore allowing them to execute with the highest priority in the system. In the same paper, an architecture was proposed for applications with hard and soft components. The proposal in [5] is to run the critical set of tasks on RTLinux, in the kernel space, and to execute the rest of the application as a regular Linux process. The communication between the hard and the soft parts has to be explicitly implemented, e.g. by means of real-time FIFO queues (RT-FIFOs), which unfortunately is very much platform-dependent.

This paper proposes an improvement to the way of implementing such architecture. Our proposal is to split the application into two different Ada partitions, one containing the hard tasks and the other one for soft tasks, and to make use of the standard Ada mechanisms described in the Distributed Systems Annex to communicate hard and soft partitions. The main goal is to hide the communication details to the programmer and to automate the process of loading the partitions in the proper layer. This idea was proposed as future work in [5]. This paper also discusses the issue of combined scheduling of hard and soft tasks in such architecture, and outlines a mechanism to implement algorithms for servicing soft tasks with a lower service time than the classical background approach. This aspect is of importance since the RTLinux approach is to run Linux in the background, as an idle task with respect to the group of real-time tasks.

The structure of the paper is the following. Section 2 presents the proposed architecture for combined hard/soft Ada applications, leaving the implementation to Section 3. Section 4 discusses scheduling issues. An example application is presented in Section 5. Finally, Section 6 presents our conclusions.

2   Architecture of the Application

Our starting point in this work is the porting of Ada to RTLinux presented in [5]. The RTLinux approach is to intercept hardware interrupts and deliver them to Linux only at points in time when the Linux kernel would become idle. The Real-Time application is part of the kernel (inserted as a Linux kernel module), therefore it resides in a higher-priority layer than the rest of processes. The goal of that porting is to execute multitask Ada applications on RTLinux, thus removing the interference of non-critical processes on the Real-Time application.

Figure 1 shows the architecture proposed for hard/soft applications. An Ada application is divided in two parts, one with hard real-time requirements (the *Ada real-time application*) and another part that is scheduled by Linux (*Ada background tasks*), since it has no strict timing requirements. In the proposal, these two parts are two different Ada programs. The link between them is via RT-FIFOs. The RT-FIFO mechanism provides a rapid way of communicating tasks in the real-time and non real-time layers. It also allows hard real-time tasks to communicate with applications written in a different language: RT-FIFOs can be seen as special devices in the /etc/dev directory.

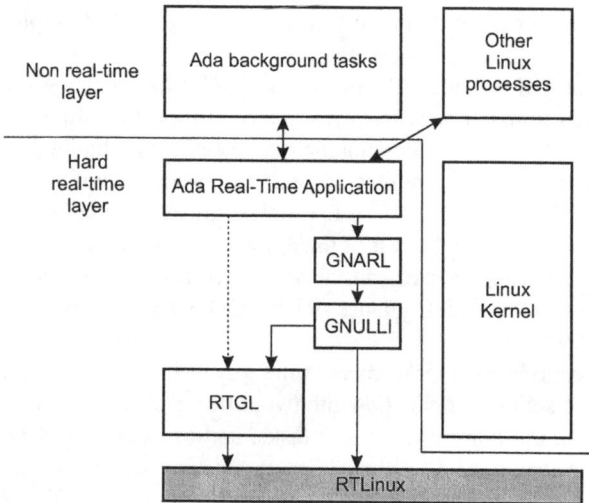

Fig. 1. Architecture of the system, with an Ada Real-Time application running on top of RTLinux and other Ada tasks running in background as a Linux process

The Ada real-time application uses the services provided by the Real-Time Gnat Layer (RTGL) only at startup, for the creation of threads (RTGL is a layer designed for the porting described in [5]). The program then uses a slightly modified version of the run-time system (layers GNARL and GNULLI) to obtain the tasking services such as rendezvous, protected objects, etc. For a more detailed description of the GNAT run-time system see [6]. The Linux kernel and other Linux processes are scheduled in the background with respect to the application's real-time components.

The architecture proposed in this paper is basically the one depicted in Figure 1, with the following considerations:

– The Ada real-time application and the set of Ada background tasks are contained in two different Ada partitions.
– The communication between the hard and soft parts is achieved by means of the mechanisms defined in the Distributed Systems Annex of the Ada standard.
– The actual implementation of the communication link may be through RT-FIFOs or other mechanisms (see Section 3.)

2.1   Inter-partition Communication

The Distributed Systems Annex (Annex E) of the Ada standard defines the possibilities for inter-partition communication in terms of categorization of the library units contained in the partitions forming the program. There exist four pragmas for the categorization of library units, namely:

– Pure. This pragma is not defined in Annex E, but it is considered a categorization pragma to complete the hierarchical relationship between categories of library units. A pure library item is preelaborable, i.e., it does not contain the declaration of any variable or named access type, except within a subprogram, generic subprogram, task unit, or protected unit. A pure library unit can depend only on other declared pure library units.

- Shared_Passive, for managing global data shared between active partitions, i.e., partitions with one or more threads of control. A shared passive library unit can be assigned to at most one partition of the distributed program and it may depend semantically only upon declared pure or shared passive library units.
- Remote_Types, for the definition of types (not variables) intended for use in communication between active partitions. A remote types library unit may depend semantically only upon declared pure, shared passive, or other remote types library units.
- Remote_Call_Interface, to provide remote subprogram calls between active partitions. The declaration of a remote call interface library unit may depend semantically only upon declared pure, shared passive, remote types, or other remote call interface library units.

The last three pragmas in this list enable to properly implement inter-partition communication at the required level, from only sharing data objects and types to remotely calling subprograms in foreign partitions. In a hard/soft real-time application, organised in different partitions as we propose, these options would allow the hard and the soft partitions to communicate in the way defined in the Ada standard, thus hiding the details of communications to the programmer (e.g., creating and managing RT-FIFOs).

3   Implementation

This section deals with the implementation details of our approach. We revise the available tools and explain how they have been modified to support distribution of an Ada application across user and kernel space in RTLinux.

3.1   GLADE: An Implementation of the Distributed Systems Annex

For the purpose described in the introduction, to distribute Ada programs in different layers of the system, we first looked for the available implementations of Annex E and found two: ADEPT and GLADE [7]. Both are based on the GNAT compiler, which was a pre-requisite for us, since our previous porting of Ada to RTLinux is also based on GNAT; but we discarded ADEPT mainly because it is no longer maintained. It was also very important for us to use a publicly licensed product, since our intention was to modify it. GLADE served our purpose sufficiently, with some changes that will be described below. Technical features of GLADE include:

- Run-time library for Annex E support.
- Management of inter-partition communication.
- Tools to define partition location and content.
- Support for heterogeneous environments.
- Data filtering (encryption, compression).
- Replication and embedded capabilities.

GLADE is basically formed by two different components: Gnatdist, the tool to distribute the application (via a configuration file) into different partitions and the GARLIC library, which implements the communication mechanisms between partitions.

Gnatdist overview. Gnatdist is the tool provided by GLADE to build and locate the different partitions forming the distributed application.

Before using Gnatdist, the application can be implemented as if it was not distributed. Once it has been tested as a non distributed application, the application's library units must be categorised according to their role in the distributed program (remote call interface, shared passive or remote types library units). Categorisation requires using the pragmas defined in Annex E.

The last step for the building of the distributed application is to write a configuration file[1] where all partitions to be created are described (name of the partitions, communication protocols used, library units belonging to each partition, how each partition has to be launched, etc.)

Gnatdist processes the configuration file and calls the GNAT compiler with the suitable parameters to build the distributed application: it generates the required stubs, performs timestamp checks for avoiding useless recompilation and makes some additional checks (e.g., all remote call interface and shared passive units must be mapped into one and only one partition.)

Changes to gnatdist. The gnatdist tool needs not to be ported to RTLinux because it will be executed as a regular Linux user application. However, there exists a limitation for our purpose: when gnatdist invokes the GNAT commpiler (gcc, gnatbind and gnatlink), it will use the versions reachable through the $PATH environment variable. This is not adequate in our case, since we need to produce two kinds of object code:

- Linux code for the soft partition. The Linux object code is produced by the GNAT version for Linux, i.e., gcc, gnatbind and gnatlink.
- RTLinux code for the hard partition. In this case, we need to use the rtlgcc, rtl-gnatbind and rtlgnatlink scripts —These tools are available in the distribution of RTLGnat [5]. These RTLinux-specific scripts call the corresponding tools with the appropriate flags.

As an example, let's look at the rtlgcc script (the flags used in the cases of rtlgnatbind and rtlgnatlink are very similar):

```
(1) #!/bin/sh
(2) GNAT_RUNTIME_DIR = /lib/gcc-lib/i686-pc-linux-gnu/2.8.1
(3) LIBS_PATH=`dirname $0`
(4) LIBS_PATH=`dirname $LIBS_PATH`$GNAT_RUNTIME_DIR
(5) RTLGNAT_LIBS=$LIBS_PATH/rts-rtlinux/
(6) gcc $@ --RTS=$RTLGNAT_LIBS
```

Lines (2) through (5) obtain the path to the RTLGnat run-time system. Line (6) invokes gcc specifying the adequate location of the run-time.

---

[1] A configuration language is provided by GLADE to specify the configuration of the distributed application.

To build the distributed application, we have added a new flag *rtlinux* to gnatdist. When this flag is set, gnatdist uses RTLGnat (rtlgcc, rtlgnatbind and rtlgnatlink) instead of GNAT to produce an RTLinux-compatible module. For example, to build a distributed program with two partitions, `Hard` and `Soft`, we need to invoke gnatdist twice:

```
gnatdist configuration_file.cfg Soft
gnatdist --rtlinux configuration_file.cfg Hard
```

With the new flag *rtlinux*, it is not necessary to install two versions of gnatdist in the same computer.

GARLIC overview. As explained above, GARLIC is the library that provides the runtime to distributed programs (communications protocols, marshalling, unmarshalling, etc.)

GARLIC has been designed as an extension of the GNAT run-time system. In fact, it substitutes dummy packages of the GNAT run-time system (e.g., `System.RPC`) with the fully implemented corresponding packages.

Currently, there is only support for the TCP protocol in GARLIC, although there exist some other communications protocols such as RT-EP [8] and UDP [9].

Changes to GARLIC. The fundamental change needed in GARLIC is to add a protocol that enables to inter-communicate Linux and RTLinux partitions. There are several options in RTLinux to achieve this goal:

- RT-FIFOs: This is the commonly used mechanism in RTLinux to communicate between RTLinux threads and Linux processes. An RT-FIFO implements a buffer shared by both parts, and a notification mechanism to RTLinux threads that enables to execute a handler every time a new message from the Linux side arrives in the RT-FIFO.
- Shared Memory is another RTLinux method to communicate RTLinux threads with Linux processes by sharing memory pages. Differently to RT-FIFO, this method does not provide any notification mechanism.
- Real-Time Light-Weight IP (RTLW-IP): This is a porting of the LW-IP stack to RTLinux [1]. It provides a full TCP/IP stack, which exceeds our requirements, and it is intended to communicate RTLinux threads residing in different computers of a network, which is not our case.
- Real-Time Linux UDP (RTL-UDP, [1]): This is a very simple UDP stack that allows direct communication of RTLinux threads with the Linux UDP stack. It is a possible candidate to build a new UDP communication protocol for GARLIC, but it has not been sufficiently tested yet.

Since RT-FIFO is the most efficient and tested known mechanism to communicate RTLinux threads with Linux processes, we have chosen it to implement a new communication protocol, called *rtfifo*, to inter-communicate Linux and RTLinux partitions. The *rtfifo* protocol is asymmetric in the sense that RT-FIFOs are viewed differently in RTLinux and in Linux. In RTLinux, there exists an API to create, destroy and use the RT-FIFOs, whereas a Linux application accesses RT-FIFOs as special devices in the

/dev directory, accessible through standard read, write, open and close functions. It is important to note that none of these standard functions will work if an RT-FIFO has not been previously created from RTLinux. Consequently, we have implemented two versions of the protocol, one to be used from RTLinux (where the hard partition resides) and another one to be used from Linux (the host of the soft partition.) It is gnatdist who instructs the linker to link with one version or the other, depending on where a partition will be hosted. The interface to the *rtfifo* protocol remains identical from the GARLIC point of view.

The *rtfifo* protocol we have implemented follows a mono-thread server model, i.e., it is only possible to establish one communication channel upon an RT-FIFO at a time. No new channels can be created until the established one is closed. A future improvement of the protocol would be to build a multi-thread server model on top of RT-FIFOs. This would allow several clients to share the services of a single server.

To implement this new *rtfifo* protocol, two new packages have been added to the GARLIC library:

- `System.Garlic.Protocols.Rtlinux` (files *s-gaprrt.ad{s|b}*). This package implements the *rtfifo* protocol itself.
- `System.Garlic.Protocols.Rtlinux.Server` (files *s-gprtse.ad{s|b}*). This package implements the creation of the task that will manage the connection. Since at the moment it is only possible to have one active channel at a time (with the current version of the *rtfifo* protocol), the task managing the channel can be statically created.

The interfaces to RT-FIFOs of the *rtfifo* protocol have been implemented in two separate files: `rtl_fifo.c` for the RTLinux partition, and `linux_fifo.c` for the Linux partition.

4   Scheduling Issues

The proposal in this paper is to execute the hard components in RTLinux and to place the soft components in a Linux partition. This isolates both parts and lets the hard partition to execute at a higher priority, in the foreground, but forces the soft partition to be scheduled in background. Background scheduling of soft tasks is acceptable from the hard real-time perspective, but other existing service policies are known to perform better than background in terms of average response time of acritical tasks.

As for today, the Ada standard does not define a dynamic priority scheduling policy, therefore we have focused on a Deadline Monotonic compatible solution to search for a basic mechanism to enhance the responsiveness of acritical tasks in our proposal. Consider for example the Deferrable Server strategy [10] in combination with Dual Priority scheduling [11]. Since the soft tasks run in Linux, if we want to execute them through a server, we need to be able to temporarily set the priority of the Linux thread to a value in the range of priorities of the hard tasks. After a certain amount of CPU time has been used by Linux (this amount of time is usually known as the *budget*), its priority would be set again to background in order not to interfere the execution of

RTLinux tasks. When the budget is replenished, the Linux priority will be set high again to reduce the servicing time of acritical tasks.

The Linux thread is accessible from RTLinux and, with RTLGnat, we can access this thread with an access object. The following package specifies a deferrable server task called DS:

```
package Acritical_Service is
   task DS;
end Acritical_Service;
```

And the body implements the mechanism, but only at a prototype level:

```
pragma Task_Dispatching_Policy(FIFO_Within_Priorities);

with Ada.Real_Time;       use Ada.Real_Time;
with System.OS_Interface; use System.OS_Interface;

package body Acritical_Service is
   Linux_Thread : pthread_t; -- Access to the Linux thread, exported by RTGL
   pragma Import (C, Linux_Thread, "linux_thread");

   task body DS is
      Next_Replenishment : Time := Clock;
      Budget_Exhaustion : Time;
      Budget : constant Time_Span := Milliseconds(100);
      Replenishment_Period : constant Time_Span := Milliseconds (500);
      High_Priority, Low_Priority : aliased struct_sched_param;
      Ret: int;
   begin
      High_Priority.Sched_Priority := 50;   -- A priority in the RTLinux band
      Low_Priority.Sched_Priority := 0;     -- Lowest priority in RTLinux
      loop
         Ret := pthread_setschedparam (Linux_Thread,SCHED_FIFO,High_Priority'Access);
         -- Wait end of budget                        -- Test code. A CPU clock is what
         Budget_Exhaustion := Clock + Budget          -- we really need to check
         delay until Budget_Exhaustion;               -- budget exhaustion
         Ret := pthread_setschedparam (Linux_Thread,SCHED_FIFO,Low_Priority'Access);
         -- Wait end of period
         Next_Replenishment := Next_Replenishment + Replenishment_Period;
         delay until Next_Replenishment;
      end loop;
   end DS;
end Acritical_Service;
```

This is a very simple prototype of a pseudo deferrable server. As commented in the code, the end of the budget is checked in terms of real time, not CPU time. We are currently working on a version that checks the CPU time consumed by the server task.

There is still another aspect of this prototype implementation to take into account: the Deferrable Server task serves Linux as a whole, i.e., all the running processes. If we want to give preference to our acritical component over the rest of Linux processes, we should assign its corresponding Linux process the highest Linux priority to ensure the budget will be used by the acritical component preferentially. Another possibility is to raise the priority of the Linux thread associated to the client, but this requires an additional programming effort.

5   An Example Application

This section presents an example of distributing a hard/soft application into critical/non-critical partitions. The application itself is a pulse width modulation (PWM) speed controller for a small DC motor.

The hard partition in this application, to be loaded as a Linux kernel module, deals with the PWM control by applying power to the motor in periodical fractions of time whose duration is proportional to the given by the *busy cycle* reference. This hard partition is also in charge of measuring the motor speed in revolutions per minute (RPM).

The busy cycle reference is aperiodically refreshed by the soft partition, to be loaded as a Linux application. This partition provides a GUI[2] for typing new reference values and also for displaying a graph showing a time window of reference and speed values. When the user types a new busy cycle the soft partition updates it to the hard partition by means of the remote call interface procedure Set_Reference, offered by the package hosted in the hard partition. To obtain the current speed of the motor, the soft partition uses a remote call interface function (Get_Speed), also provided by the hard partition.

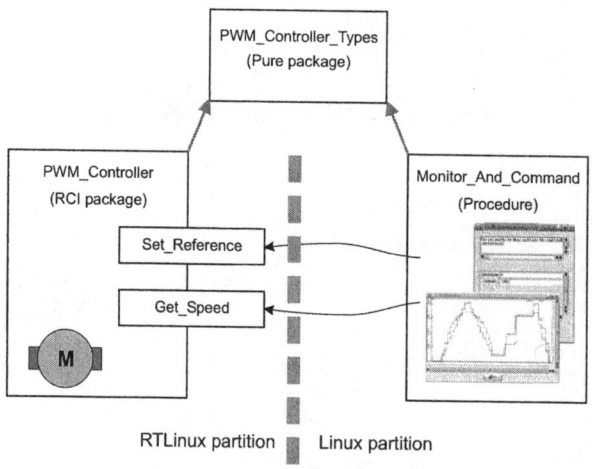

Fig. 2. Organisation of the example application

Figure 2 shows the application's organisation. It consists of three library units:

- PWM_Controller_Types is a pure package defining the types Busy_Cycle and Rpm, the measuring units for the reference and the speed, respectively. Since it is pure, this package has no state and may be duplicated to both partitions.
- Monitor_And_Command. This subprogram unit is the soft part of the application. It manages two windows: a graphic window that displays the curves of reference and speed vs. time, and a text input window to enable setting the reference busy cycle and the refresh period of the graph.

---

[2] We have used the Win_IO [12] library for implementing the GUI.

- Pwm_Controller is the hard partition. It is a remote call interface package offering Set_Reference and Get_Speed, and it hides the PWM control and speed measuring tasks.

In this example, the communication between the hard and the soft partitions is always initiated from the soft partition: function Get_Speed is periodically called from Monitor_And_Command to refresh the speed graph with the latest value whereas procedure Set_Reference is called when a new busy cycle is typed in the input window. Note that a library unit in the hard partition should not normally use synchronous remote call interface subprograms in a soft partition, since it implies suspending the calling hard task until a task in the soft partition is ready to serve the call: this would produce a probably unacceptable priority inversion to the hard task. In case the program needs to make remote procedure calls from the hard to the soft partition, pragma Asynchronous can be used to avoid blocking, although with the known limitations (i.e., only procedures with mode in parameters.)

The specification of PWM_Controller is the following:

```
with PWM_Controller_Types; use PWM_Controller_Types;
package PWM_Controller is
   pragma Remote_Call_Interface;

   procedure Set_Reference (BC : in Busy_Cycle);
   function Get_Speed return Rpm;
end PWM_Controller;
```

The pragma Remote_Call_Interface categorizes this unit as a remote call interface package, so the calls to the visible subprograms are remote procedure calls. The following configuration file instructs gnatdist to create the partitions:

```
(1)    configuration Pwm is
(2)        pragma Starter (None);
(3)
(4)        pragma Boot_Location ("rtlinux", "rtf14");
(5)
(6)        Monitor    : Partition;
(7)        Controller : Partition := (Pwm_Controller);
(8)
(9)        procedure Monitor_And_Command;
(10)       for Monitor'Main use Monitor_And_Command;
(11)       procedure Main is in Controller;
(12)   end Pwm;
```

In line (2), pragma Starter specifies the way to start a server partition when a client partition is started, in case the server has not been loaded yet. We need to set it to None, meaning that all the partitions will be manually launched. It would not be difficult to launch a hard partition in RTLinux from a soft partition in Linux (provided you have root privileges) but it is not that simple to do it the other way around.

In line (4), pragma Boot_Location indicates the inter-partition communication protocol used (*rtlinux* in our case) and the second parameter tells the partition communication subsystem what resources will be used for the communication (RT-FIFO number 14 in the example, i.e., /dev/rtf14.)

Lines (6) and (7) declare the partitions of the application. In addition, line (7) specifies the library unit contained in the partition Controller (the package Pwm_Controller.)

Lines (9) and (10) specify the name of the main procedure in partition Monitor.

Finally, line (11) specifies the name of the procedure starting the distributed program. In our case, procedure Main is null, since the PWM controller task is an internal task in package PWM_Controller.

To execute the application, it is necessary to load the hard partition as a Linux kernel module (the usual way to launch an RTLinux application), and then the soft partition is executed as any other Linux process. The order is important because RT-FIFOs must be created first, and this can only be done from the RTLinux partition.

The soft component Monitor_And_Command can be dynamically replaced with a newer version. Care must be taken to cleanly terminate the corresponding process (e.g., by means of an *exit* button in the GUI) so that it releases the communication channel: a simple *kill* signal to the process would leave the RT-FIFO busy and would not let the new version to connect with the server task.

6   Conclusions

We have presented an approach to design applications with both hard and soft real-time requirements. The approach is to build the hard/soft application as a multi-partition Ada program: a hard partition and one or more soft partitions. The partitions can communicate by means of the standard mechanisms defined in the Distributed Systems Annex of the Ada standard. All the partitions will be running on the same computer, but the partition with hard timing requirements will execute in RTLinux, therefore taking priority over the rest of Linux applications.

In our view, the advantages of this approach are:

- Clean, standard design of the application. Everything needed for this approach is in the Ada standard and the GLADE user's manual.
- Full isolation of critical and acritical components. They will share only what the programmer specifies by properly categorising the different partitions.
- The communications details remain hidden to the programmer. The interface provided by the Distributed Systems Annex is at a much higher level of abstraction than dealing with the RT-FIFO interface.
- Multiple choices for communication protocols. Besides the protocol we have implemented, other existing protocols can be added to GLADE.
- It is possible to dynamically replace clients in the soft partition. Nevertheless, a client has to be cleanly killed (execute the exit system call) to release the RT-FIFOs it uses before a new client can be launched. This is only a limitation of the current version of the *rtfifo* protocol. A more elaborated version could detect a client has been abruptly killed by a signal and manage the RT-FIFO connection consequently.
- The scheduling policy configured by pragma Task_Dispatching_Policy affects the partition where it is used. An Ada implementation defining scheduling policies other than FIFO_Within_Priorities could use them, e.g. FIFO within priorities for the *hard* partition and Round Robin for the *soft* partition.

However, we must take the following considerations into account:

- Care must be taken with respect to the communication between partitions: a hard partition should not be a client of a remote call interface subprogram in a soft partition: if the server resides in the Linux partition then RPCs are time-unbounded.
- Order of starting up the partitions is significant since RT-FIFOs can only be created from the RTLinux partition.
- The *rtfifo* protocol, in its current status, allows only one task to handle the channel. Therefore, a multiple-client architecture is not yet supported.
- It is not straightforward to distribute the designed application across different computers. For this purpose, we would need to be able to specify two different protocols for a single soft partition: an RT-FIFO protocol to communicate with the hard tasks, and a network protocol (TCP, UDP,...) to communicate soft partitions in different nodes. As far as we know, this feature is not available in GLADE or other DSA environment.
- Dynamic replacement of soft components is possible, after a clean release of the RT-FIFO, as mentioned above. Furthermore, replacing a hard, server partition is not possible while the communication channel is busy.

References

1. OCERA: Open Components for Embedded Real-Time Applications. European IST programme 35102. http://www.ocera.org/ (2002)
2. Stankovic, J.A., Rajkumar, R.: Real-Time Operating Systems. Real-Time Systems **28** (2004) 237–253
3. Barabanov, M.: A Linux-based Real-Time Operating System. Master's thesis, New Mexico Institute of Mining and Technology, Socorro, New Mexico (1997)
4. FSMLabs: RTLinux. http://www.fsmlabs.com (2004)
5. Masmano, M., Real, J., Ripoll, I., Crespo, A.: Running Ada on Real-Time Linux. In: J. P. Rosen, A. Strohmeier (Eds): Proceedings of 8th Reliable Software Technologies - Ada-Europe 2003, Toulouse, France, June 16-20, 2003. Lecture Notes in Computer Science. Volume 2655., Springer Verlag (2003) 322–333
6. J. Miranda: A Detailed Description of the GNU Ada Run-Time. http://gnat.webhop.info and http://www.iuma.ulpgc.es/users/jmiranda (2002)
7. Pautet, L., Tardieu, S.: Inside the Distributed Systems Annex. In: Lars Asplund (Eds): Proceedings of Reliable Software Technologies - Ada-Europe'98, 1998 Ada-Europe International Conference on Reliable Software Technologies, Uppsala, Sweden, June 8-12, 1998. Lecture Notes in Computer Science. Volume 1411., Springer Verlag (1998) 65–77
8. Martínez, J.M., González, M., Gutiérrez, J.J.: RT-EP: Real-Time Ethernet Protocol for Analyzable Distributed Applications on a Minimum Real-Time POSIX Kernel. In: 2nd International Workshop on Real-Time LANs in the Internet Age, RTLIA 2003, July 2003. (2003)
9. Gustavsson, U., Lundgren, T., Heerd, P., Finne, N.: GARLIC UDP package implementation (1996)
10. Lehoczky, J., Sha, L., Strosnider, J.: Enhancing aperiodic responsiveness in hard real-time environment. In: Proc. 8th IEEE Real-Time Systems Symposium, San Jose, California (1987)
11. Davis, R., Wellings, A.J.: Dual priority scheduling. In: IEEE Proceedings of 16th Real-Time Systems Symposium. (1995)
12. Michael González-Harbour: Win_IO: A set of packages for simple graphical input and output. http://www.ctr.unican.es/win_io (2004)

The Implementation of Ada 2005
Interface Types in the GNAT Compiler

Javier Miranda[1], Edmond Schonberg[2], and Gary Dismukes[2]

[1] Applied Microelectronics Research Institute,
University of Las Palmas de Gran Canaria, Spain
jmiranda@iuma.ulpgc.es
[2] AdaCore, 104 Fifth Avenue, 15th floor,
New York, NY 10011
{schonberg, dismukes}@adacore.com

Abstract. One of the most important object-oriented features of the new revision of the Ada Programming Language is the introduction of Abstract Interfaces to provide a form of multiple inheritance. Ada 2005 Abstract Interface Types are based on Java interfaces, and as such support inheritance of operation specifications, rather than the general complexity of inheritance of implementations as in full multiple inheritance. Real-time uses of Ada demand efficient and bounded worst-case execution time for interface calls. In addition, modern systems require mixed-language programming. This paper summarizes part of the work done by the GNAT Development Team to provide an efficient implementation of this language feature and simplifies interfacing with C++.

Keywords: Ada 2005, Abstract Interface Types, Tagged Types, GNAT.

1   Introduction

During the design of Ada 95 there was much debate about whether the language should incorporate multiple inheritance. The outcome of the debate was to support single inheritance only. In recent years, a number of language designs [6, 8] have adopted a compromise between full multiple inheritance and strict single inheritance, which is to allow multiple inheritance of *specifications*, but only single inheritance of *implementations*. Typically this is obtained by means of "interface" types. An interface consists solely of a set of operation specifications: the interface type has no data components and no operation implementations. A type may implement multiple interfaces, but can inherit code from only one parent type [1]. This model has been found to have much of the power of full-blown multiple inheritance, without most of the implementation and semantic difficulties.

During the last year the GNAT Development Team has been working on the implementation of Ada 2005 features [10]. For the implementation of abstract interfaces, we have adopted the design policy that the implementation must be efficient and have a bounded worst-case execution time [7–Section 3.9(1.e)]. In addition, we desire an implementation that simplifies mixed-language programming, in particular when interfacing Ada with the g++ implementation of C++.

T. Vardanega and A. Wellings (Eds.): Ada-Europe 2005, LNCS 3555, pp. 208–219, 2005.

At compile time, an interface type is conceptually a special kind of *abstract tagged type* and hence do not add special complexity to the compiler (in fact, most of the current compiler support for abstract tagged types can be reused). However, at run time, additional structures must be created to support dynamic dispatching through interfaces as well as membership tests. This paper concentrates on these issues.

The paper has the following structure: In Section 2 we summarize the main features of Ada 2005 abstract interfaces. In Section 3 we give an overview of the state of the art for implementing polymorphic calls and we sketch the GNAT implementation approach. In order to understand the proposed implementation, the reader needs to be familiar with the existing run-time support for tagged types. Hence, in Section 4 we summarize the GNAT run-time support for Ada 95 tagged types. In Section 5 we describe the implementation of abstract interfaces: Section 5.1 presents two approaches to support dynamic dispatching through interfaces, Section 5.2 presents the new layout adopted by GNAT that is compatible with the C++ Application Binary Interface in order to simplify the interfacing of Ada 2005 with C++, and Section 5.3 describes the run-time support for the membership test applied to interfaces. We close with some conclusions and the bibliography.

2   Abstract Interfaces in Ada 2005

An Ada 2005 interface type consists solely of a type declaration together with a set of operation specifications: the interface type has no data components and no implementation of operations. The specifications may be either abstract or null by default. A type may implement multiple interfaces, but can inherit operation implementations from only one parent type [1]. For example:

```
package Pkg is
   type I1 is interface;                          — 1
   procedure P (A : I1) is abstract;
   procedure Q (X : I1) is null;

   type I2 is interface and I1;                   — 2
   procedure R (X : I2) is abstract;

   type Root is tagged record ...                 — 3

   type DT1 is new Root and I2 with ...           — 4
   —  DT1 must provide implementations for P and R
   ...

   type DT2 is new DT1 with ...                   — 5
   —  Inherits all the primitives and interfaces of
   —  the ancestor
   ...
end Pkg;
```

The interface *I1* defined at –1– has two subprograms: the abstract subprogram *P* and the null subprogram *Q* (null procedures are introduced by AI-348 [2]; they behave as if their body consists solely of a *null_statement*). The interface *I2* defined at –2– has the same operations as I1, plus operation *R*. At –3– we define the root of a derivation class. At –4–, *DT1* extends the root type, with the added commitment of implementing all the subprograms of interface I2. Finally, at –5– type *DT2* extends DT1, inheriting all the primitive operations and interfaces of its ancestor.

The power of multiple inheritance is realized by the ability to dispatch calls through interface subprograms, using a controlling argument of a class-wide interface type. In addition, languages providing interfaces [6, 8] also have a mechanism to determine at run time whether a given object implements a particular interface. For this purpose Ada 2005 extends the membership operation to interfaces so that the programmer can write *O in I'Class*. Let us look at an example that uses both features:

```
procedure Dispatch_Call (Obj : I1'Class) is
begin
   if Obj in I2'Class then        — 1: Membership test
      R (I2'Class (Obj));         — 2: Dispatching call
   else
      P (Obj);                    — 3: Dispatching call
   end if;

   I1'Write (Stream, Obj)         — 4: Dispatching call to
                                  —    predefined operation
end Dispatch_Call;
```

The type of the formal *Obj* covers all the types that implement the interface *I*1, and hence at –3– the subprogram can safely dispatch the call to *P*. However, because I2 is an extension of I1, an object implementing I1 might also implement I2. Therefore at –1– we use the membership test to check at run-time whether the object also implements I2, and then call subprogram *R* instead of *P* (applying a conversion to the descendant interface type I2). Finally, at –4– we see that, in addition to user-defined primitives, we can also dispatch calls to predefined operations (that is, *'Size*, *'Alignment*, *'Read*, *'Write*, *'Input*, *'Output*, *Adjust*, *Finalize*, and the equality operator.

In the next section we briefly present the state of the art in the implementation of multiple inheritance and interfaces, and we sketch the approach followed in GNAT.

3   Implementation Strategies for Interfaces

Compiler techniques for implementing polymorphic calls can be grouped into two major categories [5]: *Static Techniques*, which involve precomputing all data structures at compile or link time and do not change those data during run time, and *Dynamic Techniques*, where some information may be precomputed at compile or link time, but which may involve updating the information and the corresponding data structures at run time. For efficiency reasons, the GNAT implementation uses only static techniques.

The static techniques for implementing polymorphic calls are: *Selector Table Indexing*, *Selective Coloring*, *Row Displacement*, *Compact Selector-Index Dispatch Tables*, and *Virtual Function Tables*. The Selector Table Indexing scheme (STI) uses a two-dimensional matrix indexed by class and selector codes (where a selector code denotes a concrete primitive operation). Both classes and selectors are represented by unique, consecutive integer encodings. Unfortunately, the resulting dispatch table is too large and very sparse, and thus this scheme is generally not implemented as described. Selective Coloring, Row Displacement, and Compact Selector-Index Dispatch Tables are variants of STI that reduce the size of the table.

The approach of Virtual Function Tables (VTBL) is the preferred mechanism for virtual function call resolution in Java and C++. The VTBL is a table containing pointers to the primitive operations of a class. Instead of assigning selector codes globally, VTBL assigns codes only within the scope of a class. In Java the implementation typically stores the VTBL in an array reachable from the class object, and searchs by name and profile for the relevant table entry at run time. Most Java compilers augment the basic search approach of the VTBL with some form of cache or move-to-front algorithm to exploit temporal locality in the table usage to reduce expected search times [3].

[3] also proposes a new interface-dispatch mechanism called the Interface Method Table. IMT is supported by Jalapeño, a virtual machine for Java servers written in Java at the IBM Research Group. The authors remark that their method is efficient in both time and space. The key idea is to convert the "Selector Index Tables" method into a hash table that assigns a fixed-sized Interface Method Table to each class that implements an interface. This approach handles collisions by means of custom-generated conflict resolution stubs (that is, subprograms with a "case" statement to determine which of the several signatures that share this slot is the desired target). These stubs are built incrementally as the program runs, and hence this technique is not considered appropriate for GNAT.

Two variants of the Virtual Function Tables (VTBL) approach have been considered for implementing dispatching calls for abstract interfaces in GNAT: 1) Permutation Maps, and 2) Multiple Dispatch Tables. In the former approach, each tagged type has one dispatch table plus one supplementary table per interface containing indices into the dispatch table; each index establishes the correspondence between the interface subprograms and the tagged type subprograms (permutation maps are discussed in [1]). Multiple Dispatch Tables, which are standard for C++ implementations, involves the generation of a dispatch table for each implemented interface. A dispatching call with an interface controlling argument locates the dispatch table corresponding to the interface (using an interface tag within the controlling argument), and then performs the usual indirect call through the appropriate entry in that table. Thus, dispatching a call through an interface has the same cost as any other dispatching call. We have written prototype implementations of both approaches. Although the second approach uses significantly more space for the tagged type than is required by permutation maps and adds complexity to the compiler, it has two major benefits: 1) Constant-time dispatching through interfaces, and 2) Simplified interfacing with C++ abstract classes and pure virtual functions. Because these two benefits are important for the Ada community, this latter approach has been selected for GNAT (further details are given in Section 5.1).

Concerning interface membership tests, [11] and [12] discuss several techniques that can be used to implement type-inclusion tests in constant time, independently of the number of interfaces implemented by a given type: *packed encoding, bit-packed encoding* and *compact encoding*. The former is the most efficient, and the latter two are more compact. Because these techniques introduce additional complexity and data structures to the run-time, we decided to evaluate their appropriateness for GNAT. For this purpose we examined the current usage of interfaces in Java, and we selected the sources available with the Java 2 Platform, Standard Edition (J2SE 5.0) [9]. Figure 1 summarizes the results: from a total of 2746 Java classes, 99.3 percent implement a maximum of four interfaces, and there is a single class (*AWTEventMulticaster*) that implements 17 interfaces. Because of these results, and also because constant-time is not really required for the interface membership test —worst-case time-cost is enough—, we have decided to implement the interface membership test in GNAT using an additional data structure: a compact table containing the tags of all the implemented interfaces (the structure of this table will be discussed in Section 5.3). Hence, the cost of the interface membership test is the cost of a search for the interface in this table, and is proportional to the number of implemented interfaces.

Number of Implemented Interfaces

0	1	2	3	4	5	6	7	8	17
22	1998	508	160	40	6	7	2	2	1

Number of Java Classes

Fig. 1. Usage of interfaces in J2SE 5.0

Before we discuss the details of the implementation of abstract interfaces in GNAT, the reader needs to be familiar with the GNAT run-time support for tagged types. This is summarized in the next section.

4   Tagged Types in GNAT

In the GNAT run-time, the *_Tag* component of an object is a pointer to a structure that, among other things, holds the *Dispatch Table* and the *Ancestors Table* (cf. Figure 2). The Dispatch Table contains the pointers to the primitive operations of the type. The Ancestors Table contains the tags of all the ancestor types; it is used to compute class-wide membership tests in constant time. For further information on the other fields, see the comments in the GNAT sources (files *a-tags.ads* and *a-tags.adb*).

Let us briefly summarize the elaboration of this structure with the help of Figure 3. On the right side, the reader can see a tagged type T with two primitive operations P and Q. On the left side of the same figure we have a simplified version of the structure described above. For clarity, only the dispatch table, the table of ancestor tags, and the inheritance level are shown. The elaboration of a root tagged type declaration carries out the following actions: 1) Initialize the Dispatch Table with the pointers to the primitive operations, 2) Set the inheritance level *I-Depth* to one, and 3) Initialize the table of ancestor tags with the *self* tag.

For derived types, GNAT does not build the new run-time structure from scratch, but starts by copying the contents of the ancestor tables. Figure 4 extends our previous example with a derived type DT. The elaboration of the tables corresponding to DT involves the following actions: 1) Copy the contents of the dispatch table of the ancestor, 2) Fill in the contents of the new dispatch table with the pointers to the overriding subprograms (as well as any new primitive operations), 3) Increment the inheritance level to one plus the inheritance level of the ancestor, 4) Copy the contents of the ancestor tags table in a stacklike manner (that is, copy the 0 to i elements of the ancestor tags table into positions 1 to $i + 1$ and save the *self* tag at position 0 of this table. Thus the *self* tag is always found at position 0, the tag of the parent is found at position 1, and so on. Knowing the level of inheritance of two types, the membership test O *in* $T'Class$ can be computed in constant time by means of the formula: $O'Tag.Ancestors\_Table(O'Tag.Idepth - T'Tag.Idepth) = T'Tag$.

In addition to the user-defined primitive operations, the dispatch table contains the pointers to all the predefined operations of the tagged type (that is, *'Size*, *'Alignment*, *'Read*, *'Write*, *'Input*, *'Output*, *Adjust*, *Finalize*, and the equality operator).

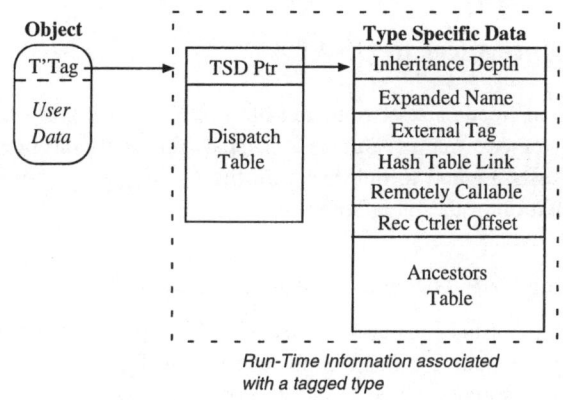

Fig. 2. Run-time data structure for tagged types

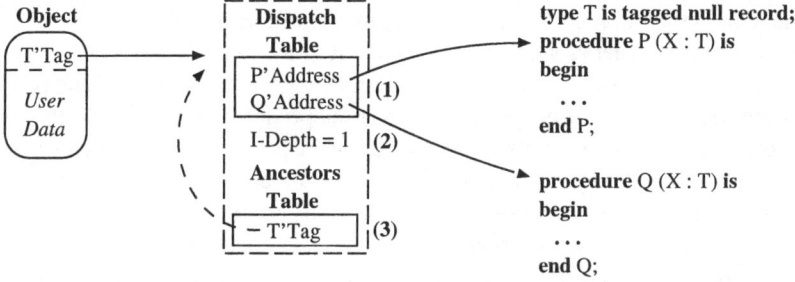

Fig. 3. Elaboration of a root tagged type

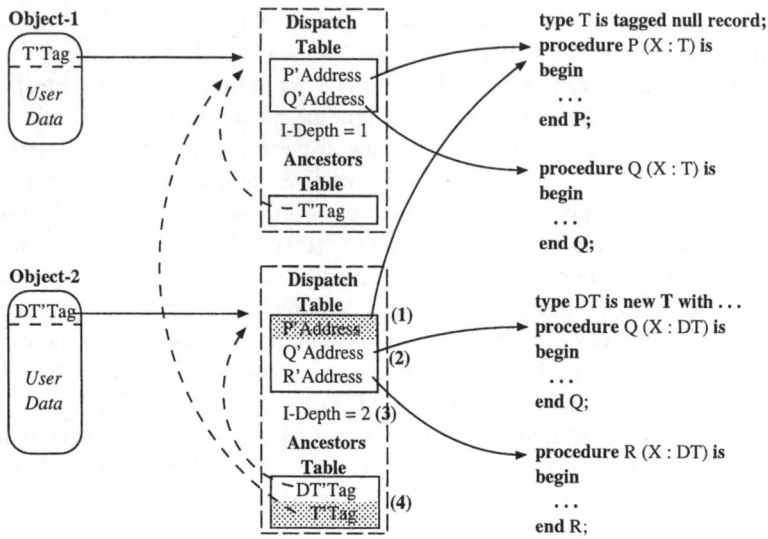

Fig. 4. Elaboration of a derived type

5   Abstract Interfaces in GNAT

As we explained in Section 2, at run time the implementation of abstract interfaces involves support for two main features: 1) Dispatching calls through interfaces, and 2) Membership Tests applied to interfaces. In the following sections we describe the GNAT implementation of these features.

5.1   Dispatching Calls Through Abstract Interfaces

Two variants of the Virtual Function Tables (VTBL) approach presented in Section 3 for implementing dispatching calls through abstract interfaces were evaluated in GNAT (cf. Figure 5): 1) Permutation Maps, and 2) Multiple Dispatch Tables. In the former approach, each tagged type has one dispatch table plus, for each implemented interface, one supplementary table containing indices into the dispatch table; each index estab-lishes the correspondence between an interface subprogram and the tagged type's im-plementation of that subprogram (permutation maps are discussed in [1]). The latter ap-proach involves the generation of a dispatch table for each implemented interface. Thus, dispatching a call through an interface has the same cost as any other dispatching call.

The implementation of the permutation map approach is simpler than the imple-mentation of multiple dispatch tables because the indices in the permutation maps never change, so they can simply be inherited directly by any descendant types. By contrast, although multiple dispatch tables require significantly more space and are more com-plex to implement (because the compiler must take care of generating additional code to create and elaborate these additional dispatch tables), it has two major benefits: 1) Constant-time dispatching through interfaces, and 2) Easier interfacing with C++. The first benefit is crucial for a real-time language like Ada, and the second benefit is impor-

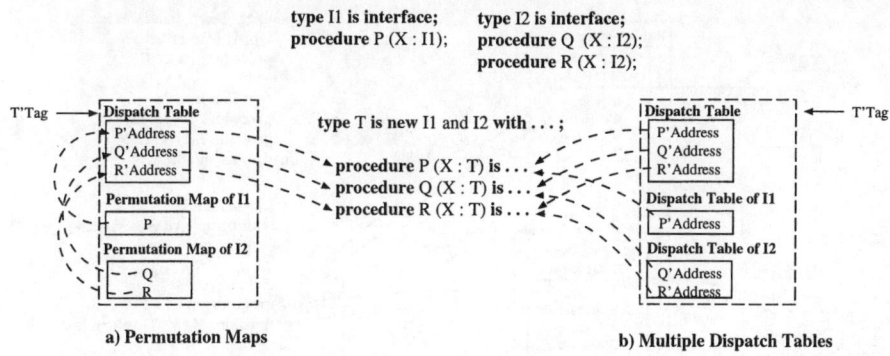

Fig. 5. Permutation Maps versus Multiple Dispatch Tables

tant for the Ada community in general because it allows interfacing with C++ abstract classes and pure virtual functions. Hence, GNAT implements interfaces by means of multiple dispatch tables.

5.2   C++ ABI Layout Compatibility

In order to have true compatibility with C++ we have modified the layout of tagged objects as well as the run-time data structure associated with tagged types to follow the C++ Application Binary Interface (ABI) described in [4]. Figure 6 presents an example with the new layout: at the top of this figure we have the layout of an object of a tagged type. Compared with the previous GNAT layout, the main difference is found in the run-time structure: the dispatch table has a header containing the offset to the top and the Run-Time Type Information Pointer (RTTI). For a primary dispatch table, the first field is always set to 0 and the RTTI pointer points to the GNAT Type Specific Data structure described in Section 4. In addition, the tag of the object points to the table of pointers to primitive operations that is available after the header.

At the bottom of Figure 6 we have the layout of a derived type that implements the interfaces *I1* and *I2*. When a type implements several interfaces, its run-time data structure contains one primary dispatch table and one secondary dispatch table per interface. Regarding the layout of the object (left side of the figure), the derived object contains all the components of its immediate ancestor followed by 1) the tag of all the implemented interfaces, and 2) its additional user-defined components. Regarding the contents of the dispatch tables, the primary dispatch table is an extension of the primary dispatch table of its immediate ancestor, and thus contains direct pointers to all the primitive subprograms of the derived type. The *offset_to_top* component of the secondary tables holds the displacement to the top of the object from the object component containing the interface tag. (This offset provides a way to find the top of the object from any derived object that contains secondary virtual tables and is necessary in C++ for *dynamic_cast*.)

In the example shown in Figure 6, the offset of the tag corresponding to the interfaces I1 and I2 are m and n respectively. In addition, rather than containing direct pointers to the primitive operations associated with the interfaces, the secondary dispatch tables contain pointers to small fragments of code called *thunks*. These thunks

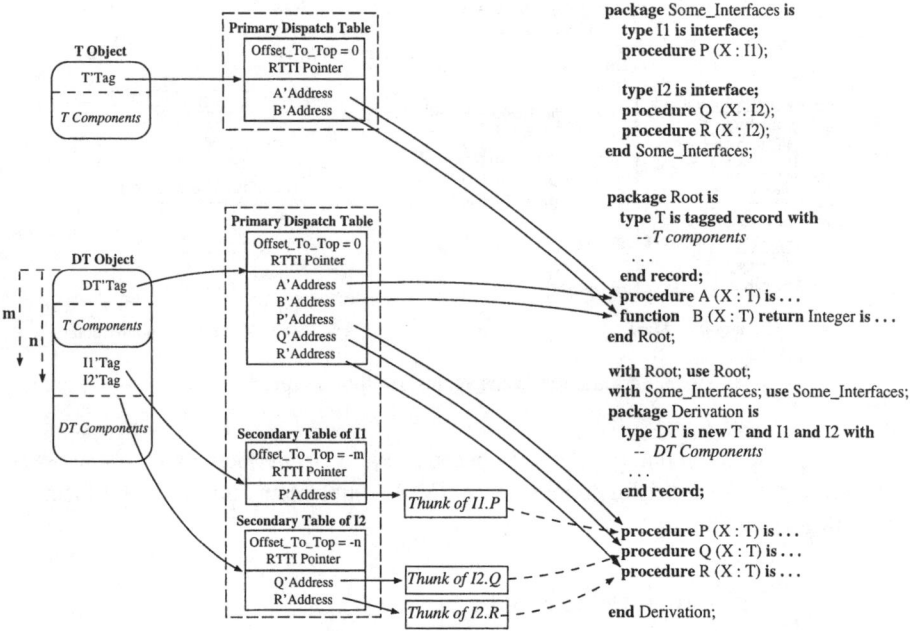

Fig. 6. Layout compatibility with C++

are used to adjust the pointer to the base of the object. To better understand its behavior, we consider an example of the use of the above run-time data structure and analyze the full execution sequence of the following code that issues a dispatching call to the subprogram *R* of the interface I2.

```
with Derivation ;        use Derivation ;
with Some_Interfaces ;   use Some_Interfaces ;
procedure Test is
    procedure Class_Wide_Call (Obj : I2 ' Class) is
        —   3: The pointer to the object received in the
        —       actual parameter is in fact a displaced
        —       pointer that points to the I2 'Tag
        —       component or the object (see Figure 6)
    begin
        —   4: Dispatch call to the thunk through the
        —       secondary dispatch table associated with
        —       the interface I2
        R (Obj);
    end Class_Wide_Call ;

    O1 : DT;                —   1: Object declaration
begin
    Class_Wide_Call (O1); —   2: Displace the pointer to
        —                          the base of the object
        —                          by n bytes
end Test ;
```

At –1– we declare an object that has the layout described in Figure 6. At –2– we have a call to a subprogram with a class-wide interface formal, and the compiler generates code that displaces the pointer to the base of the object by n bytes to point to the object component containing the I2'Tag (cf. Figure 6). This adjusted address is passed as the pointer to the actual object in the call to *Class_Wide_Call*. Inside this subprogram (at – 3–), all dispatching calls through interfaces are handled as if they were normal dispatching calls. For example, because R is the second primitive operation of the interface I2, at –4– the compiler generates code that issues a call to the subprogram identified by the second entry of the primary dispatch table associated with the actual parameter. Because the actual parameter is a displaced pointer that points to the I2'Tag component of the object, we are really issuing a call through the secondary table of the object associated with the interface I2. Rather than a direct pointer to the R subprogram, the compiler has generated code that fills this entry of the interface dispatch table with the address of the thunk that 1) subtracts the m byte displacement corresponding to I2 in order to adjust the address so that it refers to the real base of the object, and 2) jumps to the primitive subprogram R.

5.3   Interface Membership Test: *O in I'Class*

In analogy with the Ada 95 membership test applied to class-wide types (described in Section 4), at run time we have a compact table containing the tags of all the implemented interfaces (cf. Figure 7). The reasons behind the selection of this simple structure were previously discussed in Section 3. The run-time cost of the membership test applied to interfaces is the cost of a search for the interface in this table.

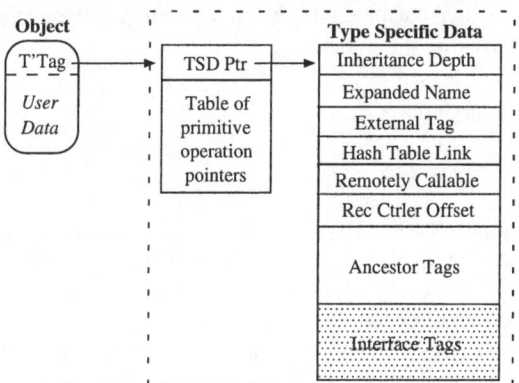

Fig. 7. The Table of Interfaces

This simple approach has the advantage that the elaboration of derived types implementing interfaces is simple and efficient. In analogy with the elaboration of the Ancestors Table (described in Section 4), we elaborate the new table of interfaces as follows: 1) Copy the contents of the table of interfaces of the immediate ancestor (because the derived type inherits all the interfaces implemented by its immediate ancestor), and 2) Add the tags of any new interfaces.

6   Conclusions

This paper summarizes part of the work done by the GNAT Development Team to implement Ada 2005 abstract interface types. Because interfaces are conceptually a special kind of *abstract tagged type*, at compile time most of the current support for abstract tagged types has been reused. At run time, additional structures were required to give support to membership tests as well as dynamic dispatching through interfaces.

We developed two prototype implementations of abstract interfaces. The first implementation uses a combination of a dispatch table for the primitive operations of a tagged type, and permutation maps that establish how a given interface is mapped onto that type's primitive operations. Although the implementation of this model was rather simple and correctly supports the Ada 2005 semantics, in order to have constant time in dispatching calls through interfaces, and also simplify the interfacing of Ada 2005 with C++ (at least for the g++ compiler), we developed an alternative prototype that is more complex and uses separate dispatch tables for all the implemented interfaces. Because of these important benefits for the Ada community, this second approach has been selected as the final version supported by GNAT.

Acknowledgments

We wish to thank Cyrille Comar and Matt Heaney for the discussions that helped us to clarify the main concepts described in this paper. We also wish to thank Arnaud Charlet, Geert Bosch, Robert Dewar, Paul Hilfinger, and Richard Kenner for helping us to clarify details of the underlying technology. Finally, we also wish to thank the dedicated and enthusiastic members of AdaCore, and the myriad supportive users of GNAT whose suggestions keep improving the system.

References

1. Ada Rapporteur Group (ARG). *Abstract interfaces to provide multiple inheritance*. Ada Issue 251, http://www.ada-auth.org/cgi-bin/cvsweb.cgi/AIs/AI-00251.TXT.
2. Ada Rapporteur Group (ARG). *Null procedures*. Ada Issue 348, http://www.adaauth. org/cgi-bin/cvsweb.cgi/AIs/AI-00348.TXT.
3. B. Alpern, A. Cocchi, S. Fink, D. Grove, and D. Lieber. Efficient Implementation of Java Interfaces: Invokeinterface Considered Harmless. *Proceedings of the Conference on Object-Oriented Programming, Systems, Languages, and Applications (OOPSLA 2001)*, ACM Press. http://www.research.ibm.com/jalapeno/publication.html, October 2001.
4. CodeSourcery, Compaq, EDG, HP, IBM, Intel, Red Hat, and SGI. Itanium C++ ABI. Technical Report Revision 1.75, www.codesourcery.com.prev/cxx-abi, 2004.
5. K. Driesen. Software and Hardware Techniques for Efficient Polymorphic Calls. *University of California, Santa Barbara (PhD Dissertation)*, TRCS99-24, June 1999.
6. J. Gosling, B. Joy, G. Steele, and G. Bracha. *The Java Language Specification (2nd edition)*. Addison-Wesley, 2000.

7. Intermetrics Inc and the MITRE Corporation. *Annotated Ada Reference Manual with Technical Corrigendum 1. Language Standard and Libraries. ISO/IEC 8652:1995(E)*. http://www.ada-auth.org/arm-files/AARM.PDF, 2000.
8. ECMA International. *C# Language Specification Standard ECMA-334 (2nd edition)*. Standardizing Information and Communication Systems, December, 2002.
9. Sun MicroSystems. Java 2 Platform, Standard Edition (J2SE 5.0). *Available at http://java.sun.com/j2se/*, 2004.
10. J. Miranda and E. Schonberg. GNAT: On the Road to Ada 2005. *ACM SigAda 2004*, November 2004.
11. K. Palacz and J. Vitek. Java Subtype Tests in Real-Time. *Proceedings of the European Conference on Object-Oriented Programming*, http://citeseer.ist.psu.edu/660723.html, 2003.
12. J. Vitek, R.N Horspoo, and A. Krall. Efficient Type Inclusion Tests. *Proceedings of the Conference on Object-Oriented Programming, Systems, Languages, and Applications (OOPSLA 97)*, ACM Press. http://citeseer.ist.psu.edu/vitek97efficient.html, 1997.

Integrating Application-Defined Scheduling with the New Dispatching Policies for Ada Tasks

Mario Aldea Rivas[1], Javier Miranda[2], and Michael González Harbour[1]

[1] Departamento de Electrónica y Computadores, Universidad de Cantabria,
39005-Santander, Spain
[2] Applied Microelectronics Research Institute, Univ. Las Palmas de Gran Canaria,
35017 Las Palmas de Gran Canaria, Spain
{aldeam, mgh}@unican.es, jmiranda@iuma.ulpgc.es

Abstract. In previous papers we had presented an application program interface (API) that enabled applications to use application-defined scheduling algorithms for Ada tasks in a way compatible with the scheduling model defined in the real-Time Annex of the language. Each application scheduler was implemented with a special task. This paper presents a new implementation in which the application scheduler actions are executed as part of the kernel on which the run-time system is based, thus increasing the efficiency. This paper also presents modifications to the proposed API that align it with the evolution of the Ada Issues being considered in the Ada 200Y standardization. First, we use the new concept of deadline as an abstract notion of urgency, to order the tasks in the scheduling queue of the underlying kernel, freeing the application scheduler of the responsibility of keeping the desired ordering of tasks, and thus simplifying it and reducing its overhead. In second place, we also consider task synchronization through protected objects using the new Stack Resource Policy proposed for the EDF task dispatching policy in Ada 200Y, which can be used in a large variety of fixed and dynamic priority scheduling policies without explicit intervention of the application scheduler.

Keywords: Real-Time Systems, Kernel, Scheduling, Compilers, Ada, POSIX.

1 Introduction[1]

Although the Ada standard allows implementations to add their own task dispatching policies, most commercial run-time systems just offer the standard fixed-priority scheduling as the mechanism to support real-time concurrency. Scheduling theory and practice shows that fixed priorities can be used to build predictable and analyzable real-time applications, but it is well known that the use of dynamic priority scheduling algorithms in which priorities may vary depending on the passage of time or on other system parameters, allows a better usage of the available processing resources [16].

---

[1] This work has been funded by the *Comisión Interministerial de Ciencia y Tecnología* of the Spanish Government under grant TIC 2002-04123-C03 and by the *Commission of the European Communities* under contract IST-2001-34140 (FIRST project).

T. Vardanega and A. Wellings (Eds.): Ada-Europe 2005, LNCS 3555, pp. 220–235, 2005.

Current scheduling theory provides enough results to allow schedulability analysis in these systems.

As a consequence, it would be desirable to have dynamic priority scheduling policies[2] available in the Ada language. A major evolution in this direction is an Ada Issue being considered for the next revision of the Ada language [10], proposing an Earliest Deadline First (EDF) task dispatching policy [13]. However, this policy by itself is not enough for real-time applications. It is important, for instance, to have a server policy that can handle aperiodic activities in a predictable way; for example, the constant bandwidth server (CBS) [1] is an example of such server. In fact the number of task dispatching policies described in the literature is quite large because dynamic priority approaches are very flexible, and they can be tailored to adapt to many kinds of application requirements. It is impractical for Ada run-time system developers to provide all of these policies in their implementations.

In the past years we have been working on application program interfaces (APIs) and implementations of application-defined scheduling services that could be used for dispatching Ada tasks [18][19]. Those APIs allow the application to install one or more task schedulers, and assigning application tasks to these schedulers. The schedulers would receive the relevant scheduling events to make the appropriate scheduling decisions, and then suspend or resume their scheduled tasks. Other authors [17][18][19] have also worked in other application-defined scheduling services, but they did not provide a full solution covering both scheduling and the associated synchronization protocols.

A previous approach [9] was flexible enough to support many kinds of application defined scheduling policies, but it had several drawbacks that potentially limit its efficiency:

- Because the application scheduler is a special thread, every scheduling decision requires a double context switch, which in some OS architectures may be too expensive.
- The application scheduler has to keep the ordering of the threads that are ready for execution, instead of leaving this task to the underlying kernel where it can be made in a more efficient way.
- Mutual exclusive synchronization requires special support.

Although the overheads measured in our MaRTE OS [2] implementation were acceptable for common applications, we realized that they could be too high in other OS architectures, and thus we worked towards eliminating these sources of inefficiency. As a result we have created a fully new implementation, with similar capabilities, but which is much more efficient than the previous approach. This paper presents the details of this implementation model.

In addition, this paper also presents a new API that aligns the application-defined scheduling proposal with the evolution of the Ada Issues being considered in the Ada 200Y standardization [10]. First, we use the new concept of deadline defined in [13]

---

[2] Although Ada offers "dynamic priority" facilities that allow the application to explicitly change the priority of a task, the term "dynamic priority policies" is usually applied to those policies in which the priority may change without explicit intervention of the application.

as an indication of urgency that is used by the underlying kernel to order the tasks in the scheduling queue. By mapping application-defined scheduling parameters into this urgency concept in a way transparent to the remainder of the application, we can free the application scheduler of the responsibility of keeping the desired ordering of tasks, and thus we can simplify it and reduce its overhead. In second place, in this paper we also consider task synchronization through protected objects using the new Stack Resource Policy proposed for the EDF task dispatching policy [13] in Ada 200Y, which can be used in a large variety of fixed and dynamic priority scheduling policies without explicit intervention of the application scheduler.

This paper is organized as follows: Section 2 gives an overview of the application-defined scheduling proposal. Section 3 discusses the use of deadlines as an abstract notion of urgency to order the tasks in the ready queue. Section 4 provides an overview of the proposed API. Section 5 discusses the implementation details: inside the kernel, the run-time system, and the compiler. Section 6 shows an example of a non-trivial application-defined scheduler. Section 7 contains an evaluation of the new implementation with performance metrics that compare it to previous implementations. Finally, we give our conclusions in Section 8.

2 Overview of the New Application-Defined Scheduling Proposal

Fig. 1 shows the proposed approach for application-defined scheduling. Each application scheduler is a special software module that is responsible of scheduling a set of tasks that have been attached to it. According to the way a task is scheduled, we can categorize the tasks as:

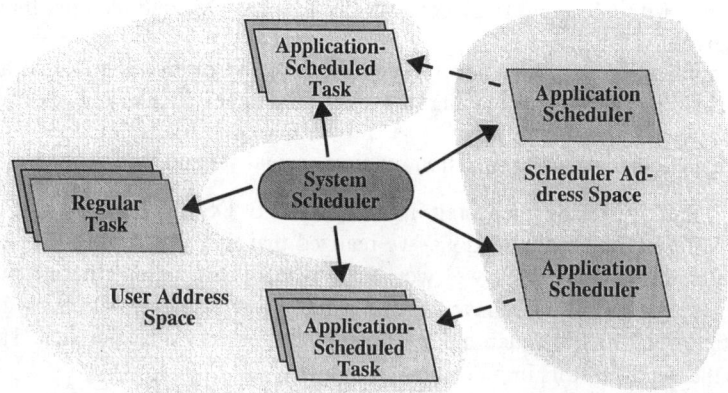

Fig. 1. Model for Application Scheduling

- *System-scheduled tasks*: these tasks are scheduled directly by the run-time system and/or the operating system, without intervention of an application scheduler.

- *Application-scheduled tasks*: these tasks are also scheduled by the run-time system and/or the operating system, but before they can be scheduled, they need to be made ready by their application-defined scheduler.

Because the scheduler may execute in an environment different than that of the application tasks, it is an error to share information between the scheduler and the rest of the application. An API is provided for exchanging information when needed. Application schedulers may share information among them.

The new scheduling API is designed to be compatible with the new task dispatching policies under the framework initially described in [16] that has evolved during the Ada 200Y standardization process [14]. In that proposal, compatible scheduling policies are allowed in the system by specifying the desired policy for each particular priority range, with the `Priority_Specific_Dispatching` pragma; three values are allowed: `Fifo_Within_Priorities`, `Round_Robin_Within_Priorities`, and `EDF_Across_Priorities` [13]. At each priority level or priority band, only one policy is available, thus avoiding the potentially unpredictable effects of mixing tasks of different policies at the same level.

We propose adding one more value that could be used with the `Priority_Specific_Dispatching` pragma: `Application_Defined`; it represents tasks that are application scheduled, in a particular priority band.

The following language-defined library package serves as the parent of other language-defined library units concerned with dispatching, including the proposed application scheduling unit [14]:

```
package Ada.Dispatching is
   pragma Pure (Dispatching);
   Dispatching_Policy_Error : exception;
end Ada.Dispatching;
```

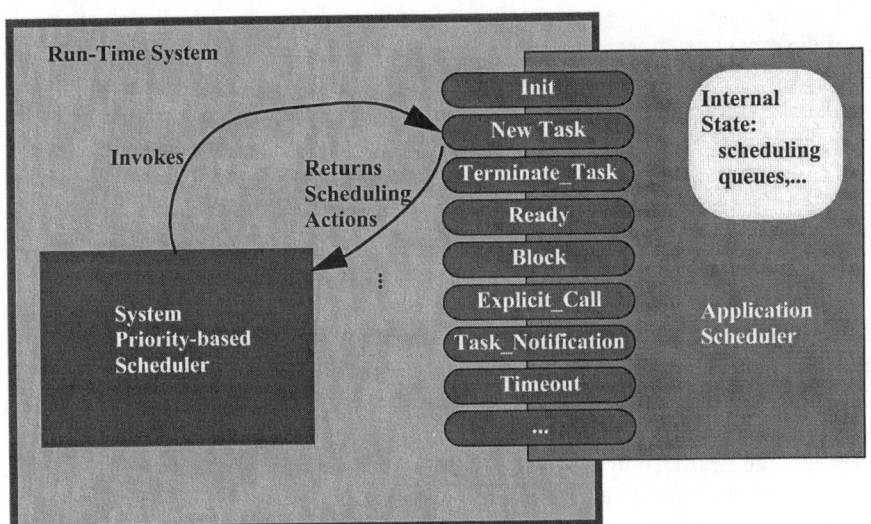

Fig. 2. Sructure of an Application Scheduler

Application schedulers have the structure shown in Fig. 2 and are defined by extending the Scheduler abstract tagged type defined in the new package Ada.Dispatching.Application_Scheduling [8]. This type contains primitive operations that are invoked by the system when a scheduling event occurs. To create an application-defined scheduler the type can be extended by adding the data structures required (for example, a ready queue and a delay queue), and by overriding the primitive operations of interest to perform the scheduling decisions required to implement the desired scheduling policy. Each of these primitive operations returns as a result an object containing a list of scheduling actions to be executed by the system, such as the requests to suspend, resume, or change the urgency of specific tasks.

When defining an application scheduler we also need to extend the Scheduling_ Parameters tagged type defined in Ada.Dispatching.-Application_ Scheduling, to contain all the information that is necessary to specify the scheduling parameters of each task (such as its deadline, execution-time budget, period, and similar parameters).

3   Abstract Ordering of the Ready Queue

In the framework proposed in [9] the application schedulers were responsible for ordering the tasks that were ready storing them in a specific queue inside the application scheduler, and required an extra overhead of invoking the scheduler for every scheduling decision. The run-time system's ready queue was not usually practical because for a given priority level it was just a FIFO queue, and dynamic priority scheduling policies usually require other orderings.

In this paper we propose taking advantage of the EDF_Across_Priorities policy defined in [13], using the deadline to order the tasks in the ready queue and interpreting it as an abstract notion of "urgency" on to which any particular scheduling parameter that the application scheduler chooses (e.g., deadline, value, quality of service, ...) can be mapped. This approach is especially suitable for scheduling policies in which the urgency or priority of the task only changes from one job to the next, but remains constant within a specific job. For example, for EDF scheduling the absolute deadline of the task does not change for a specific job, because it is defined as the release time plus the relative deadline. In any case, the approach continues to be valid for policies that do change the priority in the middle of a job, such as in the proportional time-sharing scheduler shown in the example of Section 6.

The scheduling deadline assigned to each job makes it easier to implement scheduling algorithms than in our previous application-defined scheduling proposal and, more important, the schedulers become more efficient because when a task finishes its current job it is not necessary to invoke the application scheduler again to determine the next task to execute. The system can choose the new task by itself. In this context only when a new job arrives, or when the relative priority or deadline of a job changes, it would be necessary to invoke the application scheduler.

The way chosen to inform the system about the "deadline" of a task is by adding a new parameter to the operation that adds the "ready" action:

```
procedure Add_Ready
   (Sched_Actions : in out Scheduling_Actions;
    Tid           : in Ada.Task_Identification.Task_Id;
    Urg           : in Ada.Dispatching.EDF.Deadline);
```

If this action is performed on a task that is already active, it changes the deadline of the task forcing the reordering of the ready queue.

As in the proposal for supporting deadlines and EDF scheduling in Ada 200Y [13], in our framework we have also chosen the Stack Resource Policy (SRP) [5] as the synchronization protocol for protected objects. We can use the same rules described in [13 to implement the SRP in the context of application-defined scheduling, by using the priorities in the EDF priority band as the actual preemption levels of the SRP. The priority ceilings in this band will have to be assigned according to the rules of the SRP, if we want to eliminate priority inversion effects.

4 Overview of the API

The package `Ada.Dispatching.Application_Scheduling` contains the proposed interface for the application scheduling operations.

In first place, there is an set of operations for the application scheduler to ask the system to execute scheduling decisions through what we call the scheduling "actions". We add these actions to an object of the type `Scheduling_Actions`. One of these operations is `Add_Ready`, mentioned above. The scheduling action operations are shown next:

```
type Scheduling_Actions is private;
procedure Add_Accept
   (Sched_Actions : in out Scheduling_Actions;
    Tid           : in     Ada.Task_Identification.Task_Id);
procedure Add_Reject
   (Sched_Actions : in out Scheduling_Actions;
    Tid           : in     Ada.Task_Identification.Task_Id);
procedure Add_Ready
   (Sched_Actions : in out Scheduling_Actions;
    Tid           : in     Ada.Task_Identification.Task_Id);
procedure Add_Ready
   (Sched_Actions : in out Scheduling_Actions;
    Tid           : in     Ada.Task_Identification.Task_Id;
    Urg           : in     Ada.Dispatching.EDF.Deadline);
procedure Add_Timed_Task_Activation
   (Sched_Actions : in out Scheduling_Actions;
    Tid           : in     Ada.Task_Identification.Task_Id;
    Urg           : in     Ada.Dispatching.EDF.Deadline;
    At_Time       : in     Ada.Real_Time.Time);
procedure Add_Suspend
   (Sched_Actions : in out Scheduling_Actions;
    Tid           : in     Ada.Task_Identification.Task_Id);
procedure Add_Timeout
   (Sched_Actions : in out Scheduling_Actions;
```

```
   At_Time          : in      Ada.Real_Time.Time);
procedure Add_Timed_Task_Notification
   (Sched_Actions : in out Scheduling_Actions;
    Tid           : in      Ada.Task_Identification.Task_Id;
    At_Time       : in      Ada.Real_Time.Time);
procedure Add_Timer_Expiration
   (Sched_Actions : in out Scheduling_Actions;
    T             : in out Ada.Execution_Time.Timers.Timer;
    Abs_Time      : in      Ada.Execution_Time.CPU_Time);
procedure Add_Timer_Expiration
   (Sched_Actions : in out Scheduling_Actions;
    T             : in out Ada.Execution_Time.Timers.Timer;
    Interval      : in      Ada.Real_Time.Time_Span);
```

The application-defined scheduling package provides operations for the application to directly invoke the scheduler. For instance, the usual way in which an application task informs the scheduler that it has finished its current job is by calling these operations. Information can be passed from the application task to its scheduler, and viceversa, by extending the abstract types Message_To_Scheduler and Reply_From_-Scheduler, as needed. The explicit scheduler invocation types and operations are:

```
type Message_To_Scheduler is abstract tagged null record;
type Reply_From_Scheduler is abstract tagged null record;
procedure Invoke
   (Msg    : access Message_To_Scheduler'Class);
procedure Invoke
   (Msg    : access Message_To_Scheduler'Class;
    Reply : access Reply_From_Scheduler'Class);
```

The scheduler is declared as an abstract tagged type with primitive operations that represent the code to be executed when a specific scheduling event occurs:

```
type Scheduler is abstract tagged null record;
```

The actions to be executed by the system, described above, are passed as a parameter to each of the primitive operations. The specifications of the most important of these operations are:

```
type Error_Cause is
   (SRP_Rule_Violation, Invalid_Action_For_Task);

procedure Init
   (Sched    : out     Scheduler) is abstract;
procedure New_Task
   (Sched    : in out Scheduler;
    Tid      : in      Ada.Task_Identification.Task_Id;
    Actions : in out Scheduling_Actions);
procedure Terminate_Task
   (Sched    : in out Scheduler;
    Tid      : in      Ada.Task_Identification.Task_Id;
    Actions : in out Scheduling_Actions);
procedure Ready
   (Sched    : in out Scheduler;
    Tid      : in      Ada.Task_Identification.Task_Id;
    Actions : in out Scheduling_Actions);
procedure Block
```

```
    (Sched    : in out Scheduler;
     Tid      : in      Ada.Task_Identification.Task_Id;
     Actions  : in out Scheduling_Actions);
procedure Yield
    (Sched    : in out Scheduler;
     Tid      : in      Ada.Task_Identification.Task_Id;
     Actions  : in out Scheduling_Actions);
procedure Abort_Task
    (Sched    : in out Scheduler;
     Tid      : in      Ada.Task_Identification.Task_Id;
     Actions  : in out Scheduling_Actions);
procedure Change_Sched_Param
    (Sched    : in out Scheduler;
     Tid      : in      Ada.Task_Identification.Task_Id;
     Actions  : in out Scheduling_Actions);
procedure Explicit_Call
    (Sched    : in out Scheduler;
     Tid      : in      Ada.Task_Identification.Task_Id;
     Msg      : access Message_To_Scheduler'Class;
     Reply    : access Reply_From_Scheduler'Class;
     Actions  : in out Scheduling_Actions);
procedure Task_Notification
    (Sched    : in out Scheduler;
     Tid      : in      Ada.Task_Identification.Task_Id;
     Actions  : in out Scheduling_Actions);
procedure Timeout
    (Sched    : in out Scheduler;
     Actions  : in out Scheduling_Actions);
procedure Execution_Timer_Expiration
    (Sched           : in out Scheduler;
     Expired_Timer   : in out Ada.Execution_Time.Timers.Timer;
     Actions         : in out Scheduling_Actions);
procedure Error
    (Sched : in out Scheduler;
     Tid : in Ada.Task_Identification.Task_Id;
     Cause : in  Error_Cause;
     Actions : in out Scheduling_Actions) is abstract;
--  Non-abstract operations have a null body
```

The final part of the API contains operations to handle event masks, and an operation to set the mask of events that should be filtered out. The Init primitive operation of the example shown in Section 6 illustrates the usage of these operations to create a set of events and set the event mask. The set mask operation is:

```
procedure Set_Event_Mask (Mask : in Event_Mask);
```

For an in-depth description of the API shown in this section please refer to [8].

5 Implementation Details

5.1 Changes to the Compiler and the Run-Time System

The prototype implementation of this new proposal required the implementation of the new priority dispatching mechanism proposed for Ada 200Y [14]. For this purpose we modified the GNAT GAP 1.0 compiler to give support to the new configuration pragma `Priority_Specific_Dispatching`. This pragma allows one or more priority levels to be scheduled according to a given priority policy. In addition, we modified the semantic analyser to allow the programmers the use of the `Application_Defined` policy described in this paper. Hence, the form of this pragma as well as the supported values for the policy identifier in our prototype implementation is as follows:

```
pragma Priority_Specific_Dispatching
    (Policy_Identifier,
        -- Valid policy names:
        --     FIFO_Within_Priorities          (Ada 1995)
        --     Round_Robin_Within_Priorities   (Ada 200Y)
        --     EDF_Across_Priorities           (Ada 200Y)
        --     Application_Defined             (new!)
    First_Priority_Expression, Last_Priority_Expression);
        -- Static expressions of type System.Any_Priority
```

The implementation of application-defined schedulers requires some additional mechanism that allows the programmer to register its scheduler with the run-time system. For this purpose we also give support to the following new pragma:

```
pragma Application_Scheduler
    (Application_Defined_Scheduler,
        -- Tagged type derived from
        -- Ada.Dispatching.Application_Scheduling.Scheduler
    First_Priority_Expression, Last_Priority_Expression);
        -- Static expressions of type System.Any_Priority
```

The first argument is the name of a type derived from the tagged type defined in package `Ada.Dispatching.Application_Scheduling`. In addition to the static check required to verify that all the priority levels specified in the range of priorities are allowed to have an application-defined scheduler (by means of pragma `Priority_Specific_Dispatching`), the compiler also checks that the first argument corresponds with a tagged-type derived from the correct type and that has been defined at the library level. This is required to ensure that the scheduler is available during the whole execution of the program. The implementation of pragma `Application_Defined_Sched_Parameters` is the same as was described in [9].

The information provided by these pragmas is also used by the compiler to generate additional code. For example, the arguments given in the pragma `Application_Scheduler` are used to modify the elaboration-code of the library-level package containing the definition of the application-defined scheduler: the corresponding call to the underlying operating system to create an application scheduler is performed and this scheduler is registered into the run-time for the specified range of priorities.

Concerning the run-time system, the code associated with the elaboration of the tasks has been modified. When the priority of a task is inside the range of priorities associated with an application-defined scheduler, the task is registered with it. In addition, the run-time must also take care of the re-allocation of a task to another scheduler when the priority of the task changes.

5.2 Changes to the Underlying Operating System

The implementation of the ordering of tasks by urgency in the ready queue required changing its enqueue operation. In the fixed-priority implementation, a new task was added at the tail of the queue for its priority. Now, the position depends on the urgency and the preemption level. This change is isolated to just one operation in the kernel.

In our previous implementation of application-level scheduling [9], all the scheduling operations were executed by a special task. Now, some of the scheduler operations are executed by the regular application tasks, namely `Explicit_Call`, `New_Task`, `Block`, `Yield`, and `Change_Sched_Param`. This simplification causes these operations to execute much faster because we can save the double context switch required to execute in the context of the special task, and return from it. Implementing this change has been very simple, because to accomplish the required mutual exclusion with the scheduler we just need to raise the urgency and preemption level of the task executing these operations to the same levels of that scheduler. This change of scheduling parameters does not imply reordering the queue, because the task was already executing; therefore, it is very fast.

In the new implementation, the scheduling operations triggered by asynchronous events and which cannot be executed in the context of the running task are handled by an auxiliary task created for each application scheduler. This is a kernel task that has a very simple, much faster context switch, compared to the regular Ada tasks, because it crosses less software layers. It has urgency and preemption level values higher than those of their associated application-scheduled tasks, to take precedence in execution. This auxiliary task can be eliminated completely once the "Timing events" [15] or a similar OS functionality are available. In the current implementation we don't yet have timing events available, and the only alternative to the auxiliary tasks would be the use of signal handlers, which would have more overhead than the auxiliary task.

6 Example: Proportional Share Scheduler

The following example shows the pseudocode of and application scheduler that implements a simple proportional share scheduling policy, which is useful in the context of soft real-time systems in which all tasks have to make progress but some tasks are more important than others. The policy can be easily adapted so that hard real-time tasks can coexist in the system at higher priority levels. We will make the following declaration to reduce the length of the code in this section:

```
package App_Sched renames
    Ada.Dispatching.Application_Scheduling;
```

Under the proportional share policy, each application-scheduled task has two specific scheduling parameters called "importance" and "period" that will be notified to the scheduler using the following types:

```
type Task_Importance is new Positive range 1..100;

type Share_Parameters is new
```

```
App_Sched.Scheduling_Parameters with record

Importance : Task_Importance;

Period     : Ada.Real_Time.Time_Span;

end record;
```

The application scheduler will ensure that each task has a percentage of the CPU time allocated to it, proportionally to its importance according with the following expression:

$$W_t = \frac{I_t}{\sum_{\tau \in \{T\}} I_\tau}$$

That is, the percentage or CPU time (W_t) granted to a task t is equal to its importance (I_t) divided by the sum of the importances of all the tasks scheduled by the application scheduler. That means each task will be allowed to execute at most $W_t \cdot P_t$ units of time in each period (P_t). In order to enforce that constraint, the application scheduler will make use of the execution-time timers. As soon as a task reaches its allowed execution time for its current period the application scheduler lowers its "urgency" to a background level, so that it can only execute in the case that there are no other tasks with remaining execution time. When a new period for a task starts, the application scheduler raises the "urgency" of the task to a value proportional to its importance.

The application scheduler is defined as an extension of the abstract `Scheduler`.

```
type Share_Scheduler is
  new App_Sched.Scheduler with private;
```

And then it is defined in the private part of the package to contain the total importance and a list of items with the information associated with each task:

```
type Share_Task_Data is tagged record
   Importance : Task_Importance;
   Period     : Ada.Real_Time.Time_Span;
   Next_Period_Start : Ada.Real_Time.Time;
   Budget     : Ada.Real_Time.Time_Span;
   Task_Id    : aliased Ada.Task_Identification.Task_Id;
   Timer      : access Ada.Execution_Time.Timers.Timer;
end record;

package Task_Data_Lists is new
   Singly_Linked_Lists (Share_Task_Data);

subtype Task_Data_Ac is Task_Data_Lists.Element_Ac;

type Share_Scheduler is new App_Sched.Scheduler with
record
   List            : Task_Data_Lists.List;
   Total_Importance : Natural;
end record;
```

In the body of the proportional share scheduler a new task attribute is defined as an instance of `Ada.Task_Attributes`, so that each task can access its own scheduler information, by accessing the list element represented by a value of the type `Task_Data_Ac`.

```
package Share_Data is new
     Ada.Task_Attributes (Task_Data_Ac, null);
```

The primitive operations of `Share_Scheduler` perform the following actions, illustrated with the relevant calls to the application scheduling API:

- `Init`: initializes the list of tasks and sets the event mask (with `App_Sched.Set_Event_Mask`) to filter out all the events except *New_Task*, *Execution_Timer_Expiration*, and *Task_Notification*.

```
App_Sched.Fill (Mask);
App_Sched.Delete(App_Sched.New_Task, Mask);
App_Sched.Delete(App_Sched.Execution_Timer_Expiration,Mask);
App_Sched.Delete(App_Sched.Task_Notification, Mask);
App_Sched.Set_Event_Mask (Mask);
```

- `New_Task`:
  - If there are no erroneous parameters accept the new task by adding an *Accept* action
```
App_Sched.Add_Accept (Actions, Tid);
```
  - Create an execution-time timer
```
T.Timer := new
     Ada.Execution_Time.Timers.Timer(T.Task_Id'Access);
```
  - Create a new item in the list of tasks, with information on the period, the importance, and the execution-time timer, and set the task's attribute to point to that value
```
Share_Data.Set_Value (T, Tid);
```
  - Update the total importance and recalculate the budgets of all tasks in the list
  - Activate the new task by adding a *Ready* event with an urgency equal to the importance plus the last value of importance (obtained with a trivial conversion function called `Urg_Foreground`)
```
App_Sched.Add_Ready
     (Actions, Tid, Urg_Foreground(T.Importance));
```
  - Program a timed task notification, adding a *Timed_Task_Notification* action, to occur at the next period
```
App_Sched.Add_Timed_Task_Notification
     (Actions, Tid, T.Next_Period_Start);
```
  - Program the execution-time timer
```
App_Sched.Add_Timer_Expiration
     (Actions, T.Timer.all, T.Budget);
```

- `Execution_Timer_Expiration`: This function is called by the system when the task's execution-time budget gets exhausted for the current period. It has to lower the urgency to a value equal to the importance (obtained with the trivial conversion function `Urg_Background`)

```
App_Sched.Add_Ready
    (Actions, T.Task_Id, Urg_Background(T.Importance));
```

- Task_Notification:

  - Obtain the task data using the corresponding task attribute
    ```
    T := Share_Data.Value (Tid);
    ```

  - Raise the task's urgency
    ```
    App_Sched.Add_Ready
        (Actions, Tid, Urg_Foreground (T.Importance));
    ```

  - Calculate the new ready time by adding the period to the previous one and program a task notification to occur at start of the next period
    ```
    App_Sched.Add_Timed_Task_Notification
        (Actions, Tid, T.Next_Period_Start);
    ```

  - Reprogram the execution-time timer to check the budget for the next period
    ```
    App_Sched.Add_Timer_Expiration
        (Actions, T.Timer.all, T.Budget);
    ```

The configuration pragmas in the system will be defined as follows:

```
pragma Priority_Specific_Dispatching
    (Application_Defined, 14, 18); -- for instance
pragma Locking_Policy (Ceiling_Locking);
```

And the pragma to define the application scheduler would be:

```
pragma Application_Scheduler
    (Share_Scheduling.Share_Scheduler,14,18);
```

The specification of an application-scheduler task type would be:

```
task type Share_Task_1
    (Param : access Share_Scheduling.Share_Parameters;
     Prio  : System.Any_Priority)
is
    pragma Priority (Prio);
    pragma Application_Defined_Sched_Parameters (Param);
end Share_Task_1;
```

And the body would just be the desired computation with no explicit relation with the scheduler:

```
task body Share_Task is
begin
    loop
        -- do useful work
    end loop;
end Share_Task;
```

To create a scheduler type task we would declare the importance and period inside an object of the Share_Parameters type, and then we would declare the task as:

```
T1_Paramters : aliased Share_Scheduling.Share_Parameters :=
    (Importance => 60,
     Period     => Ada.Real_Time.To_Time_Span (4.0));
T1 : Share_Task (T1_Paramters'Access,Scheduler_Priority_Low);
```

7 Evaluation

We have made some experiments to compare the overheads of the new implementation of application-defined scheduling presented in this paper with the previous one [9]. Table 1 shows some of the average results of this evaluation as measured on a 1.1 GHz Pentium III processor.

Table 1. Comparison of overhead measurements

Metric	Time (μs) old approach	Time (μs) new approach
Timed task notification event (from the execution of a user task, until the execution of the application scheduler)	1.3	1.0
Explicit scheduler invocation (from the call to the invoke operation, until the application scheduler executes)	0.9	0.23
Execute scheduling actions (switch from a running user task to a new one)	2.0	1.3
Context switch for an EDF application-defined scheduler	3.3	1.0

We can see that the timed task notification (first row in Table 1) is now smaller mainly because of the use of a kernel task, instead of a regular Ada task. The explicit scheduler invocation (second row) is much smaller because it is now executed in the context of the application task, avoiding a double context switch. Execution of scheduling actions (third row) is also faster because in the new implementation, for the application scheduler to request a context switch it is no longer necessary to suspend a task and make the new one ready, but just to lower the urgency of the task that must leave the CPU.

We have measured a common context switch time for a specific policy with the old and the current implementation. The policy chosen was EDF, and the results appear in the fourth row 4 of Table 1. The scenario measured is a typical EDF context switch in which the most urgent task finishes its current job and explicitly invokes its scheduler to notify this situation and wait for the following activation. Once that task leaves the CPU the new most urgent task starts executing. We can see that the overhead drops to around one third of that of the old implementation, from 3.3 μs to just 1.0 μs. The reason is that now the explicit invocation is done as part of the calling task, and the new task is chosen by the operating system based on its urgency, and therefore without intervention of the application scheduler. The new context switch is under the time of a context switch due to a regular delay statement (1.6 μs for the same processor). This kind of overhead is more than acceptable for common real-time applications which usually have timing requirements in the range of milliseconds or tens of milliseconds.

8   Conclusion

In this paper we have presented the implementation of the application-defined scheduling framework defined in [8], augmented with the inclusion of an abstract notion of urgency defined to enhance efficiency and simplify the development of application schedulers. To implement this notion of urgency we take advantage of the new EDF dispatching policy and associated SRP synchronization protocol proposed for Ada 200Y.

The compiler and run-time system modifications presented in [9] have been adapted to the new version of the GNAT compiler (GAP 1.0) in a straightforward manner. Also the kernel support for urgency ordering of ready queues has been implemented with only a moderate effort in our operating system MaRTE OS (a standard priority-based operating system).

To prove the flexibility and usage simplicity of our framework an example of a non-trivial application scheduler has been presented. Performance measurements show more than acceptable overheads, moreover if the important advantages of having a framework as the proposed are taken into account.

We have also shown the usefulness of the EDF task dispatching policy proposed for Ada 200Y. Although this policy by itself may not be enough for all applications, thus motivating the presence of application defined schedulers, our proposal builds on top of it and takes advantage of the notion of deadline as well as the SRP implementation for protected objects using just the priority ceilings as preemption level control values.

We believe that an application-defined scheduling framework for Ada like the one presented in this paper represents an opportunity for this language to continue to be the reference language for real-time systems, by supporting the new application requirements for more flexible and resource-efficient scheduling.

References

[1] L. Abeni and G. Buttazzo. "Integrating Multimedia Applications in Hard Real-Time Systems". *Proceedings of the IEEE Real-Time Systems Symposium*, Madrid, Spain, December 1998

[2] M. Aldea and M. González. "MaRTE OS: An Ada Kernel for Real-Time Embedded Applications". Proceedings of the International Conference on Reliable Software Technologies, Ada-Europe-2001, Leuven, Belgium, *Lecture Notes in Computer Science, LNCS 2043*, May, 2001.

[3] IEEE Std 1003.1-2003. *Information Technology -Portable Operating System Interface (POSIX)*. Institute of Electrical and electronic Engineers.

[4] IEEE Std. 1003.13-2003. *Information Technology -Standardized Application Environment Profile- POSIX Realtime and Embedded Application Support (AEP)*. The Institute of Electrical and Electronics Engineers.

[5] Baker T.P., "Stack-Based Scheduling of Realtime Processes", Journal of Real-Time Systems, Volume 3, Issue 1 (March 1991), pp. 67–99.

[6] A. Burns, M. González Harbour and A.J. Wellings. "A Round Robin Scheduling Policy for Ada". Proceedings of the International Conference on Reliable Software Technologies, Ada-Europe-2003, Toulouse, France, in Lecture Notes in Computer Science, LNCS 2655, June, 2003, ISBN 3-540-40376-0.

[7] Alan Burns, Andy J. Wellings and S. Tucker Taft. "Supporting Deadlines and EDF Scheduling in Ada". 9th International Conference on Reliable Software Technologies, Ada-Europe, Palma de Mallorca (Spain), in Lecture Notes on Computer Science, Springer, LNCS 3063, June, 2004, ISBN:3-540-22011-9, pp. 156-165.

[8] Mario Aldea Rivas and Michael González Harbour. "Application-Defined Scheduling in Ada". Proceedings of the International Real-Time Ada Workshop (IRTAW-2003), Viana do Castelo, Portugal, September 2003.

[9] Mario Aldea Rivas, J. Miranda and M. González Harbour. "Implementing an Application-Defined Scheduling Framework for Ada Tasking". 9th International Conference on Reliable Software Technologies, Ada-Europe, Palma de Mallorca (Spain), in Lecture Notes on Computer Science, Springer, LNCS 3063, June, 2004, ISBN:3-540-22011-9, pp. 283-296.

[10] Pascal Leroy. "An Invitation to Ada 2005". International Conference on Reliable Software Technologies, Toulouse, France, in Lecture Notes on Computer Science, LNCS 2655, Springer, June 2003.

[11] Ada Rapporteur Group (ARG). "Execution-Time Clocks", Ada Issue AI95-00307-1.13.
      http://www.ada-auth.org/cgi-bin/cvsweb.cgi/AIs/AI-00307.TXT

[12] Ada Rapporteur Group (ARG). "Group Execution-Time Timers". Ada Issue AI95-00354-1.8.
      http://www.ada-auth.org/cgi-bin/cvsweb.cgi/AIs/AI-00354 TXT

[13] Ada Rapporteur Group (ARG). "Support for Deadlines and Earliest Deadline First Scheduling". Ada Issue AI95-00357-1.12.
      http://www.ada-auth.org/cgi-bin/cvsweb.cgi/AIs/AI-00357.TXT

[14] Ada Rapporteur Group (ARG). "Priority Specific Dispatching including Round Robin". Ada Issue AI95-00355-1.9.
      http://www.ada-auth.org/cgi-bin/cvsweb.cgi/AIs/AI-00355.TXT

[15] Ada Rapporteur Group (ARG). "Timing events". Ada Issue AI95-00297/10
      http://www.ada-auth.org/cgi-bin/cvsweb.cgi/AIs/AI-00297.TXT

[16] Giorgio C. Buttazo. "Rate Monotonic vs. EDF: Judgment Day". Journal of Real-Time Systems, Volume 29, Number 1, Jan 2005.

[17] Y.C. Wang and K.J. Lin, "Implementing a General Real-Time Scheduling Framework in the Red-Linux Real-Time Kernel". Proceedings of IEEE Real-Time Systems Symposium, Phoenix, December 1999.

[18] Bryan Ford and Sai Susarla, "CPU Inheritance Scheduling". Proceedings of OSDI, October 1996.

[19] George M. Candea and Michael B. Jones, "Vassal: Loadable Scheduler Support for Multi-Policy Scheduling". Proceedings of the Second USENIX Windows NT Symposium, Seattle, Washington, August 1998.

The Application of Compile-Time Reflection to Software Fault Tolerance Using Ada 95

P. Rogers[1] and A.J. Wellings[2]

[1] Ada Core Technologies
rogers@adacore.com
[2] University of York, York, UK
andy@cs.york.ac.uk

Abstract. Transparent system support for software fault tolerance reduces performance in general and precludes application-specific optimizations in particular. In contrast, explicit support – especially at the language level – allows application-specific tailoring. However, current techniques that extend languages to support software fault tolerance lead to interwoven code addressing functional and non-functional requirements. Reflection promises both significant separation of concerns and a malleability allowing the user to customize the language toward the optimum point in a language design space. To explore this potential we compare common software fault tolerance scenarios implemented in both standard and reflective Ada. Specifically, in addition to backward error recovery and recovery blocks, we explore the application of reflection to atomic actions and conversations. We then compare the implementations in terms of expressive power, portability, and performance.

Keywords: Reflection, software fault tolerance, Ada, backward error recovery, recovery blocks, atomic actions, conversations.

1 Introduction

Lives and property increasingly depend on the correct operation of computer software. This dependence may be absolute because older technologies such as electromechanical, hydraulic, or pneumatic mechanisms are either inadequate or violate other system constraints, typically those of cost, weight, and power consumption. For example, the NASA Space Shuttle fleet is purely "fly-by-wire"; there is no (say) hydraulic backup control system. A larger number of people are potentially affected by fly-by-wire commercial aircraft. For example, the Boeing 737/300 and the Airbus A320, A330, and A340 aircraft are completely dependent upon reliable operation of the control software. Even more people will be affected by "drive-by-wire" automobiles as they become ubiquitous.

However, software for current and future applications – such as flight control systems – is both large and complex, such that full testing is not feasible. Furthermore, complete proofs of correctness are at best inherently limited by the potential for specification faults. Indeed, specification faults are considered the cause of the majority of safety mishaps [4]. The combination of potential specification

T. Vardanega and A. Wellings (Eds.): Ada-Europe 2005, LNCS 3555, pp. 236–247, 2005.
© Springer-Verlag Berlin Heidelberg 2005

errors and overall complexity define the problem as one of handling unanticipated software faults. "Software fault tolerance" is the use of software mechanisms to deal with these unanticipated software faults [5, Preface].

Software fault tolerance is expensive and adds to the overall complexity of the system (which may even reduce reliability as a result). Nevertheless, software fault tolerance must be explicitly considered for safety-critical applications because software faults are unavoidable, as we discussed above, and because the techniques used for hardware fault tolerance generally do not handle software faults. Hardware fault tolerance is based on replication, on the grounds that the hardware may eventually "wear out" but does not contain permanent design flaws. Software faults, on the other hand, are widely held to be permanent design mistakes. Replication would simply create multiple copies of the same permanent mistake.

One of the software technologies considered for handling software faults is "reflection". Reflection is the ability of a computational system to observe its own execution and, as a result of that observance, perhaps make changes to that execution [6, 11]. Conceptually, software based on reflective facilities is structured into distinct levels: the baselevel and one or more metalevels. The baselevel addresses the functional requirements of the application. The metalevels represent and control the baselevel. As such, the metalevels are responsible for the non-functional aspects of the system. The differences in these levels can be illustrated in terms of a stage production: the baselevel is everything seen by the audience; the considerable activity off-stage occurs in the metalevels [3].

The metalevel and baselevel are causally related: modification of one affects the other. This relationship may be achieved by making the actual baselevel implementation available to the metalevels, such that changes by the metalevels are automatically effective at the baselevel. To the degree that the implementation is made available, everything in the implementation and application – the syntax, the semantics, and the run-time data structures – is "opened" to the programmer for modification via the metalevels.

Reflection offers a clean separation of concerns with great flexibility and it has, therefore, been a focus of research in software fault tolerance. However, most of these research efforts focus on handling hardware faults and those that address software fault tolerance use languages that are limited in one respect or another. Indeed, reflection has not been applied to a language with the features integrated within Ada. Furthermore, such a language has not been used to address software fault tolerance with reflective programming even though Ada is especially appropriate for systems in which reliability is critical.

We have implemented a reflective programming facility for Ada [9] and applied it to scenarios not otherwise explored by the fault tolerance community. Specifically, in addition to backward error recovery and recovery blocks, we explore the application of reflection to atomic actions and conversations. Having implemented the scenarios using both standard and reflective Ada, we then compare the implementations in terms of expressive power, portability, and performance. In section 2 we describe the concept of compile-time reflection as applied to our reflective Ada implementation "OpenAda". Section 3 compares the results of the scenario implementations using both standard Ada and OpenAda, and section 4 provides closing remarks.

2 OpenAda

The inefficiencies incurred from reflection, especially with interpretive implementations, are a significant problem. These inefficiencies and those imposed by reifying the entire processor have led to "open compilers" that allow users to change the language's semantics without necessarily incurring performance penalties. In these compilers the internals, including parsing, the data structures, semantic analysis, and so forth, are reified such that new functionality and even new syntax may be added to the language. These changes are achieved by subclassing these reified internal classes.

A distinct alternative is to have the translation driven by a specific, individual "translator" metaclass rather than by (subclasses of) the reified compiler internals. A metaclass is, in this alternative approach, a specialization of a predefined translator class [2]. The input source code contains an annotation that affects the translation by specifying the specific metaclass to be used to perform the translation. As a result, the metaclass can be said to customize the translation of the input source code rather than customizing the compiler's internals. The resulting metaobject protocol is referred to as a "compile-time MOP". With such a MOP the metalevel code only runs during compilation: the metalevel code controls translation of the program and, thereby, albeit indirectly, run-time behaviour. The metaclass can use this MOP to inquire about the primitive operations and components of a given type, for example, and may add, remove, or arbitrarily change them as required by the goals of the metaclass. As an illustration, these changes could involve invoking an acceptance test and, if it fails, restoring state and invoking a secondary variant routine. Translating metaclasses can be reused across applications whenever the corresponding translation is required.

OpenAda is our compile-time reflection facility for Ada 95 using the "translating metaclass" approach. A pragma named Metaclass in the baselevel source code specifies the translating metaclass to be applied to that baselevel code. The metaclass alters the baselevel source to implement the non-functional requirements of the system, thereby achieving the intended separation of the source code implementing the functional and non-functional requirements.

For example, a metaclass that translates baselevel code into code that incorporates recovery blocks could be declared as follows.

```
...
with OpenAda.Meta;
with OpenAda.Syntax.Constructs;   use OpenAda.Syntax.Constructs;
with Ada.Strings.Wide_Unbounded; use Ada.Strings.Wide_Unbounded;

package Inline_Recovery_Blocks is

   type Class is new OpenAda.Meta.Class with private;

   Failure : exception;

   procedure Finalize_Translator( This : in out Class );
```

```
procedure Translate_Handled_Statements
  ( This    : in out Class;
    Input   : in out Handled_Statements;
    Control : in out OpenAda.Syntax.Visitation_Controls );

private

  type Class is new OpenAda.Meta.Class with
    record
      Required_Units           : Unbounded_Wide_String;
      Recovery_Point_Inserted : Boolean := False;
    end record;
    ...
end Inline_Recovery_Blocks;
```

The metaclass Inline_Recovery_Blocks.Class translates any handled-sequence-of-statements it encounters in the baselevel code. Specifically, it converts any pragma Recovery_Block in the baselevel into a block-statement that implements a recovery block. (See Section 0 for more details of the pragma Recovery_Block and the expanded block statement it generates.) The variants and acceptance test for any inserted recovery block are specified as pragma Recovery_Block parameters. These subprograms need not be local to the translated unit so the translator inserts with-clauses for them as necessary. The names of these units are stored in the Required_Units component of the class. Similarly, the translator inserts a with-clause for a recovery mechanism named "Recovery_Point" but only does so once for the sake of understandability. Hence a Boolean flag is used to control that insertion and is also a component of the class.

The implementation of procedure Translate_Handled_Statements verifies that the statement immediately preceding pragma Recovery_Block is a call to the procedure named as the first variant specified to the pragma. It then removes that procedure call and inserts a tailored block statement that implements recovery block semantics for the specified variants. All variant procedure names are captured and have corresponding with-clauses inserted by another routine (Finalize_Translator) if necessary.

```
procedure Translate_Handled_Statements
  ( This    : in out Class;
    Input   : in out Handled_Statements;
    Control : in out OpenAda.Syntax.Visitation_Controls )
is
  Iterator      : Parsed_Content.List_Iterator;
  Next_Item     : Any_Node;
  Prev_Item     : Any_Node;
  The_Pragma    : Any_Pragmata;
  Pragma_Args   : Parsed_Actuals;
  New_Statement : Any_Node;
  Statements    : Parsed_Content.List renames
      Sequence_of_Statements(Input'Access).Content;

  use Parsed_Content, Syntax.Utilities;
```

```
begin
   Iterator := Make_List_Iterator( Statements );
   while More( Iterator ) loop
     Prev_Item := Next_Item;
     Next( Iterator, Next_Item );
     if Next_Item.all in Pragmata'Class then
       The_Pragma := Any_Pragmata( Next_Item );
       if Image(Pragma_Name(The_Pragma),Lowercase) =
          "recovery_block"
     then
        Pragma_Args := Parsed( Args(The_Pragma) );
        -- Any preceeding statement must be a procedure call,
        -- and must be a call to the first variant listed in the
        -- pragma Recovery_Block params.
        Verify_Primary_Call( Prev_Item, Pragma_Args );
        -- replace the pragma with the recovery block
        New_Statement := New_Recovery_Block( Pragma_Args );
        Replace( Old_Node => Next_Item,
                 New_Node => New_Statement,
                 Within   => Statements );
        -- delete the preceeding procedure call
        Delete_Call( Prev_Item, Within => Statements );
        if not This.Recovery_Point_Inserted then
          Append( This.Required_Units, "Recovery_Point " );
          This.Recovery_Point_Inserted := True;
        end if;
        Append_Package_Names(This.Required_Units, Pragma_Args);
       end if;
     end if;
   end loop;
end Translate_Handled_Statements;
```

3 Comparing Standard and Reflective Ada

Compared to other mainstream languages, Ada is unusual due to its integrated support for concurrency (especially asynchronous interactions), high-integrity systems, real-time systems, and object-oriented programming. Indeed, the language provides standardized support for the typical capabilities added to other languages via reflection, namely concurrency and distribution. These integrated facilities make expression of a wide assortment of reusable fault tolerance components – particularly those involving cooperating threads – easier than in other typical languages. We have implemented a number of scenarios using common software fault tolerance facilities to determine the potential advantages offered by reflection for such a language. These scenarios are written in both standard Ada 95 and OpenAda and involve reusable components implementing backward error recovery, recovery blocks, atomic actions, and conversations. We now compare these scenario implementations in terms of expressive power, separation of concerns, and performance.

3.1 Expressive Power

Lacking a widely accepted definition, we define expressive power as a matter of implementing requirements concisely. In this subsection we compare the expressive power of standard Ada against the combination of the baselevels and the metaclass translators. We do not examine the expressive power of the metaclass code itself, but, rather, the result of applying the metaclasses to the baselevels.

Using Pragmas to Annotate Baselevel Source. Several of the reflective scenarios use metaclass-specific pragmas to annotate the baselevel code for specific treatment by the translating metaclass. The pragma Recovery_Block, for example, is expanded into code implementing the corresponding functionality. Pragmas Atomic_Action and Conversation are similarly expanded into interactions with reusable components implementing the required services. Each occurrence of pragma Conversation individually enumerates the entire set of variants to be expanded into a conversation call. These variants need not be from the same package and need not be local to the unit containing the pragmas – the metaclass determines which variants require with-clauses and generates them accordingly. These pragmas thus represent a great deal of functionality with a very simple and succinct expression. One could argue that their power exists only in combination with the metaclass translators, but that is also true of standard Ada syntax translated by a standard Ada compiler.

These annotation pragmas also help hide arcane syntax and language rules. For example, the backward error recovery implementation requires a discriminant for each recoverable object declaration. These discriminants link the recoverable application object with a controlling "recovery manager" object. A discriminant is used for the sake of robustness because the compiler ensures the linkage is specified when the object is declared. However, discriminants add syntactic weight to the code and impose rules beyond those of normal record components. Moreover, these discriminants provide a permanent linkage to a single controlling cache object even though different associations might make sense at different points in the program execution.

The reflective version of the scenario carries none of this baggage because the baselevel code does not address recovery. The metaclass programmer is responsible for inserting the discriminant specifications, not the baselevel programmer. Indeed, the metaclass could translate the code to use a procedural registration facility instead, but neither approach appears in the baselevel.

However, pragmas are not as expressive as dedicated syntax. A pragma is no more expressive than a procedure call. The Ada tasking constructs are, in part, a reaction the limitations of the expressive power of procedure calls. Prior to Ada, an application programmer made calls into an operating system to achieve concurrency. These operating system calls provided neither visibility into thread interactions nor compile-time type checking. In contrast, dedicated syntax provides explicit interactions with compile-time checking and is much more expressive than a procedural interface (as found in Java, for example).

Limitations Due to Semantics That Cannot Be Reified.   The expressive power of the reflective approach is limited by the fact that some semantics of the Ada language cannot be readily reified. A metaclass cannot alter the semantics of task activation or general object creation, for example, because there is no corresponding syntax to translate. In a reflective programming context these limitations do not compare well with other languages that use explicit syntax, such as constructors for object creation or explicit method calls for task activation, either of which are easily translated by a metaclass.

These limitations did not affect our scenario implementations because such translations were not necessary. However, had we been required to alter object creation or task activation and completion these restrictions would have been onerous. For example, one could imagine a requirement to register each task's activation for the sake of debugging.

Expressing Otherwise Inexpressible Requirements.   Atomic actions and conversions are meant to be indivisible, such that no internal state changes are discernable outside the action until the action completes. "Information smuggling" occurs when these internal state changes are inadvertently leaked. Prevention is critical because system recovery cannot be reduced to atomic action recovery if action recovery is not complete. Smuggling cannot be fully prevented in Ada because of the visibility rules [10].

A significant feature of compile-time reflective programming is the ability to do complex semantic analysis during compilation. This analysis can be applied to enforce language restrictions to a project-defined subset, for example. In the case of atomic actions and conversations, we apply such analysis to enforce the semantic requirement against information smuggling. Wellings and Burns mention the use of pragma Pure as a means of precluding smuggling by rejecting with-clauses that name library units containing state [12].   Unfortunately, using pragma Pure is neither sufficient nor entirely desirable. It is not desirable because the "purity" is required of the library units referenced, not in the unit itself where the pragma would be placed. It is not sufficient because a devious programmer could import any arbitrary Ada unit via pragma Import – including one that leaks internal state to an impure unit – thereby circumventing pragma Pure.

In our reflective implementation the metaclass explicitly checks the library units in the transitive closure of the specified baselevel unit for object declarations. However, this approach is not sufficient for the same reason that the semantics of pragma Pure are not capable of detecting potential leaks: pragma Import can be used to create an undetected leak. Therefore, the metaclass also checks for pragma Import occurrences and rejects the package if any are found. Information smuggling is thus prevented.

3.2 Separation of Concerns

In the context of this comparison, "separation of concerns" is a matter of the separation between the code meeting the functional requirements and the code meeting the non-functional requirements.

Standard Ada has extensive support for separation of interface from implementation in the form of abstract data types, physically separate interfaces and implementations, and dynamic binding. But separating interface from implementation is not the goal.

We wish to separate the code meeting the functional requirements from the code meeting the non-functional requirements.

Reflection promises a significant degree of this separation – potentially complete transparency – unless explicit interaction is intended, but in practice there are impediments to complete separation. We analyze these impediments in this subsection.

Baselevel Annotations. In some scenarios, the translating metaclass detects and expands metaclass-defined pragmas in the baselevel "inline" to implement the corresponding fault tolerance facility. For example, pragma Recovery_Block specifies the checkpoint manager object, the acceptance test function, and an unbounded list of procedures to be called as variants. The pragma is placed immediately after a procedure call that occurs in the baselevel to implement the functional requirements. For example:

```
...
Calculate_New_Position;
pragma Recovery_Block( Checkpoint,
                       Reasonable,
                       Calculate_New_Position,
                       Estimate_New_Position,
                       Reuse_Old_Position );
...
```

The metaclass removes both the pragma and the baselevel procedure call and then inserts code to implement a recovery block using the specified recovery object [8], acceptance test, and variants, with the original procedure called as the primary variant.

```
...
declare
  Variant_Failure : exception;
  Recovery_Block_Failure : exception;
  Num_Variants : constant := 3;
  use Recovery_Point;
begin
  Establish( Recovery_Data'Class(Checkpoint) );
  for Variant in 1 .. Num_Variants loop
    begin
      case Variant is
        when 1 =>
          Calculate_New_Position;
        when 2 =>
          Estimate_New_Position;
        when 3 =>
          Reuse_Old_Position;
      end case;
      if not Reasonable then
        raise Variant_Failure;
      else
        exit;
      end if;
    exception
```

```
  when others =>
     Restore(Recovery_Data'Class(Checkpoint));
     if Variant = Num_Variants then
        Discard( Recovery_Data'Class(Checkpoint) );
        raise Recovery_Block_Failure;
     end if;
  end;
end loop;
Discard( Recovery_Data'Class(Checkpoint) );
end;
...
```

As can be seen, the annotation pragmas in the baselevel indicate what operations are required and where they are required, but do not indicate how those operations are to be provided. This is the very essence of abstraction and separation of concerns. However, the pragmas do exist in the baselevel code, introducing a coupling between the baselevel and the metalevels. Essentially the pragmas are another form of explicit reference.

An alternative to the annotations is to have the metaclass automatically recognize the baselevel code to alter. In some cases the metaclasses do take this approach, for example with type and object declarations. This approach only makes sense, however, when either all such code is intended for transformation or the metaclass can distinguish between those occurrences that should be altered and those that should not. That distinction cannot be guaranteed in all cases.

Counter-Intuitive Baselevel Type Declarations. In the standard Ada version of the backward error recovery scenario, a type used for simple counting was necessarily defined as an extension to a base type providing backward recovery. In the reflective version we wanted to hide recovery from the baselevel programmers for the sake of separation of concerns. To that end we removed the recovery code from the baselevel– the type is no longer derived from a recoverable base type – but the baselevel type must still be declared as a record type because the translated usage will be as a type extension rather than a numeric type. One must wonder whether the baselevel programmer would, in practice, declare a simple numeric counter as a record type.

The intuitive reflective approach would be to declare the type in the baselevel as a simple numeric type and alter it by the metaclass to become a tagged extension type. That approach is not viable. Although overloaded operators could be declared by the metaclass, numeric literals would no longer be available within clients and value assignment would require aggregates. A metaclass could conceivably make these translations within clients but the effort is difficult to justify.

3.3 Performance

Using compile-time reflection, the reflective implementations will ideally be at least as efficient as the standard Ada versions. The reflective versions may even be more efficient than those using standard Ada due to tailored translations taking advantage of application-specific knowledge. Our benchmark programs show this expectation is valid, although performance will vary with the specific translation strategies chosen. In other words, compile-time reflection need not impose performance penalties but a poor metaclass translation may very well generate source code exhibiting lower performance.

Backward Error Recovery and Atomic Actions. After translation, the sources for the reflective versions of both the backward error recovery and atomic actions scenarios are semantically equivalent to the standard Ada versions and, as a result, the average execution times are essentially identical. This result demonstrates that reflective techniques need not impose any performance penalty whatsoever, while nonetheless providing complete separation of concerns.

Conversations. The conversations benchmarks illustrate the fact that the reflective version may be slower than the non-reflective version; in this case, about five percent slower. However, the performance penalty is not inherent in the use of reflection – it is due to the translation scheme implemented by the metaclass programmer. In this case, the source code for the two versions is not semantically equivalent. The metaclass implements a translation that is relatively easy to produce but is not as fast as the non-reflective version. This difference was not intentional, although in hindsight the implemented translation scheme is clearly not optimal. Rather than revise the metaclass, however, we left it unchanged for the sake of illustrating the potential for deleterious effects.

Specifically, the standard Ada version makes better use of generic instantiations than does the reflective version. The standard version instantiates a generic conversation role procedure template at the outermost level of the enclosing package and shares this instance across the routines exported to the calling tasks. The shared instance is, consequently, instantiated and elaborated only once. In contrast, the reflective version (after translation by the metaclass) instantiates the generic procedure within the role procedures themselves and elaborates the instances on each invocation by the tasks. This approach is necessary because the metaclass can not "know" that a single shared instance is applicable.

Recovery Blocks. The recovery blocks benchmarks provide the best illustration of performance improvements due to source tailoring based on application-specific knowledge. The reflective version is approximately 30% faster than the standard Ada version.

The speed difference is primarily due to the fact that the reusable component applied by the standard Ada version protects itself against aborts, including both task abort and aborts due to asynchronous select statements. The reflective version is tailored to ignore aborts and, as a result, does not pay the price of the unnecessary protection. (Certainly another client might need protection from abort, requiring a different translation.)

We created another standard Ada reusable recovery block component to verify that the performance difference is due to the abort protection. This component does not protect itself from aborts. The resulting performance profile is essentially identical to that of the reflective version (approximately one percent difference, i.e., within the margin of measurement uncertainty).

3.4 Comparison Conclusions

The expressive power of the reflective approach allowed the metalevel programmer to verify properties of the baselevel that cannot be expressed with standard Ada. As to separation of concerns, ample separation was achieved, although the reflective approach typically involved some degree of coupling between the baselevel and the metaclass. The code addressing non-functional requirements was, in general, both extensive and complex but did not appear in the baselevel. Finally, we saw that performance was at least that of standard Ada, given a reasonable metaclass translation approach.

Based on these comparisons we conclude that a compile-time implementation of reflective Ada does indeed provide enhanced expressive power and separation of concerns, with comparable or better performance, over that of standard Ada.

4 Concluding Remarks

We note that formal certification is a typical requirement for systems that might employ software fault tolerance techniques. Our implementations used the full Ada language, including tasks (which are inherent in atomic actions and conversations), exceptions, access types, access-to-subprogram types, dynamic dispatching, and other constructs that probably would not be allowed in certified application code. These constructs occurred both in the reusable components written in Ada 95 and the reflective and standard scenario implementations. Some of both the reflective and standard Ada scenario versions applied those reusable components as well. We have no insight into how to resolve the general conflict between certification and language subsets, other than to note that these subsets are expanding slowly over time (e.g., the ARINC-653 API [1] defines processes) and that a less reuse-oriented "inline" pragma expansion could probably have avoided prohibited features in some of the scenarios. We used the full language to avoid imposing a priori restrictions that could have unintentionally affected the later comparisons.

Finally, note that complete details about the compiler and the application to fault tolerance may be found in the Ph.D. thesis upon which this paper is based [7]. An electronic copy is available for download from the University of York as http://www.cs.york.ac.uk/ftpdir/reports/YCST-2003-10.pdf. The sources for the compiler, the fault tolerance components, and the benchmarks are available at http://www.classwide.com/OpenAda/.

References

[1] Airlines Electronic Engineering Committee, *Avionics Application Software Standard Interface, ARINC Specification 653-1*: Aeronautical Radio, Inc., 2003.
[2] S. Chiba, "A Metaobject Protocol for C++," Proc. Object-Oriented Programming Systems Languages and Applications (OOPSLA'95), Austin, Texas, 1995, pp. 285-299.
[3] G. Kiczales, J. des Rivières, and D. Bobrow, *The Art of the Metaobject Protocol*, Cambridge, Massachusetts: MIT Press, 1991.

[4] N. Leveson, "Software Safety: Why, What and How," *ACM Computing Surveys*, vol. 18, no. 2, pp. 125-163, 1986.

[5] M. Lyu, Ed. *Software Fault Tolerance*, in *Trends In Software*, vol. 3, Chichester: John Wiley & Sons, 1995.

[6] P. Maes, "Concepts and Experiments In Computational Reflection," *ACM SIGPLAN Notices*, vol. 22, no. 12, pp. 147-155, 1987.

[7] P. Rogers, "Software Fault Tolerance, Reflection, and the Ada Programming Language (YCST 2003/10)," in *Department of Computer Science*: University of York, 2003.

[8] P. Rogers and A. J. Wellings, "An Incremental Recovery Cache Supporting Software Fault Tolerance Mechanisms," *Journal of Computer Systems: Science and Engineering*, vol. 15, no. 1, pp. 33-48, 2000.

[9] P. Rogers and A. J. Wellings, "OpenAda: Compile-Time Reflection for Ada 95" in *Reliable Software Technologies -- Ada-Europe 2004*, vol. 3063, *Lecture Notes in Computer Science*, A. Llamosi and A. Strohmeier, Eds., Palma de Mallorca, Spain: Springer-Verlag, 2004, pp. 166--177.

[10] A. Romanovsky and L. Strigini, "Backward Error Recovery via Conversations In Ada," *Software Engineering Journal*, vol. 10, no. 8, pp. 219-232, 1995.

[11] B. C. Smith, "Reflection and Semantics in Lisp," Proc. 11th ACM Symposium on Principles of Programming Languages, 1984, pp. 23-35.

[12] A. J. Wellings and A. Burns, "Implementing Atomic Actions In Ada 95," *IEEE Transactions On Software Engineering*, vol. 23, no. 2, pp. 107-123, 1997.

GNAT Pro for On-board Mission-Critical Space Applications*

José F. Ruiz

AdaCore,
8 rue de Milan, 75009 Paris, France
ruiz@adacore.com

Abstract. This paper describes the design and implementation of GNAT Pro for ERC32, a flexible cross-development environment supporting the Ravenscar tasking model on top of bare ERC32 computers. The static and simple tasking model defined by the Ravenscar profile allows for a streamlined implementation of the run-time system directly on top of bare machines. The reduced size and complexity of the run time, together with its configurability, makes it suitable for mission-critical space applications in which certification or reduced footprint is needed. Software reliability and predictability is also increased by excluding non-deterministic and non analysable tasking features. Product validation has been achieved by means of a comprehensive test suite intended to check compliance with the Ravenscar profile and Ada standards, and correct behaviour of specialised features and supplemental tools. Code coverage analysis is also part of the validation campaign, with the goal of achieving 100% statement coverage.

1   Introduction

The Ada tasking model allows the use of high level abstract development methods that include concurrency as a means of decoupling application activities, and hence making software easier to design and test [23]. However, tasking capabilities have been considered as too complex for safety critical systems because accurate timing analysis is difficult to achieve. Advances in real-time systems timing analysis methods have paved the way to reliable tasking in Ada. The Ravenscar profile is a subset of Ada 95 tasking that provides the basis for the implementation of deterministic and time analysable applications on top of a streamlined run-time system.

This paper describes the design and implementation of a flexible cross-development system supporting the Ravenscar tasking model on top of bare ERC32 computers. ERC32 [13,4] is a highly integrated, high-performance 32-bit RISC embedded processor implementing the SPARC architecture V7 specification. It has been developed with the support of the European Space Agency (ESA) as the current standard processor for spacecraft on-board computer systems.

In addition to a large number of compiler features intended to detect violations of the Ravenscar profile limitations (and any other imposed restrictions) at compile time,

---

* This work has been funded by ESA/ESTEC contract No.17360/03/NL/JA and carried out in cooperation between AdaCore and the Technical University of Madrid.

T. Vardanega and A. Wellings (Eds.): Ada-Europe 2005, LNCS 3555, pp. 248–259, 2005.

the key element is the provision of a restricted Ada run time that takes full advantage of the Ravenscar profile restrictions [3]. Additional restrictions on the Ada subset to be used can be enforced in order to properly support the development of high integrity systems [17]. The purpose of such restrictions is to enable a wide range of static analysis techniques, including schedulability analysis, to be performed on the software for validation purposes.

The developed Ada run time takes full advantage of the largely enhanced modularity introduced in GNAT Pro recently. Key to achieving this goal is the fully configurable and customisable run-time library, which allows for limiting the run-time library just to those units required for the application.

The cross-development environment provides a full-featured visual programming environment that covers the whole development cycle (language-oriented editing, compiling, binding, linking, loading, graphical tasking-aware debugging).

The work described is this paper builds on some of the results of previous ESA projects which resulted in the development of UPM's *Open Ravenscar Kernel* (ORK) [9, 25], an open-source development aimed at demonstrating the feasibility of a Ravenscar-compliant Ada run time on top of a bare ERC32.

2   The Ravenscar Profile

The Ravenscar profile [7, 3, 2] defines a subset of the tasking features of Ada which is amenable to static analysis for high integrity system certification, and that can be supported by a small, reliable run-time system. This profile is founded on state-of-the-art, deterministic concurrency constructs that are adequate for constructing most types of real-time software [8]. Major benefits of this model are:

- Improved memory and execution time efficiency, by removing high overhead or complex features.
- Increased reliability and predictability, by removing non-deterministic and non analysable features.
- Reduced certification cost by removing complex features of the language, thus simplifying the generation of proof of predictability, reliability, and safety.

The tasking model defined by the profile includes a fixed set of library level tasks and protected types and objects, a maximum of one protected entry per protected object with a simple boolean barrier and no entry queues for synchronisation, a real-time clock, absolute delays, deterministic fixed-priority preemptive scheduling with ceiling locking access to protected objects, and protected procedure interrupt handlers, as well as some other features. Other features, such as dynamic tasks and protected objects, task entries, dynamic priorities, select statements, asynchronous transfer of control, relative delays, or calendar clock, are forbidden.

The compiler and run time have been developed to be fully compliant with the latest definition of the Ravenscar profile [3, 2], so that it will be compliant with the forthcoming ISO standard revision of the Ada language.

3   The High Integrity Approach

The high integrity edition of the GNAT Pro compiler is intended to reduce costs and risks in developing and certifying systems that have to meet safety standards, such as DO-178B [12], DEF Stan 00-55 [10], and IEC 61508 [15].

The centerpiece of this approach is the "configurable run time" capability. Application developers and system integrators can together define an Ada subset that closely fits the needs of the projects, thus limiting the cost of certification of the run time. Run-time subsets are defined by using three different mechanisms:

- Setting parameters in the *System* package.
- Including only a subset of available run-time system units.
- Using *pragma Restrictions*.

The compiler will then flag and reject the use of constructs that are not supported by the defined subset. Developers may use presupplied implementations of units of interest, or may develop their own alternatives. This approach gives great control over the scope of certification activities when developing in Ada.

While the configurable run time approach gives maximum flexibility, in many situations a project does not require such a level of customisation. The ERC32 toolchain therefore includes three specific instantiations of the configurable run-time library:

- The *Zero FootPrint* run time guarantees that the generated object modules contain no references to the GNAT Pro run-time library. This allows the construction of a standalone program that has no code other than that corresponding to the original source code (apart from the elaboration routine generated by the binder). The elaboration routine generated by the binder also avoids any reference to run-time routines or data. This run time is designed to reduce the cost of meeting safety certification standards for applications written in Ada. In addition, this profile is compatible with SPARK [6].
- The *high integrity Ravenscar* run time offers a multitasking programming environment (compliant with the Ravenscar profile) with maximum performances at the expense of stringent restrictions. This profile is targeted at applications aiming at certification for safety-critical use or very small footprints.
- The *extended Ravenscar* run time offers support for a larger subset of Ada 95, under the restrictions of the Ravenscar profile and the hardware constraints. This profile makes software development easier (debugging, text output, stack checking, etc.), at the expenses of a larger footprint and an increased complexity in the run time.

Although limited in terms of dynamic Ada semantics, these three high integrity profiles fully support static Ada constructs such as generic templates and child units, tagged types (at library level), and other object-oriented programming features. Users can also further restrict certain Ada features (such as dynamic dispatching, allocators, unconstrained objects, implicit conditionals and loops) through appropriate *pragma Restrictions*.

Traceability from Ada source code to object code is facilitated by giving access to different intermediate formats internally generated by the compiler. From the initial source code the compiler generates a simplified code, which is low level Ada pseudo-code (target independent) that expands complex constructs into a sequence of simpler data and code (including run-time calls). This code is then compiled into assembler code, which is later transformed into object code. The availability of these intermediate representations helps certification of object code by reducing the semantic gap between different representations. Additionally, representation information for declared types and objects is also accessible.

Full Safety and Security Annex support [1–H] is provided, including capabilities for detecting uninitialised variables [11], by means of compiler warnings and run-time errors (using *pragma Normalize_Scalars* and some additional validity checking levels that can be selected by the users).

4 Restricted Ravenscar Run Time

The run-time system is made up by several libraries that implement functionalities required by features not otherwise generated directly by the compiler. The complexity of the run time basically depends on the features supported.

A compact and efficient run time has been designed to take full advantage of the Ravenscar Profile restrictions, which is substantially different from the run time used when no such restrictions are in effect. The Ravenscar run time provides simplified, more efficient versions for the set of tasking and synchronisation operations.

The Ravenscar run time has been carefully designed to isolate target dependencies by means of a layered architecture. There is a target independent layer, called GNU Ada Run-Time Library (GNARL), which provides the interface that is known by the compiler. The part of the run time that depends on the particular machine and operating system is known as GNU Low-Level Library (GNULL), which provides a target independent interface. GNULL is some glue code that translates this generic interface into calls to the operating system interface, thus facilitating portability. On bare board targets (such as the ERC32 one), GNULL is a full implementation of this interface.

Hence, retargeting the run time to a different operating system is a matter of mapping the GNULL interface (roughly a dozen primitives for creating threads, suspending them, etc.) into the equivalent operations provided by the operating system. Retargeting the run time to a different bare board system requires reimplementing the GNULL layer on top of the Board Support Package (BSP).

4.1 Static Tasking Model

The implementation takes full advantage of the static Ravenscar tasking model, in which only library level non-terminating tasks are allowed.

First, the complete set of tasks and associated parameters (such as their stack sizes) are identified and defined at compile time, so that the required data structures (task descriptors and stacks) can be statically created by the compiler as global data. Hence, memory requirements can be determined at link time (linking will fail if available memory is not enough) and there is no need for using dynamic memory at run time.

In addition, task creation and activation is very simple and deterministic: the environment task (as part of its elaboration) creates all the tasks in the system, and once that is done all tasks are then activated and executed concurrently, being scheduled according to their priority.

Finally, only library level non-terminating tasks are allowed, so that there is no need for code for completing or finalising tasks, and no support is needed for *masters* and *waiting for dependent tasks* either.

4.2   Simple Protected Object Operations

Protected object operations can be easily implemented taking advantage of the restrictions imposed by the Ravenscar profile:

- No asynchronous operations. There are no abort statements and no timed or conditional entry calls.
- Simple creation and finalisation of protected objects. Protected objects are only allowed at library level, and allocators are not allowed for protected types or types containing protected type components.
- Simple management of entry queues. Only one entry is allowed per protected object, with at most one task waiting on a closed entry barrier. In addition, requeues are not allowed.
- Simple priority handling. Dynamic priorities are not allowed.
- Simple locking operations. On a single processor implementation (such as the ERC32), the ceiling priority rules and the strictly preemptive priority scheduling policy guarantee that protected objects are always available when any task tries to use them [16, 19] (otherwise there would be another task executing at a higher priority), and hence entering/exiting to/from the protected object can simply be done by just increasing/decreasing task's priorities.

Operations related to protected objects without entries are implemented in an even simpler manner because there is no need to check whether there is any task waiting, no need to reevaluate barriers, no need to service entry queues, etc.

In addition, efficient execution of queued protected entries is achieved by implementing what is called the proxy model [14] for protected entry execution. At the end of the execution of any protected procedure (that may change the state of the barriers), if there is a task waiting on the protected object's entry, then the barrier is evaluated, and if needed, the entry is executed by the task that opened the barrier on behalf of the queued task. It enhances efficiency by avoiding unnecessary context switches.

4.3   Exception Support

The Ravenscar profile does not place any explicit limit on the features of sequential Ada, and therefore it does not restrict the use of exceptions (in fact, some exception support is required by the Ravenscar profile [18]). Therefore, several schemes are defined for supporting exceptions, providing different levels of functionality and complexity.

The simplest exception scheme supported by the GNAT Pro run time is the "No Exceptions" one, that is called the "exclusion strategy" in [17]. Raise statements and exception handlers are not allowed, and no language-defined run-time checks are generated. Hence, program will become erroneous if a run-time exception does occur, so that the absence of erroneous states usually leading to the raising of an exception must be demonstrated.

The second choice corresponds to the "No Exception Handlers" mechanism (called "belt-and-braces" strategy in [17]). It seeks to avoid dependency on the exception mechanism, but recognises that a predefined exception may nevertheless occur for some unforeseen reason. Exception propagation is not allowed, but exception declarations and raise statements are still permitted. No handlers are permitted; a user-defined last chance exception handler (which cannot resume task execution) is introduced at the outermost scope level, and hence no run-time support is needed. If run-time checking is enabled, then it is possible for the predefined exceptions Constraint_Error, Program_Error, or Storage_Error to be raised at run time.

A third exception handling mechanism is implemented in the *extended Ravenscar Profile*, supporting the full semantics of Ada 83 exceptions; Ada 95 enhancements are not included. This run-time system supports propagation of exceptions and handlers for multiple tasks. The run-time library provided by this profile supports also limited Ada 95 exception occurrences, and Ada.Exceptions.Exception_Name. Mapping of the usual traps for hardware exceptions to Ada exceptions is also done.

The implementation of a forth alternative exception handling mechanism is being considered, supporting the "containment" strategy defined in [17], that would authorise exception handling close to the raising location. When an exception is raised, the exception handler is executed if it is located in any of the enclosing syntactic scopes up to the inner-most subprogram scope. In other words, exceptions are never propagated outside the subprogram where they were raised. Every exception not being handled within its inner-most subprogram scope forces the execution of the last chance handler. No run-time support is needed for exception propagation, so that there is no drawback either in efficiency nor in complexity of the run time.

5   Multitasking Core

The Ravenscar profile is designed to be easily supported with a small run time. Within the framework of this project we have also designed and implemented a simple Ravenscar compliant multitasking core that is in charge of task scheduling, dispatching, and synchronisation, interrupt management, and timing services (time-keeping and delays). It implements a preemptive priority scheduling policy with ceiling locking and 256 priority levels (although this number can be easily reconfigured).

It has been written in Ada (except for some low-level code written in assembler to implement context switches and trap handling). A reduced, simple, and safe subset of Ada, following the recommendations made by the ISO 15942 technical report [17], has been used.

In order to enhance portability, it has been designed a Board Support Package (BSP) layer, giving access to key hardware dependent services, that minimises and isolates specific machine dependencies. It is made up by a few assembly files and a limited and identified set of Ada packages.

5.1   Timing Services

The implementation of timing services is both accurate and efficient, providing low granularity (limited only by the oscillator) time measurements and delays together with a low overhead operation, by means of using two different hardware timers [26].

The ERC32 hardware provides two 32-bit timers (a very common arrangement on 32-bit boards) which can be programmed in either single-shot or periodic mode [4]. We use one of them as a timestamp counter and the other as a high-resolution timer. The former provides the basis for a high resolution clock, while the latter offers the required support for precise alarm handling.

Given that the maximum timestamp count that can be stored in the hardware clock is equal to 2**32 system clock ticks (215 seconds for a 20 MHz ERC32 board), which is largely insufficient for fulfilling Real-Time Systems Annex requirements [1–D.8 par. 30] of a minimum range of 50 years, a mixed hardware-software clock has been devised.

Time is represented as a 64-bit unsigned integer number of clock ticks. The hardware clock interrupts periodically, updating the most significant part (MSP) of the clock, a 32-bit unsigned integer kept in memory, while the least significant part (LSP) of the clock is held in the hardware clock register.

The 64-bit clock value very easily and efficiently, by simply concatenating the the MSP 32-bits, stored in memory. and the value stored within the hardware counter as the LSP 32-bits. Efficiency is achieved by using 32-bit operations instead of 64-bit ones (ERC32 does not provide 64-bit hardware operations). Each half of a *Time* value (MSP and LSP) is handled separately.

An efficient high resolution timer is achieved by programming the hardware timer on demand, and not periodically.

5.2   Interrupt Handling

The three major goals when designing the interrupt handling mechanisms where simplicity, efficiency, and low interrupt latency.

Simplicity and efficiency are achieved by taking advantage of the Ravenscar restrictions on a single processor system; protected procedures (together with a short prologue and epilogue) are used as low level interrupt handlers, and no other intermediate synchronisation code is required.

Thanks to the use of the ceiling locking policy, the Ravenscar profile prevents the caller from getting blocked when invoking a protected procedure. The priority of a protected object which has a procedure attached to an interrupt must be at least the hardware Interrupt_Priority of that interrupt (otherwise the program is erroneous), as it is stated in the Systems Programming Annex [1–C.3.1 par. 14].

As a result, for as long as the active priority of the running task is equal to or greater than the one of an interrupt, that interrupt will not be recognised by the processor. On the contrary, the interrupt will remain pending until the active priority of the running task becomes lower than the priority of the interrupt, and only then will the interrupt be recognised and processed.

If an interrupt is recognised, then the call to the protected procedure attached to that interrupt cannot be blocked, as the protected object cannot be in use. Otherwise the active priority of the running task would be at least equal to the priority ceiling of the protected object, which cannot be true because the interrupt was recognised.

Low interrupt latency is accomplished by allowing interrupt nesting; otherwise, interrupts would be disabled until control returns back to the interrupted task, and interrupt latency would be high since high priority interrupts would not be handled while low priority interrupts are serviced.

How stacks are organised is a critical issue when designing a nested interrupt handling mechanism. The simplest approach is to borrow the stack of the interrupted task. The problem with this approach is that it artificially inflates stack requirements for each task since every task stack would have to include enough space to account for the worst case interrupt stack requirements, in addition to its own worst case usage.

This problem is addressed by providing a dedicated "interrupt stack" managed by software. There are two fundamental methods that can be adopted. The first uses a single stack for all interrupts, and the second uses multiple stacks (the multiple stack method uses a stack for each interrupt). The single interrupt stack approach has two major disadvantages:

- It forces context switches to be delayed until the moment when the outermost interrupt (lowest priority interrupt) has finished its execution (see ORK documentation [22] for details), because otherwise interrupt handling is left in an inconsistent state. Hence, tasks which are unblocked as a result of interrupt handling may be artificially preempted by the execution of interrupts with a lower priority (priority inversion).
- It introduces an asymmetry in the way dispatching operations are executed. When a context switch is required, it is needed to check first whether we are in an interrupt handler before we actually proceed with the context switch.

The total size of the different interrupt stacks should be similar to that of the single interrupt stack, assuming that appropriate worst case analysis for maximum nesting has been accomplished for the single interrupt stack.

The multiple stack method solves the priority inversion problem that we could find with the single interrupt stack approach. By having different stacks for the different interrupts we can simply save the state of the interrupted task. Exiting from the current interrupt stack may be delayed after the context switch (until the interrupted task is executed again).

5.3   Context Switch

The Ravenscar profile provides the basis for the implementation of deterministic and time analysable applications, but to perform a precise schedulability analysis of a Ravenscar compliant application, the context switch time must be deterministic [24]. In addition, efficiency enhances system schedulability, and simplicity allows for cost-effective certification of the run time.

Efficiency has been enhanced by limiting the number of hardware registers that are saved/restored every context switch (ERC32 has 128 integer registers and 32 floating point registers accessible to the user).

The ERC32 architecture (a SPARC V7) includes the concept of register windows[4, 21]. There are two different approaches to follow for the flushing policy: either to flush all register windows or just the windows currently in use [5]. Taking advantage of the execution points at which it is not necessary to save (and also not necessary to restore) the entire state of the machine [20], the run time adopts the latter approach so as to reduce the excessive overhead of saving and restoring unused window registers. Hence, all the register windows that have been modified between two consecutive context switches are flushed on the task stack, and the new windows are loaded with the contents of the stack corresponding the the task that is about to execute.

Not only efficiency, but also the predictability of execution is a crucial concern. The worst case execution time (WCET) of the two alternative approaches is approximately the same. The adopted implementation however exhibits a better average execution time. This is of no use for timing and scheduling analysis though, which must by definition use only WCET values. Note that by automatically saving/restoring all the register windows that have been used by tasks has one interesting advantage which is predictability; before and after the context switch the state of the different register windows (as well as the current window pointer and the window invalid mask) are the same.

Another issue that has been taken into account is that not every task (and certainly not every interrupt handler) use the floating point unit. Thus, the floating point context is not flushed until necessary. The floating point state remains in the floating point registers, and does not change until another task (or interrupt handler) tries to use the floating point unit.

The ORK implementation always saves/restores the floating point registers when performing a context switch [22], leading to non-negligible performance penalties. In the case of interrupt handlers, the floating point context is saved and restored each time an interrupt is recognised, to allow user handlers the use of the floating point unit safely.

The scheme that we implement is that floating point arithmetic is disabled by default (both for tasks and interrupt handlers). Then, when getting a floating point trap the handler takes care of saving and restoring what is needed. It means that the floating point unit is disabled after every context switch, in order to avoid saving the context of the floating point unit when it is not needed.

This way, tasks and interrupt handlers that do not use the floating point unit do not have the unnecessary overhead related to saving/restoring the floating point context. Moreover, when computing worst case execution times (WCET) the overhead associated to saving and restoring the floating point context needs to be accounted only when a task (or interrupt handler) is about to use the floating point unit.

The interrupt latency is also reduced because interrupt handlers do not save the floating point context; only the integer context is saved in order to process interrupts.

6   Related Work

This project builds on some of the results of previous ESA projects which resulted in the development of ORK [9, 25]. Among others, the GNAT Pro for ERC32 compiler has the following advantages compared to ORK:

- The configurable run time capability allows for a fine grained selection of run-time entities.
- Duplicated and redundant code and data has been eliminated. Since the run time provides most of the functionality needed for tasking, some code and data are present both in the ORK kernel and in the GNAT Pro run time. Currently there is no separate kernel but a complete Ada run-time system with the needed information stored at the required level.
- Static creation of task descriptors and stacks (see Section 4.1). The compiler has been modified so that all tasking related data is created at compile time, removing the need for dynamic memory at run time.
- Task creation and activation has been largely simplified by means of adopting the Ravenscar profile restrictions.
- Several restricted exception models (see Section 4.3) are currently supported offering a wide range of choices which are with the recommendations made by the ISO 15942 [17] technical report.
- More efficient and deterministic context switches and interrupt handling. This part of the BSP has been redesigned in order to attain the simplicity and determinism required by high integrity real-time applications.
- ORK is based on a very old GNAT version (3.13), and there have been a lot of features added since then, such as a full-featured software development environment, a more efficient back-end code generator, etc.
- The validation test suite has been largely increased, including code coverage analysis (with the objective of achieving 100% statement coverage).
- Professional support and online consulting for Ada software development.

In order to have an idea of the simplification attained, it can be said that the ORK kernel is made up by around 1500 lines of Ada code (plus around 500 assembly lines), while the GNAT Pro equivalent functionality is currently implemented with around 1000 lines of Ada code (and less than 400 of assembly).

Additionally, comparing the size of a simple tasking program (including both data and code, but excluding stacks and the trap table), the resulting footprint with GNAT Pro for ERC32 (using the high integrity Ravenscar run time) is around 10KB, while the same executable compiled with ORK has a footprint of around 175KB.

7   Conclusions and Future Work

The Ravenscar profile defines an Ada subset that excludes non-deterministic and non analysable tasking features. In addition, features with a high overhead or complexity are also removed, allowing for a great simplification in the required run time. It allows for a 10KB footprint for a simple tasking program.

The fully configurable and customisable run-time library allows for a fine-grained selection of run-time features so that the footprint and complexity of the run time can be limited. This approach gives great control of the scope of certification activities, allowing for a cost-effective use in safety-critical applications where evidences of predictability, reliability, and safety must be generated. Additionally, full source code is included.

The run time has been carefully designed to isolate target dependencies, allowing its portability to new embedded architectures. We have plans for porting this work to other targets.

GNAT Pro for ERC32 is a flexible solution for large, safety-critical systems using the Ravenscar profile, allowing for developing multitasking systems for mission-critical space applications with safety requirements.

Acknowledgements

This work would not have been possible without the kind interest of Morten Rytter Nielsen, who initiated the project at the European Space Agency and supervised it as the Agency Technical Officer.

Many people at AdaCore have been involved into this project to some extent. This includes in particular Jerome Guitton and Arnaud Charlet. All my thanks to them for their support, suggestions, and reviews.

I would also like to thank the team of the Real-Time Systems Group at the Technical University of Madrid, specially to Juan Antonio de la Puente, for his help with the documentation, and Juan Zamorano, for his contributions to many design and implementation details.

Finally, I want to express my gratitude to IPL, for porting and making available *AdaTEST 95* to the *GNAT Pro for ERC32* compiler so that code coverage analysis could be achieved.

References

1. *Ada 95 Reference Manual: Language and Standard Libraries. International Standard ANSI/ISO/IEC-8652:1995*, 1995. Available from Springer-Verlag, LNCS no. 1246.
2. ARG.   New pragma and additional restriction identifiers for real-time systems. Technical report, ISO/IEC/JTC1/SC22/WG9, 2003.   Available at `http://www.ada-auth.org/cgi-bin/cvsweb.cgi/AIs/AI-00305.TXT`.
3. ARG.   Ravenscar profile for high-integrity systems.   Technical report, ISO/IEC/JTC1/SC22/WG9, 2003.   Available at `http://www.ada-auth.org/cgi-bin/cvsweb.cgi/AIs/AI-00249.TXT`.
4. Atmel Corporation. *TSC695F SPARC 32-bit Space Processor: User Manual*, 2003.
5. T.P. Baker and Offer Pazy. A unified priority-based kernel for Ada. Technical report, ACM SIGAda, Ada Run-Time Environment Working Group, March 1995.
6. John Barnes. *High Integrity Software. The SPARK Approach to Safety and Security*. Addison Wesley, 2003.
7. Alan Burns. The Ravenscar profile. Technical report, University of York, 2002. Available at `http://www.cs.york.ac.uk/~burns/ravenscar.ps`.
8. Alan Burns, Brian Dobbing, and Tullio Vardanega.   Guide for the use of the Ada Ravenscar Profile in high integrity systems.   Technical Report YCS-2003-348, University of York, 2003.   Available at `http://www.cs.york.ac.uk/ftpdir/reports/YCS-2003-348.pdf`.
9. Juan A. de la Puente, Juan Zamorano, José F. Ruiz, Ramón Fernández-Marina, and Rodrigo García. The design and implementation of the open ravenscar kernel. *Ada Letters*, XXI(1), March 2001.

10. *DEF STAN 00-55: Requirements for Safety Related Software in Defence Equipment*, August 1997.
11. Robert Dewar, Olivier Hainque, Dirk Craeynest, and Philippe Waroquiers. Exposing uninitialized variables: Strengthening and extending run-time checks in ada. In J. Blieberger and A. Strohmeier, editors, *Reliable Software Technologies — Ada-Europe 2002*, number 2361 in Lecture Notes in Computer Science. Springer-Verlag, 2002.
12. *RTCA/DO-178B: Software Considerations in Airborne Systems and Equipment Certification*, December 1992.
13. ESA. *32 Bit Microprocessor and Computer System Development*, 1992.   Report 9848/92/NL/FM.
14. Edward W. Giering, Frank Mueller, and Theodore P. Baker. Implementing ada 9X features using POSIX threads: Design issues. In *Proceedings of TRI-Ada 1993*, pages 214–228, 1993.
15. IEC. *IEC 61508: Functional Safety of Electrical/Electronic/Programmable Electronic Safety-Related Systems*, 1998.
16. Intermetrics. *Ada 95 Rationale: Language and Standard Libraries.*, 1995. Available from Springer-Verlag, LNCS no. 1247.
17. ISO/IEC/JTC1/SC22/WG9. *Guidance for the use of the Ada Programming Language in High Integrity Systems*, 2000. ISO/IEC TR 15942:2000.
18. José F. Ruíz, Juan A. de la Puente, Juan Zamorano, and Ramón Fernández-Marina. Exception support for the Ravenscar profile. In *Workshop on Exception Handling for a 21st Century Programming Language*, volume XXI, pages 76–79. ACM SIGAda, September 2001.
19. H. Shen and T.P. Baker. A Linux kernel module implementation of restricted Ada tasking. *Ada Letters*, XIX(2):96–103, 1999. Proceedings of the 9th International Real-Time Ada Workshop.
20. J.S. Snyder, D.B. Whalley, and T.P. Baker. Fast context switches: Compiler and architectural support for preemptive scheduling. *Microprocessors and Microsystems*, 19(1):35–42, February 1995.
21. Sun Microsystems Corporation. *The SPARC Architecture Manual*, 1987. Version 7.
22. UPM. *Open Ravenscar Kernel — Software Design Document*, 1.7 edition, July 2000.
23. Tullio Vardanega and Jan van Katwijk. A software process for the construction of predictable on-board embedded real-time systems. *Software Practice and Experience*, 29(3):1–32, 1999.
24. Juan Zamorano and Juan A. de la Puente. Precise response time analysis for ravenscar kernels. In *11th International Workshop on Real-Time Ada Issues*. ACM Press, 2002.
25. Juan Zamorano and José F. Ruiz. GNAT/ORK: An open cross-development environment for embedded Ravenscar-Ada software. In E.F. Camacho, L. Basañez, and J.A. de la Puente, editors, *15th IFAC World Congress*. Elsevier Press, 2002.
26. Juan Zamorano, José F. Ruiz, and Juan A. de la Puente. Implementing Ada.Real_Time.Clock and absolute delays in real-time kernels. In D. Craeynest and A. Strohmeier, editors, *Reliable Software Technologies — Ada-Europe 2001*, number 2043 in Lecture Notes in Computer Science. Springer-Verlag, 2001.

The ESA Ravenscar Benchmark*

Romain Berrendonner and Jérôme Guitton

AdaCore, 8 rue de Milan, 75009 Paris, France
{berrendo, guitton}@adacore.com

Abstract. This article presents ERB, the ESA Ravenscar Benchmark. ERB aims at providing a synthetic benchmark comparing the efficiency of various Ada Ravenscar implementations and the RTEMS C implementation featuring the native threading model. ERB is original compared to existing Ada benchmarks because it is the first Ada Ravenscar benchmark and because it provides at the same time estimates of execution time, memory footprint of the Ada runtime, and stack size requirements. ERB intends to become a reference benchmark for ERC32 Ada Ravenscar applications. To facilitate this, the European Space Agency and AdaCore plan to release it under the GNU GPL.

1 The ERB Project

1.1 Project Context

Two main trends can be identified in the European space software industry. On the hardware side, it relies for many applications on a family of radiation-hardened chips including the ERC32 SPARC V7 processor and the Leon SPARC V8 VHDL model.

On the software side, the main programming languages used for space applications are currently Ada and C, for which various tool chains exist. Some of these are self-contained, allowing the creation of self-standing applications; others rely on a kernel to provide the complete environment they need. This is particularly true for the C language, which does not provide any concurrent programming facility; the only way to do it is by providing a kernel, such as RTEMS [9] or VxWorks, and a C API.

In Ada on the other hand, the concurrency features provided by the language are rich. The Ravenscar model [13], which has now been approved by WG9 for inclusion into the imminent revision of the Ada standard, aims at providing high-integrity implementations for real-time systems, at the cost of some restrictions to the standard Ada model, which facilitate not only the schedulability analysis of programs but also allow optimization in the underlying run-time libraries.

Being relatively new, there is currently no benchmark suitable for use in this context. The goal of the ESA Ravenscar Benchmark (ERB) is therefore to provide a synthetic test suite for Ada 95 Ravenscar environments running on the ERC32. This test suite will

---

* This work has been funded by ESA/ESTEC contract No. 16962/02/NL/LvH/bj and carried out in cooperation between AdaCore, the Technical University of Madrid and the University of Padua.

T. Vardanega and A. Wellings (Eds.): Ada-Europe 2005, LNCS 3555, pp. 260–271, 2005.
© Springer-Verlag Berlin Heidelberg 2005

provide measurements of both the execution time and the memory size of test cases. Additionally, a limited set of tests running on RTEMS will be provided as a reference of C technology capabilities.

1.2   Existing Benchmarks

A variety of benchmarks are currently available to quantify the performances of a run-time system; Some of them are particularly interesting:

- *The Standard Performances Evaluation Corporation (SPEC) [10]* develops benchmark suites for C compilers. Each suite has a particular purpose, such as measuring CPU usage on workstations or the efficiency of mainstream Internet applications. For CPU usage, SPEC uses a set of high-level applications, like the BZIP or CRC algorithms, rather than synthetic tests.
- *The Embedded Microprocessor Benchmark Consortium (EEMBC)[6]* and *MiBench [4]* provide suites of benchmarks targeted to embedded systems and C compilers; they use both high-level full implementations of common algorithms and low-level simple functions.
- *lmbench [7]* is a good example of a micro-benchmark suite, used to measure the cost of specific operating system features.

The previous benchmarks are targeted to C compilers. Two well-known benchmark suites are targeted to Ada tool-chains:

- *The Performance Issues Working Group (PIWG) [8]* goal was to support performance assessment for Ada environments. To achieve this, a set of about 80 Ada 83 benchmark tests for Ada 83 was developed and distributed during the 80s and early 90s.
- *The Ada Compiler Evaluation System (ACES) [5]* was originally a joint effort by the US DoD and the British MoD to address the need for Ada 95 users to evaluate their tool-chains. This project has later been made widely available. The ACES uses the dual-loop method to provide reliable measurements of execution times, which allows measuring small chunks of code as well as full algorithms.

Whereas speed and throughput are common figures, memory measurements are rarely performed. Like EEMBC, a few benchmarks include static code size measurements, only one benchmark among all those we have studied provides information about dynamic memory: *Pennbench [3]*, which targets embedded Java and provides heap usage measurement. However, a Ravenscar application does not contain many dynamic allocations and heap allocations are allowed mostly in the initialization phase. Moreover, Ravenscar adds some other constraints on the dynamic allocation, such as forbidding constructs that require an implicit heap allocation. No benchmark, to the best of our knowledge, provides stack usage measurement.

1.3   Why a New Benchmark?

Most of the existing benchmarks first target workstation environments which disqualifies them for embedded applications. The few benchmarks targeting Ada environments, are not adapted either to modern embedded applications. The PIWG are based on Ada 83; the ACES are not Ravenscar compliant. Unfortunately, one cannot simply remove non-Ravenscar tests cases: one needs to write a new set of test cases targeting the constructs programmers would use in real embedded applications.

In such systems, memory is by every respect as important as timing. There is no point in making a careful analysis to make sure a system is able to answer in a timely fashion if a stack overflow causes the program to crash. Fitting a lot of memory may not be practical in terms of cost, weight and power consumption. To make sure the memory is sufficient, one needs to know the stack size required by each task and the runtime footprint in memory, which can be defined as the code implementing features required by the user code, such as task switching code in tasking programs. The order of magnitude of this footprint can be significant: 150 KB on ORK [2] for instance. This is why ERB provides execution time measurements as well as the above memory measures.

Finally, in order to evaluate the cost of high-level Ada features in terms of memory footprint, stack size and execution times compared to low-level C code, the Agency required that some of the tests would be ported to C on the RTEMS system.

In real life, C programmers would probably use different mechanisms when porting Ada code: they would use mutexes to control access to data and condition variables to wait on an entry barrier, instead protected objects. The fact that Ada semantics is much richer makes comparing C and Ada particularly delicate. This was solved by writing a set of C packages providing exactly the same concurrency semantics as Ada.

Another decision had to be made about using the RTEMS native threading interface against the POSIX threading interface. The native threading model was finally selected for three reasons: it is the default mode when RTEMS gets installed; Ada tasking is integrated to the runtime, and using a separate, less optimized, POSIX library would be unfair to RTEMS; the main advantage of the POSIX API over the native API is portability. Since RTEMS is used as a reference point and no port to other C environments are planned, this advantage fades.

In a nutshell, the ESA Ravenscar Benchmark (ERB) project aims at providing a new benchmark targeting Ada Ravenscar implementations on the ERC32 processor. It uses mostly synthetic tests: each of these tests is designed to exercise a particular, clearly identified, Ada feature. A set of applicative tests are provided to compensate the lack of full-fledged application. Execution time, runtime footprint and stack size estimate are provided. A subset of the Ada tests has been ported to RTEMS using C and the native threading model so that Ada can be compared to a widespread C platform. The C code is written to match closely Ada semantics.

2   Technical Overview

This section presents a quick overview of the technical choices made in the ERB project.

2.1   Portability Considerations

Portability can have many different meanings in the context of a benchmarking project. One has to consider target portability, host portability and environment portability.

Target portability is defined as the capability to use the test suite on a different target processor without significant adaptation efforts. In this case, the ERC32 was the only mandatory target, but we are considering running it on PowerPC processors. As a consequence, target portability was considered since the early stages of design: in order to facilitate adaptation to other processors, and for cost-efficiency reasons, it was decided to use a simulator. The choice for the ERC32 target was the `erc-elf-sis` ERC32 simulator. Switching to another processor should therefore be as simple as rewriting the simulator interface.

Using a simulator raises the question of the accuracy of simulation. In our context, the `erc-elf-sis` simulator is true-cycle, which means that the simulated time updates are triggered by the processor instruction unit and the FPU. This creates a strong tie between simulated time and simulated instructions and ensures a high degree of accuracy: average timing accuracy of this simulator is claimed to be around 0.5%. Other difficult issues to simulate include

- the instruction cache. On the ERC32 though, there is no cache, so this is not an issue.
- the instruction pipeline. One of the known issues with the SPARC pipeline is that write operations to a limited set of special registers may not be seen by instructions until 3 cycles have elapsed. While real ERC32 behave as described, the simulator make those immediately accessible. This has no performance impact because code usually add no-op to take this into account.
- the floating point unit. `erc-elf-sis` maps the floating point operations to host floating point capabilities. Therefore, the accuracy and generation of IEEE exceptions depend on that of the host. This should be fairly marginal taking into account the test base.

All in all, the trade off exposed above looks acceptable compared to the complexity of using hardware implementations.

Host portability can be defined as the capability to run the test harness on a different host workstation. The host is used for compiling each test, running the simulator and getting static memory information. The Agency required the test harness to be usable on Linux and Solaris; once again nothing in the design prevents it from being ported to other environments. The main harness driver is written in Ada 95, for reliability and portability. Wherever Ada was not a possible choice, Bourne Shell was used instead because it is probably the most widespread and portable interpreter available.

Environment Portability. In this document, an environment is an Ada 95 Ravenscar tool chain able to compile code for the target processor. The system has been designed so that adding support for a new environment in the harness is not difficult. Support for a particular environment is defined by:

- a configuration file containing environment-specific definitions, such as the comment delimiter in test source code or the commands used for compiling each test case.
- two scripts with a predefined interface used to first check the environment and build each test case.
- a set of specific support-packages which specification is standardized.

Adding a new Ada environment is therefore only a matter of writing those files.

Portability was not as stringent a requirement with respect to RTEMS. The goal of having a set of tests running on RTEMS is to provide a reference for comparing the efficiency of Ada 95 implementations with a classic C implementation. It is out of the scope of this project to provide a portable implementation of the test harness for C environments using the POSIX threading interface.

2.2   Timing Measurement

The approach taken by most benchmarks, which mitigates the influence of low-level issues by measuring execution time on whole applications, is not very well suited for a fine-grained analysis of the contribution of specific language features. That is why the PIWG and the ACES benchmarks use the dual-loop method.

Timing Strategies. A complete study of the dual-loop method is beyond the scope of this paper. For a complete description, the reader is welcome to read [5].

The dual-loop works with the two main timing systems that can be implemented:

- *hardware clock:* in this case the time counter is updated only by hardware means, which is possible only on systems with large time counters (typically 64 bits). Otherwise the time counter is likely to overflow.
- *alarm-clock model:* in this case, there are two different time counters. One is a hardware-managed time counter, while the other is managed by software: the operating system sets an alarm and updates the software time counter when it expires. This paradigm is convenient when the hardware time counter is small.

The dual-loop is based on a careful analysis of the possible systematic errors related to such timing systems: the jitter, which is basically the random variations of clock precisions, and the quantization error, which is mostly caused by the analog-digital conversion of the physical phenomenon used to generate the clock signal.

The first step of the dual loop strategy is to evaluate the combined order of magnitude of these errors, as measured by a program executed on the target:

- It first synchronizes on a system clock change and then counts the number of elementary ticks that can fit into one second starting from that point. These elementary ticks are counted using a Vernier, i.e. a simple loop that increases an integer counter. Using this figure, it is possible to estimate the duration of the elementary ticks.
- Then, it counts the number of elementary ticks that can fit into one clock tick a given number of times. A clock tick is defined by the Ada Reference Manual [11] as "*a real time interval during which the clock value (as observed by calling the Clock function) remains constant*".

An estimate of the combined effect of jitter and quantization is then provided by multiplying the standard deviation of the number of ticks into one clock tick by the estimated duration of an elementary tick.

One may notice that the clock can be considered as a high-resolution clock if the number of elementary ticks that can fit into a clock tick is close to 1. This allows some optimizations such as getting rid of the Vernier for time measurements.

Once the errors are estimated, the dual loop strategy repeats each test case a number of times, so that the overall execution time is significantly longer than the possible systematic errors estimates. Obviously, this must be gauged against execution time constraints and meaningfulness: a low value such as 10 is likely to provide unstable measurements, while a large figure like 10.000 would result in impractically long execution times. 100 appeared to provide a good trade off.

In order to do this, the test code is surrounded by two loop: the inner loop just executes the test code a fixed NCount number of times. NCount is fixed by the outermost loop, and keeps increasing, following a geometric series: $Ncount_{N+1} = 2 * Ncount_N + 1$ starting with $N_0 = 1$. Additionally, a maximum upper bound is provided to avoid infinite loops. NCount keeps increasing until the execution time of the inner loop meets the condition above. Once it is the case, the inner loop is executed MCount number of times with the same NCount to demonstrate that the measurement is stable. MCount is fixed so that it is lower than an arbitrary bound to avoid infinite recursion, each test does not take longer than 30 minutes of simulation time and a Student's t-test indicates that, to the requested confidence level of 90%, the timing measurements are being drawn from a sample with the same mean.

The ACES have demonstrated that the dual loop method provides very good results with the compilers they have been using, thanks to advanced heuristics to handle optimizations, processor cache issues and memory paging. But despite those efforts, the dual loop method still has some limits. In particular, it is not well suited for user code whose execution time depends on previous executions, for instance because of a side-effect, or for measuring elaboration code, which is by definition out of the reach of user instrumentation code. In order to address these issues, ERB implements two additional strategies.

The first strategy is very simple: once it is compiled, the test case is just loaded and executed on the simulator, using the simulator timing facility to retrieve the execution time. The harness is responsible for repeating the test a number of times so that it is possible to make statistically sure that the results are meaningful. This is done by checking they all fit into a 90% confidence interval. This strategy is called "external".

The second strategy is known as "single-loop". Instead of surrounding the test code by a dual loop, this method just uses the target environment timing facility to get the execution time of a single execution of the test. The harness is responsible for repeating the test a number of times, so that it is possible to make statistically sure that the results are meaningful using the same kind of proof as previously.

Common Instrumentation Code. Each test case contains some markers that are expanded in a different way depending on the actual strategy in use. They are contained in Ada comments so that unexpanded test cases are legal Ada programs. C test cases on RTEMS use the same mechanism.

- *Dual-loop:* if the harness finds the `<start_single_measure>` and `<end_single_measure>` it assumes that the test has to be run using the "external" and "single-loop" strategies: the test is not executed. If it finds the `<start_measure>` and `<end_measure>`, it assumes the dual loop strategy has to be used, and it expands them to respectively the opening part of the dual loop code, and the closing part of the dual loop code.

- *Single loop:* if the harness finds either the `<start_measure>` and `<start_single_measure>` tags on one hand or the `<end_measure>` and `<end_single_measure>` tags on the other hand, it assumes that the test has to be executed using this strategy. The `<start_[...]>` tags are expanded to take a reference time using the system clock. The `<end_[...]>` tags are expanded to the code computing the execution time.
- *External:* no expansion is made. The program is loaded on the simulator and executed.

A complete test case is shown below. It is design to use the three strategies.

```
with Support_Timing; use Support_Timing;
with Support_Types;  use Support_Types;
procedure Ar_T_A_03 is
   A_Float_1 : Float6   := Simple_Float6_Random;
   A_Fixed_1 : Afix1    := Simple_Afix1_Random;
begin
   --   <init_variables>
   --   <start_measure>
   A_Float_1 := Float6 (A_Fixed_1);
   --   <end_measure>
end Ar_T_A_03;
```

Output provides the following information:

- The name of test case. There is exactly one for individual test inside the test case;
- The minimal execution time of the test;
- The average execution time of the test;
- The standard deviation computed on the series of test case;
- The number of times each test case was executed by the inner loop (NCount);
- The number of times that each test case has been iterated NCount times by the outer loop (MCount);
- A message indicating whether the test is actually valid or not;

2.3   Footprint and Stack Measurement

For each test case, the overall size of the code and data section is computed for the support packages binary files, the test case binary file ($test.o file) and the linked test case executable file. The runtime footprint is computed by subtracting the size of the test case sections and the support packages sections to the overall binary file sections. This is an approximation, since some runtime code might be for instance inlined, but this proved sufficiently accurate.

Most of the tools used to determine post-execution the memory behavior are analyzing heap allocations. There are usually used for detection of memory leaks, but these techniques can be applied to stack measurement as well.

External monitoring: the program is run on a simulator, a virtual machine or a debugger; some inspection points are set, e.g. breakpoints. For heap usage, the inspection points are the library routines used for dynamic allocation and deallocation, e.g.

`malloc` and `free`. For stack usage, the inspection points would be set on every stack-modifying instruction. This method is very precise but it is slow because many instructions change the stack. Our preliminary tests showed that hours were needed to run a simple Dhrystone test, on a fairly fast PC machine. Moreover, this solution is highly target-dependent and technology-dependent. This is nevertheless the method used by `gnatmem` [1] and `Valgrind` [12].

Instrumentation: the user code is instrumented at some particular locations, known as inspection points, by the user, the compilation tool-chain or by a binary patching utility. If they are set in the user source code, many stack variations will be lost and the result will be highly imprecise, with no way to evaluate the error; setting them automatically is highly technology-dependent and target-dependent.

Pattern filling: memory is filled with a known pattern, before execution. After execution, the memory is read to determine the areas that have been modified. The memory can be filled either externally, by a debugger, or internally, by calling a support library. This method has several systematic errors, but they are limited and measurable as shown below. It is important to note that not all the patterns are destroyed as the stack grows into the watermarked area. This is the kind of technology GNAT's `Debug_Pools` [1] use.

For the purpose of ERB, only the third solution is practical. Therefore the project provides instrumentation routines for watermarking the stack and analyzing it after execution.

The systematic errors are mainly caused by the effects on the stack of the instrumentation routines themselves:

Bottom offset: The procedure used to fill the stack with a given pattern has itself a stack frame. The value of the stack pointer in this procedure is therefore different from the value before the call to the instrumentation procedure. In order to minimize this error, the user should get the address of a variable defined on the stack of the caller to indicate the bottom limit of the stack.

Instrumentation clobber when writing the pattern: The procedure used to watermark the stack is only able to fill it above its own stack frame. As the user passes the value of the bottom of stack to the instrumentation to deal with the bottom offset error, and as the instrumentation procedure knows where the pattern filling starts, the difference between the two values is the minimum stack usage accessible through this method. If the pattern zone has been left untouched, it is possible to conclude that the stack usage is inferior to this minimum usage.

Instrumentation clobber when reading the pattern: If this stack frame of the function used to analyze the stack is bigger than the total space used by the user code, the measured stack size will be unduly big. In order to detect such a situation, it is possible to augment this stack frame and see if it changes the measure. To do that, an additional array is allocated in this frame with a specific discriminant to change its size.

Pattern zone overflow: If the stack grows outer than the pattern zone, the outermost region modified in the pattern zone is not the maximum value of the stack pointer at execution. The difference between the outermost memory region modified in the pattern zone and the outermost bound of the pattern zone is the biggest allocation that the method could have detect, provided that there is no "Untouched allocated zone" error and no "Pattern usage in user code" error. If no object in the user code is likely to have this size, this is not likely to happen.

Pattern usage in program: The pattern can possibly be found in both the data handled by the program and the program instructions. The latter are not a problem because the instructions are contained in a different area of the memory. The former could be a problem as overwritten memory area could appear untouched by program execution. A way to avoid this is not to use the selected pattern in the test cases. One should avoid trivial patterns like 0x00000000 which could be valid value. ERB is using the 0xdeadbeef pattern which has the advantage of being unlikely to be a valid memory address and is easily recognizable by humans. Experiments carried out with other patterns have shown that the results do not depend on them.

Stack overflow: If the pattern zone does not fit on the stack, it may override the stack space of another task, leading to unpredictable results. It is sufficient to have large enough task sizes to avoid this.

Inlined instrumentation code: If the instrumentation code is inlined, the objects allocated by the instrumentation procedures are allocated on the caller stack frame, which is therefore augmented. to avoid this, none of the instrumentation procedures is inlined.

Untouched allocated zone: The user code may allocate objects that are never modified, thus keeping the pattern unchanged. Unfortunately, there is no way to detect this error. It does not happen often though, and is likely to be due to bugs in the user code. It can change the measure only if the untouched allocated zone is located in the outermost part of the stack, so it is mostly harmless.

Only one parameter of the instrumentation code is likely to change with each configuration: it indicates whether the stack grows up (from low addresses to high addresses) or down (from high addresses to low addresses). The code is designed as a general stack usage measurement library usable not only for benchmarking purposes but also for evaluating the stack usage of the tasks of any Ada application.

Here is a complete example of a test case:

```
with Support_Memory; use Support_Memory;
A : Stack_Analyzer (16#DEAD_BEEF#, Proposed_Storage_Size / 2, 0);
--  This private object is used by the memory instrumentation code.
task T is
    pragma Storage_Size (Proposed_Storage_Size);
end T;
task body T is
    Bottom_Of_Stack : aliased Integer;
    --  Bottom_Of_Stack'Address will be used as an approximation of
    --  the bottom of stack and passed to Fill_Stack.
begin
    Fill_Stack (A, To_Stack_Address (Bottom_Of_Stack));
    Some_User_Code;
    Compute_Result (A);
    Report_Result (A);
end T;
```

The output of each memory test includes:

- The name of the test being done;
- An estimate of the stack consumption. The bigger this figure, the bigger the stack space a task needs;
- The size of the space filled by the pattern that is beyond the last modified area. If it is very small, one may want to expand the watermarked area to make sure that no memory used by the program is beyond it;
- The size of the `Fill_Stack` stack frame and the size of the `Compute_Result` stack frame. If these figures are close to `Stack`, it probably means that the stack consumption figure is close to the lower limit of what the method can measure;

2.4   Test Base

In order to provide a significant test base on a cost-effective basis, we decided to leverage on the extensive test bases from existing Ada benchmarks and test suites, namely the ACES project, the PIWG project, the ACATS and the ORK project Ravenscar test suite. Most of the test cases have been adapted from the latter test suites merging specific support packages features into a united one.

Implemented test comprises 174 Ada timing tests, 92 Ada memory tests, 92 RTEMS timing tests and 50 RTEMS memory tests, divided in twelve categories, namely: high level algorithms, arithmetic tests, data storage, data structure, tasking and protected objects, exception handling, runtime checks, iterations, procedure and function calls, generics, object oriented, and miscellaneous test.

Going into more detail for the tasking and protected object tests, test cases that have been implemented so far include:

- Timing of various delay statements in main subprogram or in a separate task (priority `Priority'First` or `Priority'Last`) with positive, negative, null arguments;
- Timing of read and write operations to a protected object from a separate task, or from a task while 4 others are accessing concurrently the protected object.
- Timing of an entry call on a protected object from the main procedure or from a task with an open barrier.
- Timing of function call done by 5 different tasks.
- Timing of a calls to `'Count` from within a procedure.
- Timing of a call to `'Called` and `'Identity` from within a protected entry.

Static and dynamic memory measurement are also provided.

In order to validate the set of tests, a simple strategy of consistency checking was adopted. Since the whole point of this project is making comparison between Ravenscar tool-chains, the emphasis was not put on ensuring correctness of the test cases, but more making sure that a given test case behaves consistently on all target environments. Additionally, reusing many test cases from existing, well-known benchmarks provides a guaranty that most of the tests are correct and have a meaningful target.

3 Preliminary Results

At the time of writing, only partial Ravenscar timing results using the new GNAT Pro compiler are available. Those results have been computed on a 20 MHz emulation.

Tests involving delay statements provide sensible results. when the delay is negative or null, the delay statement can be considered as null, since the measured overhead is around 30 microsecond, no matter the delay is called from the environment task, a Priority'First task or a Piority'Last task. When the delay is 500 ms, the measured overhead is around 73 microseconds, whatever the caller is. In any event those overheads are negligible.

When measuring 1000 read and write operations to a protected object, one can notice that the operation takes twice as much time when 5 tasks are involved rather than 1. This overhead is not surprising: it is caused by the numerous context switches from one task to another.

One may notice when measuring 1000 read and write operation from a single task that it is only slightly slower to use protected routines than regular routines: the overhead is around 3%. Thanks to the Ravencar profile definition, GNAT is able to implement the lock on protected object by changing the priority of the locked task. This operation is only a matter of changing a field of the task descriptor and changing the position of the task in the task queue. Both of these operations are fast when there are only a few tasks.

One can also notice that entry call from the environment task or from within a task with open barrier condition are very close: the difference in the overhead is around 2 microseconds. The mechanism involved is the same here and as no priority needs to be changed, the operation is very fast.

The difference between a call from the environment task to a protected procedure and a protected function returning an Integer is also very small (8 microseconds) and can be overlooked. The same analysis holds when the call is done from a task.

Finally, one may notice that timing of calls to 'Count and 'Caller wrapped in functions are in the same order of magnitude than the overhead of a null function (6% longer), which means the implementation of these attributes is efficient.

4 Conclusion

Our preliminary conclusions tend to show that using the concurrent features of the Ravenscar profile with a limited number of tasks involves no significant performance penalty. However, these results needs to be refined and ERB provides a flexible framework for adding new test cases that can provide additional information on these aspects.

In order to bolster the use of ERB in the Ada 95 Ravenscar vendor community and among the users of these softwares, The European Space Agency and AdaCore agreed to make it available under the GNU Public License.

We hope that ERB will be used by compiler vendors to improve the performances of their Ravenscar implementations, and by space software developers to identify coding guidelines for producing more efficient software.

Acknowledgments

This work would not have been possible without Morten Nielsen, who initiated the project at the European Space Agency. We would also like to thank Cyrille Comar, Franco Gasperoni, Olivier Hainque, and Nicolas Roche from AdaCore, Juan-Antonio de la Puente, Juan Zamorano and Santiago Palomino from the University of Madrid, and Tullio Vardanega, from the University of Padua, for their participation in the ERB project and kind support.

References

1. Ada Core Technologies. *GNAT User's guide*, 5.02a1 edition.
   http://www.adacore.com/.
2. Juan A. de la Puente, José F. Ruiz, and Juan Zamorano. An open Ravenscar real-time kernel for GNAT. In Hubert B. Keller and Erhard Ploedereder, editors, *Reliable Software Technologies — Ada-Europe 2000*, number 1845 in LNCS, pages 5–15. Springer-Verlag, 2000.
   http://wwww.dit.upm.es/ork/.
3. G. Chen et al. Pennbench: A benchmark suite for embedded java. In *5th Workshop on Workload Characterization (WWC5)*, 2002. http://www.cse.psu.edu/~gchen/papers/wwc5.pdf.
4. Matthew R. Guthaus, Jeffrey S. Ringenberg, and Dan Ernst Todd M. Austin Trevor Mudge Richard B. Brown. Mibench: A free, commercially representative embedded benchmark suite. In *IEEE 4th Annual Workshop on Workload Characterization*, 2001.
   http://www.eecs.umich.edu/mibench.
5. High Order Language Control Facility USAF. *Ada Compiler Evaluation system Reader's Guide for Version 2.1*, February 1996. http://www.adaic.org/compilers/aces/aces-intro.html.
6. EEMBC Certification Laboratories. *The EEMBC Benchmark*.
   http://ebenchmarks.com/.
7. Larry W. McVoy and Carl Staelin. Lmbench: Portable tools for performance analysis. In *USENIX Annual Technical Conference*, pages 279–294, 1996.
8. Performance Issues Working Group (PIWG). The piwg benchmark.
   http://unicoi.kennesaw.edu/ase/support/cardcatx/piwg.htm, 1993.
9. RTEMS. *The Real-Time Operating System for Multiprocessor Systems*, v4.6.1 edition.
   http://www.rtems.com/.
10. The Standard Performance Evaluation Corporation. *SPEC CPU 2004*. http://www.spechbench.org/.
11. S.T. Taft, R.A. Duff, and E. Ploederer. *Consolidated Ada Reference Manual*. Number LNCS 2219 in ANSI/ISO/IEC-8652:1995. Springer-Verlag, 1995.
    http://www.adaic.org/standards/95lrm/html/RM-TTL.html.
12. VALGRIND. *Valgrind - a GPL'd system for debugging and profiling x86-Linux programs*.
    http://www.valgrind.kde.org/.
13. WG9. *Ravenscar profile for high-integrity systems*, March 2003.
    http://www.ada-auth.org/cgi-bin/cvsweb.cgi/AIs/AI-00249.TXT.

Author Index

Lecture Notes in Computer Science

For information about Vols. 1–3441

please contact your bookseller or Springer

Vol. 3499: A. Pelc, M. Raynal (Eds.), Structural Information and Communication Complexity. X, 323 pages. 2005.

Vol. 3498: J. Wang, X. Liao, Z. Yi (Eds.), Advances in Neural Networks – ISNN 2005, Part III. L, 1077 pages. 2005.

Vol. 3497: J. Wang, X. Liao, Z. Yi (Eds.), Advances in Neural Networks – ISNN 2005, Part II. L, 947 pages. 2005.

Vol. 3496: J. Wang, X. Liao, Z. Yi (Eds.), Advances in Neural Networks – ISNN 2005, Part II. L, 1055 pages. 2005.

Vol. 3495: P. Kantor, G. Muresan, F. Roberts, D.D. Zeng, F.-Y. Wang, H. Chen, R.C. Merkle (Eds.), Intelligence and Security Informatics. XVIII, 674 pages. 2005.

Vol. 3494: R. Cramer (Ed.), Advances in Cryptology – EUROCRYPT 2005. XIV, 576 pages. 2005.

Vol. 3493: N. Fuhr, M. Lalmas, S. Malik, Z. Szlávik (Eds.), Advances in XML Information Retrieval. XI, 438 pages. 2005.

Vol. 3492: P. Blache, E. Stabler, J. Busquets, R. Moot (Eds.), Logical Aspects of Computational Linguistics. X, 363 pages. 2005. (Subseries LNAI).

Vol. 3489: G.T. Heineman, I. Crnkovic, H.W. Schmidt, J.A. Stafford, C. Szyperski, K. Wallnau (Eds.), Component-Based Software Engineering. XI, 358 pages. 2005.

Vol. 3488: M.-S. Hacid, N.V. Murray, Z.W. Raś, S. Tsumoto (Eds.), Foundations of Intelligent Systems. XIII, 700 pages. 2005. (Subseries LNAI).

Vol. 3486: T. Helleseth, D. Sarwate, H.-Y. Song, K. Yang (Eds.), Sequences and Their Applications - SETA 2004. XII, 451 pages. 2005.

Vol. 3483: O. Gervasi, M.L. Gavrilova, V. Kumar, A. Laganà, H.P. Lee, Y. Mun, D. Taniar, C.J.K. Tan (Eds.), Computational Science and Its Applications – ICCSA 2005, Part IV. XXVII, 1362 pages. 2005.

Vol. 3482: O. Gervasi, M.L. Gavrilova, V. Kumar, A. Laganà, H.P. Lee, Y. Mun, D. Taniar, C.J.K. Tan (Eds.), Computational Science and Its Applications – ICCSA 2005, Part III. LXVI, 1340 pages. 2005.

Vol. 3481: O. Gervasi, M.L. Gavrilova, V. Kumar, A. Laganà, H.P. Lee, Y. Mun, D. Taniar, C.J.K. Tan (Eds.), Computational Science and Its Applications – ICCSA 2005, Part II. LXIV, 1316 pages. 2005.

Vol. 3480: O. Gervasi, M.L. Gavrilova, V. Kumar, A. Laganà, H.P. Lee, Y. Mun, D. Taniar, C.J.K. Tan (Eds.), Computational Science and Its Applications – ICCSA 2005, Part I. LXV, 1234 pages. 2005.

Vol. 3479: T. Strang, C. Linnhoff-Popien (Eds.), Location- and Context-Awareness. XII, 378 pages. 2005.

Vol. 3478: C. Jermann, A. Neumaier, D. Sam (Eds.), Global Optimization and Constraint Satisfaction. XIII, 193 pages. 2005.

Vol. 3477: P. Herrmann, V. Issarny, S. Shiu (Eds.), Trust Management. XII, 426 pages. 2005.

Vol. 3475: N. Guelfi (Ed.), Rapid Integration of Software Engineering Techniques. X, 145 pages. 2005.

Vol. 3474: C. Grelck, F. Huch, G.J. Michaelson, P. Trinder (Eds.), Implementation and Application of Functional Languages. X, 227 pages. 2005.

Vol. 3468: H.W. Gellersen, R. Want, A. Schmidt (Eds.), Pervasive Computing. XIII, 347 pages. 2005.

Vol. 3467: J. Giesl (Ed.), Term Rewriting and Applications. XIII, 517 pages. 2005.

Vol. 3465: M. Bernardo, A. Bogliolo (Eds.), Formal Methods for Mobile Computing. VII, 271 pages. 2005.

Vol. 3464: S.A. Brueckner, G.D.M. Serugendo, A. Karageorgos, R. Nagpal (Eds.), Engineering Self-Organising Systems. XIII, 299 pages. 2005. (Subseries LNAI).

Vol. 3463: M. Dal Cin, M. Kaâniche, A. Pataricza (Eds.), Dependable Computing - EDCC 2005. XVI, 472 pages. 2005.

Vol. 3462: R. Boutaba, K.C. Almeroth, R. Puigjaner, S. Shen, J.P. Black (Eds.), NETWORKING 2005. XXX, 1483 pages. 2005.

Vol. 3461: P. Urzyczyn (Ed.), Typed Lambda Calculi and Applications. XI, 433 pages. 2005.

Vol. 3460: Ö. Babaoglu, M. Jelasity, A. Montresor, C. Fetzer, S. Leonardi, A. van Moorsel, M. van Steen (Eds.), Self-star Properties in Complex Information Systems. IX, 447 pages. 2005.

Vol. 3459: R. Kimmel, N.A. Sochen, J. Weickert (Eds.), Scale Space and PDE Methods in Computer Vision. XI, 634 pages. 2005.

Vol. 3458: P. Herrero, M.S. Pérez, V. Robles (Eds.), Scientific Applications of Grid Computing. X, 208 pages. 2005.

Vol. 3456: H. Rust, Operational Semantics for Timed Systems. XII, 223 pages. 2005.

Vol. 3455: H. Treharne, S. King, M. Henson, S. Schneider (Eds.), ZB 2005: Formal Specification and Development in Z and B. XV, 493 pages. 2005.

Vol. 3454: J.-M. Jacquet, G.P. Picco (Eds.), Coordination Models and Languages. X, 299 pages. 2005.

Vol. 3453: L. Zhou, B.C. Ooi, X. Meng (Eds.), Database Systems for Advanced Applications. XXVII, 929 pages. 2005.

Vol. 3452: F. Baader, A. Voronkov (Eds.), Logic for Programming, Artificial Intelligence, and Reasoning. XI, 562 pages. 2005. (Subseries LNAI).

Vol. 3450: D. Hutter, M. Ullmann (Eds.), Security in Pervasive Computing. XI, 239 pages. 2005.

Vol. 3449: F. Rothlauf, J. Branke, S. Cagnoni, D.W. Corne, R. Drechsler, Y. Jin, P. Machado, E. Marchiori, J. Romero, G.D. Smith, G. Squillero (Eds.), Applications of Evolutionary Computing. XX, 631 pages. 2005.

Vol. 3448: G.R. Raidl, J. Gottlieb (Eds.), Evolutionary Computation in Combinatorial Optimization. XI, 271 pages. 2005.

Vol. 3447: M. Keijzer, A. Tettamanzi, P. Collet, J.v. Hemert, M. Tomassini (Eds.), Genetic Programming. XIII, 382 pages. 2005.

Vol. 3444: M. Sagiv (Ed.), Programming Languages and Systems. XIII, 439 pages. 2005.

Vol. 3443: R. Bodik (Ed.), Compiler Construction. XI, 305 pages. 2005.

Vol. 3442: M. Cerioli (Ed.), Fundamental Approaches to Software Engineering. XIII, 373 pages. 2005.